Conflict Prevention and Peacebuilding in Post-War Societies

Conflict Prevention and Peacebuilding in Post-War Societies provides an overview of the costs, benefits, consequences, and prospects for rebuilding nations emerging from violent conflict. The rationale for this comes from the growing realization that, in the post-Cold War era and in the aftermath of 9-11, our understanding of conflict and conflict resolution has to include consideration of the conditions conducive to sustaining the peace in nations torn by civil war or interstate conflict.

First, whereas wars between sovereign nations had dominated international politics for the previous 300 years, civil wars within nations – revolutions, secessionist wars, ethnic conflicts, and terrorism – have become the most frequent and deadly forms of armed conflict since the end of World War II. Second, the Third World – Asia, Africa, Latin America, and the Middle East – has become the site of most of the armed conflict in the last half century. Third, not only has civil war become the dominant conflict modality in the international community but once it occurs in a nation, it is highly likely to recur at some time in the future. Fourth, while the end of the Cold War has not significantly diminished the frequency and destructiveness of war, the international community has compiled an unprecedented record of mediating peaceful settlements to a number of protracted conflicts in the Third World.

These trends define a new agenda for the international community in the new century: how do we sustain the peace in nations previously torn by civil war? Each of the chapters here analyzes the prospects for building a sustainable peace from a number of different perspectives, examining: the role of economic development, democratization, respect for human rights, the potential for renewal of conflict, the United Nations, and other critical topics. In an age when "nation-building" is once again on the international agenda, and scholars as well as policymakers realize both the tremendous costs and benefits in fostering developed, democratic, peaceful and secure nations, the time has truly come for a book that integrates all the facets of this important subject.

T. David Mason is Johnie Christian Family Peace Professor, University of North Texas. He is the author of *Caught in the Crossfire: Revolution, Repression, and the Rational Peasant* (2003) and (co-edited with Abdul M. Turay), *Japan, NAFTA and Europe: Trilateral Cooperation or Confrontation?* (1994). **James D. Meernik** is Assistant Professor in the Department of Political Science, University of North Texas. He is the author of *The Political Use of Military Force in US Foreign Policy* (2004).

Contemporary security studies

Conflict Prevention and Peacebuilding in Post-War Societies

Sustaining the peace

Edited by T. David Mason and James D. Meernik

Routledge
Taylor & Francis Group

LONDON AND NEW YORK

First published 2006
by Routledge
2 Park Square, Milton Park, Abingdon, Oxon, OX14 4RN

Simultaneously published in the USA and Canada
by Routledge
270 Madison Ave, New York NY 10016

Routledge is an imprint of the Taylor & Francis Group

Transferred to Digital Printing 2009

© 2006 Selection and editorial matter, T. David Mason and James D. Meernik; individual chapters, the contributors

Typeset in Times by Wearset Ltd, Boldon, Tyne and Wear

British Library Cataloguing in Publication Data
A catalogue record for this book is available from the British Library

Library of Congress Cataloging in Publication Data
A catalog record for this book has been requested

ISBN10: 0-415-70213-5 (hbk)
ISBN10: 0-415-54495-5 (pbk)

ISBN13: 978-0-415-70213-3 (hbk)
ISBN13: 978-0-415-54495-5 (pbk)

Contents

Figures

Tables

Contributors

John A. Booth is Professor of Political Science at the University of North Texas.

Paul F. Diehl is Professor of Political Science at the University of Illinois.

Constance V. Elliott is Chief Operating Officer of Data Net Inc., a high-tech firm in Falls Church, Virginia.

V. Lani Elliott is a member of the adjunct faculty of the Joint Military Intelligence College, Washington, DC.

Andrew J. Enterline is Professor of Political Science at the University of North Texas.

The Right Honourable **Bruce George** is a Member of Parliament for Walsall South and President of the Parliamentary Assembly of the Organization for Security and Cooperation in Europe.

James L. Gibson is Professor of Political Science at Washington University, St Louis.

J. Michael Greig is Professor of Political Science at the University of North Texas.

Caroline A. Hartzell is Professor of Political Science at Gettysburg College, PA.

Seonjou Kang is Professor of Political Science at the University of North Texas.

Anthony McGee is Assistant to The Right Honourable Bruce George.

T. David Mason is Professor of Political Science at the University of North Texas.

James D. Meernik is Professor of Political Science at the University of North Texas.

Mark J. Mullenbach is Professor of Political Science at the University of Central Arkansas.

Mark Peceny is Professor of Political Science at the University of New Mexico.

Jeffrey Pickering is Professor of Political Science at Kansas State University.

Steven C. Poe is Professor of Political Science at the University of North Texas.

Jason Quinn is a PhD student at the University of North Texas.

Patricia Bayer Richard is Professor of Political Science at Ohio University.

Erum Shaikh is an instructor in Political Science at Richland Community College, Dallas.

Acknowledgments

The chapters in this book come principally from two conferences held at the University of North Texas, in Denton, Texas, in November 2003 and January 2005 on the subject of post-conflict peacebuilding. The editors would like to thank the University of North Texas, the College of Arts and Sciences and the Department of Political Science for their support for these conferences. We would also like to thank all the chapter authors for their hard work on these chapters and for contributing to such an excellent volume.

Abbreviations

ANC	African National Congress
ASI	Assembly Support Initiative
AU	African Union
BiH	Bosnia-Herzegovina
CCA	Court of Conciliation and Arbitration
CMF	Commonwealth Monitoring Force
COPAZ	Commission for the Consolidation of Peace
CSCE	Conference for Security Co-operation in Europe
DAC	Development Assistance Committee
DPA	Dayton Peace Agreement
DPED	Department of Police Education and Development
EC	European Community
ECOMOG	Economic Community of West African States Monitoring Group
ECOWAS	Economic Community of West African States
FMLN	Farabundo Marti Front for National Liberation
FSC	Forum of Security Cooperation
GNP	Gross National Product
GUNT	Transitional Government of National Unity
HCNM	High Commissioner on National Minorities
HRC	Human Rights Commission
IGO	Inter-Governmental Organization
IMF	International Monetary Fund
IMI	International Military Intervention
IOM	International Organization of Migration
LSP	Legislative Support Programme
MDTF	Multi-Donor Trust Fund
MFO	Multinational Force and Observers
MNLF	Moro National Liberation Front
MPLA	Popular Movement for the Liberation of Angola
NATO	North Atlantic Treaty Organization
NEP	New Economics Programme
NGO	Non-Governmental Organization

NP	National Party
OAS	Organization of American States
OAU	Organization of African Unity
OCHA	Office for the Coordination of Humanitarian Affairs
ODIHR	Office of Democratic Institutions and Human Rights
OMIK	OSCE Mission in Kosovo
ONUC	United Nations Operation in Congo
ONUCA	UN Observer Group in Central America
ONUMOZ	United Nations Operation on Mozambique
OSCE	Organization for Security and Co-operation in Europe
PA	Parliamentary Assembly
PBM	Peacebuilding Mission
PCF	Post-Conflict Fund
PEC	Provisional Election Commission
PITF	Political Instability Task Force
PKM	Peacekeeping Missions
PKO	Peacekeeping Operations
PMM	Peacemaking Missions
PPCF	Political Party Consultative Forums
PTS	Political Terror Scale
SPLM	Sudan People's Liberation Movement
SPMU	Strategic Police Matters Unit
SPR	Senior Police Advisor
TRC	Truth and Reconciliation Commission
UNEF I	United Nations Emergency Force
UNHCR	UN High Commission of Refugees
UNIFIL	United Nations Interim Force in Lebanon
UNITA	Union for the Total Independence of Angola
UNMIK	UN Interim Administration Mission in Kosova
UNOMIL	UN Observer Mission in Liberia
UNOSOM	UN Operation in Somalia
UNPREDEP	UN Operation in Macedonia
UNPROFOR	United Nations Protection Force
UNSOM	United Nations Operation in Somalia
UNTAC	UN Transitional Authority in Cambodia
UNTAG	United Nations Transition Assistance Group
UNTSO	UN Truce Supervision Organization
WFP	World Food Programme

Introduction

Sustaining the peace in the aftermath of conflict

James D. Meernik and T. David Mason

The US-led invasions of Afghanistan and Iraq focused the public's attention on the new forms of conflict that dominate the post-Cold War international environment. Rightly or wrongly, both wars were justified with reference to the events of September 11, 2001. Afghanistan was depicted as the long-standing safe haven and operational base of Osama Bin Laden's Al Qaeda network, and the Taliban regime was seen as Bin Laden's willing host and protector. Iraq was depicted as a rogue state that was at least sympathetic to Al Qaeda and (according to the Bush administration) an active accomplice with Bin Laden in the new international terrorist network that has replaced the Soviet Union with its nuclear arsenal as the dominant threat to the West. The invasion of Afghanistan, then, was justified on the grounds of finding and destroying the nerve center of that global network of terrorists and denying them the safe haven of Afghanistan by replacing a regime sympathetic to Al Qaeda with one that would be on track to join the community of democratic states. Similarly, the invasion of Iraq was justified on the grounds of preventing Saddam Hussein from launching or sponsoring his own 9-11 style assault and preempting his serving as a supplier of weapons of mass destruction to terror networks such as Al Qaeda. Iraq, too, would be launched on the road to democracy and serve as a beacon to the rest of the Middle East.

The aftermath of those two wars has confronted the public – and policy-makers – with the new realities of the new patterns of conflict in the post-Cold War era. Winning the wars against the Iraqs and Afghanistans of the world – in the sense of defeating their military on the battlefield and removing the offending regime from power – is relatively easy compared to winning the peace – in the sense of building a sustainable, reasonably prosperous, and democratic order out of the rubble of war. This is not to underestimate the danger and the difficulty of the initial military mission. It is simply to note that the interstate war phase of these conflicts – the war between the two US-led coalitions and the Taliban regime, in one case, and the Hussein regime, in the other – was completed in a matter of weeks with remarkable efficiency by the coalition forces. What has proven far more intractable is building a sustainable peace in the aftermath of these wars. In both nations, nominally democratic regimes have been installed. Yet both nations are torn by civil wars that threaten to erode the stability and legitimacy of these fledgling democracies and impede the sort of economic reconstruction that is essential to inoculating those societies against the appeals of local insurgents and international terrorists. As such, the survival of post-war democracy in both nations remains imperiled, and they remain ripe for revolution.

In many respects, however, the devastation wrought by decades of war in Afghanistan and the destruction resulting from the two US-led invasions of Iraq have been so deep and wide that the rebuilding efforts there are of an altogether different magnitude. If nothing else, these efforts have focused the attention of politicians and the public as never before on the complex array of humanitarian, political, economic, and cultural issues involved in remaking a nation. And the cost of these ventures dwarfs the cost of successful peacebuilding missions in several nations since 1989. Many scholars and policymakers have authored studies of the various peacekeeping, peacemaking and peacebuilding operations that have dotted the globe since the end of the Cold War. These works are too numerous to cite here, though many of them will be referenced in later chapters in this volume. Unfortunately, it appears that the hard and expensive lessons learned throughout this period do not seem to have fully registered among those most responsible for the peacebuilding efforts in Afghanistan and Iraq. Within months of the 9-11 attacks, for instance, the US Department of Defense announced plans to close its Peacekeeping Institute at the US Army War College in Carlisle, PA. While this decision was later reversed, the fact that it was announced even as US planners were preparing to invade Iraq leads one to wonder whether policymakers entered that war with a realistic awareness of what awaited them once the Hussein regime was deposed. Now more than ever, it is vitally important that we understand what works and what does not work when the international community takes over the responsibility of governing a nation. The collection of articles in this volume is intended to present an assessment of what social science theory, backed by empirical evidence, has to say about what does work and what doesn't in the enterprise of building a sustainable peace in the aftermath of civil war.

The increasing demand for knowledge about post-conflict reconstruction and reconciliation is motivated as well by the growing appreciation of changing trends in the patterns of both international and intranational conflicts. First, whereas wars *between* sovereign nations had dominated international politics for the previous three hundred years, civil wars *within* nations – revolutions, secessionist wars, ethnic conflicts, and terrorism – have become the most frequent and deadly forms of armed conflict since the end of World War II. Second, whereas Europe and the other major powers (the USA, China, Japan) had been the site of most of the world's interstate wars, the Third World – Asia, Africa, Latin America, and the Middle East – have become the site of almost all of the armed conflict that has punctuated the history of the last half century. Third, all of the more than one hundred civil wars in the Third World that began and ended between 1945 and 1997 occurred in less than 60 nations; indeed, less than half of those nations had one and only one civil war. The other, 30-plus nations experienced at least two and as many as five separate civil wars. Thus, not only has civil war become the dominant conflict modality in the international community; once it occurs in a nation, it is highly likely to recur at some time in the future.

While the end of the Cold War has not significantly reduced the frequency and destructiveness of civil war, the international community has compiled an unprecedented record of mediating peaceful settlements to a number of protracted conflicts in the Third World. Of the 55 peacekeeping operations established by the UN since its inception in 1945, 42 have been created since 1988. UN-mediated peace accords brought an end to civil wars in El Salvador, Mozambique, Namibia, Nicaragua, Guatemala, Angola, and Cambodia, to name but a few. Despite the difficulties inherent in sustaining the peace in the aftermath of civil war, most of the post-conflict regimes established by peace agreements and supported by peacekeeping missions have survived and managed to sustain the peace.

By contrast, where post-war nation-building, reconstruction, and reconciliation were not actively supported by the international community, civil war has often recurred. Moreover, in the absence of international support (in the form of peacekeeping and peacebuilding missions), a number of peace settlements have come unraveled, with a resumption of armed conflict not only inflicting more damage on the nation and its people, but complicating the prospects of ever restoring peace by undermining the warring parties' confidence in the peace process itself. At least three peace agreements have broken down in Angola in the past decade, while Liberia, Colombia, Guatemala, the Ivory Coast, Somalia, Sierra Leone, Sri Lanka, and the Sudan (among others) have experienced a resumption of armed conflict following the conclusion of a peace agreement.

These trends define a new agenda for the international community in the new century: how do we sustain the peace in nations previously torn by civil war? What factors distinguish those cases where the peace settlement endured from those where it collapsed? What measures can the international community take to ensure that peace does endure and human rights are progressively realized? Will the emerging international human rights regime continue to evolve and come to serve as an effective check on regimes' inhumane treatment of their own citizens? Can democracy be consolidated in societies that have had little or no experience of popular rule? Can economies that have been devastated by the physical destruction and capital flight that accompany civil war be rebuilt and placed on a pathway to sustainable growth? What should be done with the tyrants and war criminals who engaged in massive violations of international humanitarian law? And what role can and should the international community play in addressing and resolving these issues? Does it impose democracy and development on war-torn societies in the name of security, or does it simply facilitate and finance the work of local actors? These are the issues and the questions we will explore in this volume.

The issues we explore are all part of what we consider to be peacebuilding. Peacebuilding has been defined in various ways and for sundry purposes by policymakers and academics. The "peace" component of the term is generally understood to encompass, minimally, "negative peace" or the absence of violence. Prevention of the recurrence of conflict after war, or the emergence of other types of violence, is the necessary bedrock on which the foundation for creating and sustaining the other broader and "positive" forms of peace is based. Positive peace includes a vast array of activities designed to improve the lives of the people in conflict nations in order to make the opportunity cost of violence high and the benefits of peace substantial. Among the many types of actions that are encompassed under "positive peace" that we might find international and local actors supporting are democratization, the promotion of human rights, economic development, the repatriation of refugees, the establishment of truth commissions, and the promotion of civil society. The means by which this positive peace is pursued will differ across nations and the types of conflicts fought and so no two plans for peace will ever look exactly the same. Yet they all share a common goal. As Lewis Rasmussen (1997: 41) writes:

> Peacebuilding, whether in the post conflict resolution phase or as efforts to prevent the eruption of nascent conflict, depends on the ability to transform the conflict situation from one of potential or actual mass violence to one of co-operative, peaceful relationships capable of fostering reconciliation, reconstruction, and long-term economic and social development.

As we examine the many instances of international and local efforts to create and sustain this kind of peace, we must always remain mindful of the fact that it is this transformative element upon which the efforts must be judged. The specific goals of peacebuilding are only means to a greater end. While tasks, projects, and plans may be fulfilled, only if these actions produce peace can the effort truly be judged a success.

Our main aim in this volume is to assess how best negative peace can be sustained and how positive peace can be built in societies that have gone through periods of conflict and violence, whether transitory, episodic, or chronic. We take a decidedly empirical approach to analyzing the best available information on negative and positive peace. We do not aim to build theory here; rather, we wish to provide the reader with an analysis of what works and what doesn't in peacebuilding by evaluating the best available data on the subject. In some cases identifying the most effective peacebuilding tools can be fairly simple (if not always easy to employ), while in most instances, determining whether peacebuilding is helped or hindered by some endeavor (e.g., democratization) is fraught with complexities. Understanding these complexities, contingencies, and conditions is vitally important in recognizing when peacebuilding is most likely to succeed or fail. Thus, a full awareness of the costs and benefits, the successes and failures of peacebuilding depends on being ever mindful of these difficulties.

The plan of the book

The book is divided into two parts. Part I presents a series of chapters that explore several themes in constructing "negative peace": what can be done to bring civil wars to an end, and how we can prevent the conflict from recurring. Chapter 1 by Mason and Quinn presents an overview of the patterns of conflict in the past half century, noting, first, that civil war has replaced interstate war as the modal form of conflict in the international system and, second, that once a nation experiences one civil war, it is highly likely to experience another. They then discuss the characteristics of the conflict and the post-conflict environment that make a resumption of civil war more or less likely in a nation. Their chapter analyzes how a variety of intervention tools available to the international community can affect the incentives of both rebels and governments, first, to stop the fighting by agreeing to a negotiated settlement and, second, to sustain the peace.

Carolyn Hartzell's Chapter 2 then analyzes how civil wars can be brought to an end under the terms of a negotiated settlement. What motivates belligerents to agree to such measures? What are the terms to which civil war adversaries agree as part of a negotiated civil war settlement? And what implications do the terms of a settlement have for the ability of the post-civil war regime to sustain the peace and prevent a relapse into civil war? She presents an analysis of civil war settlement agreements that were negotiated during the years 1945–1999, with special attention to the nature of the power-sharing and power-dividing institutions that former foes construct as a means of addressing the security concerns they bring with them to the bargaining table. Settlement architects can negotiate institutions to share or divide power for any one of the four dimensions of state power that rival groups tend to be most concerned about: military, political, territorial, and economic. She finds that those settlements that have been most highly institutionalized – i.e., those that include power-sharing or power-dividing institutions grounded in several or all of these dimensions – are the most likely to produce a durable peace. The chapter concludes with a discussion of the implications of power-sharing and power-dividing institutions for democracy as well as the international community's role in the construction of negotiated settlements to civil war.

Mark Mullenbach's Chapter 3 extends the analysis of peacekeeping to the question of whether such interventions do in fact contribute to sustaining the peace in the aftermath of civil war. Since the end of World War II, and particularly since the end of the Cold War, third party actors have frequently intervened during post-conflict phases of intrastate disputes in order to enhance both prospects that the disputes do not re-escalate into military hostilities and that the disputes are peacefully resolved through negotiations between the parties. As a result of these interventions, policy-makers and scholars have debated whether third party peacebuilding (or "state-building") efforts – including providing electoral assistance, re-establishing the rule of law, providing for displaced persons and administering territory – have generally been effective or ineffective in managing and resolving intrastate disputes. Mullenbach tests a series of hypotheses regarding both short-term and long-term effectiveness of third party peacebuilding interventions on post-conflict peacebuilding. His findings are instructive with respect to the value of such interventions in preventing the relapse into armed conflict.

The Right Honourable Bruce George, a member of the British House of Commons and the President of the Organization for Security and Cooperation in Europe (OSCE) Parliamentary Assembly, has been involved as a participant in OSCE election observation missions. As a Member of Parliament, he has also participated in the deliberations of key policymakers on how to fashion post-war reconstruction programs that enhance the prospect of sustaining the peace. Chapter 4 begins with the proposition that IGO involvement in post-war reconstruction and reconciliation will not work unless the incumbent regime wants it to work. How do you persuade a government that includes former protagonists that it is in their interest to sustain the peace? George's chapter provides some insight into the role of IGOs in both brokering a peace settlement and (perhaps more importantly) monitoring the post-war situation to ensure that former protagonists do not choose to resume armed conflict rather than work to resolve the differences that inevitably arise in constructing a viable post-conflict political order. IGOs such as OSCE and the UN serve as the "eyes and ears" of the international community and, as such, provide "early warning" of the possibility of conflict resumption. The IGO presence also provides former protagonists with a third party to which they can appeal when stalemates arise over issues of institutional design and policy. The presence of a credible mediating authority that has the support of the international community can enhance the prospects of peaceful resolution to policy conflicts. In the absence of IGO involvement, former protagonists are more likely to conclude that peaceful resolution of these issues is unlikely and resuming armed conflict is preferable to policy stalemate.

Chapter 5 by Paul Diehl provides a transition to the second half of the volume, in which a series of chapters explore the elements of positive peace: once a civil war has been brought to a peaceful conclusion, what can be done to reduce the risk of conflict resuming? Paul Diehl opens Part II with an overview of the evolution of UN peacekeeping operations as a mechanism for building sustainable peace. Peacekeeping is a relatively new phenomenon in international relations, but it has nevertheless changed dramatically during its short existence. Diehl's chapter traces the origins of peacekeeping from the League of Nations to the present. Peacekeeping "epochs" are identified and the characteristics of those periods are presented. He presents descriptive statistics for post-1945 operations on several dimensions of peacekeeping missions, including the number, size, and type of missions deployed, the locations of their deployment, and other characteristics relevant to their success at preserving the peace. His analysis shows how peacekeeping has evolved from the traditional function of policing a truce between protagonists in interstate wars to the more robust, multi-dimensional peacebuilding in the aftermath of civil war.

Chapter 6 by Mark Peceny and Jeffrey Pickering examines the military interventions undertaken by the USA, the UK, France, and the UN in the post-World War II era to determine whether they have had a positive impact on democracy in target countries. Their findings demonstrate that target states are more likely to democratize and to develop stable forms of democratic governance in the wake of interventions by the USA and the UN than after interventions by the British and the French. At times, the prospects of democracy are advanced by the intervention of outside military forces, particularly those dispatched by Washington or by the UN Security Council.

Chapter 7 by Andrew Enterline and Michael Greig directly addresses the rationales for the interventions in Iraq and Afghanistan. In early spring 2003, just prior to the start of the second war against Iraq, the Bush Administration argued that democratizing Iraq through force would result in greater peace, prosperity, and democracy in the Middle East. Discussion of democratization normally centers upon the ways in which it arises indigenously and the forces that shape its success. Yet, as we have seen in both the American interventions in Iraq and Afghanistan, democracy can also be imposed from without. Not only does imposed democracy carry important ramifications for the citizens of the democratizing state itself, but policymakers have argued that imposed democracies carry important regional effects by stimulating not only democracy in neighboring states but also by promoting prosperity and a broader regional peace. In this chapter, Enterline and Greig discuss the regional impact of imposed democracies upon their neighbors and examine the evidence for the positive effects of imposed democracies.

Besides installing the formal institutions of democracy, the interventions in Afghanistan and Iraq were justified on the grounds that democracy would bring greater freedom to the citizens of those nations. James Meernik, Steven Poe, and Erum Shaikh explore this proposition in Chapter 8 by assessing the impact of military interventions on the human rights performance of regimes. Throughout history, states have used military force to impose political systems upon other societies. Indeed, the United States increasingly has used force during and after episodes of political violence to promote improvements in human rights conditions as an end itself, and as a means by which to secure the peace. Scholars are now beginning to analyze the success of attempts to impose liberal, democratic systems on nations. These analyses have largely focused on macro-level, systemic, and constitutional changes in government institutions, generally in the context of widespread political violence. In this chapter, the authors explore the degree to which uses of force by the United States have been able to effect change at the micro, or individual, level. The substance of democracy may lag behind if elected officials and citizens do not fully subscribe to critical, democratic norms such as civil liberties, tolerance, and the foreswearance of violence as a political tool. This chapter provides the first assessment of whether these uses of force have acted to improve the substance of democracy: the right to speak one's own mind, to practice the religion of one's choice and simply to live peacefully, free of the fear of imprisonment and government-sponsored violence. The findings indicate, however, that though democracy and human rights are among the considerations that determine whether the USA does use force in a particular case, uses of force are ineffective at promoting improvements in human rights. If the improvement of human rights conditions is thought to be one of the critical elements of military actions during or after civil wars, the results presented here suggest that military force alone is not sufficient for the realization of such objectives.

There is a powerful cultural dimension to sustaining the peace in the aftermath of civil war, and the next two chapters explore critical dimensions of this issue. Conflicts harden enmities and make it difficult for former enemies to contest for power peacefully through the institutions of democracy. James Gibson's Chapter 9 examines the role of post-war truth and reconciliation commissions in reducing that enmity and making it possible for reconciliation to proceed at least to the point of avoiding a resumption of armed conflict. Throughout the world, truth commissions have been (and are being) constructed in the hope that discovering the "truth" about a country's conflictual past will somehow contribute to "reconciliation." Most such efforts point to South Africa's truth and reconciliation process as an exemplar of the powerful influence of truth finding. But has truth actually contributed to reconciliation in South Africa? Until recently, no one could answer this question since no rigorous and systematic assessment of the success of the truth and reconciliation process had ever been conducted. Gibson's chapter identifies the characteristics of the truth and reconciliation process that contributed to its performance. Three factors are singled out as being critical to the success of the South African endeavor: (1) that the Truth and Reconciliation Commission (TRC) defined its objective as creating broad social change; (2) that "story-telling" hearings rather than formal trials were adopted as the primary means of ascertaining "truth"; and (3) that the TRC acted with considerable independence and evenhandedness in its efforts to discover "truth" and enhance "reconciliation."

John Booth and Patricia Bayer Richard in Chapter 10 use cross-national survey data to assess the extent to which the political culture of nations previously torn by civil war evolves, and whether a culture that is supportive of democracy can replace the culture of conflict that is often conditioned by years of civil war. Democracy, citizen participation in rule, involves citizens engaging the state through voting, demand-making, electioneering, and engaging each other in civil society. The consolidation of democracy requires, among other things, that citizens develop and maintain democratic norms and that antidemocratic attitudes decline. The political context, especially repression, institutional democracy, and levels of political violence, directly affects citizen attitudes, civil society, and political participation. The six Central American nations in the early 1990s provide a virtual laboratory for examining the impact of context (in the form of conflict) on participation, attitudes, and civil society. Levels of conflict in the region between the mid-1970s and the early 1990s varied broadly. At the stable end of a continuum was Costa Rica, which remained politically stable and free of war. At the high conflict end of the conflict continuum were Nicaragua, El Salvador, and Guatemala, which experienced lengthy civil wars. Honduras and Panama fell in between these extremes. Booth and Richard employ virtually identical surveys of the urban populations of all six Central American nations in the early 1990s to examine comparatively how conflict affected political attitudes, participation, and civil society. Evidence suggests that high levels of conflict reduced the level of support for democracy and depressed political participation and civil society. Their analysis concludes with an examination of the implications of this legacy for post-conflict Central America and its prospects for democratic consolidation.

The final two chapters examine the critical element of post-conflict economic reconstruction.

A high incidence of poverty has consistently been implicated as a cause of civil war, in the sense that the lower the level of economic well-being of a nation's citizens, the greater that nation's risk of experiencing a civil war, *ceteris paribus*. Given the fact that civil war imposes further destruction on an already weak economy, it should not be surprising that nations that experienced one civil war are at risk of experiencing another one. Therefore, a critical challenge for sustaining the peace is rebuilding the economy to the point that the opportunity costs of participating in armed conflict are too great to allow the mobilization of civil war. In Chapter 11, Seonjou Kang extends the analysis of the economics of sustaining the peace by examining the impact of international efforts at promoting economic growth in the aftermath of civil war. Poverty and underdevelopment are often causes of conflicts in the developing world, while their economically destructive consequences are numerous and severe. In that light, much of successful peace maintenance in war-affected societies will hinge on how rapidly their economies can recover. Because of the risk that these societies will relapse into civil strife, it is extremely important to understand how countries that have experienced war can achieve economic recovery and what steps the international community can take to advance development. Kang analyzes the role played by economic assistance from the international community in post-civil war economic recovery. She reviews what is known about the beneficial aspects of economic assistance on economic development in countries that have just emerged from civil wars, concluding that such efforts play a significant role in promoting economic growth, but that their effects also depend heavily upon the quality of governance in such societies.

In Chapter 12, Connie and Lani Elliott present a survey of the findings from the World Bank project on the Economics of Conflict. Those findings include some interesting implications about how post-war economic development might affect the likelihood of civil war recurring in a nation. However, the World Bank team's mandate precluded them from drawing inferences beyond what their data could support. Elliott, as a member of the team that wrote the final report of that project, extrapolates from the World Bank Project and explores the ways in which post-war economic development – and the international community's support of it – can help to immunize a nation against the recurrence of civil war.

This collection of essays is by no means comprehensive. However, we hope that it does offer a useful addition to the growing literature on post-war reconstruction and reconciliation. Much of the work on that subject is intended for policymakers and policy analysts, but this text has been written to appeal to students and all who are interested in peacebuilding. It often includes detailed case studies of specific peacebuilding operations, and evaluations of the specific dimensions of those efforts. The aim of this volume is to bring to bear theory, methods, and empirical evidence compiled by social scientists on the issue of peacebuilding. In so doing, we believe the chapters in this volume not only contribute to framing more precisely the critical issues involved in post-civil war peacebuilding but also offer some insights into how social science research can contribute to the formulation of policies and programs that have a better chance of fulfilling the goal of sustaining the peace in the aftermath of civil war.

Reference

Rasmussen, J. Lewis (1997) "The Changing Orthodoxy and Orthopraxy of Peacemaking," in I. William Zartman and J. Lewis Rasmussen (eds.) *Peacemaking in International Conflict: Methods and Techniques*. Washington, DC: United States Institute of Peace Press.

Part I

Conflict prevention

Working toward "negative" peace

1 Sustaining the peace

Stopping the recurrence of civil wars

T. David Mason and Jason Quinn

Since the end of World War II, there has not been a single day in which there was not an armed conflict of some sort going on somewhere in the world. That observation in and of itself is, unfortunately, not especially provocative or startling to anyone who reads a daily newspaper. What may not be as obvious is that the patterns of armed conflict have changed dramatically since the end of World War II. Both the predominant form and primary locus of armed conflict have shifted dramatically from the patterns that had prevailed for the previous 300 years. First, whereas war *between* nations was the modal form of conflict for the three centuries prior to World War II, since 1945 the predominant form of armed conflict has been civil war (revolution, secession, ethnic conflict); interstate war has become relatively rare. Second, whereas the interstate wars of the previous 300 years took place mainly among (and on the territory of) the members of the central power system (including Europe and North America, plus Japan and China), the civil wars of the past half century have occurred almost exclusively in the Third World (Asia, Africa, and Latin America). Indeed, until the collapse of Leninist regimes in Eastern Europe in 1989 and the disintegration of Yugoslavia and the Soviet Union in 1991, there had been no major civil wars on European soil, and only China among the major powers had experienced any conflicts of sufficient magnitude to warrant inclusion in any of the major civil war data sets.[1]

The frequency and destructiveness of this epidemic of civil war are well documented. No matter which data set one employs, there is no doubt that since 1945 civil wars have been far more frequent and destructive than interstate wars. Fearon and Laitin (2003) report that between 1945 and 1999, among all nations with populations over 500,000, there have been five times as many civil wars as interstate wars (127 to 25), and that civil wars have resulted in five times as many casualties as interstate wars (16.2 million versus 3.3 million). The latest version of the Correlates of War (COW) data set reveals similar patterns: COW2 lists 104 civil wars with a total of 13.3 million battle deaths as compared to 22 interstate wars with about 3.3 million battle deaths. To date, the end of the Cold War has not brought any substantial relief from the epidemic of civil wars: Wallensteen and Sollenberg (2001: 632) report that 104 of the 111 armed conflicts that they documented as occurring between 1989 and 2000 were civil wars. Indeed, what the end of the Cold War has brought is the diffusion of civil war to Yugoslavia and the republics of the former Soviet Union, regions of the world that had been more or less immune to armed rebellion during the Cold War.

Besides this change in the modal *form* of conflict, the predominant *locus* of conflict has shifted from Europe and the so-called central power system to Third World regions of Asia, Africa, and Latin America. Whereas Europe had been by far the most war-prone region of the world for the three hundred years prior to World War II, the end of that conflict ushered in what John Gaddis (1987) has termed "the long peace": the longest period of sustained peace among European powers since the Treaty of Westphalia in 1648. Kal Holsti (1992: 37) notes that from 1945 until 1989, there were only four instances of the use of armed force by European states against each other on European soil: the British intervention in the Greek civil war (1945–1948), the Soviet intervention in Hungary (1956), the Warsaw Treaty Organization (WTO) intervention in Czechoslovakia (1968), and the Turkish invasion of Cyprus (1974). These conflicts resulted in approximately 176,000 deaths, a figure that constitutes less than 1 percent of the 22 million battle deaths that Holsti claims occurred worldwide during that same period. All the remaining battle deaths presumably occurred on the soil of Third World nations. Of course, this long peace was less a matter of Kantian harmony than of nuclear stalemate. With Europe divided into two hostile alliances, each with nuclear arsenals sufficient to threaten the extinction of the human species, war between traditional rivals of the Euro-centric power system was simply not rational. Therefore, their rivalries were, to some extent, carried out indirectly, through intervention – direct and indirect, overt and covert – in the conflicts that erupted within and between the nations of the Third World.

Critical trends: the duration and recurrence of civil wars

Explaining the epidemic of civil wars in the Third World has been the subject of a steady stream of academic books and journal articles, and this is not the place to review that literature. What is relevant to the theme of this book – how to sustain the peace in the aftermath of civil war – are two other observable trends in the distribution of civil wars across time and space. First, the duration of civil wars has been gradually but steadily increasing over much of the post-World War II period. James Fearon has shown that the upward trend in the number of civil wars ongoing in a given year – a trend that peaked around 1994 – was not a function of any increase in the average number of new civil war outbreaks in a year.

Instead, a gradual increase in the duration of ongoing wars meant that the number of wars ending in a given year was less than the (nearly constant) number of new war onsets, resulting in the "steady accumulation of unresolved wars" (Fearon 2004: 275).

Related to the increasing duration of civil wars is what appears to be a rather robust relationship between the duration of a civil war and its outcome: the longer a civil war lasts, the less likely it is that either the rebels or the government will achieve a decisive military victory. Mason and Fett (1996) found that the strongest predictor of a war ending in a negotiated settlement (as opposed to a military victory by either side) was the duration of the war. In a follow-up study, Mason, Weingarten and Fett (1999) found that rebel victories, if they occur at all, almost always occur in the first few years of the war, and much the same holds for government victories as well: if the government does not defeat a rebel movement within the first five years or so, thereafter it becomes increasingly unlikely that the government will ever win (see also DeRouen and Sobek 2004).

These findings imply that, contrary to Edward Luttwak's (1999) "give war a chance" thesis, civil wars will not burn themselves out like brush fires, nor will the conditions of a more lasting peace emerge if the international community simply stands aside and allows the protagonists to fight it out to a decisive victory by one side or the other. The empirical evidence consistently shows that, past some point in the duration of a civil war, neither side is likely to achieve military victory. Instead, protracted conflicts settle into what William Zartman (1989) has termed a "mutually hurting stalemate," whereby both sides lack the capacity to defeat the other side but both have the capacity to deny victory to their rival. At that point, the conflicts are "ripe for resolution," lacking only the intervention of a third-party mediator to broker a settlement agreement and provide both sides with guarantees against the other side cheating on the agreement in order to achieve through surprise the victory that had eluded them on the battlefield. However, rarely are the protagonists in a civil war able to negotiate a settlement to the conflict without third-party mediation and third-party guarantees (see Walter 2002). Contrary to Luttwak's recommendation, if the international community does choose to stand aside and "give war a chance," this amounts to tacitly condoning a protracted blood-letting that is not likely to end on its own and, even if it does, will leave the nation so decimated that it immediately becomes a prime candidate for a new civil war.

This leads us to the second readily observable trend in civil war occurrence that is directly relevant to the question of how to sustain the peace in the aftermath of civil war. Since 1945 the number of nations that have experienced civil wars is considerably less than the total number of civil wars that have occurred, indicating that many nations have experienced multiple civil wars. As Table 1.1 indicates, the 104 civil wars that the Correlates of War lists as occurring between 1944 and 1997 took place in only

16   *T. David Mason and Jason Quinn*

Table 1.1 The frequency of civil war occurrences in nations, 1944–2001

Number of civil wars	Nations experiencing specified number of civil wars	
	Doyle and Sambanis (2000)	*Correlates of War 2*
1	36	28
2	18	8
3	9	13
4	5	4
5	1	1
Total wars	124	101
Total nations	69	54

54 nations. Only 28 of those nations experienced one and only one civil war. Eight had two civil wars, 13 had three, four had four, and one nation experienced five civil wars (Sarkees 2000). The Doyle and Sambanis (2000) data set of 124 civil wars occurred in just 69 nations. Only 36 of these nations had one and only one civil war, while 18 had two separate conflicts, nine nations had three, five nations had four, and one nation had five. It is evident, then, that once a nation experiences a civil war, it is very likely to experience another one.

Given these two trends, the practical task of peacebuilding in the contemporary international community is not so much a matter of developing early warning systems to predict which nations are likely candidates for a new civil war in the near future. Rather, the more practical (and probably cost-effective) task is, first, to identify those civil wars that are "ripe for resolution" (because of their duration); second, to design effective third-party intervention strategies to persuade them to negotiate and devise a mutually acceptable settlement agreement; and, third, to support that agreement with a sustained and effective post-conflict reconstruction and reconciliation program that inoculates that nation against the recurrence of civil war. In short, the challenge for sustaining the peace is how first to bring a civil war to a peaceful conclusion and, second, how to prevent it from recurring.

With these observations in mind, we turn now to the task of presenting a theoretical framework with which we can analyze the conditions that make the parties to a civil war more or less likely to agree to a negotiated settlement (as opposed to continuing to fight in anticipation of eventually achieving victory). We will then use this framework to analyze the features of the post-civil war environment that make a nation more or less susceptible to the resumption of civil war. In explaining the outcomes of civil war and the conditions that make the recurrence of civil war more likely, we will also be able to highlight those features of the civil war environment that are subject to policy manipulation by the international community in such a way as to increase the incentives of both sides to stop the killing and agree to a settlement. Similarly, in explaining the conditions that make a nation more likely to experience a relapse into civil war, we will also be able to identify those features of the post-civil war environment that are subject to intervention by the international community in such a way as reduce the incentives to resume conflict by building a post-conflict environment that can sustain the peace.

How civil wars end . . . and start again

The initiation – and recurrence – of a civil war require two general preconditions. First, what Charles Tilly (1978) has termed a *revolutionary situation* must emerge, leading potential combatants to conclude that civil war is both necessary and feasible. Tilly (ibid.: 200) describes a revolutionary situation as the emergence of a condition of *dual sovereignty*, marked by

> the appearance of contenders or coalitions of contenders, advancing exclusive alternative claims to the control over the government ...; commitment to those claims by a significant segment of the subject population ...; the incapacity or unwillingness of the government or its agents to suppress the challenger coalition.

A condition of dual sovereignty represents the structural antecedent of civil war in the sense that civil war becomes possible when dual sovereignty emerges. It also represents a necessary precondition for the recurrence of civil war as well: sustaining the peace in the aftermath of civil war will be more difficult to the extent that the outcome of the previous war preserves intact a condition of dual sovereignty, or at least makes it possible for such a condition to re-emerge with relative ease.

There is also an element of agency in the onset and recurrence of civil war: one or both of the potential combatants must conclude that renewing armed conflict is preferable to the post-conflict status quo. This implies that, for that actor, the expected benefits of eventual victory exceed the benefits of sustaining the peace, even when the benefits from victory are discounted by the probability of winning and the accrued costs that will have to be absorbed in order to achieve victory.

Tilly's concept of dual sovereignty underlies the often-cited proposition that civil wars are more likely to resume following negotiated settlements than following decisive military victories by one side or the other (Licklider 1995; Walter 1997; Hartzell and Hoddie 2003). Military victories are assumed to create a more stable (though not necessarily more abundant, democratic or humane) post-war environment because military victory by one side usually involves the destruction of the other side's ability to wage war. In effect, military victory reduces the probability of civil war recurrence by eliminating the condition of dual sovereignty.

Even among conflicts that end in negotiated settlements, the probability of civil war recurrence declines with settlement conditions that weaken or dismantle the condition of dual sovereignty. Hartzell's analysis of the sustainability of peace agreements implies that dual sovereignty must be replaced by enforceable power-sharing arrangements (see Hartzell *et al.* 2001). The power-sharing arrangements to which she refers – military, political, economic, and territorial – involve dismantling the organizational machinery of two combatant organizations and merging them under the institutions of a single state. The consistent finding across her studies is that the more dimensions of power sharing that are included in the settlement agreement, the less likely the settlement is to break down into a resumption of armed conflict. Implicit in this argument is the notion that multi-dimensional power sharing dismantles the condition of dual sovereignty.

The question of agency in the recurrence of civil wars involves the decision calculus by which potential combatants choose between sustaining the peace or resuming war. Mason and Fett (1996) presented an expected utility model of that choice, derived from the works of Wittman (1979) and Stam (1996) on how interstate wars end. This model has proven to be useful in identifying the factors that predict whether a civil war will end in a military victory or a negotiated settlement (Mason and Fett 1996), whether such conflicts will end in a government victory, a rebel victory or a negotiated settlement (Mason *et al.* 1999), the determinants of the duration of a civil war (DeRouen and Sobek 2004; Brandt *et al.* 2005), and the recurrence of civil war (Mason and Quinn 2003).

We can depict the choice to sustain peace or resume civil war as a function of the difference in the expected utility from resuming conflict versus abiding by the terms of a settlement. The payoff from resuming conflict can be depicted as follows:

$$EU_{CW} = P_V(U_V) + (1 - P_V)(U_D) - \sum_{t_i=0}^{t_v} C_{t_i}$$

where EU_{CW} is the expected utility of resuming the civil war, U_V is the expected payoff from eventual victory, P_V is the probability of achieving victory, U_D is the expected cost from defeat, $(1 - P_V)$ is the probability of defeat, C is the rate at which the costs of conflict will be absorbed from the present time ($t_i = 0$) through that time in the future in which victory is achieved, t_v. For an actor (government or rebels) to prefer a resumption of civil war to sustaining the peace, the expected utility of resuming the civil war, EU_{CW}, must be greater than the expected utility of sustaining the peace, EU_S.

The expected payoffs from sustaining the peace are depicted in Equation 2:

$$EU_S = U_S + \sum_{t_i=0}^{t_v} C_{t_i} - \sum_{t_i=0}^{t_s} C_{t_i}$$

where EU_S is the expected utility from a negotiated settlement, U_S is the payoff from the terms of the settlement. By agreeing to a settlement, the parties save the costs of achieving victory

$$\sum_{t_i=0}^{t_s} C_{t_i};$$

in effect, their utility from abiding by the terms of a post-war settlement is augmented by the costs they save from not resuming the war and fighting on to eventual victory. The only costs they have to absorb are those that accrue until t_s, the point in time when the settlement is achieved and the fighting stops ($t_s < t_v$).

This decision calculus implies that any variable which (1) decreases an actor's estimate of the probability of victory; (2) decreases the payoffs from victory; (3) increases the rate at which the costs of conflict are absorbed; (4) increases the duration of the war, or (5) increases the payoffs from sustaining the peace should increase that actor's incentive to sustain the peace rather than resume the civil war.

Combining the considerations of structure and agency, we would expect a recurrence of civil war if (1) a condition of dual sovereignty persists after the initial war ends; and (2) for at least one of the former protagonists the expected utility of resuming war is greater than the expected utility of sustaining peace. Conversely, preserving the peace can be enhanced by constructing a post-war institutional structure that dismantles the condition of dual sovereignty and reduces the incentives to resume the civil war rather than accept the peace. This theoretical framework also suggests a series of policy initiatives that the international community and post-civil war regimes can undertake to enhance the prospects for sustaining the peace and reduce the probability of a resumption of armed conflict.

Sustaining the peace and the outcome of civil wars

We begin with the proposition that the duration of a civil war and the probability of its recurrence are both in part a function of whether the initial civil war ended in a government victory, a rebel victory, or a negotiated settlement. The outcome of the civil war is arguably the single most important indicator of whether the structural conditions of dual sovereignty are preserved in the post-civil war environment. As such, the outcome of the civil war is a major determinant of whether the structural conditions exist that make a resumption of armed conflict possible, if not likely.

In terms of structure, the outcome of the prior civil war – i.e., whether it ended in a government victory, a rebel victory, or a negotiated settlement – affects the probability of civil war recurrence in that each of these three outcomes has a different effect on the extent to which a condition of dual sovereignty persists after the civil war ends. Mason and Quinn (2003) have argued that civil wars are less likely to recur following rebel victories than following government victories. Often, the defeat of an armed rebellion by the incumbent regime merely constitutes a lull in the fighting. The rebels are driven underground, where they rebuild their strength and resurface to resume the conflict at some later date. The members of a rebel organization on the verge of defeat (but not a government on the verge of collapse) can avoid annihilation on the battlefield by blending into the civilian population and awaiting that time in the future when they can muster sufficient strength to revive the conflict. Thus, any battlefield defeat short of annihilation is not likely to preempt the rebels' capacity to revive their armed challenge at some time in the future. The fact that a civil war broke out in the first place indicates the existence of a condition of contested sovereignty of sufficient severity that thousands of civilians actively supported an armed challenge to the incumbent regime, and several times that number tacitly supported the rebellion by taking no active steps to assist the government in defeating it. The rebels' defeat on the battlefield in and of itself does nothing to resolve the grievances that led that segment of the civilian population to support the rebellion in the first place, whether actively or tacitly. Therefore, they remain available for mobilization by the rebels in the future, should they restore their organizational capacity and military strength.

By contrast, a rebel victory should be less likely to be followed by a recurrence of civil war because rebel victory is more likely to eliminate the condition of dual sovereignty. Officials of the defeated government do not have the option of hiding among the civilian population. When rebel victory becomes imminent, exile is the only viable option for officials of that government and its military if they wish to avoid annihilation. In this sense, we would expect rebel victories to be more decisive than government victories, at least in the sense of eliminating the condition of dual sovereignty and thereby reducing the probability of civil war recurrence.

As noted earlier, however, military victory by either side becomes less likely, the longer the civil war lasts. Therefore, past some point in the history of a civil war, conflict settles into a mutually hurting stalemate that can persist indefinitely and likely will unless some third party intervenes to mediate a settlement to the conflict. It is at this point that the international community can bring about peace by brokering a settlement and supporting it with enforcement mechanisms (such as peacekeeping forces) and reconstruction support that make sustaining the peace more attractive than resuming the conflict for both parties. Other chapters in this volume address the particulars of how this challenge can be met.

Once peace is established through a negotiated settlement, the new regime is confronted with the challenge of preventing a relapse into conflict because, as noted earlier, negotiated settlements are more likely to break down into a recurrence of conflict than are military victories by either side. Military victory ends the condition of dual sovereignty by disrupting or destroying the organizational capacity of the defeated side's forces, making it more difficult for that party to mobilize the human and material resources necessary to renew the war effort. By contrast, negotiated settlements often preserve elements of dual sovereignty and thereby leave the nation more susceptible to a resumption of armed conflict.

However, there are features of the post-civil war environment established by a negotiated settlement that can enhance the prospects of the settlement holding and the peace lasting. As noted earlier, Hartzell has shown that the more dimensions of power sharing (i.e., military, political, territorial, and economic) that are built into the terms of the settlement agreement, the more likely the peace is to last (Hartzell 1999; Hartzell *et al.* 2001; Hartzell and Hoddie 2003). Doyle and Sambanis (2000) as well as Fortna (2004) have shown that the introduction of peacekeeping operations to enforce the terms of the settlement can sustain the peace. Negotiated settlements are more likely to hold in the presence of a peacekeeping operation that can police the disarming and demobilization of the two armed forces and provide both sides with security guarantees against their rival violating the agreement to launch a surprise attack (Walter 2002; Fortna 2004). In this manner, peacekeeping forces enhance the prospects of sustaining the peace following a negotiated settlement.

Costs and benefits of resuming the war

Besides the structural consideration of dual sovereignty, we can identify a set of conditions in the post-conflict environment that affect former combatants' estimate of the costs and benefits of resuming the conflict. Sustaining the peace, then, becomes a matter of reducing the incentives to resume combat and increasing the incentives to accept the status quo. As noted earlier, the decision calculus by which government and rebels choose between resuming the conflict or sustaining the peace implies that any factor which (1) increases the costs of resuming conflict; (2) reduces the expected benefits of victory (relative to the benefits from peace); (3) extends the time required to achieve victory through armed conflict; or (4) decreases the estimated probability of achieving victory should make the parties less likely to resume the conflict and more willing to sustain the peace.

Stakes of the conflict: ethnic divisions

Ethnic civil wars differ from ideologically based civil wars in that the stakes (i.e., the benefits of victory) are more nearly indivisible. Therefore, ethnic civil wars are less likely to be brought to an end through a negotiated settlement (Licklider 1995; Mason and Fett 1996). They also tend to last longer, all else being equal, although the findings on this question are not consistent. DeRouen and Sobek (2004: 305) suggest that the presence of ethnic issues dividing the protagonists in a civil war may impede their ability to reach a settlement and, therefore, prolong the war beyond the time it would have lasted were it not ethnically based, *ceteris paribus*. Fearon (2004) finds that "sons of the soil" rebellion by regionally concentrated ethnic minorities resisting the intrusion into their homeland of the state's authority also tend to be longer in duration, but he finds that whether or not a civil war is ethnically based in and of itself does not appear to lengthen the duration of the conflict.

Ethnically based civil wars are also more likely to recur than those that are not ethnically based. Chaim Kaufman (1996) presents the rationale as follows:

> The key difference is the flexibility of individual loyalties, which are quite fluid in ideological conflicts, but almost completely rigid in ethnic wars ... War hardens ethnic identity to the point that cross-ethnic political appeals become futile ... Ethnic wars also generate intense security dilemmas, both because the escalation of each side's mobilization rhetoric presents a real threat to the other, and even more because intermingled population settlement patterns create defensive vulnerabilities and offensive opportunities.

For these reasons, we expect ethnic civil wars to last longer, to be more difficult to bring to a conclusion through negotiated settlement, and to be more likely to recur than ideologically based civil wars, *ceteris paribus*.

War goals: secession versus revolution

Another way to conceptualize the stakes of the previous conflict is whether the goal of the rebels was revolution or secession. In a revolution, the rebels seek to overthrow the incumbent regime and take its place. In a secessionist revolt, the rebels do not seek to replace the incumbent regime but to gain independence from it; they seek to create a new sovereign nation out of a portion of the territory of the existing one. Our model of the choice between resuming conflict or sustaining the peace suggests that secessionist wars should be more likely to recur than revolutionary civil wars.

First, secessionist wars are almost always ethnically based: they are fought by regionally concentrated ethnic groups. The same logic that suggests it is more difficult to sustain the peace following an ethnic civil war would also imply that secessionist wars are more likely to recur than revolutionary conflicts. Second, secessionist ethnic groups are concentrated in territorial enclaves, which enhances their capacity to mobilize for a resumption of conflict. Regional concentration also enhances their security from the state's armed forces. In short, ethno-regional concentration preserves the basis for dual sovereignty and therefore facilitates the resumption of civil war, compared to revolutionary civil wars. For these reasons we would expect secessionist wars to last longer and be more likely to resume than revolutionary civil wars.

Costs of conflict: the destructiveness of the previous war

Because fighting a civil war consumes and destroys human and material resources, the decision to resume war will be affected by the level of resources consumed by the previous conflict. In contrast to interstate war, protagonists in civil wars draw on the same population and the same economy to sustain their military operations. Therefore, we would expect that the more destructive the previous war, the lower the probability of civil war recurrence, *ceteris paribus*.

High casualty rates in the previous war should be an especially strong deterrent to resuming the conflict for several reasons. First, with each death, the size of the pool of potential recruits available to both the government and the rebels is reduced. Second, high casualty rates create a recruitment dilemma for both the government and the rebels because high casualty rates deter potential supporters of each side from enlisting (see Walter 2004). Third, high casualty rates should reduce one or both sides' estimate of the probability of achieving victory, should they resume the conflict.

On the other hand, there is a counter-argument that higher casualty rates may actually *increase* the probability of the war recurring by hardening hatreds and distrust between former protagonists and generating a residual desire for retribution and personal revenge. As Barbara Walter (2004: 373) puts it, "wars that inflict high costs on combatants and supporters could exacerbate animosity between them and create a strong desire for retribution even if the war ends." Moreover, civil wars marked by high levels of casualties may also indicate greater willingness on both sides to pay the costs of conflict. There is some evidence to support this effect (see Walter 2004; Mason and Quinn 2003).

Duration of the previous conflict

The duration of the previous conflict affects the protagonists' choice between resuming war or preserving the peace by affecting their estimate of the length of time required to achieve victory. The longer their estimate of the time required to win, the more the benefits of victory will have to be discounted. Moreover, the duration of the war combines with the rate at which costs are absorbed in their estimate of the accrued costs required to achieve victory. Thus, even a protagonist that expects to win eventually may find a settlement now to be more attractive if victory can be achieved only after a protracted war in which the accrued costs of victory exceed the net payoffs from a settlement now. The longer the protagonists' estimate of the time required to achieve victory, the lower will be their net payoff from victory and, therefore, the lower their incentive to resume conflict. Therefore, the duration of the previous conflict should be negatively related to both sides' estimate of the probability of victory, should they resume the war.

Structures of peace

Besides the incentives and disincentives for resuming conflict, the prospects for a recurrence of civil war are affected by the ability of the post-war regime to build a structure of peace. Sustaining the peace requires the establishment of political institutions that afford former combatants a fair opportunity to pursue their interests and redress their grievances through peaceful means. It also requires the rehabilitation of the economy so that the grievances that fueled support for the initial war are reduced and the appeal of the status quo is enhanced. It is in this arena that the international community can have its greatest impact on sustaining the peace: the investment in building and sustaining the institutions of a post-war democracy and economy are, arguably, relatively cheap compared to the costs of civil war, both to the nation at conflict and to the external patrons who subsidize the war effort of either side.

Post-conflict democracy

The domestic corollary of the democratic peace proposition holds that democracies are less likely to experience civil war because the institutions and processes of democracy defuse revolutionary violence by diverting popular discontent into electoral competition and nonviolent protest (Hegre *et al.* 2001). We would expect a similar relationship to hold for civil war recurrence: A democratic post-conflict polity should be less likely to experience a relapse into civil war, *ceteris paribus*.

The establishment of post-conflict democracy should enhance the prospects of sustaining the peace because the benefits of peaceful negotiations exceed the benefits of violent conflict. Revolution is not necessary. Dissident movements do not need to resort to organized violence against the state because they can seek redress of their grievances through electoral means and other forms of nonviolent collective action. Democratic states are also less likely to repress nonviolent protest. Hence, opposition movements are not compelled by state repression to choose between withdrawing from politics in order to escape repression or shifting to violent tactics of their own in order to combat it. By contrast, weak authoritarian or semi-democratic post-conflict regimes (anocracies) lack both the institutional capacity to accommodate opposition grievances through electoral mechanisms and the coercive capacity to repress opposition movements preemptively. Therefore, post-war anocracies should be the least likely to sustain the peace. When organized opposition movements do emerge, the weak authoritarian state attempts to repress them but fails. In so doing, the state converts nonviolent opposition into revolutionary movements (Mason and Krane 1989; Mason 2004).

One note of caution on the remedial effects of post-conflict democracy concerns the special challenge of democracy in ethnically divided societies. When democracy is installed in ethnically divided societies, it often fails to inoculate the nation against the recurrence of civil war. Indeed, democratic competition can, under some circumstances, exacerbate ethnic conflict. Donald Horowitz (1985) points out that in ethnically divided democracies, parties tend to form along ethnic lines, and this makes the consolidation of democracy problematic. Any effort on the part of party leaders to form coalitions across ethnic lines or to forge multiethnic parties leaves them vulnerable to challenges from within their own ethnic group. The votes they hope to gain by making appeals across ethnic lines are fewer in number than the votes they stand to lose by being outflanked by challengers from within their own ethnic groups who "play the ethnic card." With an ethnically based party system, elections can degenerate into little more than an ethnic census. Minorities become vulnerable to the tyranny of an ethnic majority unless institutional protections are built into the constitutional arrangements. While democracy requires that losers in elections accept their defeat, it also implies that they have a reasonable expectation of winning control of the government at some point in the foreseeable future. If minority parties conclude instead that they are relegated to permanent opposition status, the payoffs from resuming conflict may come to appear more attractive than what they can expect to gain from accepting the status quo as the permanent opposition and sustaining a peace that denies them the prospect of ever leading a governing coalition. Under these circumstances, an ethnic minority may resort to extra-constitutional means to challenge the dominance of ethnic majorities. The majority ethnic group may then feel justified in repressing that minority. An escalating cycle of repression and violence may ensue, culminating in a resumption of ethnic revolution or secession.

In Sri Lanka, the Tamil minority found itself victimized by democratically enacted legislation that conferred advantages on the Sinhalese majority and institutionalized discrimination against the Tamil minority in such matters as admission to higher education, civil service positions, and officer positions in the military. A Sinhalese majority in parliament even enacted legislation making Sinhalese the official language and favoring Buddhism over Hinduism (the religion of the Tamil minority). Tamil protests were met with communal violence directed against Tamils living in predominantly Sinhalese regions of Sri Lanka. Eventually, Tamil youth became so alienated that the appeals of groups such as the Liberation Tigers of Tamil Eelam (LTTE) for Tamil secession gained enough appeal for the LTTE to build a base of support sufficient to sustain a secessionist insurgency. Attempts to resolve the conflict through negotiated settlement have so far proven fruitless (see Bush 1990; Singer 1992, 1996; Tambiah and Jayawardena 1992). Not surprisingly, most of the new post-Cold War civil wars that have erupted have been ethnically based conflicts, and many of them have occurred in new democracies that are deeply divided along ethnic lines (Wallensteen and Sollenberg 2001).

Peacekeeping and peacebuilding

We have already discussed the argument that the introduction of international peacekeeping operations does reduce the likelihood of civil war recurrence (Fortna 2004). Indeed, supporting negotiated settlements with peacekeeping forces is one factor that may resolve the oft-cited observation that negotiated settlements are more likely to break down into renewed conflict than military victories: it is settlements unsupported by third-party enforcement mechanisms (such as peacekeepers) that are most likely to break down into renewed conflict. Mason and Quinn (2003) found some tentative support for the proposition that settlements supported by peacekeeping forces are less likely to experience a relapse into civil war than are other outcomes, including military victories.

The politics of peacekeeping and the impact of peacekeeping operations on the sustainability of peace in the post-civil war environment are addressed in more detail in other chapters in this volume. We would like to add that, since the end of the Cold War, the greater willingness of the international community to sponsor peacekeeping operations (42 of the 55 peacekeeping operations established by the UN since its inception in 1945 have been created since 1988) and the expansion of peacekeeping operations beyond the traditional role of policing a truce bode well for the goal of sustaining the peace in the aftermath of civil war. "Second generation" peacekeeping has expanded to include post-conflict reconstruction and reconciliation programs. Included among these activities are installing the institutions of a post-conflict democracy through such specialized tasks as setting up and managing elections, building the institutions of police and civil administration (including training and equipping personnel), and working with non-governmental organizations (NGOs) to build the institutions of civil society that are vital to the successful operation and consolidation of democracy (Bertram 1995: 388). Peacebuilding in this sense can substantially enhance the prospects for sustaining the peace in the aftermath of civil war.

The major question that remains is whether the international community, through the UN and other IGOs, can sustain and even expand its commitment to peacebuilding missions. The expanded array of UN responsibilities in post-war reconstruction and reconciliation creates an expanded array of opportunities for failure. And failed peacekeeping operations (PKOs) can create a hangover effect that makes major powers (such as the USA) less willing to intervene in the next crisis, as evidenced by the Clinton Administration's reluctance to intervene in Rwanda following the withdrawal of peacekeepers from Somalia.

There is also a collective action problem inherent in the peacebuilding enterprise: under what conditions is it in the interest of major powers to intervene in civil wars and make a commitment to post-war reconstruction and reconciliation? The benefits to the host nation and to nations in the region that are at risk of suffering spillover effects from a civil war are apparent. However, intervention to bring a civil war to an end, broker a settlement agreement, and support it with post-war reconstruction and reconciliation requires the consent and active support of major powers (including the five permanent members of the UN Security Council). For them, the benefits of ending many civil wars may be perceived by their leaders as involving mainly collective goods, such as regional stability; there are fewer private benefits to them than to the nations directly involved in the conflict or in the neighborhood of the conflict. Therefore, the challenge for those committed to sustaining the peace in the aftermath of civil war is how to make the case that major power investment in peacebuilding is less costly to them (and potentially more beneficial) than doing nothing and "giving war a chance."

Economic well-being

In the high-risk environment following a civil war the willingness of citizens to support a resumption of armed conflict will depend to some degree on the level of economic well-being afforded them by the post-war environment. Fearon and Laitin (2003) and Collier and Hoeffler (1998) have demonstrated a strong negative relationship between the level of economic development and a nation's susceptibility to civil war onset in the first place. Civil war recurrence should also be less likely to the extent that the post-war regime is able to build a healthy economy. The greater the level of economic well-being in the post-civil war environment, the greater the opportunity costs of participating in civil war. Thus, post-war economic development makes citizens less willing to take up arms in a resumption of civil war.

In the post-civil war environment, investing in economic development is even more critical to sustaining the peace. Presumably, a nation that has experienced a civil war was already characterized by low levels of economic development and well-being. The war itself destroyed some portion of the nation's human capital and its economic infrastructure, in addition to disrupting economic production, leaving the post-civil war environment even weaker economically and, therefore, more susceptible to the recurrence of civil war. On the other hand, the economic devastation that characterizes the post-civil war environment also implies that the marginal effect of investment in post-war reconstruction by the international community is rather large: every unit increase in post-war economic well-being produces a rather substantial reduction in the probability of civil war recurring. Indeed, it seems likely that the cost of achieving a level of post-war economic reconstruction sufficient to inoculate the nation against a recurrence of civil war is rather modest compared to the military cost of fighting another round of civil war and dealing with the spillover costs to surrounding nations and, perhaps, the major powers as well.

Conclusion

The challenge facing the international community today is how to bring civil wars to a peaceful conclusion and then how to prevent them from recurring. The findings on the duration and outcomes of civil wars and the effects of third-party mediation, peacekeeping, and post-war reconstruction all suggest that the international community has at its disposal a number of tools with which it can intervene in civil wars to bring them to an earlier and less destructive conclusion. Luttwak's "give war a chance" thesis simply is not supported by the evidence on civil war duration. If civil wars are allowed to continue, they will not burn themselves out. They will simply reach a mutually hurting stalemate that persists indefinitely. This stalemate could be resolved through third-party mediation aimed at brokering a settlement and enforcing it with peacekeeping operations. Well-designed settlement agreements can significantly reduce the probability of civil war recurrence, as can the installation of effective democratic institutions. And rebuilding the war-torn economy can significantly reduce the incentives of former protagonists to resume armed conflict. While the challenges of peacebuilding are daunting, what is remarkable is the degree of success the UN and other agencies have achieved in building a sustainable peace in conflicts that most observers felt were doomed to continue and recur. The cost of building a post-civil war environment that can sustain the peace may appear expensive. However, compared to the cost of one year's budget for the US Department of Defense, the costs of all ongoing peacekeeping and peacebuilding operations since the end of the Cold War appear to be a bargain.

Note

1 On the changing patterns of conflict over time, see Holsti (1992, 1996), Mason (2004: Ch. 1).

References

Bertram, E. (1995) "Reinventing governments: The Promise and Perils of United Nations Peacebuilding," *Journal of Conflict Resolution* 39 (September): 387–418.
Brandt, P., Mason, T.D., Gurses, M., McCleod, P., Petrovsky, N., and Radin, D. (2005) "Never-Lasting Peace: Explaining the Duration of Civil Wars", paper

presented at the International Studies Association Annual Meeting, Honolulu, Hawaii, March.

Bush, K. (1990) "Ethnic Conflict in Sri Lanka," *Conflict Quarterly* 10: 41–58.

Collier, P. and Hoeffler, A. (1998) "On the Economic Causes of Civil War," *Oxford Economic Papers* 50: 563–573.

DeRouen, Jr, K.R. and Sobek, D. (2004) "The Dynamics of Civil War Duration and Outcome," *Journal of Peace Research* 41(3): 303–320.

Doyle, M. and Sambanis, N. (2000) "International Peacebuilding: A Theoretical and Quantitative Analysis," *American Political Science Review* 94: 779–801.

Fearon, J.D. (2004) "Why Do Some Civil Wars Last So Much Longer Than Others," *Journal of Peace Research* 41(3): 275–301.

Fearon, J.D. and Laitin, D.D. (2003) "Ethnicity, Insurgency, and Civil War," *American Political Science Review* 97(1): 75–90.

Fortna, P. (2004) "Does Peacekeeping Keep the Peace? International Intervention and the Duration of Peace after Civil War," *International Studies Quarterly* 48(2): 269–292.

Gaddis, J.L. (1987) *The Long Peace: Inquiries into the History of the Cold War.* Oxford: Oxford University Press.

Hartzell, C.A. (1999) "Explaining the Stability of Negotiated Settlements to Intrastate Wars," *Journal of Conflict Resolution* 43: 3–22.

Hartzell, C.A. and Hoddie, M. (2003) "Institutionalizing Peace: Power Sharing and Post-Civil War Conflict Management," *American Journal of Political Science* 47: 318–332.

Hartzell, C.A., Hoddie, M., and Rothchild, D. (2001) "Stabilizing the Peace After Civil War: An Investigation of Some Key Variables," *International Organization* 55: 183–208.

Hegre, H., Ellingsen, T., Gleditsch, N.P., and Gates, S. (2001) "Towards a Democratic Civil Peace? Democracy, Political Change and Civil War, 1816–1992," *American Political Science Review* 95(1): 34–48.

Holsti, K.J. (1992) "International Theory and War in the Third World," in B.L. Job (ed.) *The Insecurity Dilemma: National Security in Third World States.* Boulder, CO: Lynne Rienner, pp. 37–60.

Holsti, K.J. (1996) *The State, War, and the State of War.* Cambridge: Cambridge University Press.

Horowitz, D.L. (1985) *Ethnic Groups in Conflict.* Berkeley, CA: University of California Press.

Kaufmann, C. (1996) "Possible and Impossible Solutions to Ethnic Civil Wars," *International Security* 20(4): 136–175.

Licklider, R. (1995) "The Consequences of Negotiated Settlements in Civil Wars, 1945–1993," *The American Political Science Review* 89(3): 681–690.

Luttwak, E. (1999) "Give War a Chance," *Foreign Affairs* 78(4): 36–44.

Mason, T.D. (2003) "Globalization, Democratization, and the Prospects for Civil War in the New Millennium," *International Studies Review* 5(4): 461–478.

Mason, T.D. (2004) *Caught in the Crossfire: Revolution, Repression, and the Rational Peasant.* Lanham, MD: Rowman & Littlefield.

Mason, T.D and Fett, P.J. (1996) "How Civil Wars End: A Rational Choice Approach," *Journal of Conflict Resolution* 40: 546–568.

Mason, T.D and Krane, D.A. (1989) "The Political Economy of Death Squads," *International Studies Quarterly* 33: 175–198.

Mason, T.D. and Quinn, J. (2003) "Sustaining the Peace: Determinants of Civil War Recurrence," paper presented at the American Political Science Association Annual Meeting, Philadelphia, PA, August.

Mason, T.D, Weingarten, J.P., and Fett, P.J. (1999) "Win, Lose, or Draw: Predicting the Outcome of Civil Wars," *Political Research Quarterly* 52(2): 239–268.

Sarkees, M.R. (2000) "The Correlates of War Data on War: An Update to 1997," *Conflict Management and Peace Science* 18(1): 123–144.

Singer, M.R. (1992) "Sri Lanka's Tamil-Sinhalese Ethnic Conflict: Alternative Solutions," *Asian Survey* 32 (August): 712–722.

Singer, M.R. (1996) "Sri Lanka's Ethnic Conflict: Have Bombs Shattered Hopes for Peace?," *Asian Survey* 36 (November): 1146–1155.

Stam, A.C., III (1996) *Win, Lose, or Draw: Domestic Politics and the Crucible of War*. Ann Arbor, MI: University of Michigan Press.

Tambiah, S.J. and Jayawardena, L. (1992) *Buddhism Betrayed?: Religion, Politics, and Violence in Sri Lanka*. Chicago: University of Chicago Press.

Tilly, C. (1978) *From Mobilization to Revolution*. Reading, MA: Addison-Wesley.

Wallensteen, P. and Sollenberg, M. (2001) "Armed Conflict, 1989–2000," *Journal of Peace Research* 38(5): 629–644.

Walter, B.F. (1997) "The Critical Barrier to Civil War Settlement," *International Organization* 51: 335–364.

Walter, B.F. (2002) *Committing to Peace: The Successful Settlement of Civil Wars*. Princeton, NJ: Princeton University Press.

Walter, B.F. (2004) "Does Conflict Beget Conflict? Explaining Recurring Civil War," *Journal of Peace Research* 41: 371–388.

Wittman, D. (1979) "How A War Ends: A Rational Model Approach," *Journal of Conflict Resolution* 23: 743–763.

Zartman, I.W. (1989) *Ripe for Resolution: Conflict and Intervention in Africa*. 2nd edn. New York: Oxford University Press.

2 Structuring the peace

Negotiated settlements and the construction of conflict management institutions

Caroline A. Hartzell

Following two years of intense negotiations, representatives of the Sudanese government and the rebel Sudan People's Liberation Movement (SPLM) signed a peace settlement on 9 January 2005 bringing to an end Africa's longest-running civil war. Encouraged by Kenyan mediators, the current US administration, and others interested in stopping the fighting in the Sudan, the parties to the conflict worked hard to secure an end to the two-decade civil war that left two million people dead and four million homeless. Despite the heavy costs the war had imposed, however, neither the government nor the SPLM was interested in agreeing to a peace on just any terms. The two adversaries, having negotiated an end to a previous episode of civil conflict in 1972 only to see war break out again in 1983, were aware of the potential fragility of peace settlements and thus sought to protect their interests should the peace once again fail.

How can civil war opponents like the Sudanese government and the SPLM structure a peace settlement in such a manner as to safeguard their interests and foster a lasting peace? The argument of this chapter is that this is best accomplished by doing what the parties to the recent Sudanese settlement have done – construct an array of institutions that address adversaries' concerns regarding who is to exercise power and the ends for which that power will be used once the war is over. In the case of the Sudan, the institutions designed by the government and the SPLM include a coalition government, a separate army to be maintained by the southern rebels, autonomous administrative structures for the south, and revenue-sharing by the government and the SPLM from oil produced in the south. By agreeing to construct a series of institutions for the sharing and dividing of power, civil war adversaries have the opportunity to address some of the grievances that may have given rise to armed conflict as well as concerns that are produced by the war itself. Perhaps more importantly, however, by designing such institutions, antagonists help to ensure that they have a means, short of a return to war, of managing societal conflict once the shooting has stopped.

The focus of this chapter is on negotiated settlements designed to end civil wars between 1945 and 1999. Because negotiated settlements have become the dominant means of ending civil wars, there is arguably a need for the international community to learn more about this settlement type. To that end, this chapter explores the differences that exist among negotiated civil war settlements and identifies the types of settlements most likely to produce an enduring peace. Specific issues addressed in the chapter include the concerns characteristic of groups that agree to end armed conflicts through negotiated settlements, the means adversaries have devised to address these concerns, and the consequences that stem from these agreements. The chapter concludes with some thoughts regarding the role the international community is best suited to play in helping to structure an enduring peace among rivals who negotiate an end to their civil wars.

Civil war settlements (or, why does it matter how a civil war ends?)

Of the 122 civil wars that were initiated during the period between 1945 and 1999, 108 saw the fighting come to an end for at least some period of time during those years.[1] The settlements that ended these civil wars took one of four forms. First, the most common way by which civil wars have ended during the post-World War II era is through a process of *military victory*. Whether one group of actors prevails over the other(s) solely through its own efforts (e.g., Argentina's intrastate conflict in 1955) or whether foreign aid and/or foreign intervention prove crucial in leading one of the factions to triumph (e.g., Guatemala's 1954 civil war), the outcome is the same: one party claims victory and the other admits defeat. As Table 2.1 makes clear, 55 (51 percent) of the civil war settlements that were arrived at between 1945 and 1999 were military victories.[2]

Second, civil wars may end by mutual consent among adversaries who agree to a *negotiated settlement*. A negotiated settlement brings together representatives of the conflicting groups, none of which admit defeat, to discuss and agree to the terms by which they will bring the fighting to an end. One of the central features of a settlement of this nature is that adversaries directly address the question of how power is to be distributed and managed in the post-war state. Civil war opponents may negotiate a settlement on their own (e.g., Colombia in 1957) or third parties may assist in the process of such an agreement (e.g., the recent case of the Sudan mentioned at the outset of this chapter). Thirty-eight of the 108 civil wars (35 percent) that ended between 1945 and 1999 did so as a result of a negotiated settlement.

Third, *negotiated truces* have also been used as a means of stopping the fighting among groups embroiled in armed civil conflict. Eleven intrastate conflicts since the end of World War II (10 percent of the conflicts under consideration in this chapter) have been terminated, at least for some period of time, in this manner. Negotiated truces differ from negotiated

Table 2.1 Civil war settlement types, 1945–1999

Military victory	Negotiated settlement	Negotiated truce	Peace negotiated with or imposed by third parties
Afghanistan, 1978–1992	Angola, 1975–1989	Azerbaijan, 1990–1994	Cyprus, 1963–1964
Algeria, 1962–1963	Angola, 1989–1991	Burma, 1968–1982	Cyprus, 1974–1974
Argentina, 1955–1955	Angola, 1992–1994	Chechnya, 1994–1996	Israel/Palestine, 1948–1949
Bolivia, 1952–1952	Bosnia, 1991–1995	Congo/Brazzaville, 1993–94	Sri Lanka, 1983–1987
Burma, 1948–1951	Cambodia, 1978–1991	Congo/Brazzaville, 1998–99	**N = 4**
Burma, 1983–1995	Chad, 1979–1979	Congo/Zaire, 1998–1999	
Burundi, 1965–1969	Chad, 1989–1996	Croatia, 1991–1992	
Burundi, 1972–1972	Colombia, 1948–1957	Georgia/Abk, 1992–1994	
Burundi, 1988–1988	Costa Rica, 1948–1948	Georgia/S. Oss, 1989–1992	
Cambodia, 1970–1974	Croatia, 1995–1995	Moldova, 1991–1992	
Chad, 1980–1988	Djibouti, 1991–1994	Morocco, 1976–1991	
China, 1946–1949	Dominican Republic, 1965–1965	**N = 11**	
China, 1956–1959	El Salvador, 1979–1992		
China, 1967–1968	Guatemala, 1963–1996		
Congo/Brazzaville, 1997–1997	Guinea Bissau, 1998–1998		
Congo/Zaire, 1960–1965	India, 1946–1949		
Congo/Zaire, 1967–1967	Indonesia/East Timor, 1975–1999		
Congo/Zaire, 1996–1997	Iraq/Kurds, 1961–1970		
Cuba, 1958–1959	Kosovo, 1998–1999		
Ethiopia/Ogaden, 1977–1985	Laos, 1959–1973		
Ethiopia/Eritrea, 1974–1991	Lebanon, 1958–1958		
Ethiopia/ideology, 1974–1991	Lebanon, 1982–1989		
Greece, 1946–1949	Liberia, 1989–1993		
Guatemala, 1954–1954	Liberia, 1994–1996		
Hungary, 1956–1956	Malaysia, 1948–1956		
India, 1948–1948	Mali, 1990–1995		
Indonesia/MoI, 1950–1950	Mozambique, 1982–1992		

Table 2.1 Continued

Military victory	Negotiated settlement	Negotiated truce	*Peace negotiated with or imposed by third parties*
Indonesia/Darul I., 1953–1953	Nicaragua, 1981–1989		
Indonesia, 1956–1960	Papua New Guinea, 1989–1998		
Iran, 1978–1979	Philippines/MNLF, 1972–1996		
Iran, 1981–1982	Rwanda, 1990–1993		
Iraq/Shammar, 1959–1959	Sierra Leone, 1992–1996		
Iraq/Kurds, 1974–1975	Sierra Leone, 1997–1999		
Iraq/Kurds, Shiites, 1991–1991	South Africa, 1983–1994		
Jordan, 1970–1970	Sudan, 1963–1972		
Laos, 1975–1975	Tajikistan, 1992–1997		
Nicaragua, 1978–1979	Yemen/YAR, 1962–1970		
Nigeria/Biafra, 1967–1970	Zimbabwe, 1972–1979		
Nigeria/F.Islam, 1980–1984	**N = 38**		
Pakistan, 1971–1971			
Pakistan, 1973–1977			
Paraguay, 1947–1947			
Peru, 1980–1992			
Philippines/Huks, 1950–1952			
Romania, 1989–1989			
Rwanda, 1963–1964			
Rwanda, 1994–1994			
Sri Lanka, 1971–1971			
Uganda/Buganda, 1966–1966			
Uganda, 1978–1979			
Uganda/NRA, 1980–1986			
Vietnam, 1960–1975			
Yemen/YAR, 1948–1948			
Yemen/YPR, 1986–1986			
Yemen, 1994–1994			
N = 55			

settlements in two significant ways. First, negotiated truces tend to focus principally on the means by which violence is to be ended in the short term. Much of the content of negotiated truces thus consists of the design of measures designed to instill a sense of confidence in groups that laying down their weapons will not produce negative consequences, most immediate among these the death of unarmed combatants at the hands of those who might fail to abide by the truce. In other words, unlike negotiated settlements, negotiated truces seldom address the challenging question of how power is to be exercised in the post-war state and by whom. Second, negotiated truces differ from negotiated settlements in that the former often seek to delay decisions regarding explicitly political issues. Because of this, the peace secured by negotiated truces is often very indeterminate in nature. Although the fighting ends in these cases, the ultimate state of relations among combatants as well as the rules of conflict regulation remains unclear to all involved.

A final means by which civil wars may experience an end to armed hostilities comes about when an arrangement is negotiated by one of the sets of combatants with third parties involved in the conflict or a peace of sorts is imposed by third parties. *Imposed truces* are quite rare, with only four of the civil wars examined in this chapter (4 percent) coming to an end in this manner.

Although we still have much to learn regarding the consequences that follow from the different types of settlements used to end civil wars (i.e., are some settlements more likely to give rise to more democratic regimes than others? Are different levels of post-conflict economic development associated with different settlement types?), this chapter focuses on negotiated means of ending civil wars. One reason for this focus is that negotiating an end to an armed conflict has the potential to be a less costly method of stopping the killing than waiting for one side to achieve a military victory. Although the costs of civil war may be calculated in a variety of ways (i.e., the number of deaths, destruction of infrastructure, etc.), they have typically been measured in terms of the numbers of lives lost in the conflict. Based on this measure, military victory consistently appears to be a more costly means of ending civil wars than any of the three types of negotiated agreements discussed above. The intrastate conflicts brought to an end through military victories between 1945 and 1999 produced an average of 170,706 battle deaths per war during this time. On the other hand, the battle death average was 87,487 for wars in which the fighting was concluded through a negotiated settlement, 35,182 for wars ended via negotiated truces, and 15,000 for conflicts in which third parties imposed a peace.[3]

Another reason for focusing on negotiated settlements of civil wars is that this has recently become the dominant means of bringing the fighting to an end in intrastate conflicts. As Table 2.2 indicates, the majority of civil wars during the first four and a half decades of the post-World War II

36   *Caroline A. Hartzell*

Table 2.2 Trends in means of ending civil wars, 1945–1999

Settlement type	1940s (%)	1950s (%)	1960s (%)	1970s (%)	1980s (%)	1990s (%)
Military victories	5 (62.5)	11 (79)	8 (80)	13 (65)	8 (62)	10 (23)
Negotiated settlements	2 (25)	3 (21)	1 (10)	6 (30)	3 (23)	23 (54)
Negotiated truces	0	0	0	0	1 (7.5)	10 (23)
Peace negotiated with/ imposed by third parties	1 (12.5)	0	1 (10)	1 (10)	1 (7.5)	0

Note
Figures in brackets are percentages.

period were ended via military victory. During the 1990s, on the other hand, negotiated settlements became the major means used to end armed civil conflicts.

These factors – the possibility that negotiated agreements may constitute a less costly means than military victory of ending civil wars and the increasing prevalence of these agreements as a means of bringing armed conflict to a close – highlight the need for the international community to learn more about negotiated settlements as a means of ending civil wars. This chapter seeks to contribute to that effort by focusing in the sections that follow on three facets of negotiated settlements: (1) the motive groups have for agreeing to this form of war ending; (2) the shapes this form of settlement can take; (3) and how the content of such agreements may support an enduring peace.

Security concerns in the aftermath of civil war

Civil war is a form of organized social activity. Groups may be motivated to engage in this activity for a variety of reasons. Current scholarship on civil wars has focused on incentives for the initiation of intrastate conflicts ranging from so-called "grievances" (i.e., intractable ethnic hatreds) to "greed" (i.e., loot-seeking on the part of either state actors, insurgent groups, or both) (Berdal and Malone 2000; Ballentine and Sherman 2003). Social scientists have also conceptualized the initiation of armed conflict as one step in a bargaining process in which groups use civil war as a tool to help them achieve the optimal allocation of scarce goods (Reiter 2003). What these approaches to the study of civil war initiation suggest, quite reasonably, is that understanding the reasons groups start a civil war is important if we are to be able to help bring such conflicts to a close and foster a stable peace.

Understanding why groups in divided societies choose to go to war does not, however, provide a sufficient basis for helping to end civil wars and promote an enduring peace. Whatever the reasons groups have for choosing to initiate a war, once they contemplate ending it, they face a critical concern. That concern consists of ensuring the security and future survival of the groups that have participated in the war. Adversaries who have been engaged in determined efforts to kill one another need some assurance that once they put down their guns, some party to the conflict will not take advantage of that opportunity to threaten the group's continued existence. If such an assurance is not forthcoming, armed groups are unlikely to stop fighting.

In essence, civil war adversaries are caught up in a security dilemma. Accustomed to operating in an environment in which either there exists no central authority to enforce rules (e.g., failed states such as Sierra Leone and Somalia) or groups have rejected said authority as threatening to their existence, armed civil groups seek to acquire more power and capabilities to gain an extra margin of safety. The security dilemma comes to the fore when some groups perceive the security- or defense-related actions of other groups as threatening and react in kind (Herz 1950). It is only when groups are able to provide for their security through some means that does not prove menacing to the security of others that the security dilemma can be put to rest and efforts made to foster an enduring peace.

Armed opponents seeking to end a civil war face particular challenges when dealing with the security dilemma. These stem from the fact that civil adversaries must not, in a post-conflict environment, continue to rely on self-help measures to provide for their security and survival. Ending a civil war calls for the reconstruction of central authority and the exercise of that authority by the state vis-à-vis society. The state, not contending groups, must now be vested with a monopoly on the legitimate use of force, must reconstitute political power, and enforce rules for the management of the ongoing conflict that is characteristic of every society. The problem warring groups face is that it is precisely these dimensions of state power that raise for them the specter of the security dilemma. Having provided for their own security during the course of an intrastate conflict, groups in a divided society now must be concerned about the effect that the state's use of coercive force and control of political power will have on their survival. More specifically, parties to the conflict wonder what guarantee they have that the national security forces, particularly if controlled by an opposing group, will not be used against them once they lay down their weapons and disperse (Stedman 1996; Walter 1997). Groups also question whether the rules governing access to political power might not be altered in a way that is damaging to their interests, or even their survival, if an opposing party comes to power. Finally, groups worry whether once some party is in power it can be trusted not to use the resources of the state to build up its power base at the expense of other groups (Hartzell 1999).

What implications does this concern with security have for ending civil wars via a negotiated settlement? The central issue at stake for opponents considering a negotiated end to a civil war is the following: How can rival groups be convinced that, in an effort to provide an extra measure of safety for itself, some group will not use the power of the state in such a way as to threaten the security of other actors? And, as long as groups fear for their security, what can convince them to stick to the terms of a negotiated settlement? Although civil war adversaries cannot continue to rely on self-help measures when ending a war, they can seek to design settlements that minimize both security concerns and the danger that one side will renege on the agreement. The best way to do this is through the design of institutions that share or divide power among rivals in such a way as to prevent any one group from becoming dominant and exercising central authority.

All countries emerging from intrastate war are faced with the issue of institutional choice. In those cases in which civil war settlements take the form of a military victory by one side, representatives of the winning group presumably find themselves in a position to construct institutions that provide for their security and advance their interests.[4] In the event that armed antagonists seek to end an intrastate conflict through negotiation, the institutions or rules of conflict management that will regulate future behavior are the subject of intensive bargaining. The realization that civil war opponents who have not defeated each other in the course of conflict face a security dilemma when seeking to negotiate an end to a conflict provides us with significant insight into the types of institutions likely to be adopted by actors in these circumstances. Tasked with securing not just the organizational survival of the groups they represent, but in many cases their physical safety, the leaders of warring groups are likely to favor certain institutional arrangements and oppose others. More specifically, when faced with deep-rooted security concerns, groups negotiating a settlement will likely design institutions that seek to manage conflict by sharing or dividing power among competing groups (Hartzell 1999).

Negotiated settlements and conflict management institutions: addressing security concerns, signaling commitment, and reconstructing order

Institutions play three valuable roles that can help in the process of constructing an enduring peace on the basis of a negotiated civil war settlement. First, as discussed above, institutions can be designed to address rival groups' concerns regarding who is to exercise power and the ends to which that power is to be used following the end of a conflict. Antagonists will be more likely to commit to the peace if they are confident that some group will not be able to seize power and use it at the expense of others. A case in point is the 1957 National Front settlement constructed by Colombia's long-term rivals, the Conservative and Liberal Parties. The two groups fought frequently during the nineteenth and the twentieth centuries as each sought sole control of the state. Tiring of this cycle of violence, the elite representatives of the two parties resolved to end the conflict by dividing power on the basis of a 50/50 power-sharing formula. For a period of 16 years, the presidency rotated between the two parties every four years and all other elective and appointed public offices were divided evenly between the two parties (Peeler 1985). By adhering to this power-sharing arrangement, each party was placed in a position of prominence that provided the opportunity both to participate in governance and monitor the behavior of their former adversaries.

Second, the process of designing and implementing institutions as part of a negotiated civil war settlement serves to signal a commitment on the part of adversaries to the building of a lasting peace. Designing and implementing power-sharing and power-dividing institutions is not a cost-free process; adversaries typically must abandon their interest in monopoly control of the state in exchange for the compromises associated with the sharing and/or dividing of power. The degrees of willingness rival groups have for enduring these costs over time have the potential to serve as an indicator of their commitment to an enduring peace. This dynamic is apparent, for example, in the price paid by both the government of the Philippines and the Moro National Liberation Front (MNLF) to end their civil war (1972–1996). As part of the agreement that was struck, the government conceded a greater degree of political and economic autonomy to the MNLF on their home island of Mindanao than previously had been considered acceptable; at the same time, the MNLF compromised its goals by abandoning its separatist demands and instead recognizing the legitimacy of the central state's continued role in the governance of the island. The fact that both the government and the rebels willingly accepted these losses in the interest of peace served to increase the credibility of their mutual commitments to establishing a stable peace.

Third, the institutions designed as part of a civil war settlement define the means by which social conflict is to be managed in the post-war state. It is on the basis of these institutions that domestic order is reconstructed following a civil war. If a stable peace is to be secured, groups must have a means, other than relying on the use of guns, for resolving their disagreements. By making the design of institutions a central part of the process of ending an intrastate conflict, rival groups lay the foundations necessary to build an enduring peace. An example of this can be found in Malaysia. The institutions that formed the basis of that country's settlement involved communal compromises designed to give Malays a larger interest in the economy while increasing non-Malay participation in the political system. Although these institutions eventually came under challenge when post-election riots broke out in May 1969, a history of institutional accommodation made it possible for the country's communal leaders to act together to resolve the crisis. The central measure they designed to do so was a "New Economic Policy" (NEP). The NEP, announced in 1970, sought to create conditions for national unity by reducing the socioeconomic disparities that were believed responsible for inter-ethnic resentment within the state.

What are the types of conflict management institutions that groups design to help accomplish these tasks? These institutions are ones centered on the dimensions of state power rival groups tend to be most concerned about with respect to the post-war environment. The four dimensions of state power that factor most directly into the security concerns of antagonists are those associated with the political, military, territorial, and economic bases of state strength. These components of state power prove a source of apprehension to groups because each can be used or manipulated in such a way as to pose a pressing threat to the safety of groups. In addition, because these components of state power are in some ways fungible, meaning control of them can shift between different groups, they are amenable to being used to increase the power, particularly the coercive power, of any one group. Motivated by such concerns, the architects of negotiated settlements craft institutions for the sharing and/or dividing of power across these four dimensions of state power.

Political power-sharing and power-dividing institutions

Focusing on the first of these dimensions, the state's control of political power, rival groups are concerned about the possibility that politics will become a zero-sum game in which one group seizes control of the state and uses its position of influence against others. Groups fear that if they are not represented in the central government, their adversaries will be in a position to make policy choices harmful to their interests. How best can groups ensure that this does not happen? A number of scholars have focused on the issue of alternative political institutions that can be used to manage conflict within divided societies (Nordlinger 1972; Lijphart 1977; Horowitz 1985; Smooha and Hanf 1992). These institutions generally fall into three categories – electoral, administrative, and executive. Electoral rules determine the method of translating votes into seats in representative institutions, administrative rules make clear the manner in which public service appointments will be divided, and executive rules stipulate the distribution of appointments to ministerial, sub-ministerial, and cabinet-level positions. Each of these institutions thus represents a distinct component of policymaking influence within the state. Groups seeking to prevent some set of actors from gaining an advantage in the allocation of political power may focus their attention on one or some combination of these institutions (Hartzell 1999).

One of the central debates to emerge from the literature on the use of political institutions to manage conflict is between the advocates of majoritarian and proportional strategies. Supporters of majoritarianism propose that political power should be monopolized by the faction or group capable of gaining the support of a majority (or at least a plurality) of citizens. Political institutions may be structured to encourage bringing together a diverse coalition of actors in an effort to secure a majority, but those groups omitted from such an arrangement are effectively shut out of opportunities to participate in the governance of the state. Advocates of a proportional strategy, on the other hand, call for groups to share political power on the basis of some demographic (e.g., ethnicity) or political (e.g., party affiliation) principle. Groups are guaranteed a degree of representation within governing institutions by virtue of their group affiliation. A failure to achieve or maintain dominant status does not consign a group to political irrelevance; minorities have a permanent voice within the structures of the state.

Of these two sets of rules – majoritarianism and proportionalism – regarding the distribution of political power, only proportionalism provides adversaries with sufficient assurances regarding their access to political power to reduce the appeal of continued warfare or ongoing reliance on self-help mechanisms. Political institutions associated with majoritarianism largely fail to allay groups' concerns regarding becoming permanently marginalized. Timothy Sisk makes this point clear in his discussion of the meaning of majoritarian elections within divided states:

> In many divided societies, electoral competition is a contest for ownership of the state. Minorities, particularly, equate democracy not with freedom or participation but with the structured dominance of adversarial majority groups. Permanent minorities ... have feared the consequences of electoral competition, especially when the expected consequence of majority victory is discrimination against them. For minority groups, losing an election is a matter not simply of losing office but of losing the means for protecting the survival of the group.
>
> (1996: 31)

Faced with these concerns about majority rule, groups – and particularly minorities – will seek a negotiated settlement that provides them with some guarantee that they will have access to political power and/or some measure of insulation from power exercised at the center. Proportional institutions can be vital to providing such a guarantee. Electoral proportional representation, for example, does so by lowering the minimum level of voter support a candidate or party must achieve to gain political office, thus decreasing the intensity of political competition. Although the mechanics by which votes are translated into seats under electoral proportional representation systems differ, these rules share in common the aim of minimizing the disparity between a party's share of national votes and the number of parliamentary seats it occupies. A case in point is Mozambique's 1992 *General Peace Agreement*. The settlement, negotiated to end a decade-long civil war between the government (Frelimo) and the opposition (Renamo), provides for an electoral system based on the principle of proportional representation for election to the Assembly.

Administrative proportional representation expands the opportunities for political participation by increasing the access of groups to policymaking influence. Rules of this type seek to allocate decision-making and policymaking power to groups by appointing a predetermined number of their representatives to positions on courts, commissions, the civil or foreign services, and other corresponding offices. The Salvadoran peace accords signed in 1992 by the government of El Salvador and the Farabundo Martí Front for National Liberation (FMLN), for example, called for the creation of a National Commission for the Consolidation of Peace (COPAZ), which would be responsible for overseeing implementation of the political agreements reached by the parties to the settlement. The accords called for COPAZ to be composed of two representatives of the Government of El Salvador, including a member of the armed forces, two representatives of the FMLN, and one representative of each of the parties or coalitions represented in the Legislative Assembly.

In the case of proportional representation in the executive of the national government, groups are ensured a voice in the innermost circles of political power via the appointment of representatives to ministerial, subministerial, and cabinet positions. The November 1994 *Lusaka Protocol* negotiated to end the civil war in Angola placed a great deal of emphasis on this form of proportional representation. The Union for the Total Independence of Angola (UNITA), the rebel group, was allocated the ministerial posts of geology and mines, trade, health, hotel business and tourism. UNITA members were also guaranteed positions as deputy ministers of agriculture, defense, finance, home affairs, mass communication, public works, and social reintegration.

Military power-sharing and power-dividing institutions

Prior to negotiating a settlement to end a civil war, a warring group's military forces provide the greatest level of security for the group as well as its most obvious source of leverage vis-à-vis its adversaries. Rivals thus will be reluctant to give up their armed forces without some guarantee that their security will be provided for and that they will have other ways to protect their interests. A number of scholars have focused on how concerns relating to control of the military pose challenges for both the negotiation and durability of civil war settlements (Hampson 1996; Stedman 1996; Walter 2002). Highlighting the dangers groups face as they demobilize, analysts have stressed the importance of confidence-building measures meant to reassure adversaries that, once they disarm, an enemy will not be able to take advantage of the settlement and achieve the victory that had previously proven elusive on the battlefield (Fortna 2004). These confidence-building measures range from the introduction of peacekeeping troops between opposing forces to guarantees by third-party actors that those groups violating the ceasefire will be punished.

Although provisions of this type may lend greater credibility to the peace process, they do not constitute guarantees that allay this security concern. Adversaries are well aware that these measures, which entail relying on outside actors, are beyond their control and subject to failure. Opponents thus worry whether the number of peacekeeping troops will be sufficient to the task at hand (e.g., Angola's failed 1991 Bicesse Accord) or whether the third-party guarantors' commitments are truly credible (e.g., the collapsed 1979 Transitional Government of National Unity [GUNT] settlement in Chad). Most significant, such measures do not address the question of who will control the coercive powers of the state once central authority has been reconstructed.

If adversaries' concerns are to be addressed, the state's coercive forces must somehow be neutralized or balanced. Parties to the conflict must believe that a rival group will not be able to direct the security forces of the state to threaten their interests. In most cases, this guarantee will involve integrating the antagonists' armed forces into the state's security forces. This can be done either on the basis of some proportional formula representative of the size of the armed factions or, perhaps more reassuring to the weaker party to the conflict, on the basis of an absolute balance in troop numbers among the contending groups. Settlements of the conflicts in both the Philippines and El Salvador provide examples of bargains requiring the integration of state and rebel security forces. The 1996 Philippine peace agreement called for the integration of some 7,500 members of the MNLF's military wing into the national army and security forces. The accords ending the Salvadoran civil war abolished a number of the government's public security forces and founded a new National Civilian Police Force for which a quota of 20 percent each was established for former National Police officers and FMLN guerrilla troops.

Negotiated settlements may also seek to neutralize or balance the state's coercive forces by mandating the appointment of members of the subordinate group(s) to key leadership positions including general, commander, director, or defense minister in the state's security forces. This ensures that these individuals are in a position to monitor the movement and use of troops and warn of policy decisions that might harm or threaten the interests of the subordinate group. Notable examples of this type of military power sharing include the commissioning of southern Sudan People's Liberation Movement (SPLM) leader and Anya-Nya Commander-in-Chief Major-General Joseph Lagu as Major-General in the unified Sudanese Army as part of the country's negotiated settlement in 1972 and Violeta Barrios de Chamorro's retention of Sandinista General Humberto Ortega as head of Nicaragua's armed forces in 1990.

Finally, in rare cases, and although it may seem contrary to the notion of centralizing state power at a civil war's end, striking a balance between adversaries may involve allowing opposing sides to remain armed or to retain their own security forces. The settlement negotiated in 1970 that ended the Yemeni civil war between republicans and royalists allowed each side to retain its arms. The Managua Protocol on Disarmament, signed by the government of Violeta Barrios de Chamorro and the "Contras" of Nicaragua, authorized the Contras to create a security force that would provide for "internal order" within the development zones that the Nicaraguan government committed itself to create for the Contras. Finally, the 1995 Dayton Accord negotiated to end the civil war in Bosnia calls for the two entities within Bosnia and Herzegovina, the Bosniak-Croat Federation and the Republika Srpska, to maintain their own separate armies. Each of these settlements has proven stable to date.[5]

Territorial power-sharing and power-dividing institutions

The chief means of allocating power of a territorial nature among groups is through territorial autonomy. By creating forms of decentralized government that are territorially based (e.g., federalism and regional autonomy), autonomy effectively divides political influence among levels of government. This type of institution provides groups at the subnational level with some degree of power and autonomy vis-à-vis the central government. Territorial autonomy is an institution that provides a means through which compromise can be reached among adversarial groups by allowing each collectivity a regional base from which it may protect its own interests (Heintze 1997).

There are three distinct ways in which territory-based institutions reassure groups in a divided society that the power of the state will not be seized by one group and used to threaten the security and interests of others. First, territorial autonomy can serve to restrict authority at the political center by shifting decision-making power to subunits of the state. If a group considers issues such as education, language, social services, and access to governmental civil service to be essential to its survival, then it should find its ability to exercise regional control over these issues reassuring. By increasing the influence of policymakers at the subnational level, groups should also gain a sense that they possess a means of protecting themselves from the exercise of arbitrary central authority. This is particularly likely to be the case when the powers of the subunits extend to their own judiciaries and police forces, as these often serve to add to groups' feelings of autonomous capacity.

Second, and related to the above, territorial autonomy can be used to balance power among groups. Measures that ensure that territorially based groups are included in the institutions of the federal government, for example, provide these sets of actors with policymaking influence at the political center and a means of blocking other collectivities from capturing the state. These territorial devices lessen the perceived threat of centralized control by any single group by ensuring that no individual "winner" can control an entire region precisely because there is no longer a single region. In this way, "federalism operates like an electoral reform, like proportional representation," contends Donald Horowitz (1991: 124), setting "one arena off from another, making and remaking legislative majorities and minorities by adjusting the territories in which their votes are to be counted."

Third, territorial autonomy can be used to help reduce the stakes of competition among adversarial groups in a divided society. One way this is accomplished is by reducing the disparities among collectivities by enabling a minority to rise within its own state bureaucracies and educational systems. By making material resources and opportunities that did not previously exist available at the subunit level, territorial autonomy may also diffuse some of the economic power previously controlled by the political center.

Economic power-sharing and power-dividing institutions

The economic dimension of power sharing focuses on control of economic resources in the post-war state. Groups that fear for their survival as they negotiate an end to civil war have an immediate concern of an economic nature – ensuring that control of resources does not provide any one group with the means to exclude or threaten rivals. In a related manner, as they consider ending a conflict in which warfare has become the primary system of resource allocation, antagonists may become concerned about one group seizing control of economic assets that provide the source of financing for armed conflict. During the course of the Angolan civil war, for example, the oil-producing enclave of Cabinda (controlled by government forces of the Popular Movement for the Liberation of Angola [MPLA]) and the diamond-producing areas of the country (controlled by UNITA) were hotly contested by the rival forces. As the two sides tried to implement a negotiated solution to the conflict, UNITA's reluctance to cede the diamond mines it had used to finance its war efforts was seen as a hindrance to a long-term resolution to the conflict.

Faced with security fears regarding the control and use of economic resources, group representatives will seek to design rules for the distribution of wealth and income that will, if not achieve a balance among groups, at least prevent any one group from dominating economic resources. Because market competition is likely disproportionately to favor those groups that are already economically advantaged, groups concerned about the control of economic resources by rival actors are unlikely to trust market mechanisms to distribute resources. Rather, groups will seek to have the state displace or place limits on market competition, directing the flow of resources through economic public policies and/or administrative allocations to assist economically disadvantaged groups (Esman 1994).

Settlements seeking to achieve this type of distribution of material resources and economic opportunities are likely to rely on the use of preferential policies:

> laws, regulations, administrative rules, court orders, and other public interventions to provide certain public and private goods, such as admission into schools and colleges, jobs, promotions, business loans, and rights to buy and sell land on the basis of membership in a particular ... group.
>
> (Weiner 1983: 35)

Although most settlements are unlikely to specify in such detail the policies to be used to achieve the goal of distributing economic resources among rival groups, rules structuring distributive policy can range from general statements of a pattern of resource distribution to be employed by the state to more detailed formulae for resource allocation. The 1996 Philippines peace accord, for example, calls for the state to provide a Special Zone of Peace and Development in the southern Philippines with resources to foster development within the region including basic services such as water and socialized housing and entrepreneurial development support in the form of livelihood assistance and credit facilities.

Structuring a durable peace

Negotiated civil war settlements may incorporate power-sharing and power-dividing institutions rooted in anywhere from zero to all four of the dimensions of state power described above. Although a set of institutional guarantees from any one of the four dimensions is likely to help stabilize the peace, multiple sets of power-sharing institutions – or what one can refer to as highly institutionalized settlements – should prove even more reassuring. This is likely to be the case for four reasons.

First, including multiple aspects of power sharing in an agreement should have a cumulative effect on rival groups' sense of security, with the different dimensions interacting in a mutually reinforcing manner. An agreement to practice political power sharing, for example, is more likely to be implemented and to prove durable if the military is beyond the control of any single faction that might be tempted to use a coup to change the balance of power that exists in the political dimension. In a similar manner, economic power sharing may make it easier for previously disadvantaged groups to accumulate resources that will enable them to become truly competitive in future elections.

A second reason why including multiple power-sharing and power-dividing dimensions in a negotiated civil war settlement should help foster an enduring peace is that it serves as a source of insurance against the failure to implement any single power-sharing or power-dividing provision of the settlement. Parties to an agreement are likely to recognize that in the challenging transition process involved in moving from war to peace, some provisions of a peace agreement may not be implemented. By specifying multiple dimensions of power sharing as part of a settlement, the failure of any one aspect of power sharing may not result in groups becoming permanently marginalized or may not compromise their security.

Another reason settlements with power-sharing institutions rooted in various dimensions of state power are most likely to prove stable is that such settlements serve to signal groups' commitment to the peace process. Rival groups that agree to create a variety of these institutions and thus to pay the costs associated with them effectively signal to one another the seriousness with which they have embarked on the process of building a lasting peace.

Finally, a number of states in which civil war has broken out are weakly institutionalized – a problem that is likely to be even more severe in the aftermath of civil war. Designing a number of institutions that speak to the immediate concerns of groups in the post-war environment – security and the exercise of power – can help to address this problem. Not all types of institutions, it should be emphasized, will be perceived by former antagonists as effectively addressing these concerns. Groups seem most likely to commit to a set of institutions in whose design they have had a hand and which they perceive to be relevant to their survival in the aftermath of armed conflict. To the extent that power-sharing and power-dividing institutions are created with the active participation of former combatants, they can help lay the foundation for building an enduring peace.

Are negotiated settlements that call for more extensive power-sharing arrangements more likely to produce a lasting peace? Recent empirical evidence suggests this is in fact the case. Focusing on all civil wars ended via the bargaining process between 1945 and the end of 1999, Caroline Hartzell and Matthew Hoddie (2003) found that, among other factors, the more highly institutionalized agreements to end civil wars were, the longer the peace was likely to endure. Hartzell and Hoddie (2005) found that this relationship held not only for the 38 cases of fully *negotiated settlements* of civil wars that were agreed to during this period but also for what they refer to as *negotiated agreements* – the 38 negotiated settlements and 11 negotiated truces arrived at by adversaries during this 55-year period.

In seeking to identify the factors that have an impact on the duration of the peace following the signing of agreements to end civil war, Hartzell and Hoddie (2003, 2005) focus on three distinct, but not mutually exclusive, explanations for the duration of the post-civil war peace. These explanations focus on the nature of the conflict at the heart of each war, the post-conflict environment, and the terms of the settlement. With respect to the first explanation, the idea is that conflicts associated with the greatest ongoing security concerns among adversaries at the end of the war are the ones whose settlements are likely to be the most fragile and thus subject to early breakdown. Settlements that follow conflicts in which the central issue at stake in the war was one of identity (rather than ideology) and the war was short-lived and produced high numbers of casualties are hypothesized to be the ones to be followed by relatively short periods of peace. The impact that two different aspects of the post-conflict environment – the domestic environment and the international system – may have on the duration of the peace are also explored. Focusing first on the domestic environment, it is expected that both previous experience with democracy and higher levels of economic development have the potential to allay the concerns groups may have regarding the capacity of negotiated civil war agreements to provide for their safety. Factors originating in the international system are also thought to exercise an effect on adversaries' sense of security and thus on the likelihood that they will act in a manner conducive to establishing a lasting peace. More specifically, the presence of peacekeeping forces and end of the bipolar Cold War system are expected to favor increasingly durable settlements. Finally, with respect to the terms of the settlement, Hartzell and Hoddie (2003, 2005) hypothesize that the more highly institutionalized a settlement is, meaning the greater the number of different dimensions of power-sharing or power-dividing provisions a peace agreement specifies, the longer the peace is likely to prevail.

Using hazard or event history analysis, Hartzell and Hoddie (2005) examine the effects of several independent variables (representing the nature of the conflict, the post-conflict environment, and the terms of the settlement) on the duration of the peace following a negotiated civil war agreement.[6] Interestingly enough, even though they use two different sets of cases to test their hypotheses (the 38 cases of fully negotiated settlements and the 49 cases of negotiated agreements), the same three indicators – economic development, the presence of a peacekeeping operation, and settlement institutionalization – emerge as the ones that exercise a statistically significant influence on the duration of the peace following mutually constructed agreements to end a civil war. Higher levels of economic development and the presence of peacekeeping operations both reduce the risk of a return to civil war. This suggests that at least some aspects of the post-conflict environment can influence the duration of the peace, following the negotiation of agreements to end civil wars. More institutionalized settlements also lessen the risk that civil war will recur. Negotiated settlements that failed to include any power-sharing or power-dividing institutions were found to face an increased risk of a return to civil war on the order of 420 percent (negotiated agreements that failed to include any such institutions faced an increased risk of civil war recurrence of 199 percent). On the other hand, adversaries who agreed to craft all four types of power-sharing or power-dividing institutions (i.e., political, military, territorial, and economic) as part of a negotiated settlement saw a reduction in the likelihood of war breaking out again on the order of 71 percent (negotiated agreements that included all four types of power-sharing or power-dividing institutions saw the risk of war breaking out again reduced 62 percent).

Implications for ending wars and structuring peace

One positive point to emerge from the analysis of the negotiated settlement of civil wars is that it suggests that groups that until very recently have been attempting to kill one another have it within their power to exercise considerable influence over the longevity of the peace. By agreeing to construct a series of institutions that provide for their mutual security as well as spelling out the rules by which conflict is to be regulated in the future, former adversaries have the ability to structure a lasting peace. Not only do former foes seem more likely to have a stake in the peace when they themselves have played a role in designing the terms of that peace, but groups seem more likely to play by a set of rules in whose construction they have participated.

What does this analysis of negotiated civil war settlements imply for the international community's approach to ending civil wars? First of all, if, as suggested above, negotiated settlements are susceptible to being designed in such a manner as to produce an enduring peace, then the international community's current emphasis on negotiating an end to these conflicts, rather than letting them be fought to the bitter end, certainly seems appropriate. Policymakers should seek to discourage more costly means of war-ending – i.e., settlements that take the form of military victory – and, through the appropriate sets of incentives and/or pressures, move intrastate adversaries to the negotiating table.

Second, the foregoing analysis also implies that members of the international community should work to encourage civil war antagonists to design extensively institutionalized settlements. Outside actors could, for example, help provide technical or other support necessary to design institutions that not only address the security concerns of parties to the conflict but also some of the substantive issues that may originally have given rise to the conflict. At a minimum, members of the international community should take care not to pressure parties to a conflict to agree to a negotiated accord so hastily that the adversaries do not have time to design all the appropriate institutional guarantees.

Finally, outside actors are also in a position to exercise some influence over the post-conflict environment that actors who have been engaged in armed conflict will face. The international community has it within its power to make decisions regarding where it will send peacekeeping operations, for example. The knowledge that countries that negotiate an end to their civil wars are more likely to have a more durable peace if peacekeeping missions are deployed should factor into the deliberations of the international community. And, although it is obviously harder for the international community to affect a country's level of economic development in the short term, actors like the International Monetary Fund and the World Bank do have the ability, through structural adjustment and other policies, to exercise some leverage over this aspect of the post-conflict environment (Paris 2004).

Ultimately, however, the design of conflict management institutions is in the hands of the architects of negotiated civil war settlements – the groups that were parties to the conflict. These groups must identify their concerns and craft the institutions that will best address those issues. Ending a civil war and structuring a durable peace calls for more than just stopping the fighting – it calls for the design of institutions for the peaceful management of the conflict that every society experiences.

Notes

1 I make use of my own civil war data set in this chapter. The number of civil war initiations I record and the number that I classify as having ended differ from that of other major civil war data sets such as Doyle and Sambanis (2000) and Fearon and Laitin (2003) based on the different coding rules we employ. Whereas I include only those conflicts that meet the Correlates of War (see Small and Singer 1982) criterion of 1,000 battle deaths per year, the Doyle and Sambanis and Fearon and Laitin data sets classify conflicts that fall far below this threshold as civil wars. In addition, Fearon and Laitin code a civil war as ended only when it has been followed by two years of peace. Since I am interested in learning more about the factors that have an impact on the duration of the peace, I classify wars in which the fighting stopped for periods as brief as one month as having come to an end.

2 Fourteen civil wars were ongoing at the end of 1999. These cases are not listed in Table 2.1.

3 There is generally a tendency to associate longer conflicts with higher levels of death and destruction. Lasting an average of 32.79 months, however, wars that ended in military victory were shorter than conflicts that terminated in negotiated settlements (89.02 months on average), wars that ended in negotiated truces (46.18 months on average) and wars in which the peace was negotiated or imposed by third parties (an average of 15.69 months). The longer average duration of wars that end in some form of negotiated agreement is not all that surprising since it may be a feeling of stalemate that persuades combatants to end their conflict through negotiation.

4 The ability of military victors to design institutions of their choice need not mean that those that they opt to construct will provide solely for their own interests and security. As pointed out earlier, unless a civil war adversary succeeds in utterly destroying its opponent's means to resist, it is unlikely that a rival force will stop fighting unless some provision for its post-surrender security has been made.

5 The 1970 Yemeni settlement eventually was superseded by an agreement on the parts of Northern Yemen and Southern Yemen to unite.

6 Event history models are specifically designed to consider factors that might increase or decrease the length of time before a particular event occurs. In these

tests the event of interest is the failure of a civil war settlement, as indicated by the return to war. The model thus considers the duration of an episode of peace until (or if) the settlement fails.

References

Ballentine, K. and Sherman, J. (2003) *The Political Economy of Armed Conflict: Beyond Greed and Grievance*. Boulder, CO: Lynne Rienner Publishers.

Berdal, M. and Malone, D.M. (eds.) (2000) *Greed and Grievance: Economic Agendas in Civil Wars*. Boulder, CO: Lynne Rienner Publishers.

Doyle, M. and Sambanis, N. (2000) "International peacebuilding: A theoretical and quantitative analysis," *American Political Science Review* 94: 779–801.

Esman, M. (1994) *Ethnic Politics*. Ithaca, NY: Cornell University Press.

Fearon, J.D. and Laitin, D.D. (2003) "Ethnicity, insurgency, and civil war," *American Political Science Review* 97(1): 75–90.

Fortna, V.P. (2004) *Peace Time: Cease-Fire Agreements and the Durability of Peace*. Princeton, NJ: Princeton University Press.

Hampson, F.O. (1996) "Building a stable peace: Opportunities and limits to security co-operation in third world regional conflicts," *International Journal* 45: 454–489.

Hartzell, C. (1999) "Explaining the stability of negotiated settlements to intrastate wars," *Journal of Conflict Resolution* 43: 3–22.

Hartzell, C. and Hoddie, M. (2003) "Institutionalizing peace: Power sharing and post-civil war conflict management," *American Journal of Political Science* 47: 318–332.

Hartzell, C. and Hoddie, M. (2005). "Crafting Peace: Power Sharing and the Negotiated Settlement of Civil Wars," unpublished manuscript, Gettysburg College, Gettysburg, PA.

Heintze, H.-J. (1997) "Autonomy and Protection of Minorities under International Law," in G. Bachler (ed.) *Federalism against Ethnicity? Institutional, Legal and Democratic Instruments to Prevent Violent Minority Conflicts*. Zurich: Verlag Ruegger.

Herz, J. (1950) "Idealist internationalism and the security dilemma," *World Politics* 2: 157–180.

Horowitz, D. (1985) *Ethnic Groups in Conflict*. Berkeley, CA: University of California Press.

Horowitz, D. (1991) "Ethnic Conflict Management for Policymakers," in J.V. Montville (ed.) *Conflict and Peacemaking in Multiethnic Societies*. Lexington, MA: Lexington Books.

Lijphart, A. (1977) *Democracy in Plural Societies*. New Haven, CT: Yale University Press.

Nordlinger, E.A. (1972) *Conflict Regulation in Divided Societies*. Cambridge, MA: Harvard University, Center for International Affairs.

Paris, R. (2004) *At War's End: Building Peace After Civil Conflict*. Cambridge: Cambridge University Press.

Peeler, J.A. (1985) *Latin American Democracies: Colombia, Costa Rica, Venezuela*. Chapel Hill, NC: The University of North Carolina Press.

Reiter, D. (2003) "Exploring the bargaining model of war," *Perspectives on Politics* 1: 27–43.

Sisk, T.D. (1996) *Power Sharing and International Mediation in Ethnic Conflicts*. Washington, DC: United States Institute of Peace.

Small, M. and Singer, J.D. (1982) *Resort to Arms: International and Civil Wars, 1816–1980*. Beverly Hills, CA: Sage.

Smooha, S. and Hanf, T. (1992) "The diverse modes of conflict-regulation in deeply divided societies," *International Journal of Comparative Sociology* 33: 26–47.

Stedman, S.J. (1996) "Negotiation and mediation in internal conflict," in M.E. Brown (ed.) *The International Dimensions of Internal Conflict*. Cambridge, MA: MIT Press.

Walter, B. (1997) "The critical barrier to civil war settlement," *International Organization* 51: 335–364.

Walter, B. (2002) *Committing to Peace: The Successful Settlement of Civil Wars*. Princeton, NJ: Princeton University Press.

Weiner, M. (1983) "The political consequences of preferential politics: A comparative perspective," *Comparative Politics* 16: 35–52.

3 Reconstructing strife-torn societies

Third-party peacebuilding in intrastate disputes

Mark J. Mullenbach

Since the end of the Second World War, and particularly since the end of the Cold War, third-party actors have frequently intervened during intrastate disputes throughout the world to enhance the prospects that the disputes do not escalate to military hostilities and are peacefully resolved through bilateral or multilateral negotiations. When third-party interventions involve specific activities that go beyond what are referred to as "peacekeeping" missions or "peacemaking" missions, such interventions are generally referred to as "peacebuilding." In the past decade or so, peacebuilding missions have been initiated by a variety of third-party actors in nearly every region of the world.

As a result of these interventions, scholars and practitioners have debated whether third-party peacebuilding missions have been effective at managing and resolving intrastate disputes. For example, Eva Bertram suggested that the "results to date of UN peacebuilding provide reason for cautious optimism" and that in "marked contrast to some of the United Nations' riskier peace enforcement missions, none of its major peacebuilding missions has ended in disillusionment and retreat" (1995: 390). On the other hand, Roland Paris has argued that peacebuilding missions established by the international community in the post-Cold War period have "generated many unforeseen problems" and may have even had the "perverse effect of undermining the very peace they were meant to buttress" (1997: 56). Clearly, there is no consensus among scholars regarding the effectiveness of peacebuilding.

In this chapter, I focus on two questions pertaining to the ongoing debate among scholars and practitioners over peacebuilding. First, do third-party peacebuilding missions significantly decrease the likelihood of military hostilities occurring or recurring in an intrastate dispute? Second, do third-party peacebuilding missions significantly increase the likelihood of signing and implementing a peace agreement in an intrastate dispute? These questions reflect two types of "peace" that can be achieved in the context of an intrastate dispute. Some scholars have referred to the absence of violence as "negative peace" and the removal of the underlying causes of violence as "positive peace."[1]

The study of third-party peacebuilding in this chapter is motivated by the expansion of such efforts undertaken in intrastate disputes, particularly following civil conflicts, throughout the world in the past few decades. There is very little indication that the pervasiveness of third-party peacebuilding will diminish in future years. Indeed, some scholars have argued that the challenge of "rebuilding stable polities in the aftermath of civil war" is one of the most important issues currently facing the international community (Doyle and Sambanis 2000: 779). Given the importance of third-party peacebuilding, there is a need for a better understanding of its effectiveness.

This study is also motivated by the limitations in previous scholarly works on third-party peacebuilding. One of the first scholars to discuss the concept of third-party peacebuilding as a method of conflict management was Swedish sociologist Johan Galtung (1976), who argued during the 1970s that peacebuilding – along with peacekeeping and peacemaking – was one of the "three approaches to peace." Scholars largely ignored the role of peacebuilding in conflict management until two decades later when Secretary-General Boutros Boutros-Ghali submitted the report *An Agenda for Peace* to the members of the UN in June 1992. The report discussed four categories of conflict management: (1) preventive diplomacy; (2) peacemaking; (3) peacekeeping; and (4) post-conflict peacebuilding. According to Boutros-Ghali, these tools of conflict management "offer a coherent contribution towards securing peace in the spirit of the [UN] charter" (1992: 4).

Since 1992, several scholars have focused broadly on the role of third-party peacebuilding in managing political instability or conflict within countries,[2] while others have focused more narrowly on one or more of the various types of peacebuilding missions.[3] In fact, most of the research done on third-party peacebuilding in the past decade or so has been analyses of one or two case studies, including Afghanistan, Cambodia, Croatia, East Timor, Kosovo, Bosnia-Herzegovina, Haiti, Namibia, Sierra Leone, Somalia, and El Salvador.[4] The main drawback of much of the previous literature is the relative lack of broad or systematic analyses of the effectiveness of peacebuilding missions. In fact, most of this literature describes a specific case of third-party peacebuilding, and then provides one or more lessons or policy implications regarding peacebuilding in general. Although these single case studies provide valuable theoretical and empirical insights into the effectiveness of third-party peacebuilding efforts in particular locations, the conclusions or lessons drawn from such studies may not be applicable to other peacebuilding missions in other locations. In short, there is a tremendous need for more broad or systematic analyses of the effectiveness of peacebuilding missions.

The remainder of the chapter is divided into four sections. In the first section, I discuss the concept of peacebuilding and provide a formal definition of peacebuilding. In addition, I identify and describe the various dimensions of peacebuilding. In the second section, I provide a set of theoretical arguments regarding the effect of peacebuilding on the likelihood of preventing military hostilities and facilitating peaceful settlement of intrastate disputes, and I derive several hypotheses regarding the influence of peacebuilding missions from the arguments. In the third section, I analyze the hypotheses using 15 cases in which there were one or more peacebuilding efforts and 15 cases in which there were no peacebuilding efforts. Finally, I conclude in the fourth section with a summary of the case study analysis and a discussion of the policy implications of this study with respect to reconstructing and reconciling societies torn by civil strife in the twenty-first century.

Definitions and dimensions of peacebuilding

Scholars and practitioners have defined the concept of peacebuilding in a wide variety of ways, and as a consequence, there has been some difficulty in understanding the usefulness of the concept as an object of empirical analysis. Some individuals have equated "peacebuilding" with what is commonly known as "nation-building."[5] Eva Bertram, for example, suggested that "full-scale peacebuilding efforts are nothing short of attempts at nation-building; they seek to remake a state's political institutions, security forces, and economic arrangements" (1995: 389). However, others have correctly pointed out that peacebuilding and nation-building are actually two different concepts. Nation-building generally refers to broad efforts to develop "a cohesive spirit, a sense of national identity, as well as the instruments of modern government" (Jacobson 1964: 76). The two concepts intersect when the absence of a fully developed national identity within a country is at least partly responsible for civil strife. Although peacebuilding and nation-building may be interrelated in some situations and have been used interchangeably by many individuals in the past, the two concepts are generally not treated as synonymous in this study.

Much more closely related to peacebuilding is the concept of "statebuilding," which, according to Richard Caplan, refers to "efforts to reconstruct, or in some cases to establish for the first time, an effective indigenous government in a state or territory where no such capacity exists or where the capacity has been seriously eroded" (2004: 53). According to this definition, third-party state-building might include some peacebuilding activities such as temporary administration and election monitoring. In fact, Carrie Manning suggested that "peacebuilding can fruitfully be viewed as part of or dependent upon a process of statebuilding" and that "statebuilding must be taken to include the practical establishment of state authority throughout the national territory" (2003: 26).

Even focusing narrowly on peacebuilding reveals that there are some important differences among scholars in terms of the definition of the concept. Many individuals consider peacebuilding to be a tool of conflict management used primarily following military hostilities between parties to an intrastate dispute.[6] In fact, UN Secretary-General Boutros Boutros-Ghali's 1992 *An Agenda for Peace* specifically referred to the concept of "post-conflict peacebuilding," and defined it as "action to identify and support structures which will tend to strengthen and solidify peace in order to avoid a relapse into conflict" (ibid.: 4). Along the same lines, Gareth Evans (1994) suggested that peacebuilding referred to efforts to prevent the "recurrence of hostilities" following an intrastate conflict. On the other hand, others have argued that peacebuilding efforts "should not be limited to postconflict societies" (Call and Cook 2003: 240). For example, Ronald Fisher suggested that peacebuilding could be defined as "developmental and interactive activities, often facilitated by a third-party actor, which are directed toward meeting the basic needs, de-escalating the hostility, and improving the relationship of parties engaged in protracted social conflict" (1993: 252). Similarly, Laurence Baxter defined peacebuilding as "a set of political, economic, military or social activities conducted by any party before or after hostilities that contribute to creating conditions of mutual consent and lasting stability" (1998: 5).

Notwithstanding the issues discussed above, most definitions of third-party peacebuilding contain one or more of the following three elements: (1) peacebuilding efforts are generally initiated during crisis (pre-conflict) or post-conflict phases of intrastate disputes; (2) third-party actors, such as countries and international organizations, play a critical role in the peacebuilding process;[7] and (3) the main goal of most peacebuilding efforts is to prevent the occurrence or recurrence of hostilities and to facilitate the peaceful settlement of a dispute. Therefore, peacebuilding is defined here as:

> efforts by third-party actors during crisis phases or post-conflict phases of intrastate disputes which are initiated to deal with the underlying problems or basic needs of the parties to the dispute, to foster conditions that enhance the likelihood that the dispute will not escalate or re-escalate to military hostilities, and to enhance the likelihood that the dispute will be peacefully settled by the parties.

Given the above definition of peacebuilding, it is necessary to identify specific types of peacebuilding activities undertaken by third-party actors. Roland Paris suggested that third-party peacebuilding involves

> [a] broad range of activities, from disarming former belligerents to providing financial and humanitarian assistance, monitoring and conducting elections, repatriating refugees, rebuilding physical infrastructure, advising and training security personnel and judicial officials, and even temporarily taking over the administration of an entire country.
>
> (1997: 55)

These and other third-party peacebuilding activities can be categorized into five dimensions: economic, humanitarian, legal, military, and political.[8] Each of these dimensions of peacebuilding includes a set of specific third-party activities with the overall goal of meeting the "basic needs" of a society, preventing military hostilities, and facilitating the peaceful settlement of an intrastate dispute. In short, the main purpose of third-party peacebuilding efforts is to lay the foundation for a long-lasting and stable peace in a country that has been torn by civil strife.

The economic dimension of peacebuilding involves third-party efforts to repair and rebuild the damaged infrastructure of the strife-torn country, including roads, bridges, sewers, schools, and hospitals. This reconstruction work can be done either directly by personnel representing the third-party country or organization or indirectly through the financing of reconstruction projects managed and undertaken by local personnel. According to Dan Smith, "[e]conomic reconstruction has to start with short-term needs while laying the foundation for long-term prosperity without gross differences between megawealth and extreme poverty" (2002: 446). In addition to the immediate need for rebuilding infrastructure, the economic dimension of peacebuilding also includes long-term assistance for sustainable development in the form of grants, loans, and technical assistance.

The humanitarian dimension of peacebuilding involves third-party efforts to provide emergency assistance (or humanitarian assistance) to those individuals who are adversely affected by strife within a country. Michael Schloms defined humanitarian assistance as "the provision of basic requirements which meet people's needs for adequate water, sanitation, nutrition, food, shelter and health care" (2003: 43). In addition to basic necessities, third-party humanitarian efforts might also include repatriation of displaced individuals to their homes or places of origin. In fact, several scholars have discussed the importance of dealing with refugee problems as an integral part of the overall peacebuilding process in a strife-torn country. For example, B.S. Chimni suggested that the "return of displaced persons ... lends greater legitimacy to the subsequent democratic and state-building process" (2002: 163). In other words, the results of democratic elections or a constitutional referendum, for example, may not be perceived as legitimate if thousands of eligible voters are unable to participate due to their displacement. Ultimately, the perception of illegitimacy of a government or political system could undermine the building of peace and could lead to the resumption of instability in a strife-torn country.

The legal dimension of peacebuilding focuses on a variety of third-party efforts that are intended to strengthen the "rule of law" in a strife-torn country, including the training and monitoring of civilian police personnel and the promotion and monitoring of human rights conditions within the country. Chetan Kumar has argued that the "rule of law and the availability of security and justice for the common person are clearly important determinants of the degree to which democracy can emerge and be stabilized in a postconflict situation" (2004: 124). Indeed, the legal dimension also involves activities that are intended to promote justice and reconciliation in countries with a legacy of serious human rights abuses and crimes against humanity. In these situations, third-party personnel may be asked to establish (or take part in the establishment of) and participate in a "truth commission" or a "war crimes tribunal." In fact, Abdul Rahman Lamin (2003) suggested that societies making the transition from war to peace are faced with two options regarding past human rights abuses and crimes against humanity: retributive justice and restorative justice. According to Lamin, retributive justice refers to punishment of "perpetrators of past human rights abuses through criminal prosecution in a national or international setting," while restorative justice refers to a "non-punitive approach that emphasizes 'truth-telling' usually under the auspices of a truth commission or other such designated bodies" (2003: 298–299). In either case, the "truth" about past human rights abuses and crimes against humanity is often a necessary step before peace can ultimately be built in societies dealing with such tragic legacies. Occasionally, these societies look to third-party personnel to take a leading or supporting role in the truth and reconciliation process.

The military dimension of peacebuilding focuses on third-party efforts to reconstruct the military forces of a strife-torn country, including providing professional training and advice to government military personnel. In addition, countries dealing with civil strife often have thousands of landmines placed in various locations by the parties to a dispute. According to B.S. Chimni, "landmines represent a key obstacle to the return of refugees and displaced persons and to reconstruction activities" (2002: 170). In order to assist in the overall peacebuilding process, third-party military personnel are often deployed to assess a landmine situation and to assist with the clearing of landmines. Although considered by some scholars as part of the military dimension of peacebuilding, the supervision by third-party personnel of disarmament and demobilization programs are considered in this study as types of third-party "peacekeeping" missions because such personnel are normally assigned to perform such tasks.

Finally, the political dimension of peacebuilding involves third-party efforts to assist in holding a referendum on a new constitution or constitutional amendments and efforts to assist in holding "free and fair" elections, including monitoring or supervising voting during such elections. These third-party efforts might also include specific activities necessary for ensuring that elections are conducted in a professional and fair manner, including pre-election training or assessment of some aspect of a country's electoral system (e.g. registration of voters). Indeed, Neil Kritz has argued that the "international role in elections can be extremely important," and he suggested that international activities "include providing education and training in advance of elections, helping to draft election laws, and sending delegations to observe the elections to ensure their fairness" (1996: 592). The political dimension might also involve a third-party actor temporarily administering or governing a country during a transitional period culminating in democratic elections and self-government.

Theoretical arguments

As mentioned earlier, this study focuses on two questions: (1) Do third-party peacebuilding missions decrease the likelihood of military hostilities occurring or recurring in an intrastate dispute?; and (2) Do third-party peacebuilding missions increase the likelihood that a peace agreement will be signed by the parties and the provisions of the peace agreement will be implemented?

The main argument pertaining to these questions is that third-party peacebuilding efforts decrease the likelihood of military hostilities ("negative peace") and increase the likelihood that parties to an intrastate dispute will sign and implement a peace agreement ("positive peace"). The primary reason for the influence of peacebuilding is the considerable focus of such missions on the "basic needs" of the parties to the dispute (Fisher 1993: 259). Unlike peacemaking and peacekeeping, third-party peacebuilding efforts actually address underlying grievances and injustices perceived by the parties. These grievances and injustices – and the perceived lack of attention paid to them – are at least what partly motivates the parties to resort to violence. Once some or all of these underlying issues have been addressed, the likelihood that the parties will seek a peaceful resolution of their political differences is significantly higher. One of the main assumptions behind this argument is that since the underlying issues in an intrastate dispute are normally multidimensional (e.g. poverty and economic disparities, refugees and internally displaced persons, human rights abuses, etc.), the potential for building lasting peace in a strife-torn country is enhanced only if the overall peacebuilding process is also multidimensional (i.e. the overall third-party effort involves two or more dimensions of peacebuilding). The following hypotheses are derived from the main argument:

> Hypothesis 1a: *The likelihood of preventing military hostilities in an intrastate dispute is higher when a multidimensional third-party peacebuilding effort has been undertaken.*

> Hypothesis 1b: *The likelihood of peaceful settlement of an intrastate dispute is higher when a multidimensional third-party peacebuilding effort has been undertaken.*

The theoretical and empirical literature on third-party peacebuilding suggests additional hypotheses regarding peacebuilding and the likelihood of preventing military hostilities and facilitating peaceful settlement. First, some scholars have argued that for peacebuilding efforts to be successful there must be an international effort to deal with the security situation in the country.[9] For example, Naomi Weinberger (2002) concluded that "establishing a modicum of security by deploying international peace-keepers is often a necessary but not sufficient condition for addressing short-term humanitarian emergencies and initiating longer-term recon-struction efforts." Peacekeeping missions are often established by or under the auspices of a UN body, but *ad hoc* groups of countries and regional inter-governmental organizations (IGOs) are also capable of establishing peacekeeping missions in intrastate disputes.[10] The primary purpose of most third-party peacekeeping missions established within countries is to maintain a secure and stable environment, usually but not necessarily following the cessation of military hostilities. It would not be difficult to point out one or more cases in which a peacekeeping effort was vital to the success of a peacebuilding process in a strife-torn country. Indeed, recent events in Afghanistan and Iraq arguably indicate that without the presence of North Atlantic Treaty Organization (NATO) and US troops in Afghanistan, and US-led "coalition of the willing" troops in Iraq, peace-building activities in these countries would have less chance of success. This argument suggests the following set of hypotheses:

> Hypothesis 2a: *The likelihood of preventing military hostilities in an intrastate dispute is higher when one or more third-party peacekeeping missions have been established simultaneously with the establishment of a multidimensional peacebuilding mission.*

> Hypothesis 2b: *The likelihood of peaceful settlement of an intrastate dispute is higher when one or more third-party peacekeeping missions have been established simultaneously with the establishment of a multidimensional peacebuilding mission.*

Similar to the argument above, some scholars have argued that in order for third-party peacebuilding efforts to be successful, one or more simulta-neous third-party peacemaking efforts are necessary.[11] As with peacekeep-ing, third-party peacemaking efforts such as mediation may be initiated by representatives of countries, inter-governmental organizations, and non-governmental organizations. In her study of the peaceful settlement of civil wars, Barbara Walter argued that "one would expect all successful settlements to involve mediation and those that failed to have suffered from its absence" (1997: 348). The basic assumption underlying this argu-ment is the notion that while peacebuilding involves dealing with the underlying issues of an intrastate dispute, it would be difficult, if not impossible, to deal with the underlying issues in an intrastate dispute without negotiations. In fact, third-party mediation often is necessary to bring parties to the negotiating table, and that without the diplomatic skills and leverage of the mediator, there is a higher likelihood that parties will resort to military hostilities. Likewise, it is assumed that without third-party mediation, there is little likelihood of peaceful negotiations and dispute settlement.

> Hypothesis 3a: *The likelihood of preventing military hostilities in an intrastate dispute is higher when one or more third-party peacemaking efforts have been initiated simultaneously with the establishment of one or more peacebuilding missions.*

> Hypothesis 3b: *The likelihood of peaceful settlement of an intrastate dispute is higher when one or more third-party peacemaking efforts have been initiated simultaneously with the establishment of one or more third-party peacebuilding missions.*

Finally, some scholars have argued that the likelihood of preventing military hostilities and facilitating peaceful settlement is influenced by whether or not third-party peacebuilding activities are effectively coordinated. In fact, many individuals have pointed to the lack of coordination among the various third-party peacebuilding agencies and efforts as being a serious impediment to successful peacebuilding.[12] It is especially problematic when the goals of two or more peacebuilding missions are contradictory. In her critical analysis of the peacebuilding efforts undertaken in Central America in the 1990s, Jenny Pearce pointed out that

> [the] lack of coordination between economic policy-making institutions, notably the World Bank, International Monetary Fund and Inter-American Development Bank and humanitarian organizations, i.e. the UN, prevented any discussion of the way budget cuts and trade liberalisation, for example, might affect the poor and peacebuilding in the fragile conditions of a war-torn society.
>
> (1999: 57)

Similarly, Bruce Jones concluded that "absent effective coordination by the UN, a comparable regional or international organization or a lead state, the effectiveness of implementation efforts will be heavily constrained" (2002: 89). The following set of hypotheses is based on the assumption that two of the main goals of peacebuilding – preventing military hostilities and facilitating peaceful settlement – are more likely to be achieved if peacebuilding activities are coordinated by an international organization.

> Hypothesis 4a: *The likelihood of preventing military hostilities in an intrastate dispute is higher if the United Nations or a regional*

inter-governmental organization (IGO) is largely responsible for coordinating the peacebuilding process.

Hypothesis 4b: *The likelihood of peaceful settlement of an intrastate dispute is higher if the United Nations or a regional IGO is largely responsible for coordinating the peacebuilding process.*

Case study analysis

In order to test the preceding hypotheses, I examine a total of 30 cases of *crisis phases* or *post-conflict phases* of intrastate disputes since 1970, including six cases from each of the five regions of the world (Asia/Pacific, Europe/Former Soviet Union, Middle East/North Africa/Persian Gulf, Sub-Saharan Africa, and Western Hemisphere). The cases were selected from an existing data set containing a total of 256 intrastate disputes that are disaggregated into some 1,475 dispute phases.[13] The 30 disputes phases selected for this study are listed on the left-hand column of Table 3.1. For each region, I have selected three cases in which a multidimensional peacebuilding mission (PBM) was established by one or more third-party actors and three cases in which a multidimensional PBM was not established.[14] The situations in Cambodia (1991–1998) and Rhodesia/Zimbabwe (1979–1983) represent two types of cases – the first involving several dimensions of peacebuilding in a post-conflict situation and the second involving only one dimension of peacebuilding. In the case of Cambodia, the UN launched several peacebuilding efforts beginning in early 1992 following a destructive civil war that lasted more than 12 years, resulting in the deaths of some 175,000 Cambodians and the displacement of more than two million. The UN-coordinated effort consisted of specific missions involving each of the five dimensions of peacebuilding: financial assistance for reconstructing the infrastructure; repatriating refugees and other displaced Cambodians; monitoring and training civilian police and monitoring human rights conditions; clearing mines; and providing transitional administration and election supervision. Simultaneously, the UN deployed some 16,000 peacekeeping personnel from more than 30 countries between February 1992 and September 1993.[15]

In the case of Rhodesia/Zimbabwe, the Commonwealth of Nations had mediated an end to a civil war lasting seven years between rival groups in the British colony in late 1979. The organization then established the Commonwealth Monitoring Force (CMF), which consisted of some 1,500 peacekeeping personnel from Britain, Australia, Fiji, Kenya, and New Zealand, to monitor a ceasefire and demobilization of combatants. In addition, a small group of Commonwealth personnel monitored parliamentary elections that took place in February 1980. Within three months of arriving in the country, the CMF had largely withdrawn from Zimbabwe. Beyond the election monitoring mission, neither the

Table 3.1 Cases of crisis/post-conflict phases of intrastate disputes, 1970–present

Country (years)	Phase type	Multi-dimensional peacebuilding?	Peacekeeping mission?	Peacemaking?	Coordination?	Hostilities? (5 years)	Hostilities? (10 years)	Settlement? (5 years)	Settlement? (10 years)
Sri Lanka/Tamils (1987–1990)	Post-Conflict	Yes	Yes	No	No	Yes	Yes	No	No
Cambodia (1991–1999)	Post-Conflict	Yes	Yes	Yes	Yes	No	No	No	No
Indonesia (1996–present)	Crisis	Yes	No	No	No	No	n.a.	No	n.a.
Bangladesh (1997–present)	Crisis	No	No	No	No	No	n.a.	No	n.a.
PNG/Bougainville (1994–1996)	Post-Conflict	No	Yes	Yes	No	Yes	Yes	No	Yes
Philippines (1986–1987)	Post-Conflict	No	No	No	No	Yes	Yes	No	No
Albania (1997–1999)	Crisis	Yes	Yes	Yes	No	No	n.a.	Yes	n.a.
Georgia/Abkhazia (1993–present)	Post-Conflict	Yes	Yes	Yes	No	No	No	No	No
Tajikistan (1996–present)	Post-Conflict	Yes	Yes	Yes	No	No	n.a.	Yes	n.a.
Bulgaria (1984–1991)	Crisis	No	No	No	No	No	No	No	No
Cyprus (1974–present)	Post-Conflict	No	Yes	Yes	No	No	No	No	No
Serbia/Kosovo (1998–1999)	Post-Conflict	No	Yes	Yes	No	Yes	n.a.	No	n.a.
Yemen (1994–present)	Post-Conflict	Yes	No	No	No	No	No	No	No
Morocco/W. Sahara (1991–present)	Post-Conflict	Yes	Yes	Yes	Yes	No	No	No	No
Chad (1996–1998)	Post-Conflict	Yes	No	No	Yes	Yes	Yes	No	No

Table 3.1 Continued

Country (years)	Phase type	Multi-dimensional peacebuilding?	Peacekeeping mission?	Peacemaking?	Coordination?	Hostilities? (5 years)	Hostilities? (10 years)	Settlement? (5 years)	Settlement? (10 years)
Lebanon (1976–1977)	Post-Conflict	No	Yes	Yes	No	Yes	Yes	No	No
Sudan/Anya Nya (1972–1983)	Post-Conflict	No	No	No	No	No	No	Yes	Yes
Syria (1982–present)	Post-Conflict	No	No	No	No	No	No	No	No
Rwanda (1994–present)	Post-Conflict	Yes	Yes	Yes	Yes	No	No	No	No
Mozambique (1992–1994)	Post-Conflict	Yes	Yes	Yes	Yes	No	No	Yes	Yes
Liberia (1996–2000)	Post-Conflict	Yes	Yes	Yes	Yes	Yes	n.a.	No	n.a.
Côte d'Ivoire (1999–2002)	Crisis	No	No	Yes	No	Yes	n.a.	No	n.a.
Rhodesia/Zimbabwe (1979–1983)	Post-Conflict	No	Yes	No	No	Yes	Yes	No	No
Tanzania (1995–1999)	Crisis	No	No	Yes	No	No	No	Yes	Yes
El Salvador (1990–1994)	Post-Conflict	Yes	Yes	Yes	Yes	No	No	Yes	Yes
Haiti (1991–1996)	Crisis	Yes	No	Yes	Yes	No	No	No	No
Suriname (1992–present)	Post-Conflict	Yes	No	No	No	No	No	Yes	Yes
Chile (1973–1978)	Crisis	No	No	Yes	No	No	No	No	No
Bolivia (1978–1982)	Crisis	No	No	No	No	No	No	No	No
Nicaragua (1979–1981)	Post-Conflict	No	No	No	No	Yes	Yes	No	No

Note
n.a. = not applicable.

Commonwealth nor another third-party actor had initiated any substantial peacebuilding effort during the transitional period between the end of the civil war and the withdrawal of the CMF.

Multidimensional peacebuilding missions (PBMs)

To start, I examine whether or not the establishment of a multidimensional PBM influences the occurrence or recurrence of military hostilities. As shown in Table 3.1, only ten of the 30 cases (33 percent) escalated to military hostilities within five years of the beginning of a dispute phase. For example, military hostilities between Sri Lankan government troops and ethnic Tamil rebels resumed in June 1990, some three years after a ceasefire had temporarily ended conflict in July 1987. With one exception, all the disputes that escalated to military hostilities at any time after the beginning of a dispute phase did so within five years (the dispute between the Sudanese government and the Anya Nya secessionist movement escalated to military hostilities some 11 years after the end of conflict in 1972).

Of the 15 cases involving a multidimensional PBM, only three cases (20 percent) escalated to military hostilities within five years. In the case of Chad, the UN repatriated some 10,000 refugees who had fled to neighboring countries and provided electoral assistance during a post-conflict phase beginning in January 1996. Although peace agreements were signed by representatives of the government and several opposition groups during this period, military hostilities resumed between government troops and a rebel group in northern Chad in September 1998. Of the 15 cases that did not involve a multidimensional PBM, seven cases (46.6 percent) escalated to military hostilities. Therefore, the rate of escalation to military hostilities was more than twice as high for the cases not involving multidimensional PBMs than the cases involving multidimensional PBMs.

What effect does the establishment of a multidimensional PBM have on the likelihood that the parties will formally settle their dispute? The concept of "dispute settlement" includes not only the official signing of a peace agreement, but also implementation of the provisions of the peace agreement. Dispute settlement occurred in only seven of 30 cases (23.3 percent) within five years of the beginning of a dispute phase (and eight of 30 cases within ten years). The case of Mozambique is an example of an intrastate dispute that was officially settled after 15 years of civil war between government troops and rebels from 1977 to 1992. Representatives of the parties signed a peace agreement mediated by the Italian government, the Vatican, and Sant 'Egidio Community in Rome in October 1992, and the major provisions of the peace agreement, including combatant demobilization, refugee repatriation, and democratic elections, were implemented with the assistance of the international community during the following 26 months.[16]

As shown in Table 3.2, five of the 15 cases (33 percent) involving

Table 3.2 Multidimensional peacebuilding, military hostilities, and dispute settlement

Multidimensional peacebuilding?	Military hostilities? (five years)		Dispute settlement? (five years)	
	Yes	No	Yes	No
Yes	Sri Lanka/Tamils Chad Liberia	Cambodia Indonesia Albania Georgia/Abkhazia Tajikistan Morocco/Western Sahara Yemen Rwanda Mozambique El Salvador Haiti Suriname	Albania Tajikistan Mozambique El Salvador Suriname	Sri Lanka/Tamils Cambodia Indonesia Georgia/Abkhazia Yemen Morocco/Western Sahara Chad Rwanda Liberia Haiti
No	Papua New Guinea/ Bougainville Philippines Serbia/Kosovo Lebanon Côte d'Ivoire Rhodesia/Zimbabwe Nicaragua	Bangladesh Bulgaria Cyprus Sudan/Anya Nya Syria Tanzania Chile Bolivia	Sudan/Anya Nya Tanzania	Bangladesh Papua New Guinea/ Bougainville Philippines Bulgaria Cyprus Serbia/Kosovo Lebanon Syria Côte d'Ivoire Rhodesia/Zimbabwe Chile Bolivia Nicaragua

multidimensional PBMs were officially settled within five years of the beginning of a dispute phase. At the same time, only two of the 15 cases (13.3 percent) not involving a multidimensional PBM were officially settled within five years. One of these two cases involved a secessionist conflict between the government of Sudan and the Anya Nya rebels in southern Sudan. After a civil war lasting some eight years and resulting in the deaths of some 500,000 individuals, Emperor Haile Selassie of Ethiopia facilitated the signing of a peace agreement between the parties in February 1972. Beyond the repatriation of some 150,000 Sudanese refugees by the UN, there were no substantial peacebuilding efforts by third-party actors in the strife-torn country. Nevertheless, the parties implemented the peace agreement during the 1970s (although conflict re-emerged in the 1980s). Overall, the evidence regarding the relationship between multidimensional PBMs and dispute settlement is similar to the evidence regarding the relationship between multidimensional PBMs and military hostilities. The rate of dispute settlement was more than twice as high for cases involving multidimensional PBMs than cases not involving multidimensional PBMs.

Peacekeeping missions (PKMs)

Next, I examine whether or not the establishment of PKMs during dispute phases influences the likelihood that intrastate disputes will subsequently escalate to military hostilities. As shown in Table 3.1, third-party actors established one or more PKMs in 15 of the 30 cases selected for this study, usually for the purpose of monitoring ceasefires or demobilization processes. In six of these 15 cases (40 percent), escalation to military hostilities occurred within five years of the beginning of a dispute phase. Among the remaining 15 cases in which third-party actors did not establish PKMs, four cases (26.6 percent) escalated to military hostilities within five years. This evidence suggests that PKMs alone do not decrease the likelihood of military hostilities, probably because peacekeeping personnel are normally deployed by third-party actors in the situations that, for one reason or another, are at a higher risk of escalating to military hostilities.

Is there any evidence that simultaneous multidimensional PBMs and PKMs decrease the likelihood of military hostilities? The evidence from the 30 cases suggests that this combination may indeed reduce the risk of military hostilities (see Table 3.3). Of the ten cases involving both multidimensional PBMs and PKMs, only two cases (20 percent) – Sri Lanka/ Tamils and Liberia – escalated to military hostilities. In the case of Liberia, the Economic Community of West African States (ECOWAS) mediated a ceasefire in August 1996 between representatives of six rival factions that had waged a devastating civil war beginning in December 1989, resulting in the deaths of some 175,000 individuals and displacement of some

Table 3.3 Multidimensional peacebuilding × peacekeeping, military hostilities, and dispute settlement

	Military hostilities? (five years)		Dispute settlement? (five years)	
	Yes	*No*	*Yes*	*No*
Multidimensional peacebuilding × peacekeeping? **Yes**	Sri Lanka/Tamils Liberia	Cambodia Albania Georgia/Abkhazia Tajikistan Morocco/Western Sahara Rawanda Mozambique El Salvador Indonesia	Albania Tajikistan Mozambique El Salvador Sudan/Anya Nya	Sri Lanka/Tamils Cambodia Georgia/Abkhazia Morocco/Western Sahara Rwanda Liberia Indonesia
No	Papua New Guinea/Bougainville Philippines Serbia/Kosovo Chad Lebanon Côte d'Ivoire Rhodesia/Zimbabwe Nicaragua	Bangladesh Bulgaria Cyprus Yemen Sudan/Anya Nya Syria Tanzania Haiti Suriname Chile Bolivia	Tanzania Suriname	Bangladesh Papua New Guinea/Bougainville Philippines Bulgaria Cyprus Serbia/Kosovo Yemen Chad Lebanon Syria Côte d'Ivoire Rhodesia/Zimbabwe Haiti Chile Bolivia Nicaragua

750,000 individuals. Following the ceasefire, the UN coordinated a multi-dimensional PBM involving repatriating some 80,000 refugees and monitoring national elections during the post-conflict period from August 1996 to July 2000. Both the UN and ECOWAS maintained peacekeeping personnel to monitor the ceasefire and demobilization of combatants.[17] Military hostilities resumed between government troops and rebels beginning in July 2000.

As shown on the left-hand side of Table 3.3, eight of the 20 cases (40 percent) that did not involve both multidimensional PBMs and PKMs escalated to military hostilities. One of these eight cases was Nicaragua, where the government of President Somoza Debayle was toppled by Sandinista rebels following a 21-month civil war in July 1979. Although the World Bank provided reconstruction assistance to the Sandinista government, neither a multidimensional PBM nor a PKM was established in Nicaragua during the post-conflict phase. A civil war broke out between the Sandinista government and opposition groups (i.e., *contras*) funded by the US government in August 1981. Overall, the rate of escalation to military hostilities was twice as high for the cases not involving simultaneous multidimensional PBMs and PKMs. There is also evidence that the combination of multidimensional PBMs and PKMs affects the likelihood of dispute settlement, as shown on the right-hand side of Table 3.3. Four of the ten cases (40 percent) involving both multidimensional PBMs and PKMs were peacefully settled within five years, while only three of the 20 cases (15 percent) not involving both multidimensional PBMs and PKMs were peacefully settled within five years.

Peacemaking missions (PMMs)

I now examine whether or not there is evidence that third-party peacemaking efforts influence the likelihood of military hostilities. As shown in Table 3.1, there were third-party peacemaking efforts undertaken during 17 out of the 30 cases selected for this study, including five cases (29.4 percent) that escalated to military hostilities within five years and 12 cases (70.6 percent) that did not escalate within five years. One of the five cases that escalated to military hostilities is Papua New Guinea, where the Bougainville Revolutionary Army, headed by Francis Ona, had waged a secessionist struggle on the island of Bougainville beginning in 1988. Following a ceasefire that went into effect in September 1994, Australian government officials facilitated negotiations between government and Bougainville representatives between September and November 1995. Nevertheless, negotiations failed and military hostilities resumed in March 1996.

There were no third-party peacemaking efforts undertaken during the remaining 13 out of 30 cases, including five cases (38.5 percent) that escalated to military hostilities within five years and eight cases (61.5 percent) that did not escalate to military hostilities within five years. Among the cases that escalated to military hostilities was the Philippines, where government troops and communist rebels fought a civil war between January 1969 and December 1986. There were no third-party peacemaking efforts initiated following the ceasefire in December 1986, and military hostilities resumed only a couple of months later. While it is true that the rate of military hostilities was somewhat lower for cases involving PMMs (such as Papua New Guinea/Bougainville) compared to the cases not involving PMMs (such as the Philippines), the difference between the two categories is not particularly significant.

Third-party peacemaking alone may not have a substantial effect on the likelihood of a dispute escalating to military hostilities, but does the combination of peacemaking and multidimensional peacebuilding have a substantial effect? In fact, there is considerable evidence that this combination does have an effect. Of the ten cases that involved both multidimensional PBM and PMM, only one case (10 percent) escalated to military hostilities within five years (see Table 3.4). In the case of Liberia, the UN undertook simultaneous peacebuilding and peacemaking efforts throughout much of the post-conflict phase beginning in August 1999. As mentioned earlier, military hostilities resumed in July 2000. Of the remaining 20 cases that did not involve both multidimensional PBMs and PMMs, eight cases (40 percent) escalated to military hostilities within five years. Included among the eight cases was the situation in Côte d'Ivoire, where a political crisis developed following a military coup that toppled the government of President Henri Konan-Bedie in December 1999. Although third-party actors did not establish a multidimensional PBM, there were several third-party peacemaking efforts undertaken during the crisis, including a UN special envoy, a UN commission of inquiry, and a good office commission established by the non-governmental organization, Parliamentarians for Global Action. Nevertheless, the crisis escalated to military hostilities between government troops and Patriotic Movement of Ivory Coast rebels beginning in September 2002.

As shown on the right-hand side of Table 3.4, there is also evidence that the combination of multidimensional PBMs and PMMs influences the likelihood of dispute settlement. Of the ten cases that involved simultaneous multidimensional PBMs and PMMs, four of the cases (40 percent) were peacefully settled within five years. In the case of El Salvador, the UN-coordinated multidimensional peacebuilding and peacemaking efforts following the signing by representatives of the government and leftist rebels of a framework for peace negotiations in Geneva in April 1990. On the other hand, only three of the 20 cases (15 percent) that did not involve simultaneous multidimensional PBMs and PMMs were peacefully settled.

Table 3.4 Multidimensional peacebuilding × peacemaking, military hostilities, and dispute settlement

	Military hostilities? (five years)		Dispute settlement? (five years)	
	Yes	No	Yes	No
Multidimensional peacebuilding × peacemaking?				
Yes	Liberia	Cambodia Albania Georgia/Abkhazia Tajikistan Morocco/Western Sahara Rwanda Mozambique El Salvador Haiti	Albania Tajikistan Mozambique El Salvador	Cambodia Georgia/Abkhazia Morocco/Western Sahara Rwanda Liberia Haiti
No	Sri Lanka/Tamils Papua New Guinea/ Bougainville Philippines Serbia/Kosovo Chad Lebanon Côte d'Ivoire Rhodesia/Zimbabwe Nicaragua	Indonesia Bangladesh Bulgaria Cyprus Yemen Sudan/Anya Nya Syria Tanzania Suriname Chile Bolivia	Sudan/Anya Nya Tanzania Suriname	Sri Lanka/Tamils Indonesia Bangladesh Papua New Guinea/ Bougainville Philippines Bulgaria Cyprus Serbia/Kosovo Yemen Chad Lebanon Syria Côte d'Ivoire Rhodesia/Zimbabwe Chile Bolivia Nicaragua

Multidimensional peacebuilding missions (PBMs) and coordination

Finally, I examine whether or not multidimensional PBMs coordinated by the UN or a regional IGO influence the likelihood of escalation to military hostilities and dispute settlement. As shown in Table 3.1, eight of the 30 cases (26.7 percent) selected for this study involved multidimensional PBMs coordinated by the UN or a regional IGO. For example, the UN and the Organization of American States jointly coordinated a multidimensional PBM in Haiti during a political crisis that began with the overthrow of President Jean-Bertrand Aristide in September 1991. The multidimensional PBM included reconstruction assistance, human rights monitoring, civilian police monitoring and election monitoring between September 1991 and February 1996. Of the eight cases that involved coordinated multidimensional PBMs, only two cases (25 percent) escalated to military hostilities within five years (see Table 3.5). The two cases both involved UN-coordinated PBMs established after civil wars in African countries – Chad and Liberia. Of the 22 cases that did not involve coordinated multidimensional PBMs, eight cases (36.4 percent) escalated to military hostilities. Although not a significant difference, there is some evidence that the risk of military hostilities is at least somewhat lower when the UN or a regional IGO coordinates a multidimensional PBM. On the other hand, coordinated multidimensional PBMs do not seem to matter when it comes to dispute settlement. Of the eight cases that involved coordinated multidimensional PBMs, two cases (25 percent) were peacefully settled within five years. Similarly, five cases out of the 22 cases (22.7 percent) that did not involve coordinated multidimensional PBMs were peacefully settled.

Conclusion

The analysis of 30 cases of crisis and post-conflict phases of intrastate disputes in this study suggests the following preliminary findings: (1) multidimensional PBMs decrease the likelihood of military hostilities and increase the likelihood of peaceful settlement; (2) although PKMs alone are not necessarily effective, simultaneous multidimensional PBMs and PKMs decrease the likelihood that an intrastate dispute will escalate to military hostilities and increase the likelihood that parties will peacefully settle their dispute; (3) simultaneous multidimensional PBMs and PKMs decrease the likelihood of military hostilities and increase the likelihood of peaceful settlement; and (4) multidimensional PBMs coordinated by third-party actors decrease somewhat the likelihood that an intrastate dispute will escalate to military hostilities, but have little if any effect on the likelihood that parties will peacefully settle their dispute.

While there is some evidence in support of seven out of eight of the

Table 3.5 Multidimensional peacebuilding × coordination, military hostilities, and dispute settlement

	Military hostilities? (five years)		Dispute settlement? (five years)	
Multidimensional peacebuilding × coordination?	*Yes*	*No*	*Yes*	*No*
Yes	Chad Liberia Sri Lank/Tamils	Cambodia Haiti El Salvador Morocco/Western Sahara Rwanda Mozambique Indonesia	Mozambique El Salvador Albania	Cambodia Haiti Morocco/Western Sahara Chad Rwanda Liberia Sri Lanka/Tamils Indonesia
No	Papua New Guinea/Bougainville Philippines Serbia/Kosovo Lebanon Côte d'Ivoire Rhodesia/Zimbabwe Nicaragua	Bangladesh Tajikistan Bulgaria Cyprus Yemen Sudan/Anya Nya Syria Tanzania Suriname Chile Bolivia Albania Georgia/Abkhazia	Tajikistan Sudan/Anya Nya Tanzania Suriname	Bangladesh Papua New Guinea/ Bougainville Philippines Bulgaria Cyprus Serbia Yemen Lebanon Syria Côte d'Ivoire Rhodesia/Zimbabwe Chile Bolivia Nicaragua Georgia/Abkhazia

hypotheses developed in this study, two important caveats are in order. First, although this study was broader than many case study analyses of the effectiveness of third-party peacebuilding, it was neither as broad nor systematic as it could have been. There are in fact dozens of cases of crisis and post-conflict phases of intrastate disputes since 1970, not to mention since the end of the Second World War, that were not analyzed in this study. It is possible that an analysis of a different set of 30 cases or a statistical analysis of more than 30 cases would yield a different set of results.

Second, this study involved bivariate analyses of independent and dependent variables. A more systematic analysis would test each of the hypothesized relationships in a multivariate manner, controlling for other factors that could potentially influence the occurrence or recurrence of military hostilities and dispute settlement. For example, some scholars have argued that the likelihood of preventing military hostilities and facilitating peaceful settlement is influenced by the timing of democratic elections in a strife-torn society (Steiner 2003: 5–6). Specifically, some scholars have argued that elections should be held only when specific conditions are met. For example, Terrence Lyons suggested that "[d]emocratization requires time and will be encouraged by a slower pace that place elections at the end of a sequence of events such as demilitarization, repatriation of refugees and displaced persons, and rebuilding the basics of a functioning state" (2002: 231).

What are the policy implications of these preliminary findings? First, although costly both in financial and human terms, multidimensional PBMs established by third-party actors are worth the significant costs of such missions to the international community. While not all cases of dispute phases involving multidimensional PBMs lead to peace and not all dispute phases not involving multidimensional PBMs lead to war, it is clear that the cases involving multidimensional PBMs are more likely to result in peace than cases not involving multidimensional PBMs. Second, it is important for the international community to do what it can to enhance the likelihood of peace during crisis and post-conflict phases of intrastate disputes by combining multidimensional PBMs with peacekeeping and peacemaking whenever feasible. Indeed, the goals of multidimensional PBMs are more likely to be achieved if one or more third-party actors are simultaneously providing for a secure environment through the deployment of peacekeeping personnel. In addition, the goals of multidimensional PBMs are more likely to be achieved if one or more third-party actors are simultaneously engaged in facilitating or mediating negotiations between the parties. Finally, the international community should attempt to coordinate multidimensional PBMs in order to maximize the efficiency and effectiveness of such missions. While only minimal evidence of a positive effect of coordination was found in this study, it is reasonable to conclude that it would be counterproductive for competing third-party actors to initiate and undertake contradictory or inconsistent peacebuilding efforts in strife-torn societies. While the UN is the obvious choice to co-ordinate multidimensional PBMs, there is no reason why regional IGOs such as the OAS and the African Union (AU) cannot also successfully coordinate multidimensional PBMs.

Ultimately, it is up to the parties to an intrastate dispute themselves to make the decisions and commitments necessary to bring both "negative peace" and "positive peace" to strife-torn societies, but third-party actors can, and frequently do, make important contributions to the peace process of such societies.

Notes

1 See J. Goodhand and D. Hulme, "From Wars to Complex Political Emergencies: Understanding Conflict and Peace-Building in the New World Disorder," *Third World Quarterly* 20 (1999): 14–15; O. Ramsbotham, "Reflections on UN Post-Settlement Peacebuilding," *International Peacekeeping* 7 (2000): 171–172.

2 See L. Baxter, "An All-Encompassing Approach for Peacebuilding – The Internal Conflict Cycle," *Peacekeeping & International Relations* 27 (1998): 3–6; E. Bertram, "Reinventing Governments," *Journal of Conflict Resolution* 39 (1995): 387–418; E. Cousens and C. Kumar, with K. Wernester (eds.) *Peacebuilding as Politics: Cultivating Peace in Fragile Societies* (Boulder, CO and London: Lynne Rienner Publishers, 2001); A. B. Fetherston, "Peacekeeping, Conflict Resolution and Peacebuilding: A Reconsideration of Theoretical Frameworks," *International Peacekeeping* 7 (2000): 190–218; R. Fisher, "The Potential for Peacebuilding: Forging a Bridge from Peacekeeping to Peacemaking," *Peace and Change* 18 (1993): 247–266; Goodhand and Hulme, "From Wars to Complex Political Emergencies," pp. 13–26; D. Last, "Organizing for Effective Peacebuilding," *International Peacekeeping* 7 (2000): 80–96; C. Manning, "Local Level Challenges to Post-Conflict Peacebuilding," *International Peacekeeping* 10 (2003): 25–43; B. Pouligny, "Building Peace after Mass Crimes," *International Peacekeeping* 9 (2002): 202–221; Ramsbotham, "Reflections on UN Post-Settlement Peacebuilding," pp. 169–189.

3 See M. Flournoy and M. Plan, "Dealing with Demons: Justice and Reconciliation," *The Washington Quarterly* 25, no. 4 (Autumn 2002): 111–123; M. Griffin and B. Jones, "Building Peace through Transitional Authority: New Directions, Major Challenges," *International Peacekeeping* 7, no. 4 (Winter 2000): 75–90; Kritz, "The Rule of Law in the Postconflict Phase," 1996, pp. 587–606; M. Matheson, "United Nations Governance of Postconflict Societies," *American Journal of International Law* 95, no. 1 (January 2001): 76–85; D. Mendeloff, "Truth-Seeking, Truth-Telling, and Postconflict Peacebuilding: Curb the Enthusiasm," *International Studies Review* 6 (2004): 355–380; C.L. Sriram, "Truth Commissions and the Quest for Justice: Stability and Accountability after Internal Strife," *International Peacekeeping* 7, no. 4 (Winter 2000): 91–106; R. Wilde, "From Danzig to East Timor and Beyond: The Role of International Territorial Administration," *American Journal of International Law* 95, no. 3 (July 2001): 583–606.

4 See M. Monshipouri, "NGOs and Peacebuilding in Afghanistan," *International Peacekeeping* 10, no. 1 (Spring 2003): 138–155; M. Doyle, "Peacebuilding in Cambodia: Legitimacy and Power," in E. Cousens and C. Kumar, with K. Wermester (eds.) *Peacebuilding as Politics: Cultivating Peace in Fragile Societies* (Boulder, CO: Lynne Rienner Publishers, 2001), pp. 89–111; J. Smoljan,

"Socio-Economic Aspects of Peacebuilding: UNTAES and the Organization of Employment in Eastern Slavonia," *International Peacekeeping* 10, no. 2 (Summer 2003): 27–50; P. Candio and R. Bleiker, "Peacebuilding in East Timor," *The Pacific Review* 14, no. 1 (2001): 63–84; J. Mertus, "Improving International Peacebuilding Efforts: The Example of Human Rights Culture in Kosovo," *Global Governance* 10, no. 3 (July–September 2004): 333–351; E. Cousens, "Building Peace in Bosnia," in Cousens and Kumar, *Peacebuilding as Politics*, pp. 113–152; C. Kumar, "Peacebuilding in Haiti," in Cousens and Kumar, *Peacebuilding as Politics*, pp. 21–51; L.M. Howard, "UN Peace Implementation in Namibia: The Causes of Success," *International Peacekeeping* 9, no. 1 (Spring 2002): 99–132; K. Powell, "Sierra Leone: A Peacebuilding Success Story?," *Ploughshares Monitor* 23, no. 3 (Autumn 2002): 9–11; A. Jan, "Somalia: Building Sovereignty or Restoring Peace?," in Cousens and Kumar, *Peacebuilding as Politics*, pp. 53–88; D. Holiday and W. Stanley, "Building the Peace: Preliminary Lessons from El Salvador," *Journal of International Affairs* 46, no. 2 (Winter 1993): 415–438.

5 See G. Dempsey with R. Fontaine, *Fool's Errand: America's Recent Encounters with Nation Building* (Washington, DC: CATO Institute, 2001); M. Ignatieff, "Nation-Building Lite," *New York Times Magazine* (July 28, 2002): 26–34; H. Strohmeyer, "Collapse and Reconstruction of a Judicial System," *American Journal of International Law* 95, no. 1 (January 2001): 47; A. Suhrke, "Peacekeepers as Nation-Builders: Dilemmas of the UN in East Timor," *International Peacekeeping* 8, no. 4 (Winter 2001): 1–20; K. von Hippel, "Democracy by Force: A Renewed Commitment to Nation-Building," *The Washington Quarterly* 23, no. 1 (Winter 2000): 95.

6 See C. Santiso, "Promoting Democratic Governance and Preventing the Recurrence of Conflict: The Role of the United Nations Development Programme in Post-Conflict Peace-Building," *Journal of Latin American Studies* 34, no. 3 (August 2002): 555–586; N. Weinberger, "Civil-Military Coordination in Peacebuilding: The Challenge in Afghanistan," *Journal of International Affairs* 55, no. 2 (Spring 2002): 245–275.

7 See C. Crocker and F.O. Hampson, "Making Peace Settlements Work," *Foreign Policy* no. 104 (Fall 1996): 55.

8 O. Ramsbotham also categorized peacebuilding into five "dimensions", including the military/security dimension, political/constitutional dimension, economic/social dimension, psychological/social dimension, and international dimension. See his "Reflections on UN Post-Settlement Peacebuilding," *International Peacekeeping* 7, no. 1 (Spring 2000): 182.

9 See J. Hamre and G. Sullivan, "Toward Postconflict Reconstruction," *The Washington Quarterly* 25, no. 4 (Autumn 2002): 92; Smith, "Europe's Peacebuilding Hour?," p. 446.

10 Peacekeeping is defined by UN Secretary-General Boutros-Ghali in *An Agenda for Peace* as "the deployment of a United Nations presence in the field, hitherto with the consent of all of the parties concerned, normally involving United Nations military and/or police personnel and frequently civilians as well."

11 Peacemaking is defined by UN Secretary-General Boutros-Ghali in *An Agenda for Peace* as "action to bring hostile parties to agreement, essentially through such peaceful means as those foreseen in Chapter VI of the Charter of the United Nations." The "peaceful means" suggested in Chapter VI of the UN Charter include good offices, fact-finding, mediation, and conciliation.

12 See A. de Soto and G. del Castillo, "Obstacles to Peacebuilding," *Foreign Policy* no. 94 (Spring 1994): 79; Hamre and Sullivan, "Toward Postconflict Reconstruction," p. 93; A. Schnabel, "Post-Conflict Peacebuilding and Second-

Generation Preventive Action," *International Peacekeeping* 9, no. 2 (Summer 2002): 16; B. Jones, "The Challenges of Strategic Coordination," in S. Stedman, D. Rothchild, and E. Cousens (eds.) *Ending Civil Wars: The Implementation of Peace Agreements* (Boulder, CO: Lynne Rienner Publishers, 2002): 89.

13 See Third-Party Interventions in Intrastate Disputes (TPI-Intrastate Disputes) Project website located at: http://faculty.uca.edu/~markm/tpi_homepage.htm.

14 A multidimensional peacebuilding mission (MPM) refers to any third-party peacebuilding effort involving two or more different dimensions of peacebuilding, including economic, humanitarian, legal, military, and political.

15 See information regarding the United Nations (UN) peacekeeping and peacebuilding activities in Cambodia located at: http://www.un.org/Depts/dpko/dpko/co_mission/untac.htm.

16 "Council Endorses October Elections: New Parliament Installed," *UN Chronicle*, March 1995, 13–15.

17 The Economic Community of West African States (ECOWAS) established a monitoring group (ECOMOG) consisting of some 12,500 military personnel from nine West African countries on August 24, 1990. ECOMOG was withdrawn from Liberia on October 23, 1999. The UN Security Council established the UN Observer Mission in Liberia (UNOMIL) consisting of more than 300 military observers on September 22, 1993. UNOMIL was disbanded on September 30, 1997.

References

Baxter, L. (1998) "An All-Encompassing Approach for Peacebuilding – The Internal Conflict Cycle," *Peacekeeping & International Relations* 27: 3–6.

Bertram, E. (1995) "Reinventing Governments: The Promise and Peril of United Nations Peacebuilding," *Journal of Conflict Resolution* 39: 387–418.

Boutros-Ghali, B. (1992) *An Agenda for Peace: Preventive Diplomacy, Peacemaking, and Peacekeeping, Report of the Secretary-General*. New York: United Nations.

Call, C. and Cook, S. (2003) "On Democratization and Peacebuilding," *Global Governance* 9: 233–246.

Candio, P. and Bleiker, R. (2001) "Peacebuilding in East Timor," *The Pacific Review* 14(1): 63–84.

Caplan, R. (2004) "International Authority and State Building: The Case of Bosnia and Herzegovina," *Global Governance* 10: 53–65.

Chimni, B.S. (2002) "Refugees and Post-Conflict Reconstruction: A Critical Perspective," *International Peacekeeping* 9: 163–180.

Cousens, E. (2001) "Building Peace in Bosnia," in Elizabeth M. Cousens and Chetan Kumar, with Karin Wernester (eds.) *Peacebuilding as Politics: Cultivating Peace in Fragile Societies*. Boulder, CO: Lynne Rienner Publishers, pp. 113–152.

Cousens, E. and Kumar, C., with K. Wernester (eds.) (2001) *Peacebuilding as Politics: Cultivating Peace in Fragile Societies*. Boulder, CO: Lynne Rienner Publishers.

Crocker, C. and Hampson, F.O. (1996) "Making Peace Settlements Work," *Foreign Policy* 104: 54–71.

Dempsey, G. with R. Fontaine (2001) *Fool's Errand: America's Recent Encounters with Nation Building*. Washington, DC: CATO Institute.

de Soto, A. and del Castillo, G. (1994) "Obstacles to Peacebuilding," *Foreign Policy* 94: 69–83.

Doyle, M. (2001) "Peacebuilding in Cambodia: Legitimacy and Power," in Elizabeth M. Cousens and Chetan Kumar, with Karin Wermester (eds.) *Peacebuilding as Politics: Cultivating Peace in Fragile Societies*. Boulder, CO: Lynne Rienner Publishers, pp. 89–111.

Doyle, M. and Sambanis, N. (2000) "International Peacebuilding: A Theoretical and Quantitative Analysis," *American Political Science Review* 94: 779–801.

Evans, G. (1994) "Cooperative Security and Intrastate Conflict," *Foreign Policy* 96: 3–20.

Fetherston, A.B. (2000) "Peacekeeping, Conflict Resolution and Peacebuilding: A Reconsideration of Theoretical Frameworks," *International Peacekeeping* 7: 190–218.

Fisher, R. (1993) "The Potential for Peacebuilding: Forging a Bridge from Peacekeeping to Peacemaking," *Peace and Change* 18: 247–266.

Flournoy, M. and Plan, M. (2002) "Dealing with Demons: Justice and Reconciliation," *The Washington Quarterly* 25(4): 111–123.

Galtung, J. (1976) "Three Approaches to Peace: Peacekeeping, Peacemaking, and Peacebuilding," in *Peace, War and Defense: Essays in Peace Research II*. Copenhagen: Christian Ejlers, pp. 292–304.

Goodhand, J. and Hulme, D. (1999) "From Wars to Complex Political Emergencies: Understanding Conflict and Peace-Building in the New World Disorder," *Third World Quarterly* 20: 13–26.

Griffin, M. and Jones, B. (2000) "Building Peace through Transitional Authority: New Directions, Major Challenges," *International Peacekeeping* 7(4): 75–90.

Hamre J. and Sullivan, G. (2002) "Toward Postconflict Reconstruction," *The Washington Quarterly* 25(4): 85–96.

Holiday, D. and Stanley, W. (1993) "Building the Peace: Preliminary Lessons from El Salvador," *Journal of International Affairs* 46(2): 415–438.

Howard, L.M. (2002) "UN Peace Implementation in Namibia: The Causes of Success," *International Peacekeeping* 9(1): 99–132.

Ignatieff, M. (2002) "Nation-Building Lite," *New York Times Magazine* (July 28): 26–34.

Jacobson, H. (1964) "ONUC's Civilian Operations: State-Preserving and State-Building," *World Politics* 17: 75–107.

Jan, A. (2001) "Somalia: Building Sovereignty or Restoring Peace?," in Elizabeth M. Cousens and Chetan Kumar, with Karin Wernester (eds.) *Peacebuilding as Politics: Cultivating Peace in Fragile Societies*. Boulder, CO: Lynne Rienner Publishers, pp. 53–88.

Jones, B. (2002) "The Challenges of Strategic Coordination," in Stephen John Stedman, Donald Rothchild, and Elizabeth M. Cousens (eds.) *Ending Civil Wars: The Implementation of Peace Agreements*. Boulder, CO: Lynne Rienner Publishers, pp. 89–115.

Kritz, N. (1996) "The Rule of Law in the Postconflict Phase," in Chester A. Crocker and Fen Osler Hampson, with Pamela Aall (eds.) *Managing Global Chaos: Sources of and Responses to International Conflict*. Washington, DC: United States Institute of Peace Press, pp. 587–606.

Kumar, C. (2001) "Peacebuilding in Haiti," in Elizabeth M. Cousens and Chetan

Kumar, with Karin Wernester (eds.) *Peacebuilding as Politics: Cultivating Peace in Fragile Societies*. Boulder, CO: Lynne Rienner Publishers, pp. 21–51.

Kumar, C. (2004) "Sustaining Peace in War-Torn Societies: Lessons from the Haitian Experience," in William J. Lahneman (ed.) *Military Intervention: Cases in Context for the Twenty-First Century*. Lanham, MD: Rowman & Littlefield Publishers, pp. 105–132.

Lahneman, W.J. (ed.) (2004) *Military Intervention: Cases in Context for the Twenty-First Century*. Lanham, MD: Rowman & Littlefield Publishers.

Lamin, A.R. (2003) "Building Peace Through Accountability in Sierra Leone: The Truth and Reconciliation Commission and the Special Court," *Journal of Asian and African Studies* 38: 295–321.

Last, D. (2000) "Organizing for Effective Peacebuilding," *International Peacekeeping* 7: 80–96.

Lyons, T. (2002) "The Role of Postsettlement Elections," in Stephen John Stedman, Donald Rothchild, and Elizabeth M. Cousens (eds.) *Ending Civil Wars: The Implementation of Peace Agreements*. Boulder, CO: Lynne Rienner Publishers, pp. 215–235.

Manning, C. (2003) "Local Level Challenges to Post-Conflict Peacebuilding," *International Peacekeeping* 10: 25–43.

Matheson, M. (2001) "United Nations Governance of Postconflict Societies," *American Journal of International Law* 95(1): 76–85.

Mendeloff, D. (2004) "Truth-Seeking, Truth-Telling, and Postconflict Peacebuilding: Curb the Enthusiasm," *International Studies Review* 6: 355–380.

Mertus, J. (2004) "Improving International Peacebuilding Efforts: The Example of Human Rights Culture in Kosovo," *Global Governance* 10(3): 333–351.

Monshipouri, M. (2003) "NGOs and Peacebuilding in Afghanistan," *International Peacekeeping* 10(1): 138–155.

Paris, R. (1997) "Peacebuilding and the Limits of Liberal Internationalism," *International Security* 22: 54–89.

Pearce, J. (1999) "Peace-Building in the Periphery: Lessons from Central America," *Third World Quarterly* 20: 51–68.

Pouligny, B. (2002) "Building Peace after Mass Crimes," *International Peacekeeping* 9: 202–221.

Powell, K. (2002) "Sierra Leone: A Peacebuilding Success Story?," *Ploughshares Monitor* 23(3): 9–11.

Ramsbotham, O. (2000) "Reflections on UN Post-Settlement Peacebuilding," *International Peacekeeping* 7(1): 169–189.

Santiso, C. (2002) "Promoting Democratic Governance and Preventing the Recurrence of Conflict: The Role of the United Nations Development Programme in Post-Conflict Peace-Building," *Journal of Latin American Studies* 34(3): 555–586.

Schloms, M. (2003) "Humanitarian NGOs in Peace Processes," *International Peacekeeping* 10: 40–55.

Schnabel, A. (2002) "Post-Conflict Peacebuilding and Second-Generation Preventive Action," *International Peacekeeping* 9: 7–30.

Smith, D. (2002) "Europe's Peacebuilding Hour? Past Failures, Future Challenges," *Journal of International Affairs* 55: 441–460.

Smoljan, J. (2003) "Socio-Economic Aspects of Peacebuilding: UNTAES and the Organization of Employment in Eastern Slavonia," *International Peacekeeping* 10: 27–50.

Sriram, C.L. (2000) "Truth Commissions and the Quest for Justice: Stability and Accountability after Internal Strife," *International Peacekeeping* 7(4): 91–106.

Stedman, S., Rothchild, D., and E. Cousens (eds.) (2002) *Ending Civil Wars: The Implementation of Peace Agreements.* Boulder, CO: Lynne Rienner Publishers.

Steiner, M. (2003) "Seven Principles for Building Peace," *World Policy Journal* 20: 87–93.

Strohmeyer, H. (2001) "Collapse and Reconstruction of a Judicial System," *American Journal of International Law* 95(1): 46–63.

Suhrke, A. (2001) "Peacekeepers as Nation-Builders: Dilemmas of the UN in East Timor," *International Peacekeeping* 8(4): 1–20.

von Hippel, K. (2000) "Democracy by Force: A Renewed Commitment to Nation-Building," *The Washington Quarterly* 23(1): 95–112.

Walter, B. (1997) "The Critical Barrier to Civil War Settlement," *International Organization* 51: 335–364.

Weinberger, N. (2002) "Civil-Military Coordination in Peacebuilding: The Challenge in Afghanistan," *Journal of International Affairs* 55(2): 245–275.

Wilde, R. (2001) "From Danzig to East Timor and Beyond: The Role of International Territorial Administration," *American Journal of International Law* 95(3): 583–606.

4 The OSCE's approach to conflict prevention and post-conflict rehabilitation

Bruce George and Anthony McGee

> The validity of the concept of post-conflict peacebuilding has received wide recognition. The measures it can use – and they are many – can also support preventive diplomacy. Demilitarization, the control of small arms, institutional reform, improved police and judicial systems, the monitoring of human rights, electoral reform and social and economic development can be as valuable in preventing conflict as in healing the wounds after conflict has occurred.
>
> (Boutros-Ghali 1995: 47)

With the dramatic rise in conflict that has been seen since the end of the Cold War the Organization for Security and Co-operation in Europe (OSCE) has been faced with the same challenge as all international organisations, namely creating new competences for itself in order that it may address the new challenges to security which have emerged. A crucial aspect of this work is post-conflict peacebuilding or the rehabilitation of states. The job of rehabilitation involves much more than just rebuilding infrastructure such as roads, schools or hospitals. The OSCE's comprehensive approach dictates that it means addressing the structures and institutions of a state which were absent or failed, allowing tensions within or between states to escalate into conflict. Former UN Secretary-General Boutros Boutros-Ghali makes the point that effective rehabilitation should not just relieve the suffering caused by conflict, it should also put in place democratic structures and institutions in an effort to ensure that conflict is not allowed to return. This chapter is intended to describe the principles and practices of the OSCE to this effect.

While the OSCE's forerunner, the Conference for Security Co-operation in Europe (CSCE) ostensibly came into being under the provisions of the 1975 Helsinki Act, its roots can in fact be traced back to the mid-1950s and Russian attempts to hold a pan-European conference that would relieve the tensions of post-war Europe by settling the German question. The notion of dialogue between the East and West outside the context of the respective military alliances once again became a possibility in 1969 when Finland, benefiting from its neutral status, took advantage of the détente in East–West relations to propose convening a conference to discuss European security in Helsinki. The idea was accepted by all the concerned parties and CSCE negotiations began with a meeting of Foreign Ministers from the 35 participating countries in July 1973.

The three main parties to the conference – the Soviet states, the USA and the West European states – each approached the conference with particular agendas. The Soviet Union was keen to increase levels of co-operation and technology transfer between the East and West; the USA was concerned that the conference contribute to the ongoing process of arms negotiations and the parallel negotiations on Mutual Balanced Force Reductions while the European states were preoccupied with the question of human rights and the increased contacts between the populations on either side of the Iron Curtain. These respective agendas were reflected in the three so-called "baskets" into which the conference divided its work. The work of the conference culminated in the signing by the heads of the 35 participatory states of the Helsinki Final Act in late July 1975. The centre-piece of the Act was its ten key principles which the signatory states agreed should guide future inter-state relations: (1) the sovereign equality of states; (2) respect for the rights inherent in sovereignty; (3) refraining from the threat or use of force; (4) inviolability of frontiers; (5) territorial integrity of states; (6) peaceful settlement of disputes; (7) non-intervention in internal affairs; (8) respect for human rights and fundamental freedoms; (9) equal rights and self-determination of peoples: and (10) co-operation among peoples and the fulfilment in good faith of obligations under international law (OSCE 1975).

The Final Act was signed at the high point of East–West Cold War détente. However, as the détente began to fade post-1975, the enthusiasm which had surrounded the Helsinki Act began to dissipate.[1] The co-operative spirit on which the Act was based was replaced by a more combative use of its provisions. The West consistently used its proclamations on human rights as a stick with which to beat the Soviet Union which in return bemoaned the West's failure to respect its right of sovereignty.

Given the dominating role of military security in the Cold War, inevitably NATO was the leading actor in terms of security policy. However, the subtle role of the CSCE throughout the period in forming an overarching security structure and exposing the "internal bankruptcy" (Nolan 1999: 311) of the Soviet system is often underestimated as a contributory factor to the eventual collapse of the Soviet Union.

> Many activists of the day ... remain convinced that the human rights pressure brought to bear at a critical time by the CSCE was crucially important. They cite the CSCE role in encouraging activism by, and in offering some measure of protection to Soviet bloc non-governmental organisations.
>
> (ibid.)

Throughout this period post-conflict reconstruction was understandably given little thought by Europe's international organisations. Soviet hegemony had placed something of a straitjacket on Eastern Europe, effectively freezing potential conflicts while doctrines such as Mutually Assured Destruction ensured that in a post-conflict scenario between East and West, there would be little left on which to rebuild.

The fall of the Berlin Wall and the collapse of the Soviet Union was for the CSCE, as for other international organisations, the cause of much celebration if not euphoria, as is reflected in the preamble to the Charter of Paris in 1990:

> We the Heads of State or Governments for the States participating in the Conference on Security and Co-operation in Europe have assembled in Paris at a time of profound change and historic expectations. The era of confrontation and division of Europe has ended.
>
> (OSCE 1990: 3)

The Charter of Paris contained a commitment on the behalf of the participating states to "seek effective ways of preventing conflicts, through political means, which may yet emerge" and to define "appropriate mechanisms for the peaceful resolution of any disputes which may arise" (ibid.: 9). Such commitments were indicative of an appreciation that the CSCE would have to adapt to meet the challenges of the changing dynamic of European security, but were essentially secondary to the overwhelming feeling among states that the eruption of violence in the region was unimaginable: "the threat of conflict in Europe has diminished" (ibid.). Accordingly in this environment of hope and optimism about the absence of conflict in Europe, consideration or discussion of the need for a post-conflict capability in the CSCE was entirely absent.

However, in the wake of the Paris Summit as events first in Yugoslavia and then elsewhere rapidly began to unfold, the 'historic expectation' of Paris gave way to the realisation that the dynamic of post-Cold War Europe would present just as pressing, if very different, challenges for those concerned with security on the Continent. It became clear to the member states of the CSCE that it had become necessary to re-orientate the conference to ensure its ability to face these new challenges. The 1972 Helsinki Final Act made various provisions for the prevention of conflict. However, the task it had addressed was of preventing conflict which would most likely spring from accidental or inadvertent escalation. Yugoslavia was an early example of the new breed of conflict which would, and continues, to engulf areas of the OSCE region. The CSCE, to its credit, quickly realised that future conflict would largely be of an ethno-political and often intrastate character involving sub-state actors and erupting with little warning. The CSCE, in common with other international organisations, had been unprepared and was ill-equipped to respond. As this became more and more apparent, the CSCE set about endowing itself with the appropriate institutions, structures and instruments to set about tackling the new challenges of conflict prevention over the course of ministerial meetings and at the summits of Helsinki, Stockholm, Rome and Budapest.

While there had been a creeping institutionalisation of the conferences, the early 1990s saw a deliberate acceleration of the process as for the first time genuinely permanent structures were put into place (Nolan 1999: 314). A Secretariat was founded, as was the position of Secretary General; a Permanent Council was put in place; the High Commissioner on National Minorities (HCNM) was created, as was the Forum for Security Cooperation (FSC); the Office of Free Elections was created and then strengthened to become the Office of Democratic Institutions and Human Rights (ODIHR); plans for a Court of Conciliation and Arbitration (CCA) were put in place and the Parliamentary Assembly (PA) was formed.

What emerged from this period was a new, more sophisticated approach to conflict prevention which entailed creating institutions, structures and tools to address the specific needs of the different stages of the conflict cycle. The creation of a High Commissioner on National Minorities (HCNM) was an innovative approach to the task of early warning which was to be complemented by the work of the Conflict Prevention Centre. The creation of a capability for peacekeeping and rapporteur missions, outlined at Helsinki, would contribute to the Conference's crisis management capabilities, and the proposed creation of the Court of Conciliation and Arbitration would facilitate the settlement of disputes (OSCE 1992: 14). By the time of the Budapest Summit, it was decided by the participating states that the degree of institutionalisation that the CSCE had undergone and the level of permanence that it had been given by these new institutions was such that it was no longer appropriate to talk of the arrangements in terms simply of a conference:

> The new era of security and co-operation in Europe has led to a fundamental change in the CSCE and a dramatic growth in its role in reshaping our common security area. To reflect this the CSCE will henceforth be known as the Organization for Security and Co-operation in Europe.

> (ibid.: 1)

This move from 'conference' to 'organisation' did not alter the politically binding nature of the organisation's commitments or the legal status of the organisation. Rather, the change was representative of the determination of member states to make the organisation more "operational and effective"[2] and to "give a new political impetus to the CSCE thus enabling it to play a cardinal role in meeting the challenges of the twenty-first century" (ibid.). Central to meeting these challenges would be the OSCE's conflict prevention work. At Budapest the participating states gave the organisation further responsibility in this field by both declaring that it would be a "primary instrument for early warning, conflict prevention and crisis management in the region" (ibid.: 2) as well as for the first time including "post-conflict rehabilitation, and reconstruction" among its conflict prevention duties (ibid.: 1).

While many of the institutions and tools which were provided for at Helsinki, Stockholm and Rome would come to be central to the OSCE's activities in post-conflict societies, Budapest represented the first commitment of the OSCE to undertake work in the area. This reflects in part the fact that it was only by 1994 that a settlement of any of the OSCE region's disputes had become a possibility such as to merit consideration of what the OSCE's role would be in a post-conflict era. Nevertheless, post-Budapest, the inclusion of "post-conflict rehabilitation" among the OSCE's commitments to conflict prevention has been consistent, and as will be discussed below, the size and range of activities in the field have continued to grow.

The OSCE approach to security: comprehensive and co-operative

Since its inception in the 1970s the OSCE has differed from all other international organisations by its comprehensive approach to security; the range of issues it considers as impacting on security and its determination to establish a competence with regard to all of them. As such, the OSCE has been termed *"the* classic institution in terms of exemplifying the concept of comprehensive security" (George 2004). From its inception and the creation of three security baskets through the Helsinki process, the organisation has consistently pressed for a more holistic approach to what constitutes security, stressing the interdependence of the politico-military, economic and human dimensions of security. The OSCE's commitment to comprehensive security was reiterated at Helsinki in 1992:

> Our approach is based on our comprehensive concept of security as initiated in the Final Act. The concept relates to the maintenance of peace to the respect for human rights and fundamental freedoms. It links economic and environmental solidarity and co-operation with peaceful inter-state relations. This is equally valid in managing change as it was necessary in mitigating confrontation.
>
> (OSCE 1992: 10)

This comprehensive commitment which the organisation has taken on has direct consequences for its potential as a post-conflict actor. The requirement that it develop competencies for itself across the security spectrum taking in politico-military, economic, human dimension and environmental issues has resulted in it being qualified to assist post-conflict societies in a number of ways across such a range of issues that it can arguably be matched by no other single organisation. In operational terms, the OSCE is equipped to assist with a variety of post-conflict challenges from integrating armies to irrigation. The comprehensive ethos also tends to work against the undue dismissal of factors, which, under a less holistic ethos, may be considered inconsequential.

Alongside comprehensive security is the OSCE's commitment to the co-operative pursuit of security in the region. The OSCE is a co-operative security forum

> proceeding from the assumption that nations, even adversaries, have an interest in reducing each other's insecurity ... By promoting the ideas of mutual reassurance instead of deterrence, and co-operation instead of confrontation, co-operative security arrangements seek to prevent crises from happening and/or reducing the risk of already existing situations from getting worse.
>
> (Kemp 1994: 2)

Co-operative security presupposes non-hegemonic behaviour by the OSCE's member states, and rejects the idea that any can consider themselves to be pre-eminent in the provision of security or consider any part of the OSCE region as being its sphere of influence. This co-operative approach is reflected in the equal status given to all OSCE states in the decision-making process and the consensual basis on which the OSCE conducts the great bulk of its work (OSCE 2000). Again, the co-operative ethos can be seen in the OSCE work in post-conflict settings promoting dialogue through seminars and roundtables, encouraging transparency, fostering conciliation and civic re-integration.

Further underlying the theory of co-operative security is the assumption that security is indivisible. No single state can, or should, attempt to pursue its security at the expense of another. Equally, co-operative security dictates that instability in one region or even within one state is a threat to the stability of the entire region and as such states have a responsibility to act in unison in response. When combined with the comprehensive interpretation of threats to security, the OSCE is given a broad scope for action. Exemplary of this is the proclamation made at the 1991 Moscow Meetings of the Conference on the human dimension of the CSCE by the participating states

> [to] categorically and irrevocably declare that the commitments undertaken in the field of human dimension of the CSCE are matters of direct legitimate concern to all participating States and do not belong exclusively to the internal affairs of the State concerned.
>
> (OSCE 1991: 29)

The result is that the OSCE's areas of legitimate concern allow it to be extremely intrusive in its examination of a state, so much so that it has been argued that no domestic institution or norm is beyond the scope of the OSCE (Buergenthal 1991). In the post-conflict setting such a power of examination can be a valuable tool both in rooting out potential institutional problems or weaknesses, and highlighting them before they have a chance to generate undue tension.[3]

OSCE peacekeeping operations and missions of long duration

As the OSCE went about the task of reforming itself to deal with the new generation of threats which were emerging in post-Cold War Europe, it was clear to the participating states that in addition to the institutional and structural developments that were being implemented, the organisation would have to develop practical vehicles through which it would be able to use its new capabilities.

Within the terms of the Helsinki document, provision was made for two separate methods of intervention, which can perhaps be termed the "hard" and "soft" options. The hard option was contained in the detailed provision within the Helsinki document for the OSCE to mount peacekeeping operations (PKOs): "CSCE peacekeeping activities may be undertaken in cases of conflict within or among participating States to help maintain peace and stability in support of an ongoing effort at a political solution" (OSCE 1992: 17). This can be considered the "hard" option in the sense that it entails using armed forces as an instrument of the OSCE, although the use of the organisation's forces for enforcement or coercion activities is explicitly ruled out.[4] However, the drafters of Helsinki also clearly envisaged a role for the PKOs beyond simply that of a traditional UN blue helmet operation:

> A CSCE peacekeeping operation, according to its mandate, will involve civilian and/or military personnel, may range from small to large scale, and may assume a variety of forms including observer and monitor missions and larger deployments of forces. Peacekeeping activities could be used, *inter alia,* to supervise and help maintain cease-fires, to monitor troop withdrawals, to support the maintenance of law and order, to provide humanitarian and medical aid and to assist refugees.
>
> (ibid.: 18)

The attention given to peacekeeping in the Helsinki document suggests that the participating states clearly intended the peacekeeping function to be a well-used one. In modern peacekeeping parlance, the activities outlined here include peace support operations, conflict prevention and peacebuilding.[5] However, in practice, the OSCE has never mandated a formal PKO, despite occasionally coming close.[6] Under the provisions of Helsinki, the basic principles of OSCE peacekeeping were laid out to be the consent of all parties concerned, impartiality and the use of force only in self-defence. As mentioned above, these principles rule out operations that might be termed peacemaking or peace enforcement. This more passive approach to PKO has been cited by some analysts as a significant explanatory factor in the under-use of the organisation's PKO competence (Homan 2003). In practice, states have been unwilling to undertake peacekeeping under the aegis of the OSCE. Experiences such as that of UNPROFOR in Bosnia and Herzegovina and UNSOM in Somalia have demonstrated that the complexities of modern, usually intrastate, peacekeeping demand robust rules of engagement which go beyond the "self-defence" provisions of Helsinki.[7]

Despite the failure to use formal PKO thus far, there is sustained enthusiasm among sections of the OSCE membership, not least Russia, to make better use of the competence. In the Charter for European Security adopted at the 1999 Istanbul Summit, member states outlined a desire to "explore options for a potentially greater and wider role of the OSCE in peacekeeping" (OSCE 1999: 12). More recently, the OSCE Ministerial in Porto tasked the permanent Council with conducting a review of peacekeeping and examining opportunities for greater OSCE involvement in the future. In response, the "Informal Open-ended Group of friends of the chair on the OSCE Role in the field of Peacekeeping Operations" was established. However, it failed to come to any agreement over the updating of the Helsinki PKO provisions.[8]

While formal PKO mandates have not been forthcoming, the organisation has in fact undertaken much peacekeeping-related activity such as border patrols and verification work. These activities have usually been undertaken as part of the work of its long-term missions. Fact Finding and Rapporteur Missions, as they were initially titled at Helsinki, began as an extremely fluid concept intended to be used as *ad-hoc* responses to problems as they arose rather than the central vehicle for OSCE activity that they have become. Former Secretary General Wilhelm Hoynock has noted that long-term missions now account for 84 per cent of the OSCE's budget. If the potential of these Fact Finding and Rapporteur Missions was recognised by the participating states at Helsinki, it was certainly not reflected in the meagre attention given to them in the Helsinki document. Nevertheless, the value of the missions quickly became apparent. A month after the summit the worsening situation in Yugoslavia persuaded the Senior Council[9] to adopt a series of decisions related to missions, included in which was the decision to establish missions in Kosovo, Sandjak and Vojvodina (Bloed 1993).

In the years since the issue of the first mandate, OSCE missions have taken a pivotal role in the delivery of the OSCE's capabilities. The missions receive their mandate from the Permanent Council and are deployed with the permission of the host country. No two mission mandates are the same, and the size and composition of missions vary greatly. Prior to its closure, the mission to Ukraine consisted of only four people, while the ambitious OSCE mission to Kosovo entailed 350 internationally seconded staff assisted by some 1,150 local staff.

The OSCE's long-term missions offer the organisation a singularly invaluable tool in the modern business of post-conflict rehabilitation and state building. While the tendency of missions to overrun their mandate and the absence of "benchmarks" or an exit strategy for mission withdrawal from a region have been a source of concern, the longevity of missions also offers great advantage, particularly in the field of post-conflict rehabilitation (Huber *et al.* 2003). The initial post-conflict stage of the conflict cycle is usually the time when most offers of support and messages of solidarity are sent to the affected state. Other states and organisations keen to be associated with the euphoria of peace, or implored by their population upon seeing the usually devastating consequences of conflict, are eager to give messages of solidarity and offer aid, largely in economic form. However, much of this short-term interest inevitably fades as the realities of the complex, painstaking and time-consuming task of mending civic wounds and rebuilding institutions and infrastructures unfolds. In these circumstances the low profile but enduring nature of OSCE missions, some lasting more than a decade, is crucial to the eventual success of post-conflict societies. The long-term mission's continuing presence on the ground throughout the re-building process in post-conflict states offers it an insight into needs and capabilities unavailable to those who observe periodically or from less proximity.

The OSCE's contribution to post-conflict societies

Defining a post-conflict state is a troublesome business. In some cases a political settlement may theoretically have been reached while, in practice, violence continues, while in others violence may be periodic, regional or of an extremely low level so that while the state remains technically conflicted, the impact of this status may in practice be negligible for much of the population.[10] As is often the case with a politically minded organisation such as the OSCE, in response to this question of definition it has preferred to adopt a "constructively obscure" approach. As discussed above, since Budapest, the OSCE commitment to the overall activity of conflict prevention has usually acknowledged a specific responsibility in the field of "post-conflict rehabilitation," however, it has never explicitly outlined what "post-conflict" means and where the lines are drawn between conflict management, conflict settlement and rehabilitation activities. While this obscurity no doubt in part arises from convenience and an eagerness to avoid protracted academic debates among drafting states, it also in part reflects the impossibility of neatly delineating the different aspects of the OSCE's overall commitment to the work of conflict prevention. While we are seeking to examine post-conflict rehabilitation as a distinct functional category, it is worth noting that each of the organisation's conflict prevention functions inevitably contains some of the characteristics associated with other functions. This is particularly true of post-conflict activities that are undertaken in the often tense, if not volatile surroundings of post-conflict societies.

Politico-military factors

While the OSCE's comprehensive approach to security demands that it address a broad range of factors when attempting to redress the weaknesses that have allowed conflict to occur, inevitably a basic degree of security must be ensured before the work of rehabilitating the human and economic dimensions can begin.

> if military aspects of security remain volatile they continue to inhibit the state, individuals and society at large. Under these conditions no progress can be made in addressing the causes of conflict e.g. facilitate a more participatory form of government or the reinvigoration of economic capacities.

> (Huber 2003)

The remnants of wartime military forces pose significant hurdles to the rehabilitation of societies. Oversized and unwieldy armies with little or no civilian control or oversight, irregular and paramilitary forces and the abundance of weaponry and ammunition can greatly add to the volatility of post-conflict environments and potentially serve to re-ignite violence even more quickly than it originally occurred (Newman and Schnabel 2002). In post-war Bosnia the combined expenditures of the previously warring factions were unsustainable and running at several times the proportion of national income spent by NATO countries. As such, a key goal for the OSCE in conjunction with other international organisations became reducing the size of forces and integrating the hitherto separate command structures (Barry 2002).

Despite being the first international organisation to react at the outset of conflict in the former Yugoslavia, the OSCE did not play a major role in the settlement of the conflict prior to the signing of the Dayton Peace Agreement (DPA) which marked the end of formal hostilities in the country.[11] Nevertheless, the role assigned to the organisation by the main architects of the Peace Agreement, the European Community (EC)[12] and the United Nations (UN) was a significant one. A central facet of the OSCE's involvement in the post-conflict process in Bosnia-Herzegovina was that of consolidating military stabilisation in the region through promoting confidence- and security-building measures as well as facilitating and overseeing disarmament by parties to the conflict.[13]

In the months following Dayton, the OSCE oversaw negotiations on confidence-building measures.[14] The final document which emerged from these negotiations provided for the restrictions on deployments of certain kinds of weapons, exchanges of data on heavy weaponry, the temporary restriction of military manoeuvres and the institution of reciprocal inspections of military installations. In addition, it was agreed that both the Bosnian Serbs and the Bosnian Federation forces should appoint liaison officers to improve communication between the two factions (Sica 1997). Sica has noted that the delegation of military stabilisation tasks to the OSCE probably had much to do with its experience in arms control negotiations,[15] and the process of disarmament and the principles which emerged for maintaining intrastate peace in BiH certainly had much in common with the principles it had for some time employed to bolster inter-state security through the Forum for Security Co-operation (FSC). Since being established under the terms of the Helsinki document in 1992 the FSC has been a forum for weekly meetings in Vienna of representatives from all the OSCE participating states to discuss and consult on arms controls and negotiations, disarmament, security building and the implementation of arms treaties.[16]

Building on its work fostering confidence between the factions, the OSCE has concentrated much of its efforts in BiH on the demobilisation and reintegration of former combatants. These tasks are crucial in post-conflict societies as the former combatants can be in a position of making or breaking efforts at rehabilitation (Ball 1997). The OSCE was instrumental in the first significant wave of demobilisation in 2002 which saw a reduction in the number of troops from 33,000 to 19,000. In BiH it has attempted to guard against the potential risks arising from such large-scale demobilisation through various social and educational measures. In conjunction with the International Organisation of Migration (IOM), it has implemented a resettlement and transition programme converting military barracks and offering advice to military personnel seeking civilian employment (Sweden 2004). This first wave of demobilisation has been followed by a further reduction in 2004 from 19,000 to 12,000 professional troops and a reduction in the number of reserves from 240,000 to 60,000 and an ongoing process of reintegrating the separate command structures of the old armies.

In addition, the OSCE's activities in the field of military reform and stabilisation have involved bringing the states' military structures and institutions back within the bounds of democratic control and oversight. Here the OSCE's Code of Conduct plays an important role providing a normative framework and benchmarks for developing states to work towards. The code outlines in some detail what constitutes democratic control of forces. Its principles include the "primacy of constitutionally established authorities vested with democratic legitimacy over military power . . . political neutrality of armed forces and the respect of civil rights of individual members" and the "prohibition of acquisition by paramilitaries of combat mission capabilities in excess of that for which they were established."[17]

In BiH the OSCE has worked to strengthen the democratic control of armed forces in part through fostering improved parliamentary oversight of the military. This has been achieved through the strengthening of BiH parliamentary defence-related committees and the institution of fact-finding and information-sharing missions to neighbouring parliaments (OSCE 2004).

Democratic governance and institution building

A key feature of the OSCE's approach to post-conflict rehabilitation is its emphasis on democratic governance. The theory behind this emphasis is that states that have well-functioning, representative and responsive intuitions provide channels for the frustration of dissatisfied or disaffected sections of their population and remove the tendency on the part of those sections of the population to resort to the use of violence in pursuit of redress. In a great number of cases, particularly in the OSCE area, conflict does not emerge as a result of a total absence of democracy. Rather, it emerges because the institutions of the state are to a greater or lesser extent flawed. The rise of nationalism witnessed since 1990 has often meant that institutions of the state have failed to represent, respond to or even recognise minorities within a state. Where the minorities have held sufficient power in a region of the state and it has failed to recognise or respond to grievances, for instance, by refusing to devolve power, the result has been conflict surrounding efforts by that region to cede and wrest control from the centre. Where those who are failed by the state are more dispersed or fewer in number, the failure of institutions can generate terrorism or insurgencies. If the aggrieved constituency of a state is sufficient in size or resources, conflict can take the form of civil war. Conflicts "signify failed political systems that could not perform essential governance functions, thereby generating political insurgencies. The need, therefore, is not to go back to pre-crisis conditions but to move in a different direction" (OSCE 2004: 87).

As the OSCE sets about the business of assisting the repairing of the war-torn institutions of a state, its job is also crucially one of analysis. There is little worth in perpetuating or rebuilding institutions, which in the form that they exist have contributed to the eruption of conflict, and may threaten the often fragile peace that exists in post-conflict scenarios. But nor is it feasible or desirable to begin from a blank canvas, and disassemble elements of the state's apparatus that have not contributed to the overall failings or are receptive to reform. The nature of the OSCE's long-term presence in a state through its missions gives it a distinct advantage here by allowing it to distinguish between institutions worth saving, those which are obsolete, and where demand justifies the creation of new institutions (Huber 2003b).

Institution building was a central facet of the mandate for the OSCE Mission in Kosovo (OMIK). Institution building has taken place with the goal of the "development of democratic structures which represent and work on behalf of society."[18] Institutions are divided into those which deliver governance, those which support political life and those which support public life. The work the OSCE has undertaken with the Municipal Authorities elected in 2001 is typical of its support for institutions in the field of governance. The Assembly Support Initiative (ASI) was created to help overcome the problems facing the fledgling Municipal Assemblies and have focused on the development of effective and representative legislatures.

With regard to political life, OSCE assistance has involved work with political parties and has been primarily with the aim of strengthening their organisational capacity to develop policy platforms that enable them to participate in the political process. To this end, the OSCE has hosted Political Party Consultative Forums (PPCF) as a means of facilitating dialogue between respective political parties and with their equivalents in the international community. In addition, training schemes aimed at increasing the capacity of parties have focused on their various roles, as opposition, their relations with the media, and representing minority sections of their constituencies. The OSCE's work with institutions of public life has involved fostering civic identity and enabling community participation in decision-making. This work has in part taken the form of establishing and supporting community centres based mostly in smaller communities. The community centres serve as a focal point for the sharing of information and expression of views. They also serve as a vehicle through which training to assist community-based initiatives and nurture democratic development can be delivered.[19]

The rule of law

A further central tenet of the OSCE's approach to rehabilitation has been a commitment to restoring and bolstering the rule of law. Ensuring that the rule of law is effectively applied is a factor in almost all OSCE missions. However, work in the field has particular relevance in post-conflict situations as failure or deficiencies in the rule of law have consistently been significant contributing factors to the outbreak of conflict, and strengthening the rule of law has been central to preventing the re-emergence of conflict. The OSCE's commitments on the rule of law stem from the Copenhagen document of 1990, which declares that participating States are "determined to support and advance those principles of justice which form the basis of the rule of law" and that:

[they] consider that the rule of law does not mean merely a formal legality which assures regularity and consistency in the achievement and enforcement of democratic order, but justice based on the recognition and full acceptance of the supreme values of human personality and guaranteed by institutions providing a framework for its fullest expression.[20]

The fundamental principle underlying the organisation's interpretation of the rule of law is the fair and equitable treatment of human beings. The process of making law must be transparent and invite participation from all concerned groups. The citizens of a state should be made aware of what the law prevents them from doing, but also crucially what it entitles them to expect. The law should apply equally and fairly to everyone. Factors such as ethnicity should not affect a citizen's experience of the legal process or make them more likely to experience it. Equally nobody should be exempt or given preferential treatment.

Under the nationalist regimes which spread through parts of the OSCE region throughout the 1990s, the rule of law was often undermined by non-participatory legislating which excluded ethnic minorities. This problem was at times compounded by inequalities in access to law and the politicisation of the judiciary. In such circumstances, when faced with injustice, minorities could not take recourse to law which could in any case have been drafted to their disadvantage. The potential for such circumstances to inflame afflicted sections of the population is clear and, as such, the OSCE's post-conflict work invariably attempts to address such institutionally rooted threats to the rule of law. The responsibility for much of this work lies with the Office for Democratic Institutions and Human Rights (ODIHR) and, more specifically, its Rule of Law Unit.

To address weaknesses in the rule of law stemming from the legislative process, the OSCE's work has involved offering legislative support to transitional states, working from the premise that the conditions necessary for respect for human rights, democracy and the rule of law cannot improve without an adequate legal basis. Legislation and the legislative process itself are thus crucial to the entrenchment of the rule of law and the success of democratisation more generally. ODIHR's long commitment to legislative reform has in recent times manifested itself in the form of the Legislative Support Programme (LSP) which offers assistance in the form of reviews of draft legislation and advice on best legislative practice for OSCE states.

The OSCE has further been engaged in work aimed at ensuring fair trials for citizens. A fair trial involves the right to a fair and public hearing within a reasonable timeframe. Deficiencies in post-conflict societies have a tendency to be more pronounced for a variety of reasons. In the first place, fair trials require access to professional legal advice and representation. Such access can be severely limited in post-conflict states. As conflict erupts, elites, such as academic elites, are often the first to leave conflicted states. The professional classes are often forced to join the military, seek refuge in neighbouring states or are chased from their homes, becoming internally displaced.[21] The effect of this can be a "brain drain" in professions such as the legal profession that severely limits the number of properly qualified individuals available. The right to a fair trial is often lacking in post-conflict societies where the re-emerging judiciaries are often charged with undertaking tasks, such as overseeing the prosecution of war-criminals, which would present challenges for the most established legal systems.

In Croatia the mission has highlighted the ongoing organisational and efficiency problems in the judiciary, which have in part caused a backlog of 1.4 million cases. In an attempt to address these deficiencies the Croatian government, assisted by the OSCE, adopted a five-year plan for judicial reform in 1992. Included in the plan were measures aimed at changes to the practice of both civil and criminal law, increasing the number of legal staff, improving legal education standards and improving academic facilities for the judiciary and legal professionals more generally. In addition, the mission has conducted seminars on the principles of fair trials for local court judges. The mission has also highlighted problems with the Constitutional Court and its failure to give sufficient weight to human rights issues, particularly in the case of minorities.[22]

Since its initial mandate was outlined, the OSCE's rule of law work in Croatia has involved the monitoring of war crimes cases appearing before Croatian courts. Initially, the wars crimes process was marked by the much higher number of cases pursued against Serbs accused of crimes against Croats. These trials often lacked fundamental guarantees of impartiality and involved accepting questionable evidence and convicting defendants *in absentia*. While the discrepancy between the treatment of Serbs and Croats is less pronounced, the OSCE has continued to highlight the application of double standards between ethnic groups at each stage of the judicial process and applied pressure on the Croatian authorities to address the disparity.

In the aftermath of conflict the most serious and practically apparent obstacle to the rule of law may be the inability of the state to enforce the law and hold to account those responsible for crime and corruption. For much of the post-Cold War period international organisations have paid insufficient attention to the problematic contribution made by crime to instability within and between states, the perpetuation of conflict and the further complication of the post-conflict rebuilding process. It has been argued quite plausibly that closer inspection of many conflicts reveals that the crucial events which marked the escalation from tension to violence have often surrounded the motives of profits and personal gain by key actors (Monk 2000). Conflict is often sustained by elites who stand to gain in terms of money, power and status after the general appetite for retribution has diminished and post-conflict societies are almost always marked by abundant black market activity and high degrees of organised crime (Monk 2000).

The conditions which precipitate the slide to conflict such as institutional failures and a lack of authoritative and legitimate governance also invite predatory criminals who are able to thrive in the lawlessness and the demand for a black economy that accompany conflict. However, the end of conflict is rarely itself enough to break the patterns of highly organised crime which may have emerged throughout and, as such, the OSCE, particularly in South-Eastern Europe, has placed great emphasis on building domestic policing capabilities in post-conflict states:

> There is overwhelming evidence to show that good policing has a vital role to play in the prevention of conflict (particularly secondary conflict), the preservation of social stability during political crises and the post-conflict rehabilitation of societies. Without effective law enforcement, respect for the rule of law and the operation of institutions responsible for upholding it, there can be little likelihood of social, political or economic development in any State.
>
> (OSCE 2002b)

The inability of states to effectively and equitably enforce law can have devastating effects by frustrating the reconciliation process, deterring outside investment and, in the worst cases, leading to the resumption of conflict. In its Charter for European Security the OSCE outlined a commitment to develop its competencies in relation to policing: "We will work to enhance the OSCE's role in civilian police-related activities as an integral part of the Organization's efforts in conflict prevention, crisis management and post-conflict rehabilitation" (OSCE 1999: 11). This commitment has since been regularly re-stated[23] and has manifested itself in the creation of a Strategic Police Matters Unit (SPMU) within the OSCE secretariat and headed by the Senior Police Advisor (SPR) Richard Monk.[24] Since its creation, the SPMU has worked to create a capacity for the OSCE to assist participating states with various aspects of their policing with some of special importance to post-conflict scenarios. In order to ease the reconciliation process and build confidence both between communities and in the police force, the OSCE has worked on multi-ethnic police training and assisting states to increase the proportional representation of forces to reflect the communities they police. Additionally, Community Policing promotes the concept of people taking an active stake in the detection and prevention of crime by building relationships with local forces and fostering civic co-operation, which is often lacking in post-conflict societies. As a means of helping war-torn states protect themselves from the ongoing influx of traffickers, terrorists and fugitives which they may have attracted in the chaotic atmosphere of conflict, the OSCE has also focused on border policing. It offers advice on building the infra-structures and organisational systems necessary to tighten borders and protect communities living close to borders from intimidation. The most ambitious of the OSCE's police-related programmes has been that under-taken by the OSCE mission in Kosovo (OMiK). As the institution-building partner in the UN Interim Administration Mission in Kosovo (UNMIK), the OSCE mission has undertaken the development of an entirely new and democratic police force in the country. Through the establishment of the Department for Police Education and Development (DPED), the mission has undertaken to train 6,533 Kosovo police officers through a 20-week basic course involving training on Kosovo's penal codes and initiatives on organised crime and community policing.[25]

Post-conflict elections

As a community of countries committed to democracy, the OSCE places great emphasis on promoting democratic elections. Democratic and free elections, as outlined in the Copenhagen document, are a cornerstone of the democratic tradition which characterizes the organisation. To this end, the OSCE has developed considerable expertise in administering elec-tions, providing technical assistance to states which are inexperienced in administering them, and monitoring them. Despite their central role in functioning democracies, the process of elections does not by itself equal democracy. While they are inevitable in any genuine programme of democratisation, if used insensitively, particularly in the post-conflict context, elections are as likely to undermine democratisation efforts as to contribute to them. While elections can be tools for conciliation and can be designed to prevent so-called "winner takes all" outcomes, they are essentially by their nature divisive instruments necessitating competition and generating winners and losers. It is this fact that has led some to ques-tion the viability of elections in the wake of conflict: "most war-torn soci-eties lack the political climate, social and economic stability, institutional infrastructure and even political will to mount successful elections" (Kumar 1998: 7). Often the greatest pressure for election comes from the international community keen to be able to demonstrate the results of the resources they have invested in bringing violence to an end and advertise, accurately or otherwise, that the state in question is on the road to demo-cracy. "Many people – in government, international organizations, acade-mia, and non-profit assistance organizations – see elections as mechanisms for transplanting democracy ... This is 'electoralism'" (Rose 2001: 95).

While the OSCE places great weight on fair and free elections, the vast range of indicators by which it judges democratisation and its commit-ment, not least through the missions of long duration, surely mean that the charge of electoralism as outlined by Rose is not one that can be fairly lev-elled at the organisation. Nevertheless, there must come a point, if states are to progress, that post-conflict elections become necessary: "the over-arching challenge of international electoral assistance is to build or re-build a sustainable democratic state that can function without direct international involvement. Elections are crucial in achieving this" (Reilly 2003: 13).

For the OSCE, elections are a hurdle that must be overcome if a post-conflict state is to go on to be a self-sufficient well-functioning democracy. Timing is thus the crucial factor in its administration of post-conflict elections, although not always one which is within its control. Held too soon and elections may serve only to turn generals into politicians, delayed too long and the international community loses patience and aspects of rehabilitation which depend on elections are stunted. The OSCE's experience in BiH is evidence of how complex post-conflict elections can be:

> 1. OSCE. The Parties request the OSCE to adopt and put in place an elections program for Bosnia and Herzegovina as set forth in this Agreement.
> 2. Elections. The Parties request the OSCE to supervise, in a manner to be determined by the OSCE and in co-operation with other international organizations the OSCE deems necessary, the preparation and conduct of elections for the House of Representatives of Bosnia and Herzegovina; for the Presidency of Bosnia and Herzegovina; for the House of Representatives of the Federation of Bosnia and Herzegovina; for the National Assembly of the Republika Srpska; for the Presidency of the Republika Srpska; and, if feasible, for cantonal legislatures and municipal governing authorities.
>
> (OSCE 1995: Annexe 3, Articles I and II)

Under the terms of the Dayton Peace Agreement negotiated by the UN and the EU, the OSCE was given an electoral task unprecedented in scale. Essentially the task was to supervise and give assistance in preparation for elections in BiH, to certify the country's readiness for elections, to set a date and then observe the elections. The work of the OSCE was to be carried out in conjunction with the Bosnian parties through the Provisional Election Commission (PEC) which would contain three experts and three representatives from Bosnian political parties. The PEC was to be chaired by Robert Frowick, the head of the OSCE mission in the country, whose job it would be in practice to certify when the country had reached sufficient maturity to host elections. Crucially, Annexe 3 contained the proviso that: "Timing. Elections shall take place on a date ('Election Day') six months after entry into force of this Agreement or, if the OSCE determines a delay necessary, no later than nine months after entry into force" (OSCE 1995: Annexe 3, Articles I and II).

As the OSCE set about the task of preparing for elections, the legacy of the conflict which had raged throughout the region generated various serious difficulties that cast doubts on the country's readiness for elections. It became clear that the nine-month deadline for the elections was "unrealistically short – reflective more of the drafters' desire to secure rapid transformation to formally democratic government than of conditions on the ground" (Goldston 1997: 8). In practice, in BiH as the election deadline approached, arbitrary police controls continued to be exercised limiting freedom of movement and generating a stream of reports of ethnic discrimination, intimidation and aggression. Freedom of expression and association were undermined by the difficulties opposition parties had in accessing the media, which was dominated by inflammatory nationalist propaganda. The return of refugees remained slow with only 80,000 displaced person returning to the country, and then only returning to areas where their ethnic group had power, leaving 2,000,000 Bosnian refugees potentially disenfranchised (Sica 1997). Despite all these difficulties and the continued presence and political activity of indicted war criminals, the international community placed considerable pressure on the OSCE to give certification of the readiness for elections. US President Bill Clinton, who was in an election year himself, had promised a "quick fix" for the turmoil in the region. Under such international pressure, the OSCE despite its reservations, as demonstrated by its decision to repeatedly postpone municipal elections, found itself with little option other than to certify conditions ready for the presidential elections, despite the ongoing problems. When announcing his decision to certify conditions as suitable for the elections on 25 June 1996, Chairman in Office Cotti made reference to the fact that elections were the will of the international community, and that if they were further postponed, IFOR's presence could not be ensured (Sica 1997).

The OSCE mounted a huge election monitoring mission in BiH in the hope of minimising the divisive impact of elections. In the report which followed, reference was made to the problems that were a feature of the election, albeit in the restrained and relatively diplomatic parlance of election observation. While the OSCE has since taken great strides in the effective administration of the various elections that have followed in BiH by helping the country agree to an election law, and creating domestic capacity for effective election administration in the form of the BiH Election Commission and its secretariat, the problems that arose from the 1996 election remain with the country. While the continued support for monolithic nationalist parties undoubtedly reflects in part the mood of the country, it has also been attributed to the early voting patterns established by premature post-conflict elections.[26] Support for such nationalist parties continues to frustrate broader efforts at reconciliation and reconstruction in post-conflict BiH.

While the BiH experience is an example of the problems of post-conflict elections, it is perhaps also an example of the limits of what international organisations and democratisation can achieve if they do not attempt, or do not succeed in engendering, support for their efforts at the grassroot levels of society. For the OSCE's part, it has increasingly attempted to do this through work with civil society organisations in parallel with its work relating to field institutions. It remains the case that without an appetite for peace and inclusion among the population of a post-conflict society, there is only so much in the way of democratisation that can be achieved.

Conclusion

However, where this basic desire does exist or there is room for it to be nurtured, there is much that international organisations can contribute to post-conflict societies and some roles that can be effectively undertaken only by them. While space here does not permit a further examination of the many, many activities and projects in which the OSCE is involved in post-conflict societies, the examples used will hopefully outline the basic principles that underpin the organisation's efforts in the area. The OSCE and its unique characteristics mean it is very well placed to undertake the work of post-conflict rehabilitation. Its comprehensive approach to security means it undertakes the work of rehabilitation not through a sense of charity or at the whim of participating states' publics. Rather, the work is undertaken based on the conviction that bad governance and the failure of politics which facilitate conflict, as well as crime and instability, are a threat to the stability of the whole OSCE region. This grounding for the organisation's efforts mean it is less vulnerable to the vagaries of public support and less motivated by short-term results and early exit strategies. While in post-conflict areas such as BiH, the OSCE has a very high visibility and the merit of its work is widely recognised, it is only small elements of the organisation's work such as its election monitoring missions that gain any international profile.[27] Nevertheless, the OSCE's co-operative ethos and comprehensive long-term approach mean, in practice, it is one of the most effective post-conflict actors in the European security architecture.

Notes

1 For an interesting insight into US attitudes of the period towards the CSCE and the Helsinki Act, see Kissinger (1999).
2 A commitment first made in *Challenges of Change* (OSCE 1992: 6).
3 For more discussion on the conflict prevention ethos of the OSCE, see Cohen (1999) and Bloed (1997).
4 "CSCE missions will not entail enforcement action" (Homan 2003: 319–320).
5 Sub-definitions of peacekeeping have become almost a science in themselves. For a useful guide to the various definitions, see United Kingdom (2004: 3–50). For an excellent outline of the issues involved in modern peacekeeping more generally, see Bellamy *et al.* (2004).

6 The 1994 Budapest Summit took the decision to send a PKO to intervene in the Nagorno-Karabakh region. Extensive planning was done for the operation but the failure to establish a ceasefire eventually prevented deployment, see Mooradian (1998).

7 More rigorous enforcement action could in theory be undertaken by the OSCE with a Chapter VIII mandate from the UN but this function has also remained unused.

8 For analysis of contemporary efforts to reinvigorate OSCE PKOs, see Milinkovic (2004).

9 Then called the Committee of Senior Officials.

10 De Zeeuw makes the point that the blurred reality which is neither war nor peace in many war-torn states makes the prefix "post-conflict" almost obsolete, see de Zeeuw (2001).

11 In fact the OSCE has been the subject of criticism for its perceived ineffectiveness in Yugoslavia prior to Dayton, see, for example, Anderson (1995).

12 Now the European Union.

13 DPA, Annexe 1.

14 As required by Annexe 6, Article II of the DPA.

15 Sica (1997) suggests, among others Hirschfeld (1992), and Berg and Rotfeld (1986) as interesting historical perspectives of the OSCE's work in the area.

16 For more on the work of the FSC, see Schmid and Klepsch (1997: 299–305).

17 The OSCE Code of Conduct on Politico-Military Aspects of Security, 91st Plenary Meeting of the Special Committee of the CSCE Forum for Security Co-operation, Budapest, 1994. Section VII: The democratic control of armed forces, Para 20. For a through commentary on the entire code, consult Ghebali and Lambert (2005).

18 Taken from the OMIK website.

19 For a more in-depth analysis and review of the OSCE's institution-building work in Kosovo in particular, see Everts (2001).

20 Second meeting of the Conference on the Human Dimension of the CSCE, Copenhagen, 1991, p. 3.

21 These very short-term problems are often compounded in the longer term by the emergence of a "dreadfully under-educated post-war generation" resulting from the disruption to education inherent in conflict arising from shortage of teachers, disrupted schedules, damage to schools, etc. (Newman and Schnabel 2002).

22 The OSCE's mission to Croatia has its own website (as do all the missions) which is a particularly useful source of information: http://www.osce.org/croatia/

23 For example, in the consolidated document resulting from the Ninth Meeting of the Ministerial Council, Bucharest, December 2001 (OSCE 2001: 33).

24 Although it is perhaps important to note that the SPMU had a problematic first few months with the OSCE failing to provide a budget for it.

25 For more on the work of all the OSCE mission which encompass police-related activity, see the yearly reports of the Secretary General on OSCE Police-Related Activities which are submitted in accordance with Decision 9, paragraph 6, of the Bucharest Ministerial Council Meeting, 4 December 2001 (OSCE 2001).

26 For more on the ethnic voting patterns of BiH and the international community's involvement in the Balkans more generally, see Poletti and Korski (2004).

27 Typical example are the recent Short Term Observation Missions to Georgia and Ukraine which were headed by Bruce George MP.

References

Anderson, J. (1995) "EU, NATO, and the CSCE Response to the Yugoslavia Crisis: Testing Europe's New Security Architecture," *European Security* 4(2): 328–340.

Ball, N. (1997) "Demobilizing and Reintegrating Soldiers: Lessons from Africa," in K. Kumar (ed.) *Rebuilding War-Torn Societies: Critical Areas for International Assistance*. Boulder, CO: Lynne Rienner.

Barry, R. (2002) "The OSCE: A Forgotten Transatlantic Security Organization?" British American Security Information Center. Report 2002.3, July 31, 2002. Available at: http://www.basicint.org/europe/pubs.htm

Bellamy, A.J., Williams, P. and Griffin, S. (2004) *Understanding Peacekeeping*. Cambridge: Polity Press.

Berg, A. and Rotfeld, D. (1986) *Building Security in Europe: Confidence-Building Measures and the CSCE*. New York: Institute for East–West Security Studies.

Bloed, A. (1993) *The Conference on Security and Cooperation in Europe: Analysis and Basic Documents, 1972–1993*. Dordrecht: Kluwer.

Bloed, A. (1997) "The Main Political Bodies of the OSCE and their Role in Conflict Prevention and Crisis Management," in M. Bothe, N. Ronzitti and A. Rosas (eds.) *The Role of the OSCE in the Maintenance of Peace and Security: Conflict Prevention, Crisis Management and Peaceful Settlement of Disputes*. The Hague: Kluwer Law International.

Boutros-Ghali, B. (1995) *An Agenda for Peace*, 2nd edn. New York: United Nations.

Buergenthal, T. (1991) "The CSCE Human Rights System," *The George Washington Journal of International Law and Economics* 25(5): 333–386.

Cohen, J. (1999) *Conflict Prevention in the OSCE: An Assessment of Capabilities*. Clingendael, The Hague: The Netherlands Institute of International Relations.

de Zeeuw, J. (2001) *Building Peace in War Torn Societies: From Concept to Strategy*. Clingendael, The Hague: Conflict Research Unit.

Everts, D.W. (2001) "The OSCE Mission in Kosovo – Two Years into Institution Building," *Helsinki Monitor* 12(4): 245–256.

George, B. (2004) "Introduction," in B. George (ed.) *Mediterranean Security and Beyond*. Available at: http://www.rthonbrucegeorgemp.co.uk/table_of_contents.html

Ghebali, V.Y. and Lambert, A. (2005) *The OSCE Code of Conduct on Politico-Military Aspects of Security: Anatomy and Implementation*. Leiden: Martinus Nijhoff Publishers.

Goldston, J. (1997) "The Role of the OSCE in Bosnia: Lessons from the First Year," *Helsinki Monitor* 3: 6–36.

Hirschfeld, T.J. (1992) *Helsinki II: The Future of Arms Control in Europe*. Santa Monica, CA: RAND Corp.

Homan, K. (2003) "Moldova: A Litmus Test for the Viability of OCSE Peacekeeping," *Helsinki Monitor* 14(4): 319–320.

Huber, M. (2003a) "Workshop on Post-Conflict Management: Timing, Sequencing and Prioritisation," OSCE Conflict Prevention Centre, Vienna.

Huber, M. (2003b) "The Effectiveness of OSCE Missions," *Helsinki Monitor* 14(2): 125–135.

Huber, M., Lewis, D., Oberschmidt, R. and du Pont, Y. (2003) *The Effectiveness of*

OSCE Missions: The Cases of Uzbekistan, Ukraine and Bosnia Herzegovina. Clingendael, The Hague: Conflict Research Unit.

Kemp, W. (1994) *Making Sense of the CSCE.* Federal Trust Discussion Paper. London.

Kissinger, H. (1999) *Years of Renewal.* New York: Simon and Schuster.

Kumar, K. (1998) "Post-Conflict Elections and International Assistance," in K. Kumar (ed.) *Post Conflict Elections, Democratization and International Assistance.* Boulder, CO: Lynne Rienner.

Milinkovic, B. (2004) "OSCE Peacekeeping: Still Waiting to Perform!" *Helsinki Monitor* 15(3): 193–201.

Monk, R. (2000) "Policing the Peace: Military Police Interaction in the Field: The Case of the Balkans," Presentation. Available at: http://www.janes.com/press/pc001027-2.shtml

Mooradian, M. (1998) "The OSCE: Neutral and Impartial in the Karabakh Conflict?" *Helsinki Monitor* 9(2): 6–17.

Newman, E. and Schnabel, A. (2002) "Introduction: Recovering from Civil Conflict," *International Peacekeeping* 9(2): 1–6.

Nolan, C.J. (1999) "The OSCE: Non-military Dimensions of Cooperative Security in Europe," in C.C. Hodge, (ed.) *Redefining European Security.* New York: Garland Publishing.

Organization for Security and Co-operation in Europe (1975) *Final Act of Helsinki: Summit of Heads of State or Government.* OSCE, Vienna. Available at: http://www.osce.org/documents/mcs/1975/08/4044_en.pdf

Organization for Security and Co-operation in Europe (1990) *Charter of Paris for a New Europe: Summit of Heads of State or Government, Paris, 19–21 November 1990.* Available at: http://www.osce.org/mc/13017.html

Organization for Security and Co-operation in Europe (1991) *Moscow Meetings of the Conference on the Human Dimension of the CSCE, 1991.* OSCE, Vienna. Available at: http://www.osce.org/documents/odihr/1991/10/13995_en.pdf

Organization for Security and Co-operation in Europe (1992) *Challenges of Change: Summit of Heads of State or Government, Helsinki.* OSCE, Vienna. Available at: http://www.osce.org/mc/13017.html

Organization for Security and Co-operation in Europe (1994) *Towards a Genuine Partnership in a New Era: Summit of Heads of State or Government, Budapest, December 1994.* OSCE, Vienna. Available at: http://www.osce.org/mc/13017.html

Organization for Security and Co-operation in Europe (1995) The General Framework Agreement for Peace in Bosnia and Herzegovina. OSCE, Vienna. Available at: http://www.oscebih.org/overview/gfap/eng/

Organization for Security and Co-operation in Europe (1999) *Charter for European Security, Istanbul, 1999.* OSCE, Vienna. Available at: http://www.osce.org/mc/13017.html

Organization for Security and Co-operation in Europe (2000) OSCE Handbook 3rd edn. OSCE, Vienna. Available at: http://www.osce.org/publications/osce/2005/04/13858_222_en.pdf

Organization for Security and Co-operation in Europe (2001) *Ninth Meeting of the Ministerial Council, Bucharest, December 2001.* OSCE, Vienna. Available at: http://www.osce.org/mc/13017.html

Organization for Security and Co-operation in Europe (2002a) *Police Development Unit, Annual Report 2002.* OSCE, Vienna. Available at: http://www.osce.org/item/13999.html

Organization for Security and Co-operation in Europe (2002b) *Annual Report of the Secretary General on Police-Related Activities.* OSCE, Vienna. Available at: http://www.osce.org/

Organization for Security and Co-operation in Europe (2004) Annual Report on OSCE Activities 2003. OSCE, Vienna. Available at: http://www.osce.org/secretariat/documents.html

Poletti, A. and Korski, D. (2004) "Stabilizing the Balkans: Cataloguing the International Community's Efforts," in B. George (ed.) *Mediterranean Security and Beyond.* Available at: http://www.rthonbrucegeorgemp.co.uk/table_of_contents.html

Reilly, B. (2003) "International Electoral Assistance: A Review of Donor Activities and Lessons Learned," Working Paper 17. Clingendael: Conflict Research Unit. Available at: http://www.clingendael.nl/cru/project/publications/pdf/Working_Paper_17.pdf

Rose, R. (2001) *International Encyclopedia of Elections.* London: Macmillan Press.

Schmid, W.J. and Klepsch, M. (1997) "On the Path to a European Security Architecture: the Contribution of the Forum for Security Co-operation," in *OSCE Yearbook 1997.* Baden-Baden: Institute for Peace Research and Security Policy at the University of Hamburg.

Sica, M. (1997) "The Role of the OSCE in the Former Yugoslavia after the Dayton Peace Agreement," in M. Bothe, N. Ronzitti and A. Rosas (eds.) *The OSCE in the Maintenance of Peace and Security.* The Hague: Kluwer International Law Institute.

Sweden (2004) "Contribution from the Philippean Embassy in Stockholm," the Stockholm Initiative on Disarmament, Demobilization and Reintegration. Available at: http://www.sweden.gov.se/content/1/c6/03/55/42/fc6359f7.pdf

United Kingdom (2004) *The Military Contribution to Peace Support Operations,* 2nd Joint Warfare Publication, Ministry of Defence, UK. Available at: http://www.mod.uk/linked_files/jdcc/publications/jwp3_50.pdf

Part II

Peacebuilding

Working toward positive peace in
post-conflict societies

5 Paths to peacebuilding

The transformation of peace operations

Paul F. Diehl

Introduction

The focus of most diplomatic efforts, especially those carried out by the global community, historically has been to prevent war and, should war occur, stop the fighting as soon as possible. From a normative standpoint, it is hard to argue with this strategy. Preventing or stopping armed conflict can save countless lives; this includes not only those directly involved in the combat, but civilian populations that may also be affected by the fighting. Furthermore, war may create conditions that make it difficult to resolve future conflicts peacefully, as domestic populations harden to the idea of compromise with an enemy. Despite the desirability of early intervention in a conflict, the international community is often slow to react to impending crises. Even when international organizations and leading states do respond to a war, it is often too late to prevent violent conflict and they are faced with the job of cleaning up in the aftermath of that conflict.

Over time, there has been a shift in strategies by the international community from an exclusive focus on conflict prevention and conflict management towards an emphasis on what has come to be referred to as "peacebuilding," or assisting states in recovering from war. International organizations have been at the forefront of such efforts, as recent activities in Haiti, Sierra Leone, East Timor, and elsewhere attest. Yet such activities were hardly envisioned by the founders of those organizations, and in most cases there are no provisions for such activities in the charters of regional and global organizations. It is the contention of this chapter that peacebuilding represents a significant break from past collective security and peacekeeping practices. Yet, at the same time, peacebuilding is not entirely *de novo*, but rather its components can be traced to the certain changes in international community practice over a broad period of time.

This chapter traces the evolution of international peace operations and related activities to the present-day practice of peacebuilding. I begin with a brief discussion of the essential components of peacebuilding. The focus of the chapter is on peacebuilding efforts, primarily from the vantage point of the global community. Thus, peacebuilding does not necessarily encompass the full range of reconstruction and reconciliation activities, nor does it encompass unilateral actions carried out by states operating as occupying powers (for example, see Jackson 2004). I trace the development of peacekeeping operations from their earliest origins through several epochs until the present-day emphasis on peacebuilding. In each phase, I describe the predominant modes of how the global community collectively responded to threats to international peace and security, as well as what precedents for later actions are set. Finally, I conclude by describing some patterns in modern international peacekeeping, noting its evolution away from traditional peacekeeping toward peacebuilding.

The concept of peacebuilding

Peacekeeping analyses are notorious for their conceptual muddles. It is common for the terms peacekeeping, peacebuilding, peace enforcement, peacemaking, and a host of other terms to be used interchangeably. Even when distinctions are made, there is not necessarily agreement among scholars and practitioners on the conceptual components of a given term. Given that, it is impossible to specify a single, universally agreed-upon definition of peacebuilding. Nevertheless, there is some intersubjective consensus on some of the relevant dimensions of peacebuilding operations.

A useful place to begin is the definition put forward by then UN Secretary-General Boutros Boutros-Ghali (1995), the standard or baseline conceptualization of peacekeeping-related definitions used by scholars and policymakers. Boutros-Ghali speaks of "peacebuilding" as the "creation of a new environment," not merely the cessation of hostilities facilitated by traditional peacekeeping. His analysis and those of other scholars seem to suggest a series of characteristics or dimensions by which peacebuilding can be compared with other concepts.

The first dimension concerns the goal(s) of peacebuilding. Most seem to agree with Boutros-Ghali (1995) that, minimally, the purpose of peacebuilding is to prevent the recurrence of conflict. Yet there is some disagreement over whether this idea of "negative peace" (the absence of violent conflict) should be extended to include elements of "positive peace," including reconciliation, value transformation, and justice concerns. This distinction is critical because virtually all differences in conceptualizations of peacebuilding can be traced back to disagreements on this point.

The second dimension of peacebuilding includes the strategies and accompanying activities designed to achieve the goal(s). Not surprisingly, these vary somewhat according to whether one pursues goals broader than preventing conflict recurrence or not. A minimalist strategy of preventing conflict recurrence adopts strategies consistent with conflict management. That is, peacebuilding is partly concerned with decreasing the "opportunity" (Most and Starr 1989) to resort to violence. Thus, some peacebuilding activities include disarming warring parties, destroying weapons, and training indigenous security personnel. One might also include the use of traditional peacekeeping forces to separate combatants in the short run as a precursor or supplement to such activities. Minimalist approaches are also dedicated to creating mechanisms under which conflicts can be managed peacefully rather than through violence. Thus, facilitating elections, repatriating refugees, and strengthening government institutions are peacebuilding activities consistent with this strategy (see Boutros-Ghali 1995, for these and other examples).

A broader conception of peacebuilding leads to a somewhat different strategies and sets of activities. Some (Cockell 2000; Doyle and Sambanis 2000; Cousens 2001) see peacebuilding as addressing the "root causes of conflict." Minimalists expect conflict to occur, but want to manage it peacefully. In contrast, the maximalist strategy does not merely promote management, but *conflict resolution*, that is eliminating the "willingness" (Most and Starr 1989) of parties to use violence. Accordingly, many peacebuilding activities are designed for attitudinal changes by disputants and their constituents. These include programs to promote economic development and human rights protection. Ramsbottom (2000) arranges peacebuilding activities in several categories (military/security, political/constitutional, economic/social, psycho/social, and international) as well as according to whether they are designed to be short-, medium-, or long-term measures (for a broad list of activities, see also Cockell 2000; Newman and Schnabel 2002).

A third dimension concerns the timing of such activities. Most conceptions of peacebuilding envision its activities to occur following some type of peace settlement between warring parties. Preventive diplomacy and its accompanying actions are supposed to be put in place *before* significant levels of violence occur (Lund 1996). Coercive military intervention takes place in the context of ongoing armed conflict. Traditional peacekeepers (e.g., the UN forces in the Golan Heights) are usually deployed after the cessation of violence, but prior to any peace settlement (hence their primary roles as ceasefire monitors). Peacebuilding then takes place *after* prevention has failed, *after* traditional peacekeeping (if it has occurred), and *after* peacemaking.

In some sense, peacebuilding shares some elements with preventive diplomacy in that both occur in the absence of violent conflict and both are designed to prevent its outbreak. Nevertheless, there is an implicit assumption in peacebuilding that the existence of a prior war has fundamentally changed the relationship (and relative risk of future conflict) such that the strategies and activities pursued must be different; diplomatic initiatives alone are likely to be inadequate. Positive peace advocates note that there is no reason to confine peacebuilding activities to post-settlement, as many could be employed with positive results in earlier phases of conflict as well. They are certainly correct in this asser-tion and indeed instances of such (e.g., NATO actions in Kosovo) have occurred, but, empirically, peacebuilding, at least by international govern-mental organizations, is predominantly a post-war set of actions.

A fourth dimension is the context in which peacebuilding should be carried out. Boutros-Ghali (1995) envisions that peacebuilding could occur following either interstate or intrastate conflict; he also notes some activ-ities appropriate to each context. *De facto*, however, most of the discussion of peacebuilding has assumed that it would be employed in a civil context, following an intrastate war, significant ethnic conflict, or even in a failed state (see Maley *et al.* 2003). In practice, we should recognize that the dis-tinctions between intrastate and interstate conflict break down when neighboring states intervene in civil conflicts, best illustrated by the Congo war starting in the 1990s.

The fifth and final dimension is the actors that will carry out the peace-building actions. As Pugh (2000) notes, peacebuilding seems to assume that external actors will play a significant, if not exclusive role, in this enterprise. Again, an examination of the strategy and activities would not seem to preclude local actors, and indeed some elements (e.g., truth and reconciliation commissions) may be more successful when external actors are not the driving forces. Also implicit in the peacebuilding notion is that such actors will act in an impartial fashion for the greater good of the society, exercising some moral authority rather than pursuing private interests. Normatively, most regard peacebuilding as an altruistic enter-prise, but as Pugh (2000) argues, such conceptions may still promote particular ideologies (e.g., democracy, neo-capitalism, and the like – see also Paris 1997, for an elaboration).

Pre-World War II

For analytical purposes, the history of peace operations is divided into dif-ferent epochs or phases (see also Wiseman 1987; James 1990; Goulding 1993; Segal 1995; Schmidl 2000; Malone and Wermester 2000; Jakobsen 2002; Bellamy *et al.* 2004; Talentino 2004).

The nineteenth century and earlier

Schmidl (2000) identifies a dozen or so multinational missions carried out by major powers prior to World War I. These range from joint actions against pirates to interventions in civil conflicts such as the Greek War of Independence (during the 1820s) and the Boxer Rebellion (1900). Early international efforts at collective military action shared a number of characteristics. First, they operated on an *ad hoc* basis, organizing and dis-banding according to the crisis at hand. This attribute persists with modern peacekeeping and peacebuilding operations to this day. Second, beyond the *ad hoc* arrangements, these early actions had little precedent to follow. Thus, they operated without specific guidelines, often with little coordination between national units. This circumstance would change in the twentieth century, when operations relied heavily on guidelines established by previous operations in terms of personnel, deployment, and conduct. Finally, early efforts went forward primarily without the approval or the direction of an international body, virtually because international organizations as we know them today did not exist. The protection of international peace and security was largely indistinguishable from the interests of the major powers in the world.

The League of Nations period

The creation of the League of Nations was an important turning point in the development of international peace operations. The Covenant of the League is perhaps the first document to explicitly recognize an international obligation to maintain peace and security, and to provide for collective action in meeting that responsibility. Article 10 states:

> The Members of the League undertake to respect and preserve as against external aggression the territorial integrity and existing political independence of all Members of the League. In case of any such aggression, the Council shall advise upon the means by which this obligation shall be fulfilled.

The provisions of that Article, however, are a far cry from installing discretionary power in an international police force to meet threats to international security.

At first glance, such provisions seem unrelated to modern peacebuilding activities; after all, the Covenant envisioned only coercive actions (collective security) and provided strict conditions for their authorization. Nevertheless, they reinforce some earlier precedents as well as break new ground that would influence UN provisions for peace and security years later. First, the operations were to be organized on an *ad hoc* basis, much as were their historical predecessors, further reinforcing the preference not to create permanent organizational structures, at least in the security realm. Second, and on a related point, any operations would probably not be under the control of the League or be truly international forces. At this stage, multilateral security action was controlled at the authorization and execution stages by the leading states in the system. Still, League provisions were a significant break with the past in that they supplied the *legal* authority for the League to take collective military action.

The collective security mechanisms of the League failed to meet a series of challenges to international peace and security (i.e., the Japanese invasion of Manchuria, the Italian invasion of Ethiopia, German rearmament).

Despite these failures, the League of Nations was active in several disputes and crisis. During these disputes, the League began to perform some peace observation functions that were to evolve into the peacekeeping strategy in later years. The League Covenant makes no mention of peace observation, yet Article 11, authorizing the League to "take any action that may be deemed wise and effectual to safeguard the peace of nations," opened the door to actions not specifically mentioned in the Covenant or envisioned by its authors. Furthermore, Article 15 provided for the Council to report on the facts of disputes and make recommendations on how those disputes might be settled peacefully. These two articles would form the basis for League actions that combined the missions of fact-finding and observation.

The first League action came in a dispute over the Aaland Islands between Sweden and Finland and led the League to create a commission of inquiry to investigate the situation and recommend solutions to the controversy (Barros 1968). One might think a fact-finding mission would seem to offer few precedents for future peace observation. Yet this simple case established a precedent that the League could successfully intervene in a dispute and act in a neutral fashion in pursuit of a peaceful solution. The acceptance, albeit without enthusiasm, of the fact-finding report by the protagonists also helped establish the League's reputation as a fair arbiter. This case indicates that the international community can legitimately intervene in a conflict even when fighting is not ongoing, at least *prior* to the outbreak of violence. Yet the opportunity for intervention *after* serious conflict is terminated would not be legitimized until many years later.

Throughout the 1920s, the League involved itself in a number of disputes. The usual method was to create fact-finding commissions that would report back to the Council, following the strategy outlined in the Covenant and the precedent established in the Aaland Islands case. In the dispute between Poland and Germany over Upper Silesia, troops were sent to supervise the plebiscite in the area (James 1990). Although such action did not resemble later peace observation missions, it did represent a key instance of the use of internationally sanctioned forces in a supervisory role. Most importantly, this case is perhaps the first to include an internationally supervised popular election as a key component of conflict resolution. Today, some peacebuilding operations have democratic elections as part of the process in rebuilding societies.

The Greek-Bulgarian crisis of 1925 provided another opportunity for League involvement and the establishment of another precedent that would later form the basis of later peace operations (Barros 1970). Before the Council authorized a fact-finding mission, it insisted that there be a ceasefire, which was subsequently achieved. This became a virtual requirement for authorizing peacekeeping operations. The recommendations of the commission of inquiry included the pullback of forces and their separation at a safe distance, supervised by neutral observers. A committee composed of representatives from both disputants and some neutral parties was to discuss problems with the ceasefire and limit the escalation potential of hostile incidents. The construction of a buffer zone and the establishment of such a committee became standard operating procedures for traditional peacekeeping operations.

Shortly after the Aaland Islands dispute, a more serious conflict arose between Poland and Lithuania over the province of Vilna. More than just deploying a fact-finding mission this time, the League was successful in negotiating a provisional line of demarcation and a neutral, demilitarized zone between the disputants, thus setting the physical and political conditions for the introduction of an international force. An international force of 1,500 troops from states that had no seat on the Council (in marked contrast to the Upper Silesia force) was designed to supervise a plebiscite in the area. Unfortunately, such a force never assumed those roles. The action by the League of Nations in the Saar may be the first true example of an international peace observation force (Wambaugh 1970). Yet the conditions under which the operation functioned were extraordinary and indeed helped contribute to the success of the mission. The Saar, lying between France and Germany, was to be an internationally administered territory for a period of some years following World War I, at which time a plebiscite would decide the final disposition of the area. Thus the usual problem of obtaining permission of the host country for the stationing of an international force was not an issue in this case: the League was the equivalent of the host state. Note that this augurs later UN operations in territories such as East Timor.

Unlike previous missions in which nations maintained control of units, the Saar force was under the direction of the League through its appointed commander. Although the troops were to maintain order prior to and during the plebiscite, they did not function as an international police force. They patrolled the territory but would only take action in emergency situations and then only in response to a request by the local authorities. The level of military force was to be kept at a minimum, reflecting what would become the standard for limitations on the use of military force in peacekeeping missions. The Saar operation is far from the full range of activities carried out by peacebuilding operations, but we still have an important instance of the international community being involved in the disposition of a given territory with the goal of preventing future conflict.

Beyond peace observation, the League of Nations was also an important progenitor of peacebuilding by virtue of its Mandate System (see Murray 1957). This system was designed to take the colonies of the losing states in World War I and prepare those territories for eventual independence rather than distributing the territories to members of the victorious coalition, a long-standing tradition in wars. A trustee (an advanced state, most often France and the United Kingdom in practice) was appointed to guide the former colonial territory. One might recognize some of the

Mandate purposes and functions as similar to modern peacebuilding activities. Trustees sought to build institutions, train personnel, and conduct other activities so as to facilitate the self-governance of former colonies. Such actions did not follow wars within those areas, but they are similar to peacebuilding activities in failed states and are related to later UN actions in East Timor. Thus, in a limited way, the League established the idea that the international community had an interest and would take action to promote peaceful self-governance within (potential) states.

Most historians regard the League of Nations as a failure. Yet from its successes in peace observation and inquiry, the League established procedures and precedents about the proper timing and form of international intervention. First, its activities, with the Saar exception, took place in smaller states, at the periphery of major power competition. Second, the League was more successful in intervention when hostilities had not reached full-scale war; this reinforced the idea that international organizations had the greatest roles to place at times other than the height of violence, although a post-war role was still not envisioned. Third, although the focus was still on *inter*state conflict, there was recognition through the Mandate System that *intra*state concerns were also important to peace and security and there were times that the international community needed to step in to assure self-determination so that peoples could govern themselves.

The Cold War

The early years

The UN provisions for conflict intervention resemble those of the League, but are laid out more explicitly and rely on an increasingly coercive sequence of actions. According to Chapter VI of the UN Charter, protagonists are given a number of dispute resolution alternatives to the use of military force. These techniques were primarily envisaged as occurring prior to conflict escalation, although there is nothing inherent in the approaches that necessitates this. Chapter VII of the UN Charter lists some courses of action for UN members to take should peaceful methods of settlement outlined in Chapter VI fail. Article 42 directly identifies the collective security option: "[the Security Council] may take such action by air, sea, or land forces as may be necessary to maintain or restore international peace and security." The UN Charter did not mention the notion of peace observation, and peacekeeping operations were yet to be created. International organizations still lacked formal options between enforcement measures and mediation. Nevertheless, this necessitated some adaptation on the part of the organization, given that it became paralyzed by Cold War tensions, and therefore incapable of dealing with many threats to peace in ways outlined by the Charter.

First, the United Nations continued the tradition of peace observation that had begun under the League of Nations (see Wainhouse 1966, for details). As collective security proved unworkable, these missions provided the new organization with experience in conflict intervention and, in a few instances, offered guidelines that would be adopted under peacekeeping. Civil instability in Greece after World War II provided the first opportunity for peace observation. In line with League experience, a UN fact-finding mission was dispatched. Yet because Greek Communists were involved in the civil unrest, the conflict became part of the emerging Cold War at the international level. As a consequence of the Soviet veto in the Security Council, the General Assembly had to take the lead and set up an observation force, with several posts at Greek borders. The force did not maintain continuous supervision of the border areas, as would a peacekeeping force, but did make frequent inspections to discourage the supply of rebel troops from abroad. This mission reinforced the notion that the UN and international organization had a role to play in civil conflicts.

The first UN attempt at truce supervision was in assisting Indonesian independence from the Netherlands. Observers were placed at the disposal of the "good offices" commission that was trying to negotiate a peaceful withdrawal of Dutch forces from Indonesia. Having secured an agreement for the independence of Indonesia, the observers later monitored the demobilization and withdrawal of Dutch forces, a common function assigned to peace forces today in the aftermath of a peace settlement.

Peace observation began to be a rountinized activity for the organization, even as the individual missions remained *ad hoc*. Following the 1948 war in the Middle East, the UN Truce Supervision Organization (UNTSO) was charged with observing the truce and its limitations on the movement of troops and material. In conjunction with a fact-finding and mediation mission that achieved a ceasefire in 1949, a UN team was dispatched to Kashmir in the center of the Indo-Pakistani conflict and stationed with regular Indian and Pakistani troops. The observer force investigated complaints, provided information on troop movements and actions, and helped local authorities to maintain order. Both of these operations remain in place today. The United Nations had begun to deploy forces *following* conflict, rather than as a preventive mechanism. Still, such observer forces were not put in place following some type of peace settlement, a characteristic of peacebuilding that was still decades away.

UNEF I and the first "golden age" of UN peacekeeping

The Suez Crisis prompted a fundamental change in thinking about the UN role in and mechanisms for dealing with active threats to international peace and security. In June 1956, the British handed over control of the Suez Canal to Egypt. A little more than a month later, President Nasser

nationalized the canal, setting off the Suez Crisis. UN and other diplomatic efforts failed to resolve differences between Israel, Egypt, Britain,
and France. Israel invaded Egypt on October 29, setting off the second
Arab-Israeli war in a decade. One day later, Britain and France issued an
ultimatum to Egypt and Israel demanding that forces be moved away from
the canal and that British and French troops fill the void to ensure free
passage. Egypt rejected this ultimatum. Because of a stalemate in the
Security Council, the General Assembly faced the circumstances that
peace observation was inadequate to the task, but collective enforcement
was politically impossible. Furthermore, Britain and France insisted on
some sort of international police force before they withdrew their troops.
On November 4, 1956, the General Assembly passed the seminal Resolution 998, which authorized the Secretary-General to set up a UN force to
be dispatched to the region (see Rosner 1963, for details).

Specifically, the United Nations Emerging Force (UNEF I) was charged
with monitoring the ceasefire between forces and supervising the withdrawal of these forces from the area. It later acted as a buffer against the
future engagement of Arab and Israeli forces. Importantly, its mission was
limited to these functions. It played no role in reopening the canal or in
the delicate negotiations that followed concerning the management of the
canal, in contrast to the fact-finding and conciliation functions often tied to
peace observation. Although limited in mandate, UNEF I was a dramatic
innovation: armed international soldiers were now charged with specific
functions in an interstate conflict, including monitoring military force
withdrawal.

The period from 1956 (the advent of the UNEF I operation) until 1978
is popularly known as the first "golden age" of peacekeeping. This is so
because it was the period during the Cold War in which the greatest
number of peacekeeping operations were authorized. In these two
decades, the UN deployed ten different peacekeeping or observation missions to different areas of the world (for a review of many of these operations, see United Nations 1990; Diehl 1994) Although some areas were
excluded (the superpower spheres of influence), traditional peacekeeping
and observation were the predominant operational methods by which the
international community responded to threats to international peace.

With the notable exception of the Congo operation (see below), most
peacekeeping operations in this period shared a number of characteristics,
most in contrast to contemporary peacebuilding operations. These operations were put in place prior to a peace settlement, but following a ceasefire; this is consistent with earlier peace observation missions. The duties
of the peacekeeping forces were very limited. Traditional peacekeepers
acted as interposition forces, separating combatants in order to deter military engagements. Peacekeepers also monitored ceasefires and helped
resolve any disputes that arose over the terms of the halt in fighting. Additional activities, such as clearing transportation routes and providing

medical assistance to local populations occurred, but they tended to be incidental, certainly not part of the mandate granted to them. Traditional peacekeeping operations were also deployed almost exclusively in inter-state conflicts, quite unlike the peacebuilding operations that would occur decades later.

If traditional peacekeeping operations in the first golden age were so different from peacebuilding missions, what role did the former play in stimulating the latter? It was certainly not the tasks that the peacekeepers performed. Rather, this series of operations routinized and legitimized the norm of the international community intervening in international conflicts. Collective security actions were moribund and peace observation missions were still infrequent. Traditional peacekeeping became the baseline response to threats to international peace, albeit only ones that did not directly involve either of the superpowers. The fundamental characteristics of traditional operations (lightly armed forces, impartial) would later be modified according to new threats to peace, but the important point is that peacebuilding operations were not created *de novo*, but rather as deviations from the standard peacekeeping profile.

The Congo operation: a proto-peacebuilding operation?

The UN operation in the Congo or ONUC (1960–1964) was, in several ways, a very different operation from all other peacekeeping missions in this era (see Lefever 1967; Abi-Saab 1978). The collapse of law and order following Congalese independence led the Belgian government to deploy troops in order to protect Belgian nationals. At the same time, the province of Katanga declared itself independent from the Congo, apparently with some support from Belgium. The United Nations organized ONUC and dispatched it to the capital city to help ensure the territorial integrity of the Congo, assist in restoring law and order, and supervise the withdrawal of Belgian forces. ONUC was not deployed following a peace settlement, but in the middle of active combat. Nevertheless, this operation is perhaps the first instance in which UN peacekeeping troops (as opposed to observers) were sent to a civil war. The exceptions were mixed cases involving decolonization, but these still involved extant states. The Congo operation also involved decolonization, and the presence of Belgian troops was a motivating factor for UN intervention, but UN troops stayed after the Belgian withdrawal and were intimately involved in what was a struggle between different factions for control of Katanga and indeed the country as a whole. Involvement in civil conflicts is now the most common context for peacebuilding, but the Congo operation was really a convention-breaking operation and opened the door for actions that seemed to permeate the hard shell of state sovereignty.

Several of the initial and subsequent actions by ONUC were similar to later peacebuilding activities, and far from the narrow mandate of traditional operations of ceasefire monitoring. First, ONUC troops were sent to Katanga with the job of restoring order and facilitating the withdrawal of Belgian troops. This was similar to some peacebuilding actions in which troops perform some civilian police functions and monitor the disarmament of local forces (for example, Holm and Eide 1999). When the civil war spread beyond Katanga, ONUC's mandate was expanded to include reconvening the Congolese parliament. The move also allowed the United Nations to use offensive military force as a last resort in order to prevent an all-out civil war. The United Nations established a conciliation commission to find a way to make peace between the warring factions. ONUC succeeded in getting a ceasefire between the parties as well as an agreement on a new unified government for the country. In a limited way, ONUC was assisting in creating government machinery to run the country after its withdrawal, something later peacebuilding operations would attempt as well. Katanga remained in rebellion, and the United Nations expanded the mandate of ONUC even further, authorizing ONUC to use all means necessary, including military force, to control Katanga. ONUC launched offensive military actions in Katanga and seized most of the province. The UN never quite operated government machinery or provided the services as it would in later peacebuilding operations, but nevertheless ONUC was the principal mechanism for establishing local order until a peace agreement finally held and the central government was strong enough to take over in 1964.

In some ways, ONUC was a precedent-setting operation. It established that the United Nations could intervene in civil conflicts and that UN peacekeepers could perform functions far beyond those connected to ceasefire monitoring. Many of the activities represent limited versions of what we associate now with peacebuilding. Nevertheless, disagreements between the major powers (primarily the United States, the Soviet Union, and France) over the Congo operation and the backlash from newly independent African states led the United Nations away from trying to duplicate the Congo operation in other civil conflicts. Indeed, it would be almost 25 years before the UN would again venture in peacekeeping that involved civil conflicts and quasi-peacebuilding actions.

A discussion of the development of peacebuilding would not be complete without a mention of the United Nations Security Force (UNSF) in New Guinea. West New Guinea was in the process of decolonization in the early 1960s and it would be transferred to Indonesia. Yet there was a transition period following the end of colonial rule by the Netherlands in which an administrative arm of the peacekeeping operation governed the territory for over six months. This operation established few precedents and is largely forgotten today in peacekeeping analyses. It also was an operation that had more to do with decolonization (a well-established norm in the international system) than issues of civil conflict or piercing state sovereignty. Nevertheless, it is an instance in which the international community took responsibility for running government operations in a territory, something similar to what would occur in East Timor decades later and what must be regarded as toward the end of the peacebuilding continuum today.

The "lost decade" and the thawing of the Cold War

If the period from the onset of UNEF I until the deployment of UNIFIL (United Nations Interim Force in Lebanon, first authorized in 1978) in southern Lebanon could be called the golden age of peacekeeping, the ten years that followed (1979–1988) might easily be referred to as the "lost decade." No new UN peacekeeping operations were deployed during this time, and many observers regarded peacekeeping in general as moribund – the latter is probably incorrect because previously authorized operations in Cyprus and the Middle East continued to operate and were generally successful at conflict abatement.

The lost decade might be attributable to a number of different factors. First, much of the so-called demand for peacekeeping came from conflicts in which it was least likely to be authorized. Conflicts in Afghanistan, Panama, Grenada, and the like directly involved the superpowers, and traditional peacekeeping was generally excluded from conflicts within the superpowers' spheres of influence. Second, ongoing hotspots (e.g., India-Pakistan, Arab-Israeli) were already covered by one or more UN peacekeeping and observation missions. Third, renewed Cold War tensions in the early 1980s and dissatisfaction with extant operations made peacekeeping a less attractive option during this period.

Toward the end of the 1980s, the logjam would be broken and a flood of UN and other peacekeeping operations would emerge in the next two decades. Auguring the development of peacebuilding operations were several new ventures, most notably in Namibia, but also elsewhere, that involved election supervision. This was not necessarily a completely new idea as League of Nations observers had previously monitored plebiscites. Still, these operations were a gateway to the establishment of peacebuilding operations.

The United Nations operation in Namibia (United Nations Transitional Assistance Group or UNTAG) exhibited in a limited fashion many of the peacebuilding characteristics noted above. First, it was a peacekeeping force deployed *following* a peace agreement between different groups (both local actors and the South African government). Previously, peacekeeping operations had occurred prior to peacemaking. Peacekeeping forces would now be charged with the implementation of an agreement, usually a first step or prerequisite for more expansive peacebuilding activities. Second, UNTAG carried out several activities associated with peacebuilding, most notably monitoring disarmament and supervising the electoral process. Unlike later peacebuilding efforts, however, UNTAG did not have full control over these functions. The small number of troops (approximately 4,000) was inadequate to monitor troop movements and repatriation efforts, especially early in the process. Furthermore, South African forces maintained some control over the country until election day as well as portions of the election process. In addition, Namibia was not really a purely intrastate conflict, but merged together concerns with decolonization and foreign intervention, as well as internal conflict. Nevertheless, despite such problems, most regard the outcome of the Namibian election as free and fair, and perhaps this is why international decision-makers sought to repeat and expand this role in future operations.

The Namibian success would spawn similar operations, sometimes with more expansive activities. In 1989 and 1990, the UN Observer Group in Central America (ONUCA) monitored the military disengagement of opposing forces before and following elections in Nicaragua. More significant was the United Nations Transitional Authority in Cambodia or UNTAC. Its name was indicative of the broader powers and functions assigned to the operation. Much like the Namibian operation, it was a post-settlement mission in an internationalized civil conflict and the centerpiece of the mission was to be supervising elections, which would follow supervised disarmament of various protagonists. Nevertheless, UNTAC was another incremental step toward contemporary peacebuilding because of its other characteristics (see Doyle 1995).

UNTAC did not merely monitor elections in a passive fashion. It had the mandate of repatriating refugees, maintaining law and order, and conducting some governmental functions. Furthermore, it was charged with authority to construct the election system, register voters, and conduct the election, not merely deter or report on election-day irregularities. Mirroring later peacebuilding operations, UNTAC was supplemented by 7,000 additional UN personnel, most notably civilian police who supervised local police and investigated human rights abuses.

What began in 1978 as the seeming death of peacekeeping was transformed into what is now referred to the second golden age of peacekeeping 10–15 years later. Peacebuilding was not yet the term used to describe these new forms of peacekeeping, but nevertheless many of the aspects of peacebuilding were already in place by the time of the Cambodia operation. Peacebuilding, however, would reach fruition with the Somalia operations and several other post-Cold War operations.

The post-Cold War period

Somalia and the birth of peacebuilding

Many trace the first use of the term peacebuilding to the first edition of Boutros-Ghali's *An Agenda for Peace*, released in 1992. In that book, he may have coined the phrase, but he also described some peacebuilding activities as well as distinguishing peacebuilding from other kinds of peace operations, such as traditional peacekeeping and peacemaking. Although I have argued the peacebuilding elements really precede this date, many regard US and UN actions in Somalia as the first true peacebuilding operations. Others, often with expanded duties, would follow in Bosnia, Haiti, and elsewhere, but Somalia was a watershed moment for peacebuilding.

The UN Operation in Somalia (UNOSOM) was first deployed in 1992 in response to the breakdown of order in that country and a humanitarian crisis of colossal proportions. Phase I of the operation was superseded later that year by Operation Restore Hope, an American-led military operation designed to guarantee the distribution of food and medical supplies. UNOSOM II, deployed in 1993, facilitated the transition of peacekeeping and relief duties from a US-centered operation to a UN-directed one.

US and UN efforts in Somalia went beyond election supervision missions in Namibia and Cambodia, even as Somalia involved no electoral process. First, the Somalia crisis was purely internal, at least to the extent that no other state was militarily involved in the country or responsible for a broader threat to international peace and security. Earlier operations in Cambodia and Namibia also included the involvement of powerful neighbors, and international responses to those conflicts had regional security as part of their impetus. Except for some concern about refugees, there were few "negative externalities" associated with this conflict (Lepgold 2003). Indeed, the collapse of the Somali state had the desirable effect of ending its militarized rivalry with Ethiopia. Second, on a related point, the Somalia crisis was primarily a humanitarian one. That is, the international community was motivated more by concerns for "human security" than it was for traditional security matters. Appropriately, peacebuilding strategies were consistent with this motivation, whereas missions involving interposition forces or even election supervision, previously the staple of peace operations, would do little to address the suffering taking place in Somalia. Third, the operations lacked host state consent, largely because in the face of state collapse there was no national government to give its approval. Fourth, the Somali operation provided for more intrusive peacebuilding activities, perhaps because of the absence of a central government authority. These activities involved emergency relief (in terms of distribution of food and medical supplies) as well as trying to establish law and order in the country. Local reconciliation efforts were also part of the mix (see Menkaus 1996). UN operations also involved greater coordination with NGOs, previously less common in peace operations and more reflective of pure humanitarian assistance missions.

The evolution of peace operations continued after Somalia. The second golden age of peacekeeping may have ended shortly after the genocide in Rwanda and the failure of the UN and its members to prevent it. Still, Rwanda had more the effect of causing UN members to be reluctant to enter conflicts at all or to do so only after certain conditions were present. The retrenchment, however, does not necessarily seem to include a scaling back of the peacebuilding duties assigned to operations that are approved. Many peace operations have been deployed in the past two decades, and I will not review them all here. Rather, the next section provides an overview of some of the changes in peace operations in the post-Cold War era, and these are juxtaposed against standard practice in earlier eras.

Trends in post-Cold War peacekeeping

There have been a number of notable changes in peace operations with the advent of peacebuilding operations. Below, I summarize some of the primary changes, many (but not all) of which are related to the rise of peacebuilding (see also Diehl 2000).

Frequency and geography

The most obvious change in peace operations is their significantly greater numbers in the post-Cold War era. In the period from 1945–1988, there were only about 13 peace operations conducted under UN auspices (and few others conducted by other actors); this is roughly one new operation every three years. Since that time, however, the UN has authorized 46 operations, or almost three new operations per year, through 2004 (data taken from UN website: http://www.un.org/Depts/dpko/). Many of the recent missions are clustered in the 1988 to 1993 period, with a lull in new missions shortly thereafter. Nevertheless, whatever impact the legacies of failures in Somalia and Rwanda had, including bringing about the end of the second golden age of peacekeeping, they did not linger long; there was again an upsurge in new peace missions at end of the decade. In addition, other organizations (e.g., NATO) have carried out peace operations as well. This is not merely a function of more crises or wars in the international system, but a real increase in the willingness of the international community to carry out these missions.

Beyond sheer numbers, peace operations have expanded to new regions. In the Cold War era, peace operations were largely excluded from superpower spheres of influence. More recently, peace operations have been found in all regions of the world, notably in the Western Hemisphere and in eastern Europe. Africa has also seen a dramatic increase in operations, suggesting that an adversion to peace operations stemming from the ONUC experience has been overcome.

Organization

The traditional organizing agency for most peacekeeping operations has been the United Nations. There were occasional forays into peacekeeping by regional organizations during the Cold War era (e.g., OAU in Chad, OAS in the Dominican Republic) and multinational efforts (e.g., Multinational Force and Observers – MFO – in the Sinai) but these tended to be isolated occurrences amid the dominant pattern of UN-sponsored peacekeeping. Although still most common, UN operations have been supplemented by those carried out by regional organizations, including NATO, ECOWAS, and the African Union. There are also individual state efforts at peace operations, including those by Britain in Sierra Leone and Australia in East Timor. Regardless of the organizing entity, however, soldiers deployed in such operations remain almost exclusively under national command, something that has changed little since the early days of peace operations.

In addition to the primary organizing agency of peace operations, there have been two other notable changes in the composition of peace operations. First, peace operations now necessitate a larger number of soldiers than older peacekeeping operations (Green *et al.* 1998). Newer operations cover a wider geographic area and perform a broader range of duties than Cold War operations. The deployment of troops during ongoing conflict also requires more soldiers than in the past. Second, major power states now are among the primary troop contributors to some operations. Previously, leading states were excluded from providing troops, leaving neutral countries and "middle powers" to provide the bulk of forces. The requirements of new peacebuilding missions, however, have necessitated that major powers assume a greater role on the ground, perhaps at some risk to impartiality. Third, other UN agencies and NGOs are an integral part of most new peace operations. Their functions vary, but generally they are partners in the broad range of new peacebuilding activities, including those related to humanitarian assistance and building civil society (for example, see Terry 2003).

Timing

Cold War peacekeeping was generally characterized by deployment following a ceasefire between disputants, but prior to a final resolution (often indicated by a peace treaty or agreement for elections). More recent peacekeeping operations have broadened the range of choice of when to intervene. The UN operation in Macedonia (UNPREDEP) is the only true empirical example of preventive deployment. UNPREDEP's purpose was to monitor and report any developments in the border areas and deter the spread of conflict into the former Yugoslav Republic of Macedonia. Intervention during the second conflict phase, while military hostilities are ongoing, has occurred on several occasions, most notably in Bosnia. The final phase of conflict, after a peace settlement is achieved, is increasingly common for peace operations. For example, ONUMOZ (United Nations Operation in Mozambique) helped implement a peace agreement in Mozambique following the end of civil war in that country. Many of the peacebuilding missions presume some measure of stability before activities such as elections, economic development, and reconciliation can occur.

Host state consent

During the Cold War, before a peacekeeping operation could be deployed, the state upon whose territory the peacekeepers would be placed had to agree to the operation. In the post-Cold War era, peacekeeping operations may be deployed in conflicts in which host state co-operation is complete or those in which it is absent (and at several points in between). Host state consent is all but an oxymoron in the context of failed states; the absence of any organized governing authority means that no government exists to provide its consent for a peacekeeping deployment. In other cases, different groups in a civil war may agree to peacebuilding operations, but no formal government exists or at least the post-settlement period begins with a clean slate with respect to legal authority. It is often the charge of peacebuilding operations to build or revitalize that legal authority, rather than be subjects of its approval *per se*.

Mission

During the Cold War era, peacekeeping missions could be classified largely by the political context of the disputes with which they dealt (see James 1990, for a typology). Nevertheless, they all roughly shared the same mandate or mission. Peacekeeping operations were dedicated to being interposition forces (i.e., separating combatants) who performed ceasefire monitoring functions. Some peace observation missions were too small in number and were unarmed and therefore did not necessarily function as a buffer between the disputants. Nevertheless, the passive monitoring of a temporary peace agreement was the hallmark of traditional operations.

Traditional peace operations are still being authorized; witness the peacekeeping force sent to the Ethiopia–Eritrean border area. Yet most new peace operations are multifunctional, encompassing some of the activities lumped under the peacebuilding rubric. These missions are not only dramatically different from past mandates, but many of the peacebuilding activities themselves are very different from one another in terms of their roles and orientations toward the conflict parties, even if they are lumped together as peacebuilding activites. Diehl, Druckman, and Wall (1998) discovered that many of the missions were drastically different from one another and necessitated very different training regimens, rules of engagement, and need for impartiality; whether these roles are compatible in a single peacebuilding operation is an open question. In practice, peace operations have become more complex over time, and individual operations are taking on more roles and activities rather than fewer.

Type of conflict

Finally, a significant portion of peace operations authorized since the end of the Cold War have involved a significant civil conflict component. In the Cold War era, perhaps only four (or about 30 percent) of peace observations were sent to conflicts that involved significant internal conflict – and this includes Cyprus, whose threats to peace and security were as much interstate as they were intrastate. Since 1988, however, more than 90 percent of the peace operations have involved civil conflict; in a number of cases (e.g., Haiti), deployment was in an area facing exclusively internal violence, with little likelihood of foreign intervention from neighbors.

Explanations for the development of peacebuilding

I have portrayed the development of peacebuilding operations as the product of an evolutionary process, with many precedents found in prior peace operations. Nevertheless, peacebuilding does not come to full fruition until the 1990s, raising the question of why such operations emerged then and with such frequency. There are several explanations in the scholarly literature, all of which are explicitly or implicitly related.

The most common explanation for the emergence of peacebuilding is the end of the Cold War, conventionally designed at occurring approximately in 1989 (better understood as a process, however, rather than a fixed point). As noted above in the historical narrative and description of historical trends, peace operations change dramatically after this time (Malone and Wermester 2000). The end of the Cold War is said to be associated with superpower retrenchment in providing aid to other states and a reluctance to intervene in civil conflicts; the vacuum created paved the way for more expansive peace operations that could address the conflicts "dumped" on them by the superpowers. The thawing of the superpower rivalry also broke the stalemate in the UN Security Council that had historically limited peace operations in number and scope.

The end of the Cold War seems better able to predict the dramatic increase in the number of peace operations than it does the expansion of their duties. There was greater willingness on the part of the permanent members of the Security Council, and indeed the international community of states as a whole, to let the United Nations (and increasingly other international organizations) handle conflicts. Nevertheless, the new functions assigned to peace operations were not those carried out by the superpowers in the past, nor were aid programs provided by those leading powers designed to address similar problems. The end of the Cold War provides the opportunity to conduct peacebuilding and other operations, but it does not necessarily follow that the actions taken are related to greater co-operation among the leading states in the system.

A second explanation focuses on the demand side of the equation, namely that peacebuilding arises because most of the threats to international peace and security in the 1990s and beyond are civil conflicts, including failed states. There is clear empirical evidence that civil conflicts have been more prevalent that interstate ones (Gleditsch *et al.* 2002), and failed or disrupted states are indeed a recent phenomena. Yet the UN and other actors do not automatically respond to all emergencies. Furthermore, the mode of response can vary substantially as peacebuilding activities are only among the menu of options available to the international community. Certainly, peacebuilding could not be possible without the kinds of conflicts manifest in the last two decades. Still, the choice of actions is better accounted for by other explanations.

Recently, scholars have emphasized two, largely interrelated explanations based on normative change and globalization, respectively, to account for the rise of peacebuilding. The normative change argument has several variants. Paris (2004) argues that the ideology of liberalism is the guiding force behind peacebuilding operations. The promotion of democracies and open markets represents attempts to transform states so that they would become peaceful and productive members of the international community. This is consistent with the notion of peacebuilding as a set of activities for peaceful conflict management. A consensus on liberalism, of course, only comes about globally with the end of the Cold War.

A somewhat different normative argument is based on the idea that there has been a transformation to greater concern for the individual, human rights, and government legitimacy, and a corresponding decline in the strength of state sovereignty (Talentino 2004; see also Finnemore 2003). A norm of humanitarian intervention has been established and the international community has an obligation to take action to redress wrongdoing. In this context, peacebuilding activities become a logical extension of military interventions, which alone can solve the problems encountered. This approach also recognizes global democratization as a key element, but puts more emphasis on international humanitarian norms.

Jakobsen (2002) tries to make an integrative argument, using globalization as the central explanation for the rise of peacebuilding; he contends that globalizing forces are the significant and intervening variable connecting the end of the Cold War with the transformation of peace operations. Although somewhat vague on what he means by globablization, he argues that it has produced the normative changes in the areas of human rights and democracy that other scholars cite. Yet he also argues that economic liberalism in the international system, and accompanying conditionality in aid programs, have created increased conflict and state failure in underdeveloped states. In addition, globalization has increased media coverage of human suffering and thereby pressures for intervention and actions to deal with such problems (see also Jakobsen 1996).

In summary, there are a series of non-mutually exclusive explanations why peacebuilding has become the predominant form of peace operations in the past two decades. One argument that has little explanatory capability is that of experiential learning, that is, peacebuilding evolved as a result of successes and failures. There is little evidence to support this explanation, given there have been few clear successes in peacebuilding from which actors could build upon (Talentino 2004); perhaps only East Timor is a clear success. Amidst repeated failure, the international community did not abandon peacebuilding or cast aside problematic functions, but actually continued activities and expanded into others. Such an observation suggests that future evolutions of peace operations will not necessarily be a function of past efforts, even as scholars, policymakers, and other analysts devote extensive attention to "lessons learned."

References

Abi-Saab, G. (1978) *The United Nations Operation in the Congo*. London: Oxford University Press.

Barros, J. (1968) *The Aaland Islands Question: Its Settlement by the League of Nations*. New Haven, CT: Yale University Press.

Barros, J. (1970) *The League of Nations and the Great Powers: The Greek-Bulgarian Incident*. Oxford: Oxford University Press.

Bellamy, A., Williams, P., and Griffin, S. (eds.) (2004) *Understanding Peacekeeping*. Cambridge: Polity Press.

Boutros-Ghali, B. (1995) *An Agenda for Peace*. 2nd edn. New York: United Nations.

Cockell, J. (2000) "Conceptualising peacebuilding: human security and sustainable peace," in M. Pugh (ed.) *Regeneration of War-Torn Societies*. London: Macmillan, pp. 15–34.

Cousens, E. (2001) "Introduction," in E. Cousens and C. Kumar, with K. Wermester (eds.) *Peacebuilding as Politics: Cultivating Peace in Fragile Societies*. Boulder, CO: Lynne Rienner Publishers, pp. 1–20.

Diehl, P.F. (1994) *International Peacekeeping*. Revised edn. Baltimore, MD: Johns Hopkins University Press.

Diehl, P.F. (2000) "Forks in the road: theoretical and policy concerns for 21st century peacekeeping," *Global Society* 14: 337–360.

Diehl, P.F., Druckman, D., and Wall, J. (1998) "International peacekeeping and conflict resolution: a taxonomic analysis with implications," *Journal of Conflict Resolution* 42: 33–55.

Doyle, M. (1995) *UN Peacekeeping in Cambodia: UNTAC's Civil Mandate*. Boulder, CO: Lynne Rienner Publishers.

Doyle, M. and Sambanis, N. (2000) "International peacebuilding: a theoretical and quantitative analysis," *American Political Science Review* 94: 779–802.

Durch, W. (ed.) (1993) *The Evolution of UN Peacekeeping*. New York: St Martin's Press.

Finnemore, M. (2003) *The Purpose of Intervention: Changing Beliefs About the Use of Force*. Ithaca, NY: Cornell University Press.

Goulding, M. (1993) "The evolution of United Nations peacekeeping," *International Affairs* 69: 451–464.

Gleditsch, N.P., Wallensteen, P., Eriksson, M., Sollenberg, M., and Strand, H. (2002) "Armed conflict 1946–2001: a new data set," *Journal of Peace Research* 39: 615–637.

Green, D., Kahl, C., and Diehl, P.F. (1998) "Predicting the size of UN peacekeeping operations," *Armed Forces and Society* 24: 485–500.

Holm, T.T. and Eide, E.B. (1999) "Peacebuilding and police reform," Special issue of *International Peacekeeping* 6.

Jackson, R. (2004) "International engagement in war-torn countries," *Global Governance* 10: 21–36.

Jakobsen, P.V. (1996) "National interest, humanitarianism, or CNN: what triggers UN peace enforcement after the Cold War?" *Journal of Peace Research* 33: 205–215.

Jakobsen, P.V. (2002) "The transformation of United Nations peace operations in the 1990s: adding globalization to the conventional 'end of the Cold War explanation,'" *Cooperation and Conflict* 37: 267–282.

James, A. (1990) *Peacekeeping in International Politics*. London: Macmillan.

James, A. (1994) "The Congo controversies," *International Peacekeeping* 1: 44–58.

Lefever, E. (1967) *Uncertain Mandate: Politics of the UN Congo Operation*. Baltimore, MD: Johns Hopkins University Press.

Lepgold, J. (2003) "Regionalism in the post-Cold War era: Incentives for conflict management," in P.F. Diehl and J. Lepgold (eds.) *Regional Conflict Management*. Lanham, MD: Rowman and Littlefield, pp. 9–40.

Lund, M. (1996) *Preventing Violent Conflicts: A Strategy for Preventive Diplomacy*. Washington, DC: United States Institute of Peace Press.

Mackinlay, J. and Chopra, J. (1992) "Second generation multinational operations," *Washington Quarterly* 15: 113–131.

Maley, W., Sampford, C., and Thakur, R. (eds.) (2003) *From Civil Strife to Civil Society: Civil and Military Responsibilities in Disrupted States*. Tokyo: United Nations University Press.

Malone, D. and Wermester, K. (2000) "Boom and bust?: The changing nature of UN peacekeeping," *International Peacekeeping* 7: 37–54.

Menkaus, K. (1996) "International peacebuilding and the dynamics of local and national reconciliation in Somalia," *International Peacekeeping* 3: 42–67.

Most, B. and Starr, H. (1989) *Inquiry, Logic, and International Politics*. Columbia, SC: University of South Carolina Press.

Murray, J.N. (1957) *The United Nations Trusteeship System*. Urbana, IL: University of Illinois Press.

Newman, E. and Schnabel, A. (eds.) (2002) "Recovering from civil conflict: reconciliation, peace, and development," Special issue of *International Peacekeeping* 9.

Paris, R. (1997) "Peacebuilding and the limits of liberal internationalism," *International Security* 22: 54–89.

Paris, R. (2004) *At War's End: Building Peace After Civil Conflict*. Cambridge: Cambridge University Press.

Pugh, M. (2000) "Introduction: the ownership of regeneration and peacebuilding," in M. Pugh (ed.) *Regeneration of War-Torn Societies*. London: Macmillan, pp. 1–12.

Ramsbottom, O. (2000) "Reflections on UN post-settlement peacebuilding," *International Peacekeeping* 7: 167–189.

Ratner, S. (1995) *The New UN Peacekeeping*. New York: St Martin's Press.

Rosner, G. (1963) *The United Nations Emergency Force*. New York: Columbia University Press.

Schmidl, E.A. (2000) "The evolution of peace operations from the nineteenth century," in E.A. Schmidl (ed.) *Peace Operations Between Peace and War*. London: Frank Cass.

Segal, D. (1995) "Five phases of United Nations peacekeeping: an evolutionary typology," *Journal of Political and Military Sociology* 22: 65–79.

Shaw, T. (1996) "Beyond post-conflict peacebuilding: what links to sustainable development and human security?" *International Peacekeeping* 3: 36–48.

Suhrke, A. (2001) "Peacekeepers as nation-builders: dilemmas of the UN in East Timor," *International Peacekeeping* 8: 1–20.

Talentino, A. (2004) "One step forward, one step back?: The development of peacebuilding as concept and strategy," *Journal of Conflict Studies* 25: 33–60.

Terry, F. (2003) "Reconstituting whose social order?: NGOs in disrupted states," in W. Maley, C. Sampford, and R. Thakur (eds.) *From Civil Strife to Civil Society*. Tokyo: United Nations University Press, pp. 279–299.

United Nations (1990) *The Blue Helmets: A Review of United Nations Peace-Keeping*. 2nd edn. New York: United Nations.

Wainhouse, D. (1966) *International Peace Observation*. Baltimore, MD: Johns Hopkins University Press.

Wambaugh, S. (1970) *The Saar Plebiscite*. Cambridge, MA: Harvard University Press.

Wiseman, H. (1987) "United Nations peacekeeping: an historical overview," in H. Wiseman (ed.) *Peacekeeping: Appraisals and Proposals*. New York: Pergamon Press, pp. 19–63.

6 Can liberal intervention build liberal democracy?

Mark Peceny and Jeffrey Pickering

George Bush proclaimed that the invasion of Iraq was a war to liberate that country from the tyranny of Saddam Hussein and transform it into a liberal democracy. In less visible efforts, the British sent nearly 1,000 troops to Sierra Leone in 2000 to end that nation's civil war and bring free elections. In late 2002, France sent 4,000 troops to Côte D'Ivoire to broker a ceasefire among warring parties and prepare for free and fair elections. Can soldiers dispatched by such liberal powers help to propel countries on a path toward democracy? Can liberal intervention build liberal democracy?

Most scholars doubt that military intervention can lead to democracy. Many are skeptical because they see the fundamental causes of democracy as internal. Rich, equitable, ethnically homogeneous states that value liberal ideals are more likely to sustain democracy than are poor, inequitable, divided societies with illiberal cultural values. Most targets of military intervention contain numerous domestic impediments to democratization that external intervention will rarely overcome. From this perspective, democracy cannot be implanted in infertile soil. Furthermore, the logic of war fundamentally undermines the prospects for democracy because democracy is most likely to flourish in a peaceful rather than war-torn environment. Still others are doubtful because they see military interventions as guided primarily by the material interests of the intervenor. Since democracy may threaten the control exercised by the intervening power, intervention is often expected to focus more on the creation of stable and friendly governments than on the promotion of democracy.

Although these ideas dominate the debate, they have not gone unchallenged. In fact, some scholars assert that the opposite is true: military intervention can help to promote the democratization of target states. Some democracies may be pushed by militant interpretations of liberal norms to fight wars to liberate oppressed peoples. Even if democracies are not driven by messianic zeal, they may assume that promoting democracy serves their material interests by creating new governments that will be friendly, stable, and co-operative allies. Whether the intervenor is driven to promote democracy by ideals or interests, military interventions can remove tyrants from power, disrupt existing patterns of authoritarian rule, dismantle domestic barriers to democracy, and/or provide incentives for autocratic allies to liberalize their regimes. For adherents of this view, serious efforts by outside powers to promote democracy can succeed, even in relatively barren soil.

This chapter looks at the relationship between military interventions launched by liberal actors and democratization in target countries over a 50-year period. It asks the following questions: Does intervention by liberal states lead to political liberalization? Does it lead to full democracy? And, most importantly, do the answers to the previous questions depend on which liberal actor intervenes? We examine in detail the post-World War II military interventions of the United States, the United Kingdom, and France to see whether military intervention by these liberal great powers has helped to foster some movement toward democracy in target states. We also consider whether intervention by the United Nations has helped to democratize target states.

We argue that military intervention by these liberal actors can create opportunities for the liberalization of authoritarian regimes and at times for full democratization, but that the scope of regime change is often quite limited. In part, the impact of intervention on democracy is limited by the domestic impediments to democracy in target states. Liberal intervenors also face a number of strategic dilemmas that can undermine attempts to democratize target states. One of the most notable dilemmas concerns the fundamental task of placing a friendly and stable regime in power in the target country. If liberalizing reform threatens the stability of allied regimes in client states, liberal states may decide to forego democracy promotion during their military interventions. Indeed, the USA seems to have chosen stability over democratization during a number of its Cold War military interventions.

At the same time, however, liberal decision-makers have frequently concluded that the promotion of democracy in target states can serve the intervenor's material as well as its ideological interests, because liberal states tend to forge peaceful and co-operative relationships with one another. In addition, even when liberal ideals are not a central motivation for intervention, democratically elected leaders often must respond to local constituents and international allies who care about the promotion of liberal values. Therefore, leaders often promote democracy in order to legitimate interventions launched for other reasons to domestic and international audiences. This combination of motivations has led the United States to adopt pro-liberalization policies during military interventions throughout the twentieth century, including a sizable number during the Cold War.

We further argue that grasping the way that liberal intervenors tend to respond to these strategic dilemmas is crucial for understanding the prospects for democratization in target countries. Other things being equal, the probability of democratization should be higher when the intervening power strives to liberalize the target country's political system than when it eschews this objective. We contend that some liberal intervenors have pursued the goal of democratization more consistently and earnestly than others in the post-1945 era. Countries that have been targets of the former set of actors, those that have been more prone to make democracy promotion a centerpiece of their foreign military missions, should stand more chance of experiencing political liberalization than countries that were the targets of the latter group of actors.

We use an updated version of Pearson and Baumann's (1993) International Military Intervention data set for our universe of cases of military intervention. Our dependent variable is drawn from the Polity IV collection. We examine whether targets of liberal intervention moved toward or away from democracy in the wake of liberal interventions. We also look at whether any of these states surpassed a conventional threshold denoting the ascendance to full democracy. Our results largely support our argument. They show that liberal intervention has limited potential to democratize target countries and that it matters which liberal actor intervenes. The targets of hostile US or supportive UN intervention have been more likely to experience political liberalization and democratization than have targets of either type of British or French intervention, though our analysis unexpectedly suggests that even French military intervention may lead to the liberalization of target states.

Liberal intervention and democracy

Building an understanding of how liberal intervention might lead to the liberalization of authoritarian regimes requires a focus on two related issues. First, we must examine why liberal states might decide to promote democracy during their military interventions. Then we need to discuss how international actors might affect local conditions in ways that can facilitate democratization.

Liberal states intervene in other countries' affairs with military force for many reasons. At times, these actors may be driven to promote democracy by missionary zeal to spread the blessings of liberty. Most liberals embrace a norm of humanitarian intervention to stop massive human rights abuses or genocide. Most also accept the legitimacy of counterintervention against those who have attacked liberal states or intervention in support of wars of national liberation (Doyle 1997: 396–402). Mill (1973) argued for the legitimacy of liberal imperialism because he felt that only external force could embed the prerequisites necessary for successful democratization in target countries. These arguments have surely influenced decision-makers in the powerful liberal actors we analyze at different points in time. For example, some assert that the United States is driven by the "American creed" to promote democracy abroad (Huntington

1982; Packenham 1973; Quester 1982). Others suggest that liberal values encouraged the British to promote republican institutions of governance as a central element of their colonial practice (Huntington 1991). These liberal impulses may find an echo in France's "civilizing mission." Over the past decade and a half, the United Nations has explicitly proclaimed its commitment to liberal norms and the promotion of free and fair elections and other liberalizing reforms as part of its peacekeeping operations (Paris 1997; Kumar 1998; Doyle and Sambanis 2000).

The idea that democracy should be spread by force of arms has not gone uncontested in liberal states, however. Prominent strains of liberal thought condemn claims that democracy should be imposed from the outside. The philosophical foundation of Kant's original formulation of liberal internationalism rests on mutual respect for self-determination. The forceful imposition of democracy, therefore, contradicts core principles of liberal philosophy. Furthermore, the liberal impulses of great powers often exhibit tendencies that militate against successful promotion of democracy. Hartz (1955), for example, argues that America's "liberal totalitarianism" pushed it to embrace a virulent anti-communism that led to a variety of illiberal foreign polices. Britain's liberal imperialism was usually coupled with the racism and paternalism of the "white man's burden." France's overseas policy often emphasized the forging of strong, administratively capable governmental institutions in target countries and the spread of French language and culture (Shafer 1988). In general, British and French interventions may be driven by a normative or cultural sense of "family" responsibility to care for their former colonial "children" that has very little to do with the spread of liberalism (Brysk *et al.* 2002). The primacy of liberal ideology and traditions in a state thus does not mean that its decision-makers will attempt to spread democracy when dispatching soldiers overseas. In fact, the opposite may often be the case. History is littered with examples of liberal states pursuing illiberal policies abroad.

They do so in part because states intervene not only to further ideological goals, but also for material and strategic gain. Even decision-makers in countries where liberal ideals are firmly entrenched send troops to foreign lands to enhance their state's power, protect its security, acquire more territory, increase their prosperity, and/or pursue a variety of other material interests. Such material goals may at times be served by the promotion of like-minded regimes in target countries because similar regimes tend to engage in more peaceful and co-operative relationships with one another, whether this involves monarchs supporting other monarchs during the Concert of Europe, Soviet interventions to spread socialism, or democracies expanding the scope of the liberal pacific union (Kramer 1997; Oren and Hayes 1997; Russett and Oneal 2001; Owen 2002). But material interests can also compete with, and supplant, aspirations to restructure government institutions in target states. Much depends on the strategic perceptions that prevail in the intervening state and the broader international context. Democracies like the USA, for example, propped up decidedly undemocratic regimes with military force during the Cold War so long as these states remained in the Western camp. France has used military force to bolster friendly authoritarian regimes in Africa and elsewhere. Bueno de Mesquita *et al.* (2003) even claim that democracies should be especially prone to create puppet governments.

Of course, the fact that liberal policymakers take decisions to intervene abroad for multiple reasons, not all of them commendable, is hardly a revelation. We contend, however, that decision-makers in liberal powers tend to balance the goal of spreading democracy and other foreign policy objectives in fairly consistent ways over time and that these proclivities vary by state. This variation might be explained by liberal traditions that differ in subtle but important ways across countries. It might also be part of a larger phenomenon. Walker (1987) and Shafer (1988) maintain that succeeding generations of state decision-makers tend to absorb mores about their state's historic role in the world, which often influence state policy. Geography may play a foundational role in this process by helping to mold the state's strategic orientation (Thompson 2000) and perhaps even something akin to a collective psychology in the country (Pastor 1999). Whatever the specific cause, decision-makers in certain liberal great powers may tend to place a higher priority on the democratization of target governments when dispatching troops overseas than their counterparts in other liberal powers.

For example, most scholars argue that post-1945 French and British military interventions have often been driven by a realpolitik logic that rarely emphasizes democratization. During much of the post-World War II era, British troops were dispatched to stabilize post-colonial governments and to shore up faltering regimes in areas of British influence, most notably those along the 'east of Suez' network of bases that stretched from the Middle East to Asia (Bartlett 1972; Van Wingen and Tillema 1980; Carver 1992; Pickering 1998). This overseas military role guaranteed access to oil and other strategic resources while it simultaneously buttressed Britain's great power status. When London abandoned this military network in the early 1970s, British military interventions became increasingly rare.

French intervention in Sub-Saharan Africa has reflected similar realpolitk goals. Nearly 80 percent of unilateral French military interventions were in Francophone Africa from 1946 to 1996, and all unilateral French interventions since 1987 have been into this region. At its core, French policy in Africa followed national interest and was designed to maintain or enhance French power (Berdal 1998; Schraeder 1996). Gregory (2000: 436) observes:

> In post-colonial Africa, France found an exclusive sphere of influence ... on which to base its claims of *grandeur* and great power status ...

In Africa France found strategic resources, in particular oil and uranium, and a ready market for French goods ... With Francophone Africa, France was always more than a middle-sized European state.

French intervention thus tended to be designed to "protect French nationals, subdue rebellion (irrespective of its legitimacy), and prop up pro-French rulers, including some of the most despotic and murderous individuals in post-colonial African history" (Gregory 2000: 437). The democratization of target countries was not a priority. The French military's role in Africa did not fully change with the end of the Cold War. The Rwandan genocide of 1994 exposed the motivations of French policy, for during that episode, "France had supported and equipped a corrupt, undemocratic government, had sent troops to defend it from rebellion, and had established safe havens for Hutus – including perpetrators of genocide – to protect 'friends' of France from public scrutiny and accountability" (Utley 2002: 132).

Analysts of US military intervention have revealed numerous examples of precisely these kinds of motivation in US interventions since World War II. The US, however, has also made significant efforts to promote the liberalization of target regimes during a sizable proportion of its twentieth-century military interventions. Meernik (1996), Hermann and Kegley (1998), and Peceny (1999) even find a statistically significant relationship between US military intervention and the democratization of target states over different twentieth-century time periods. This need not imply that US interventions are guided by liberal idealism rather than material interests. Indeed, scholars of the promotion of democracy in US policy have emphasized the security rationale of this policy as a central component of a broad strategy of "national security liberalism" (Smith 1994; Cox *et al.* 2000). Whatever the motivation, the USA has often included democracy promotion in its security policies during military interventions in ways that differ from other liberal states. The UN has also supported democratization during its peacekeeping missions, particularly over the past decade and a half. The UN's commitment to the promotion of democracy and human rights involved not only an expression of liberal ideals but also a security rationale that the promotion of democratic institutions was the most appropriate strategy for bringing peace to societies torn by civil war (Doyle and Sambanis 2000).

The four liberal actors we analyze thus seem to have often had different motives for intervening and different goals for target states. Divergent goals may not, however, always lead to divergent outcomes. A bevy of international and local factors help to shape the prospects for democratization in target states. In a number of post-1945 US military interventions, for example, the pressures associated with the Cold War pushed aspirations to democratize the target regime to the sidelines. Moreover, most of the states that have experienced military interventions since 1945 have been non-democracies (Hermann and Kegley 1996; Tures 2002). They tend to be younger, poorer, more inequitable, more war-prone, more ethnically fragmented, and more culturally illiberal than states which have not experienced military intervention. To the extent that skilled strategic pact-making can forge democracy despite domestic structural impediments (O'Donnell and Schmitter 1986), states which have experienced military intervention are often ones where such domestic pact-making has proven unsuccessful. All these characteristics should make such societies unlikely candidates for democratization regardless of the motivations of the intervenors. This has been a common refrain of the many scholars who have cautioned about the challenges inherent in "exporting democracy" (Lowenthal 1991).

Worse still, the application of military force may itself undermine democratization efforts. Much recent scholarship emphasizes the way external force tends to weaken democracy. Peace is thought to provide the political space necessary for successful democratization (Colaresi and Thompson 2003), while interstate conflict strengthens local militaries and authoritarian elites (Tilly 2003), encourages the abuse of civil liberties, and allows leaders to divert attention from the need for domestic reform (Mansfield and Snyder 1995). If the use of armed force does not make democratization impossible, liberal intervenors may flinch when the full implications of their democratizing missions become apparent. In cases where the intervening power suspects that free and fair elections are likely to lead to the selection of candidates antagonistic to their interests, they may forgo elections altogether. Alternatively, they may try to manipulate the electoral process in ways designed to empower their preferred candidates or to limit the powers of the institutions inhabited by hostile elected officials (Carothers 2003). True, lasting democracy is not likely to emerge in this context.

These daunting barriers to democratization should not, however, lead us to conclude that liberal intervenors with democratizing missions will tend to fail. The positive relationship between US intervention and the political liberalization of target states found in previous studies not only suggests that the obstacles to democratization can be overcome, but that external military force may help to overcome them (Meernik 1996; Hermann and Kegley 1998; Peceny 1999). The most obvious way external intervenors can further the democratization process is to oust an authoritarian ruler who would have been otherwise difficult to remove. If this effort evolves into a full-blown war, loss in war has been demonstrated to increase the likelihood of regime change (Stein and Russett 1980; Bueno de Mesquita *et al.* 2003). Of course, this is the image that first springs to mind when one considers the possibility of forging democracy at gunpoint, but there are other ways external force can prove important. It has been shown, for example, that revolutionary counterelites in civil war settings can force democratization if they fight authoritarian regimes to a stalemate

(Wood 2000; Call 2002). Foreign soldiers can help them to do so. Even when liberal states intervene to bolster authoritarian actors, they may use a range of positive inducements to encourage liberal reforms in the target country (Ikenberry and Kupchan 1990; Carothers 2003). Liberal intervention thus has the potential to break down authoritarian rule either through force of arms or more subtle suasion and socialization.

This potential is only likely to be met if democratization is a priority for decision-makers in the intervening state. If it is not, the domestic barriers to liberalization will often prove insurmountable. Thus, in this chapter, we determine if the different ideological traditions of the liberal powers are important when they send their troops to foreign lands. We anticipate starkly different governing structures to emerge in the wake of foreign military interventions by the USA and UN, on the one hand, and the British and French, on the other. Given the different causal paths implied by the military overthrow of authoritarian regimes and the socialization of authoritarian allies, we also examine the potentially divergent impacts of hostile and supportive interventions.

Measuring democracy and military intervention

We use the Polity data set to measure democracy. This data set codes each polity along nine dimensions, five of which are used to construct a composite score of the democratic characteristics of political regimes. The first two elements characterize the competitiveness and openness of executive recruitment. A third codes the political constraints imposed on the executive. The final components measure the regulation and competitiveness of participation. Polity classifies states as institutionalized democracies on an 11-point scale if the executive is chosen in open elections, is subordinated to or constrained by an elected legislature, and political participation is competitive. It classifies states as institutionalized autocracies on a different 11-point scale if an executive possessing unlimited decision-making authority is selected in a closed process and political participation is restricted and/or suppressed. Specifically, we use the *polity* variable in Polity IV, which subtracts Polity's autocracy scores from its democracy scores to produce a single scale ranging from -10 to 10, to measure democracy (Jaggers and Marshall 2004).

For Tables 6.1–6.4, we code cases based on the *polity* score of each target of intervention in the year before the intervention $(t-1)$ and three years after the intervention $(t+3)$. In cases of interruptions (-66 in *polity*), interregnums (-77), or transitions (-88), we generally use the first available score in either the pre- or post-intervention period. Each table categorizes cases based on whether their *polity* decreased by at least one point, stayed the same, or increased by at least one point from year $t-1$ to year $t+3$. Of course, states can move up the *polity* scale without ever becoming full democracies. Many cases listed in the tables involve clearly autocratic regimes becoming only slightly less autocratic in the wake of an intervention. We, therefore, also examine whether countries exceeded a score of six on the *polity* scale, a common threshold used to distinguish non-democracies from democracies. States that can be considered democracies by this criterion in either the pre- or post-intervention period are listed in **bold** in the tables.

One must be cautious when using Polity measures as dependent variables. Polity assembles evaluations about actors' distinct institutional characteristics into a single scale. As Munck and Verkuilen (2002: 23) observe, it thus forces "a multidimensional phenomenon into a common metric." Relevant information such as political and cultural context can be lost in the process of aggregation. For that reason, different countries' movement up or down the scale cannot be interpreted as equivalent processes and Polity IV cannot be considered a perfect continuum (Gleditsch and Ward 1997). A country scoring an eight on the scale may not be more democratic than one with a seven. They may merely be different types of democracies with distinct institutional characteristics. Keeping in mind Polity IV's limitations, our dependent variables nonetheless provide a rough sense of movement from more autocratic to more liberal political structures. Each increment of change in political liberalization may not be equal, but states that move nearer the high end of the *polity* index generally possess political institutions of a more democratic hue than those nearer the low end. Similarly, each episode when states cross the threshold to full democracy will not be the same, but all of the affected states have nonetheless met broadly accepted standards for democratic governance.

Foreign military intervention is operationalized with Pearson and Baumann's (1993) International Military Intervention (IMI) data set. The original IMI collection spanned the years 1946 to 1988, but has recently been updated to 1996 (Pickering 2002). The collection records all verifiable instances when "troops or forces ... move into the territory ... of another country" to pursue political, economic or strategic objectives (Pearson and Baumann 1993: 1). IMI includes military missions ranging from the evacuation of nationals stranded in war-torn countries to operations to lend support to friendly, yet faltering, foreign governments and from brief border clashes to long, draining military occupations. In the IMI conceptualization, the single most important characteristic of a foreign military intervention is political authorization at the national level. Foreign military intervention is considered first and foremost to be a policy tool, which is the result of a policy decision by national leaders. Consequently, troops involved in training missions and military advisors are excluded from the database. Their missions do not involve the direct application of military force to influence the course of events in another country. If, however, national decision-makers order soldiers engaged in exercises or military advisers to rescue nationals overseas or to become actively involved in combat, these troops are considered participants in a foreign military intervention. Soldiers concentrated in foreign bases, in transit, on leave, or transporting materials are omitted from the IMI dataset for similar reasons. While the IMI includes episodes when national air forces penetrated the air space of another country or when naval forces entered the territorial waters of another state, conventional wisdom suggests that "boots on the ground" may be essential to subdue non-democratic forces and to provide the incentives and the consistent pressure needed to instill democracy in target societies (Hermann and Kegley 1998). We, therefore, exclude the air and naval interventions in the Pearson and Baumann data set from our analyses. If a country experiences political liberalization or democratizes in the wake of a foreign military intervention coded in IMI, it is likely the result of conscious policy decisions by national leaders that dispatched ground troops for this purpose.

IMI is useful for our analysis because it is the only data collection on military interventions that distinguishes between hostile and supportive interventions and, therefore, allows us to examine the different causal relationships between intervention and democracy that emerge in these two very different contexts. A six-category variable in IMI labeled "direction of the intervention" is used to distinguish supportive and hostile military interventions. If the intervention neither directly supports nor opposes the target government, the original six-part variable is coded "0." It is coded "1" if the intervention is intended to support the target government; "2" if it opposes rebels or opposition groups; "3" if it is intended to oppose the target government; "4" if it supports rebel or opposition groups; "5" if it supports or opposes a third party government; and "6" if it supports or opposes rebel groups in a sanctuary. We dichotomize the original IMI direction variable for this study. Scores of "3" or "4" on the original variable are considered hostile to the target government, while all remaining outcomes on the original direction variable are considered supportive of or neutral toward the target government. We refer to the latter as supportive interventions and examine them separately from hostile interventions in our analyses. Hostile interventions are distinguished from supportive interventions in the tables by being listed in *italics*. Our final inventory of interventions includes 153 supportive interventions and 80 hostile interventions from 1946 to 1996.

Intervention and democracy

Can liberal intervention build liberal democracy? Our examination of the record of the post-World War II era finds evidence that liberal intervention is positively related to both political liberalization and the democratization of target regimes, but that it matters which liberal actor has intervened and whether that intervention was supportive or hostile. Among the liberal states, US intervention has most often led to the democratization of target regimes, though this is most true of the targets of hostile US interventions. The British have the worst record, with interventions undertaken by the UK often leading to movement away from democracy. French military intervention has been associated with the liberalization of target regimes, but almost never to their full democratization. The United Nations has the best record among all the actors surveyed here, with UN supportive interventions often leading to the liberalization and/or democratization of target regimes.

Table 6.1 reviews the evidence for US military interventions. Almost twice as many targets of US intervention liberalized in the wake of US intervention than moved in the opposite direction. This result is driven mostly by the cases of hostile intervention. US policies probably played an important role in the liberalization of allied regimes in El Salvador and Honduras during the 1980s, but there are as many cases of movement away from democracy as toward democracy among targets of supportive US military interventions. In contrast, hostile US interventions have led both to political liberalization and to the installation of regimes that earned at least a 6 on the *polity* scale three years after the US intervened. Even these seemingly strong results should be interpreted with caution. Three cases in the Caribbean Basin help account for these findings. In 1961, the United States participated covertly in the assassination of Rafael

Table 6.1 US military interventions and political liberalization

Negative change	No change	Positive change
South Korea 1950	Liberia 1947	*Cuba 1959*
Laos 1961	*North Korea 1950*	***Dominican Republic 1961***
Dominican Republic 1965	Philippines 1951	Cambodia 1969
Cambodia 1975	Lebanon 1958	*Iran 1980*
Thailand 1975	South Vietnam 1961	**El Salvador 1983**
Guyana 1978	Thailand 1962	**Honduras 1988**
	Cambodia 1964	***Panama 1988***
	Laos 1965	***Panama 1989***
	South Vietnam 1965	***Haiti 1994***
	Lebanon 1982	Tanzania 1994
	Italy 1985	Rwanda 1994
	Philippines 1989	
	Liberia 1990	
	Iraq 1991	
	Kuwait 1993	
	Dem. Rep. of Congo 1994	
	Central African Rep. 1996	
	Kuwait 1996	
	Rwanda 1996	
6	19	11

Notes
Names in bold reached a polity score of 6 or above.
Names in italics were the targets of hostile interventions.

Trujillo in the Dominican Republic and then overtly intervened to ensure that members of his family would not succeed him. This made possible the liberalization of the Dominican regime and the brief democratic interlude under the presidency of Juan Bosch. The United States subsequently accepted Bosch's overthrow in a military coup and then actively intervened in 1965 in opposition to a military rebellion that had proclaimed the restoration of Bosch as its central goal. Thus, the impact of US intervention on Dominican democracy was decidedly ambiguous.

The US efforts to forge democracy at gunpoint in Panama in 1989 and Haiti in 1994 are somewhat more straightforward than the Dominican case. In Panama, the USA overthrew the military dictatorship of Manuel Noriega and placed Guillermo Endara, the rightful winner of the 1989 presidential elections in Panama, in office. The transition to democracy in Panama was a direct result of US intervention. Panama has sustained democratic rule since 1989, including the election of two presidents from Noriega's former party. In 1994, the USA reinstalled President Jean-Bertrand Aristide in office three years after he had been removed from office in a military coup. While Haitian democracy lasted the three-year period we use as a cutoff in our analyses, democratic rule crumbled soon afterward. Two additional cases of liberalization after a US military intervention reflect "successes" that most US policymakers would not embrace. Polity IV gives both Fidel Castro's Cuba and Ayatollah Khomeini's Iran better *polity* scores than the US-backed regimes of Fulgencio Batista and the Shah that they replaced.

In contrast to the US record, Table 6.2 shows that only one target of

Table 6.2 British military interventions and political liberalization

Negative change	No change	Positive change
Oman 1957	Netherlands 1946	Jordan 1948
Cyprus 1963	Iraq 1946	
North Yemen 1963	Oman 1952	
Congo 1964	*North Yemen 1954*	
Uganda 1964	*Egypt 1956*	
Kenya 1964	Libya 1958	
Zambia 1965	Jordan 1958	
North Yemen 1966	*North Yemen 1958*	
Kenya 1982	Tanzania 1964	
	Oman 1966	
	Mauritius 1968	
	Lebanon 1982	
	Ireland 1985	
	Iraq 1991	
9	14	1

Notes
Names in bold reached a polity score of 6 or above.
Names in italics were targets of hostile interventions.

British military intervention, Jordan in 1948, had experienced significant liberalization within three years of the intervention. Nine countries became more autocratic in the wake of British intervention. For some cases, like Oman in 1957, British intervention clearly contributed to the strengthening of autocratic rulers. In other cases, like North Yemen, autocratization flowed from British weakness. British military ventures outside of their base in Aden in 1966 were in response to challenges from a rebel group that eventually controlled the federal government. Britain failed to prevent a victory by these forces and instead withdrew from Yemen, leaving a government more autocratic than the one that preceded it. The British were thus attempting to thwart further autocratization, but failed. Through these very different paths, the United Kingdom systematically managed to leave target states more autocratic in the wake of their interventions.

The results for French intervention are perhaps the most surprising of our findings. Table 6.3 shows that nine targets experienced some liberalization in the aftermath of French interventions, while only two moved in the opposite direction. This finding appears to stand in stark contrast to the secondary literature on post-1945 French military activity overseas, particularly in sub-Saharan Africa. This finding, however, should be interpreted with some

Table 6.3 French military interventions and political liberalization

Negative change	No change	Positive change
Syria 1946	*Egypt 1956*	*Morocco 1956*
Congo Brazzaville 1963	Spain 1958	*Comoros 1989*
	Cameroon 1960	Gabon 1990
	Tunisia 1961	Chad 1990
	Gabon 1964	Rwanda 1990
	Central African Rep. 1967	**Benin 1991**
	Chad 1968	Chad 1991
	Zaire 1978	Djibouti 1992
	Chad 1978	Rwanda 1993
	Central African Rep. 1979	
	Lebanon 1982	
	Chad 1983	
	Chad 1986	
	Zaire 1991	
	Iraq 1991	
	Zaire 1993	
	Dem. Rep. of Congo 1994	
	Rwanda 1994	
	Cameroon 1994	
	Comoros 1995	
	Central African Rep. 1996	
2	21	9

Notes
Names in bold reached a polity score of 6 or above.
Names in italics were targets of hostile interventions.

caution. Only one country that experienced a supportive French military intervention made a transition to democracy, Benin in 1991. Only one other case of political liberalization in the wake of French intervention involved a significant movement to a positive *polity* score, when the French military ousted a French mercenary, Bob Denard, who had taken control of the government of the Comoros in a 1989 coup. The country's first democratic elections were held shortly thereafter. All the other cases of political liberalization involved the marginal liberalization of undemocratic target governments supported by France. Nevertheless, the French intervention in Comoros was crucial for the subsequent liberalization of that country's polity and the importance of the partial liberalization of France's autocratic allies in the region should not be fully discounted. It is difficult to conclude that troops dispatched from Paris tended to be a positive influence on democratization over the entire 1946–1996 period, but the interventions in Benin and Comoros suggest that this record may have begun to change in recent years.

Table 6.4 demonstrates that the UN has the strongest record of any of

Table 6.4 UN military interventions and political liberalization

Negative change	No change	Positive change
Indonesia 1947	Lebanon 1948	Jordan 1948
Greece 1948	Egypt 1948	Pakistan 1949
Syria 1948	Israel 1948	**Cyprus 1964**
South Korea 1950	India 1950	Egypt 1973
North Yemen 1963	*North Korea 1950*	**Cyprus 1974**
Afghanistan 1988	Egypt 1956	**Pakistan 1988**
Croatia 1992	Lebanon 1958	**Honduras 1989**
Yugoslavia 1992	Congo 1960	**El Salvador 1989**
	Netherlands 1962	**Namibia 1990**
	India 1965	**El Salvador 1991**
	Pakistan 1965	Morocco 1991
	Israel 1973	Kuwait 1991
	Saudi Arabia 1973	Cambodia 1991
	Syria 1974	**Mozambique 1992**
	Lebanon 1978	**Haiti 1993**
	Iran 1988	Georgia 1993
	Iraq 1988	Liberia 1993
	Guatemala 1989	Uganda 1993
	Costa Rica 1989	Rwanda 1993
	Angola 1989	Chad 1994
	Nicaragua 1991	Tajikistan 1994
	Iraq 1991	**Croatia 1996**
	Somalia 1992	
	Libya 1994	
	Bosnia 1995	
8	25	22

Notes
Names in bold reached a polity score of 6 or above.
Names in italics were targets of hostile interventions.

intervenors discussed here. The UN generally claims that the primary purpose of its military interventions is to pursue conflict resolution, usually at the request of both parties engaged in civil war. This divergence from the practice of intervention by liberal great powers may explain why the UN is the only actor whose supportive interventions have led to greater political liberalization as well as democratization in target countries. Approximately 40 percent of all targets of UN intervention liberalized in the context of UN interventions. Eight countries achieved *polity* scores of six or above, qualifying as full democracies for the purposes of this analysis. Only one of these eight cases of democratization appears to be unrelated to the UN intervention. While the UN did dispatch troops to Pakistan in 1988, the year parliamentary democracy was restored to that country, their presence had little to do with that restoration. Two small outposts of UN peacekeepers were established on Pakistan's western border to monitor cross-border activities with Afghanistan while Soviet troops withdrew from that country. In seven other cases, however, the UN played a constructive role in the crafting of nascent democracies: Cyprus, Honduras, El Salvador, Namibia, Haiti, Mozambique, and Croatia. Only Honduras crossed the threshold to full democracy the same year that UN troops arrived, while the others crossed this watershed at some point in the three years following the intervention. These countries remained democratic through 1996 (and all but Haiti remained democratic through 2003, the last year coded in Polity).

Conclusion

It matters which liberal actor intervenes in a target state. Military missions authorized by either decision-makers in Washington, DC, or the UN Security Council stand a greater chance of democratizing target governments than missions initiated by Paris or London. That said, Washington and the UN Security Council take starkly different paths to reach similar outcomes in target states. While supportive UN intervention tends to help democratize governments, Washington achieves similar results only when US troops are dispatched in opposition to the target regime. US interventions launched in support of target governments have no strong relationship with either liberalization or democratization. Indeed, none of the liberal great powers examined in this study exhibited a strong record of liberalization or democratization in target states in the wake of their interventions in support of governments. Moreover, in contrast to the image portrayed in much of the secondary literature, British rather than French military interventions were most prone to autocratize target governments. The French could even claim credit for the political liberalization of regimes in some of the states in which they intervened.

Our analyses suggest that when liberal great powers are faced with the dilemma of whether to impose democratic change on friendly regimes, they are usually reluctant to impose democracy on friendly tyrants. Decision-makers in liberal interveners may have to choose between democracy, on the one hand, and target state stability and fealty on the other. Since the initial stages of democratization are not commonly associated with political tranquility or predictability, liberal decision-makers appear to often choose to forgo political liberalization in lands that are strategically or economically vital. In contrast, the UN, with its mandate to pursue conflict resolution and post-conflict political, social, and economic reconstruction, is the only actor examined here with a record of success for its democracy promotion efforts in the wake of supportive interventions. In an era when the UN is often criticized for its ineffectiveness, our results suggest that it has succeeded in nurturing democracy in some countries emerging from devastating civil conflicts.

Where the USA stands in contrast to the British, and to a lesser extent the French, is in its efforts to forge democracy at gunpoint in the wake of some of its hostile military interventions. As our analysis suggests, the empirical foundations of this finding represent a thin reed on which to make strong generalizations. Nevertheless, the United States has at times decided that the promotion of democracy is the most appropriate way to serve its ideological goals and material interests and to legitimate its hostile military interventions to international and domestic audiences. In at least some cases, this has led to the democratization of target states. Taken together, the fact that the USA and UN have successfully helped to democratize at least half a dozen countries suggests that even if it is not the most common path to liberalization and democratization, external military force cannot be ignored as part of the explanation for the transitions to democracy that have swept the globe during the third wave of democracy.

References

Bartlett, C.J. (1972) *The Long Retreat: A Short History of British Defense Policy, 1945–1970.* New York: St Martin's Press.

Berdal, M. (1998) "Peacekeeping in Africa: The Role of the United States, France, and Britain," in O. Furley and R. May (eds.) *Peacekeeping in Africa.* Brookfield, VT: Ashgate.

Brysk, A., Parsons, C., and Sandholtz, W. (2002) "After Empire: National Identity and Post-Colonial Families of Nations," *European Journal of International Relations* 8: 267–305.

Bueno de Mesquita, B.M., Morrow J.D., Smith, A., and Siverson, R.M. (2003) *The Logic of Political Survival.* Cambridge, MA: MIT Press.

Call, C. (2002) "War Transitions and the New Civilian Security in Latin America," *Comparative Politics* 35: 1–20.

Carothers, T. (2003) "Promoting Democracy and Fighting Terror," *Foreign Affairs* 82: 84–97.

Carver, M. (1992) *Tightrope Walking: British Defense Policy since 1945.* London: Hutchinson.

Colaresi, M. and Thompson, W.R. (2003) "The Economic Development-Democratization Relationship: Does the Outside World Matter?," *Comparative Political Studies* 36(4): 381–403.

Cox, M., Ikenberry, G.J., and Inoguchi, T. (eds.) (2000) *American Democracy Promotion: Impulses, Strategies, and Impacts.* New York: Oxford University Press.

Doyle, M. (1997) *Ways of War and Peace.* New York: W. W. Norton.

Doyle, M. and Sambanis, N. (2000) "International Peacebuilding: A Theoretical and Quantitative Analysis," *American Political Science Review* 94: 779–803.

Fukuyama, F. (1994) "Comments on Nationalism and Democracy," in L. Diamond and M.F. Plattner (eds.) *Nationalism, Ethnic Conflict, and Democracy.* Baltimore, MD: The Johns Hopkins University Press, pp. 23–28.

Gleditsch, K.S. and Ward, M.D. (1997) "Double-Take: A Re-Examination of Democracy and Autocracy in Modern Polities," *Journal of Conflict Resolution* 41: 361–383.

Gregory, S. (2000) "The French Military in Africa: Past and Present," *African Affairs* 99: 435–448.

Hartz, L. (1955) *The Liberal Tradition in America: An Interpretation of American Political Thought since the Revolution.* New York: Harcourt, Brace, Jovanovich.

Hermann, M.G. and Kegley, C.W. Jr. (1996) "Ballots, A Barrier Against the Use of Bullets and Bombs: Democratization and Military Intervention," *Journal of Conflict Resolution* 40: 436–460.

Hermann, M.G. and Kegley, C.W. Jr. (1998) "The US Use of Military Intervention to Promote Democracy: Evaluating the Record," *International Interactions* 24: 91–114.

Horowitz, D.L. (1994) "Democracy in Divided Societies," in L. Diamond and M.F. Plattner (eds.) Nationalism, Ethnic Conflict, and Democracy. Baltimore, MD: The Johns Hopkins University Press, pp. 35–55.

Huntington, S. (1982) "American Ideals vs. American Institutions," *Political Science Quarterly* 97: 1–37.

Huntington, S. (1991) *The Third Wave.* Norman, OK: University of Oklahoma Press.

Ikenberry, G.J. and Kupchan, C. (1990) "Socialization and Hegemonic Power," *International Organization* 44: 283–315.

Jaggers, K. and Marshall, M. (2004) "Polity IV Project," http://www.cidcm.umd.edu/inscr/polity.

Kegley, C.W. Jr. and Hermann, M.G. (1997a) "Putting Military Intervention into the Democratic Peace: A Research Note," *Comparative Political Studies* 30: 78–107.

Kegley, C.W. Jr. and Hermann, M.G. (1997b) "A Peace Dividend? Democracies' Military Interventions and their External Political Consequences," *Cooperation and Conflict* 32: 339–368.

Kramer, M. (1997) "The Prague Spring and the Soviet Invasion of Czechoslovakia: New Interpretations," Cold War International History Project Working Paper Series. Woodrow Wilson Center for International Scholars. http://cwihp.si.edu/publications.htm.

Kumar, K. (ed.) (1998) *Postconflict Elections, Democratization and International Assistance.* Boulder, CO: Lynne Rienner.

Lowenthal, A. (ed.) (1991) *Exporting Democracy.* Baltimore, MD: Johns Hopkins University Press.

Mansfield, E. and Snyder, J. (1995) "Democratization and the Danger of War," *International Security* 20: 5–38.

Meernik, J. (1996) "United States Military Intervention and the Promotion of Democracy," *Journal of Peace Research* 33: 391–402.

Mill, J.S. (1973) "A Few Words on Nonintervention," in G. Himmelfarb (ed.) *Essays on Politics and Culture*. Gloucester: Peter Smith, pp. 368–384.

Munck, G.L. and Verkuilen, J. (2002) "Conceptualizing and Measuring Democracy: Evaluation Alternative Indices," *Comparative Political Studies* 35: 5–34.

O'Donnell, G. and Schmitter, P. (1986) *Transitions from Authoritarian Rule:* vol. 4: *Tentative Conclusions about Uncertain Democracies*. Baltimore, MD: Johns Hopkins University Press.

Oren, I. and Hayes, J. (1997) "Democracies May Rarely Fight One Another, but Developed Socialist States Rarely Fight At All," *Alternatives* 22: 493–521.

Owen, J.M. IV (2002) "The Foreign Imposition of Domestic Institutions," *International Organization* 56: 375–410.

Packenham, R. (1973) *Liberal America in the Third World: Political Development Ideas in Foreign Aid and Social Science*. Princeton, NJ: Princeton University Press.

Paris, R. (1997) "Peacebuilding and the Limits of Liberal Internationalism," *International Security* 22: 54–89.

Pastor, R.A. (ed.) (1999) *A Century's Journey: How the Great Powers Shape the World*. New York: Basic Books.

Pearson, F.S. and Baumann, R.A. (1993) "International Military Intervention, 1946–1988," Inter-University Consortium for Political and Social Research, Data Collection 6035, University of Michigan.

Peceny, M. (1999) *Democracy at the Point of Bayonets*. University Park, PA: Pennsylvania State University Press.

Pickering, J. (1998) *Britain's Withdrawal from East of Suez: The Politics of Retrenchment*. Houndmills: Macmillan.

Pickering, J. (2002) "War Weariness and Cumulative Effects: Victors, Vanquished, and Subsequent Interstate Intervention," *Journal of Peace Research* 39: 313–337.

Pickering, J. and Thompson, W.R. (1998) "Stability in a Fragmenting World: Interstate Military Force, 1946–1988," *Political Research Quarterly* 51: 241–263.

Quester, G. (1982) *American Foreign Policy: The Lost Consensus*. New York: Praeger.

Rasler, K. and Thompson, W.R. (1999) "Predatory Initiators and Changing Landscapes for Warfare," *Journal of Conflict Resolution* 43: 411–433.

Reiter, D. (2001) "Does Peace Nurture Democracy?" *Journal of Politics* 63: 935–948.

Robinson, W. (1996) *Promoting Polyarchy: Globalization, U.S. Intervention, and Hegemony*. New York: Cambridge University Press.

Russett, B. and Oneal, J. (2001) *Triangulating Peace: Democracy, Interdependence, and International Organizations*. New York: W. W. Norton.

Schraeder, P. (1996) "Removing the Shackles? U.S. Foreign Policy Toward Africa after the End of the Cold War," in E.J. Keller and D. Rothschild (eds.) *Africa in the New International Order*. Boulder, CO: Lynne Rienner.

Shafer, D.M. (1988) *Deadly Paradigms*. Princeton, NJ: Princeton University Press.

Smith, T. (1994) *America's Mission: The United States and the Worldwide Struggle for Democracy in the Twentieth Century.* Princeton, NJ: Princeton University Press.

Snyder, J. (2000) *From Voting to Violence: Democratization and Nationalist Conflict.* New York: W. W. Norton.

Stanley, W. (1996) *The Protection Racket State.* Philadelphia, PA: Temple University Press.

Stein, A.A. and Russett, B.M. (1980) "Evaluating War: Outcomes and Consequences," in T.R. Gurr (ed.) *Handbook of Conflict Theory and Research.* New York: Free Press.

Thompson, W.R. (2000) *The Emergence of the Global Political Economy.* London: Routledge.

Tillema, H.K. (1994) "Cold War Alliance and Overt Military Intervention, 1945–1991," *International Interactions* 20: 249–278.

Tilly, C. (2003) *The Politics of Collective Violence.* New York: Cambridge University Press.

Tures, J.A. (2002) "The Dearth of Jointly Democratic Interventions," *International Studies Quarterly* 46: 579–589.

Utley, R. (2002) "'Not to do less but to do better ...': French Military Policy in Africa," *International Affairs* 78: 129–146.

Van Wingen, J. and Tillema, H.K. (1980) "British Military Intervention after World War II: Militance in a Second-Rank Power," *Journal of Peace Research* 17: 291–303.

Walker, S.G. (ed.) (1987) *Role Theory and Foreign Policy Analysis.* Durham, NC: Duke University Press.

Wood, E. (2000) *Forging Democracy from Below.* New York: Cambridge University Press.

7 Just the good, no bad and ugly?

The regional impact of externally imposed democracy

Andrew J. Enterline and J. Michael Greig

The chapters in this volume focus principally on the peacemaking process following a conflict, principally those conflicts that occur within states. Often, central to this peacemaking process is a change in the political system governing a post-conflict society. Historically, these changes in the political institutions in states afflicted with conflict are instigated or shepherded by third party actors, such as the United Nations, the major power states, or states neighboring the state experiencing the internal conflict. During, but principally following, the Cold War, the democratization of former autocratic states was argued to be an important component of a general strategy to prevent the recurrence of intrastate conflicts, as well as cultivating political systems that would have beneficial regional effects.

Recently, the claim that externally cultivated democratic institutions translate into positive regional benefits has been elaborated to suggest that this democratization promises rewards for the geographic regions into which democratic polities are introduced, such as greater peace, prosperity, and democracy. Furthermore, these regional outcomes are argued to be causally entwined and reinforcing, such that democracy increases peace, and peace and democracy provide the basis for stable and prosperous economic markets central to prosperity, and prosperity reinforces the desirability and effectiveness of democratic forms of governance, and so on. In light of developments in contemporary international relations, specifically the international occupations and democratization of Afghanistan and Iraq in 2002 and 2003, respectively, the regional implications of democratic institutions cultivated by third party states and international organizations is an important, yet rarely studied, aspect of models of conflict resolution and peacemaking. We discuss our scientific inquiry into the veracity of this claim regarding the link between externally imposed democracy and the regional outcomes of peace, democracy, and prosperity in the remainder of this chapter.

Imposed democracy and regional peace, democracy and prosperity

In February 2003, American policymakers sought to place a possible war against Iraq in a broader, and more importantly, regional policy context.

This important shift in policy was generally interpreted in the media as a strategy by American policymakers to garner greater support from European and Middle Eastern allies for the use of military force against Iraq (Bumiller 2003). In formulating a broader policy, one that we refer to hereafter as the *regional-level* argument, American, and later British, policymakers sought to link war with Iraq, and implicity, military victory, and the eventual democratization of Iraq with a broad recipe for conflict resolution in the Middle East region, including greater interstate and intrastate peace, democracy, and economic prosperity.[1]

As stated publicly, policymakers sought first and foremost to reduce the interstate security threat posed by Hussein's Iraq and the destabilizing effect that policymakers argued this authoritarian regime had on other conflicts in the Middle East. Policymakers reasoned that the cultivation of a democratic regime in Iraq would address this problem, in part, because democratic polities, policymakers assumed, are more likely to exhibit peaceful foreign polities. Moreover, democratic polities are more likely to resolve disputes with other states through negotiation and compromise rather than resort to military force. This positive relationship between democracy and pacific foreign policy is fortified by several auxiliary assumptions implicit in contemporary policy statements and we discuss each in turn.

First, democratic polities are assumed to be less likely to support terrorist organizations, or pursue destabilizing policies in neighboring states, thereby providing a foundation for stable regional relations. Second, democratic polities reflect more inclusive political arenas in which ethnic, religious, and political differences between groups are moderated by inclusive, representative political institutions that preclude the need for groups to ground political mobilization in cultural identity. As a result, democratic states are less likely to experience domestic political instability, instability that is linked to interstate friction and militarized conflict. Finally, the very process of imposing democracy has important implications for regional politics. Specifically, democratizing authoritarian regimes through military force signals to non-democratic states, as well as to non-state actors supported by non-democratic states, that further pursuit of destabilizing regional policies might result in forceful responses by the international community, including further democratization of states through war.

Current scholarly research tends to substantiate the plausibility of the first assumption as it pertains to the regional-level argument. For example, Gleditsch and Hegre (1997) report evidence of a global system threshold at which point system democracy eventually begins to exert a negative effect on militarized conflict at the level of the interstate system. Crescenzi and Enterline (1999) confirm this finding, but conclude that there is considerable regional heterogeneity in the parabolic relationship between system democracy and war. Similarly, McLaughlin, Gates and Hegre

(1999) conclude that while an increase in system democracy eventually corresponds to a decrease in system war, a fully parabolic relationship fails to materialize. Ray (2000) argues that the level of conflict in the global system is, in part, a function of how the shrinking population of non-democratic states responds to an increasingly democratic system, one that very well might be construed by non-democratic polities as threatening, thereby increasing the likelihood of militarized conflict.

The second dimension of the regional-level argument links the presence of an imposed democracy with further regional democratization. This relationship is grounded in the demonstrative properties of imposed democratic polities that flow out of the assumption that the more proximate a democratic polity, the greater the likelihood that liberal democratic ideals will become an issue of intellectual and public debate in neighboring non-democratic states. In turn, this public debate is anticipated to increase the pressure on non-democratic regimes to liberalize. Additionally, the presence of a liberal democracy in a region demonstrates the viability of democratic institutions in regions that are not traditionally democratic, thereby overcoming historical impediments to democratization such as colonial legacies and non-democratic regimes installed during the Cold War.

Finally, the regional-level argument assumes that individuals in all societies possess aspirations, if latent, for the liberties and institutions associated with liberal democracy. As a result, all societies can liberalize, even if the end product of this liberalization process varies significantly in form from the democratic institutions in the West European and North American states. As a result, the presence of an imposed democracy can act as a catalyst for further democratization in regions resistant to liberalization during previous waves, or surges, of democratization in the modern state system.

Again, current research suggests tangential support for the demonstration properties of imposed democracies. For example, in his well-known study, Huntington (1991) concludes that "snowballing" of national political systems occurs regionally. Similarly, Starr (1991, 1995) finds evidence of positive spatial dependence between democratic transitions, such that democratization can diffuse across, or spill over, national borders. More recently, Starr and Lindborg (2003) find further evidence that democratic and autocratic changes increase the likelihood of similar changes in neighboring states (i.e., democratization leads to further democratization, and autocratization leads to further autocratization), a finding that squares with the analysis of the domestic and international causes of democratization reported in Colaresi and Thompson (2003).

Other research emphasizes that state-system characteristics influence the probability of further democratization. The argument that imposed democracy promotes regional democracy is consistent with the conception of diffusion as emulation described by Siverson and Starr (1991). Thompson (1996) suggests that the emergence of "zones of peace" regionally can spur democratization. Pevehouse (2002) finds that state membership in democratic international organizations increases the odds that member states will democratize. Gleditsch (2002) finds strong evidence of spatial clustering among democracies within the international system. Kadera, Crescenzi and Shannon (2003) conclude that the greater the democratic community's power in a state-system, the more likely democratic polities are to persist, findings that square with the earlier work of Modelski and Perry (1991). Finally, Cederman and Gleditsch (2004), drawing upon the innovations in Gleditsch (2002), conclude that as the frequency of democracies within a geographic region increases, the more likely non-democratic states in the region are to democratize.

In general, current research provides indirect, if consistent, support for the contemporary regional-level policy claim that imposed democratic polities provide a demonstration of liberal political ideals and institutions, a process that encourages further regional democratization. Indeed, this body of research, coupled with the oft-cited cases of West Germany and Japan following World War II, provides relatively strong evidence that the forceful democratization of authoritarian regimes can stimulate further regional political liberalization. However, aside from this tangential evidence reflected in the scholarly literature, as well as the anecdotal cases of post-WWII Germany and Japan, no direct test of relationship exists in the current literature.

Closely related to the theory linking imposed democracy with further regional democratization is the causal logic underlying the relationship between imposed democracy and regional prosperity. This causal linkage is achieved because the process of demonstration is one of liberal ideas and behavior in general, rather than solely the demonstration of democratic political institutions. Indeed, the political and economic dimensions of liberal thought, particularly the emphasis on individual agency, are mutually reinforcing. Therefore, in several ways, the regional impact of an imposed democratic, market-oriented state is a function of a causal logic that is similar to the logic identified in the discussion of regional democratization, wherein an imposed democracy demonstrates liberal ideas and debate as well as the general viability of liberal political institutions to citizens in non-democratic states.

In addition to the causal processes flowing from demonstration by imposed democracies, the economic dimension of the regional impact of imposed democracy is also anchored to the diffusion processes associated with economic interactions. The presence of a liberal, market economy in a region will, much like its impact on political thinking, demonstrate the viability and benefits of this economy to countries with non-market economies. Additionally, the presence of a market-oriented economy in a region functions as a foil for the economic stagnation that is often associated with centralized, nondemocratic economies. Much as the citizens of East European countries were subject during the Cold War to media reflecting the superior economic performance in the Western European democracies, the presence of a prosperous market economy in a region demonstrates the potential for greater economic prosperity to citizens in states with poor, centrally controlled economies. In turn, this positive economic foil encourages citizens of states in non-market economies to pressure their governments for greater economic liberalization. Finally, market economies are closely associated with foreign trade, and trade is also central to this diffusion argument. The presence of a liberal trading state encourages non-liberal states to engage in trade, a process that should increase the likelihood of further political and economic liberalization in non-democratic states.

Of the three causal claims advanced in the regional-level argument, the link between imposed democracy and regional prosperity is perhaps the least studied in the scholarly literature. Some scholarly research does examine the regional economic impact of post-WWII Japan and Germany, and these cases appear to provide support for this aspect of the regional-level argument. For example, during the post-war period, Japan steadily increased its regional economic influence such that by the 1980s in "almost every country in the region [Asia], Japan was simultaneously the largest investor; the largest exporter; the largest source of tourism; the largest foreign-aid donor; and the largest buyer of raw commodities" (Fallows 1995: 247). This expansion of Japanese economic influence in the region stimulated and coincided with increasingly market-oriented Asian economies and rapid economic growth in many countries. Similarly, West Germany played an important role in promoting economic and social change within Eastern Europe following World War II. For example, Lane (1995) argues that the West German policy of *Ostpolitik* increased the openness of the societies of Eastern Europe to new ideas and influences by stimulating contacts between Western Germany and Eastern Europe. The view from West Germany was that these linkages would open the societies of Eastern Europe to new ideas and influences.

Studies of the relationship between imposed political regimes and regional prosperity default to the familiar examples identified by American policymakers, i.e., the post-WWII democratic and capitalist success stories of West Germany and Japan.[2] In turn, the cases of West Germany and Japan appear to suggest firm evidence of the regional benefits that imposed democratic states can have on regional prosperity. However, beyond these two notable cases, little research exploring the relationship between imposed democratic regimes and regional prosperity exists.

Testing the regional-level argument

To verify empirically the regional-level argument, we identified a set of 27 externally imposed democratic polities (i.e., political institutions) during the twentieth century.[3] Externally imposed democratic polities are those political institutions that are installed in a state by one or more third party actors, including states or international organizations (e.g., democratic institutions installed by the United States in Japan following World War II). The 27 externally imposed polities that we analyze are reported in Table 7.1. In addition to exploring the general relationship between imposed democracies and regional outcomes, we wish to investigate whether this relationship is moderated by the strength or presence of democratic institutions in imposed democratic polities. To this end, we refer to imposed democracies with strong democratic institutions as "bright democratic beacons," and we refer to imposed democracies with weak democratic institutions as "dim democratic beacons." In testing the regional-level argument, we consider each regional outcome – i.e., peace, democracy, and prosperity – in turn, and with respect to the impact of bright and dim democratic beacons.

With respect to the relationship between externally imposed democratic polities and regional interstate war, our empirical analysis indicates

Table 7.1 Externally imposed democratic polities in the twentieth century

State	Start	End
Austria	1920	1934
Austria	1946	1994
Botswana	1966	1994
Canada	1867	1994
Cuba	1901	1955
Cyprus	1960	1994
West Germany/Germany	1949	1994
Guyana	1966	1978
Haiti	1918	1935
Honduras	1908	1936
Ireland	1922	1994
Jamaica	1959	1994
Japan	1952	1994
Kenya	1963	1969
Lebanon	1941	1990
Lesotho	1966	1970
Malaysia	1957	1994
Mauritius	1968	1994
New Zealand	1857	1994
Nigeria	1960	1966
Philippines	1935	1972
Singapore	1959	1965
Sri Lanka	1948	1994
Sudan	1954	1958
Syria	1944	1950
Uganda	1962	1967
Zimbabwe	1923	1987

Source: McLaughlin *et al.* (1998).

that a state's war propensity declines by approximately 32 percent when it is geographically contiguous to a bright democratic beacon. By contrast, this relationship attenuates when we consider states beyond those directly contiguous to an externally imposed democracy. As encouraging as these results are regarding the relationship between imposed democracy and regional interstate war, further analysis suggests the need for caution. First, although the analysis for the twentieth century suggests a significant pacifying effect by bright democratic beacons on neighboring states, this effect is considerably weaker in a sample corresponding to the post-WWII period. Indeed, we find that bright democratic beacons have their weakest impact on regional peace during precisely that historical interval, the post-WWII period.

Most striking, however, are the findings corresponding to the performance of dim democratic beacons during the post-WWII interval. Specifically, it appears that rather than enhancing regional peace, these beacons actually undermine regional peace. Indeed, a state neighboring a dim democratic beacon is 87 percent more likely to engage in war in any given year relative to a state that is not. In general, our analysis suggests that the degree to which an imposed democratic polity is democratic has significant implications for regional war. The brighter the imposed democratic beacon, the greater the negative impact on regional war; conversely, the dimmer the democratic beacon, the greater the regional tendency toward war.

In sum, our analysis of regional peace suggests that externally imposed democratic polities can stimulate regional peace, but only under conditions in which imposed democratic beacons burn brightly. If an imposed democracy reflects strong democratic institutions, then this bright democratic beacon does reduce conflict among its closest neighbors, stimulating greater regional peace and conflict resolution. Yet, our analysis suggests that dim democratic beacons do not merely exert a benign impact on the regions in which they reside. Rather, our analysis suggests that these dim democratic beacons increase their own conflict propensity, as well as the war-proneness of neighboring states, a dynamic that undermines regional peace, ongoing peacemaking processes, and general political stability.

Next, we now consider the impact of such polities on regional democratization. In general, our empirical analysis suggests little empirical support for the claim that the presence of imposed democratic polities stimulates further democratization in the regions that they occupy. Indeed, there appears to be no significant effect of these polities upon the likelihood of democratization of states in their region. While bright democratic beacons do not seem to influence regional democratization, dim democratic beacons negatively influence the democratization of their neighbors.

Interestingly, dim democratic beacons do not appear to have the same effect upon the states directly contiguous to them as they do to other non-contiguous neighbors. Indeed, our analysis suggests that states geographically contiguous to dim democratic beacon are neither more nor less likely to experience democratization. At first glance, this result seems surprising since it makes sense to expect that imposed regimes are likely to have the most direct effect upon the bordering states. Yet, these results may reflect the presence of two opposed effects that dim democratic beacons potentially exert upon their immediate neighbors. On one hand, the weak form of democracy associated with dim democratic beacons, as well as the instability that these polities seem to interject into the regions they occupy, would likely decrease the likelihood of further regional democratization. Conversely, the military presence of the imposing state or states (e.g., the United States in Iraq) in the state receiving the imposed polity, a presence that would encourage democratization both within the imposed polity and the region at large, would be felt most directly by states directly contiguous to the dim democratic beacon. Such an explanation might explain the two effects that would account for the null findings for states directly contiguous to dim democratic beacons.

Our third and final theoretical expectation links the presence of imposed democratic polities with increased regional prosperity, a concept that we operationalize with per capita Gross National Product (GNP). Our analysis of prosperity suggests that the variable describing the minimum distance of a state to the nearest bright democratic beacon is negative and statistically significant. This finding indicates that per capita GNP growth becomes more likely the *nearer* a state is to a bright imposed democratic beacon. Indeed, we find that states that are proximate, but not contiguous, to a bright democratic beacon are approximately 13 percent more likely to experience GNP growth than other states. Interestingly, states contiguous to a bright democratic beacon were neither significantly more or less likely to experience GNP growth. Similar to our analysis of regional democracy, dim democratic beacons have a negative effect on prosperity in the regions they occupy, such that the presence of a dim beacon within a 1–950 kilometer band of a state reduces the likelihood of growth in per capital GNP in given year by approximately 16 percent.

In sum, our analysis lends additional support to the conjecture that factors associated with dim democratic beacons exert two separate effects upon their immediate neighbors. On one hand, the influence of the imposing power may have a spill-over effect upon the states contiguous to the imposed state, promoting greater stability and, in turn, increasing the likelihood of economic growth. At the same time, based on our analysis of peace, above, the presence of dim democratic beacons seems to promote instability in neighboring states. As a result, the null findings obtained for states contiguous to dim democratic beacons may reflect the impact of these two cross-cutting influences.

Conclusion

In crafting the policy argument for the invasion of Iraq, policymakers repeatedly referenced the post-World War II experiences of Germany and Japan as epicenters of subsequent peace, democracy, and prosperity in their respective geographic regions. Our study of this regional-level policy claim with data for the twentieth century leads us to conclude that, under conditions in which bright democratic beacons persist in a region, regional peace and prosperity are promoted, but democratization is not. Furthermore, we find that imposed democratic polities that are weakly democratic generally reduce the odds that a region will achieve greater peace, prosperity, and democracy.

Based on these general findings, our analysis provides some insight into the likely regional impact of a post-Hussein democracy in Iraq. On the positive side, if Iraq emerges as a bright democratic beacon, there exists a chance for greater regional peace and prosperity. Such an achievement in a region racked by recurring, high-intensity conflict would without a doubt be a favorable development. However, the road to a fully functioning democracy on the order of Germany or Japan, i.e., quintessential bright democratic beacons, is likely to be difficult, given Iraq's ethnic and religious cleavages, near absence of a democratic tradition, the impact of the American occupation, and the potential hostility of Iraq's neighbors. Under conditions of a dimly lit democratic beacon in Iraq, our analysis suggests that regional peace, prosperity, and democracy are unlikely to follow in the Middle East.

The implications of our analysis of externally imposed democratic polities for thinking about peace in post-conflict societies are significant. As we know, nation–states do not exist in isolation. Rather, virtually every nation–state in the modern state system has some geographic, economic, social, or political links to other nation–states in this system. Therefore, attempts by the international community to resolve disputes between and within states do have important implications beyond the state where democratic political institutions are imposed. Indeed, our study indicates that the translation of imposed democracy into positive regional outcomes turns on the strength of the democratic institutions in an imposed democracy. If the beacon of democracy is strong, then most, but not all, of the promised benefits have, on average, accrued regionally. Conversely, if the beacon of democracy is weak, then the regional byproducts of imposed democracy are alarming and likely to be counter-productive. Ultimately, despite the positive regional benefits derived from the presence of bright democratic beacons, we conclude that relying on externally imposed democracy as a vehicle for regional conflict resolution is a risky strategy for achieving regional conflict resolution, democracy, and prosperity.

Notes

1 The most explicit outline of this policy shift is reflected in two speeches by American President George W. Bush in 2003 (Bush 2003a, 2003b).
2 See President George W. Bush's speech to the American Enterprise Institute (Bush 2003a).
3 Detailed coding rules for identifying these polities, as well as more extensive reporting of our empirical tests of the regional-level argument, are reported in Enterline and Greig (forthcoming). Due to data limitations, we define the twentieth century to include the period 1909–1994.

References

Bumiller, E. (2003) "Bush Says Ousting Hussein Could Aid Peace in the Middle East," *New York Times* February 27.

Bush, G.W. (2003a) "In the President's Words: 'Free People Will Keep the Peace of the World,'" *New York Times* February 27.

Bush, G.W. (2003b) "Iraqi Democracy Will Succeed," *New York Times* November 6.

Cederman, L. and Gleditsch, K.S. (2004) "Conquest and Regime Change: An Evolutionary Model of the Spread of Democracy and Peace," *International Studies Quarterly* 48: 603–629.

Colaresi, M. and Thompson, W.R. (2003) "The Economic Development-Democratization Relationship: Does the Outside World Matter?," *Comparative Political Studies* 36 (4): 381–403.

Crescenzi, M.J.C. and Enterline, A.J. (1999) "Ripples from the Waves? A Systemic, Time-Series Analysis of Democracy, Democratization, and Interstate War," *Journal of Peace Research* 36: 75–94.

Enterline, A.J. and Greig, J.M. (2005) "Beacons of Hope? The Impact of Imposed Democracy on Regional Peace, Democracy and Prosperity," *Journal of Politics* 67(4): 1075–1098.

Fallows, J. (1995) *Looking at the Sun: The Rise of the New East Asian Economic and Political System*. New York: Vintage.

Gleditsch, K.S. (2002) *All International Politics Is Local: The Diffusion of Conflict, Integration, and Democratization*. Ann Arbor, MI: University of Michigan.

Gleditsch, N.P. and Hegre, H. (1997) "Peace and Democracy: Three Levels of Analysis," *Journal of Conflict Resolution* 41: 283–310.

Huntington, S.P. (1991) *The Third Wave: Democratization in the Late Twentieth-Century*. Norman, OK: University of Oklahoma.

Kadera, K.M., Crescenzi, M.J.C., and Shannon, M.L. (2003) "Democratic Survival, Peace, and War in the International System," *American Journal of Political Science* 47: 234–247.

Lane, C. (1995) "Germany's New Ostpolitik," *Foreign Affairs* 74: 77–89.

McLaughlin, S., Gates, S., and Hegre, H. (1999) "Evolution in Democracy-War Dynamics," *Journal of Conflict Resolution* 43: 771–792.

McLaughlin, S., Gates, S., Hegre, H., Gissinger, R., and Gleditsch, N.P. (1998) "Timing the Changes in Political Structures: A New Polity Database," *Journal of Conflict Resolution* 42: 231–242.

Modelski, G. and Perry, G. (1991) "Democratization in Long Perspective," *Technological Forecasting and Social Change* 39: 23–34.

Pevehouse, J.C. (2002) "Democracy from the Outside-In? International Organizations and Democratization," *International Organizations* 56: 515–49.

Ray, J.L. (2000) "On the Level(s): Does Democracy Correlate with Peace?" in John A. Vasquez (ed.) *What Do We Know About War?* Lanham, MD: Rowman and Littlefield.

Siverson, R.M. and Starr, H. (1991) *The Diffusion of War: A Study of Opportunity and Willingness.* Ann Arbor, MI: University of Michigan.

Starr, H. (1991) "Democratic Dominoes: Diffusion Approaches the Spread of Democracy in the International System," *Technological Forecasting and Social Change* 35: 356–381.

Starr, H. (1995) "D2: The Diffusion of Democracy Revisited," paper presented at the International Studies Association Meeting, Chicago, Illinois, February 20–26.

Starr, H. and Lindborg, C. (2003) "Democratic Dominoes Revisited: The Hazards of Governmental Transitions, 1974–1996," *Journal of Conflict Resolution* 47: 490–519.

Thompson, W.R. (1996) "Democracy and Peace: Putting the Cart Before the Horse?" *International Organization* 50: 141–174.

8 The use of military force to promote human rights

James D. Meernik, Steven C. Poe, and Erum Shaikh

Introduction

Among the major, stated goals of the military action in Iraq has been the US administration's desire to replace the Saddam Hussein dictatorship with a regime that would serve as a model for human rights and democracy in the Middle East. Thought controversial by many because it may represent a bad precedent, as well as a sea change in American foreign policy, the use of force for these purposes is really not that unusual in a broad historical context. Throughout history, states have frequently used military force to impose political systems upon other societies. Owen (2002: 375) chronicled 198 such cases that have occurred since 1555. And like the current case, most such efforts have involved the forceful imposition of a regime by a powerful country on a weaker target state. And in most of these the powerful state has sought to impose on the target country a set of political institutions that more closely resembles its own.

The extent to which such uses of force have been successful at bringing about more human rights in societies is debatable. Scholars are now beginning to analyze the success of attempts to impose liberal, democratic systems on nations (Fossedal 1989; Smith 1994; Peceny 1995, 1999; Meernik 1996; McDougall 1997; Hermann and Kegley 1998; Whitcomb 1998). Such research has emphasized the extent to which a system of democratic governance has been established in a nation whose prior regime did not subscribe to democratic norms. These analyses have largely focused on macro-level, systemic and constitutional changes in government institutions. We are interested, however, in exploring the degree to which these uses of force have been able to effect change at the micro, or individual level. While regime change may presage an improvement of conditions in a society, the changes may only be in law and not in fact. The procedural aspects of democratization may be realized in the course of these military interventions, as new constitutions are written and elections held. Yet the substance of democracy may lag behind if elected officials and citizens do not fully subscribe to critical, democratic norms such as civil liberties, tolerance, and the foreswearance of violence as a political tool.

One aim of this chapter is to provide the first assessment of whether these uses of force have acted to improve the substance of democracy – the right to speak one's own mind, to practice one's religion and simply to live peacefully, free of the fear of imprisonment and government-sponsored violence. As such, this study also constitutes a useful addition to the literature that seeks to ascertain the relationship between human rights and a variety of foreign policy tools (e.g., Stohl Carleton and Johnson 1984, Stohl and Carleton 1985; Cingranelli and Pasquarello 1985; McCormick and Mitchell 1988; Regan 1995; Poe and Sirirangsi 1994; Blanton 1994; 2000; Apodaca and Stohl 1999). Given the fact that the literature has examined the impact of foreign economic and military aid and arms transfers in some detail, it is rather surprising that no one has yet systematically analyzed the relationship between human rights and US uses of force, which are arguably the most serious of foreign policy commitments, and certainly the most visible.

Most importantly of all, we seek to deepen our understanding of one of the key elements of a sustainable peace in nations that have undergone conflict – their level of human rights protection. Governments that abuse their citizens' human rights may well be more likely to experience repeated patterns of internal and/or external forms of violence and conflict. Their abusive policies may precipitate challenges from within and attempts from without to impose a new government more respectful of human rights. Thus, evaluating the extent to which uses of force result in an improvement of the human rights situation in the target state is critical to understanding the prospects of a sustainable peace in that society.

Toward this end, we will examine uses of force by the United States across all nations of the world, using data for the period 1977–1996. We find that the regimes that are subjected to uses of force by the United States are a distinct set of nations, distinguished from others by their regime types. Having examined which nations the USA has used force in, we next analyze our primary question of interest: the impact of such military actions on the lives of people in the target nation. We argue that if US uses of force are indeed successful at promoting human rights, then the success or failure of uses of force is apt to be a function of their type, size, and duration. Our findings indicate that though democracy and human rights are among the considerations that determine whether the USA does intervene in a particular case, these uses of force are ineffective at promoting improvements in these conditions.

Explaining the use of military force by the United States

To explain the consequences of US uses of military force, we begin by examining the events to which the USA is responding. We make one *seemingly* obvious, but important assumption – that United States foreign policymakers are more interested in some foreign crises than others. Our purpose is not to enumerate all the types of events and conditions that make some events of concern to US foreign policymakers and not others. Instead, we seek to explain how a nation's domestic political system and regime policies affect US foreign policy toward that nation. Are US foreign policymakers' perceptions of the importance of a threat posed by some nation influenced in any degree by these domestic, political conditions in that country? And do such interests increase the likelihood that the United States will use military force to influence events in these nations? We believe the answer to both questions to be "yes." The first step in our analysis of the relationship between human rights and the use of force is to explain why we believe internal political conditions influence the likelihood of US military action.

The promotion of liberalism and the US use of force

The United States has long been interested in promoting liberalist values in its foreign policies (Fossedal 1989; Smith 1994; Peceny 1995, 1999; Meernik 1996; McDougall 1997; Hermann and Kegley 1998; Whitcomb 1998). In contrast to realists, who would argue that promoting democracy or human rights is rare in a security-oriented, anarchic international system, many of these scholars have found that the United States has increasingly used force to remake other societies. This is not altogether surprising for other researchers have argued that there are substantial opportunities and incentives for a powerful state to remake the world in its own image (Krasner 1978: 340) and to socialize leaders in other states to its norms and values (Ikenberry and Kupchan 1990). Indeed, even Hans Morgenthau (1973: 10) once wrote, "All nations are tempted—and few have been able to resist the temptation for long—to clothe their own particular aspirations and actions in the moral purposes of the universe." Recent research by Owen (2002) confirms that states have forcibly imposed domestic institutions on other states throughout history. Ideologically inspired military interventions have seemingly become more feasible and prevalent with the end of the Cold War, but as Peceny (1999) demonstrates, the USA embarked on such missions during and before the Cold War as well. Peceny finds that in almost one-third of US military interventions in the twentieth century, presidents sought to achieve liberal democratic aims abroad. Most recently, one of the five major objectives of US military strategy in the Annual Defense Report 2000 is fostering an international environment in which "Democratic norms and respect for human rights are widely accepted."[1]

First, we hypothesize that the United States will be interested in the extent to which a nation subscribes to liberal, democratic values. The democratic peace research program has shown that democratic regimes tend not to make war on each other (Maoz and Russett 1993; Owen 1994; Bueno de Mesquita and Lalman 1992). More recently, scholars are finding that when democracies do enter conflicts, it is often because they are targeted by non-democratic states (Leeds and Davis 1999; Prins and Sprecher 1999). Democratic regimes also tend to be more co-operative in general in their international behavior (Benoit 1996; Leeds and Davis 1999). Huth (1998) finds that major powers are more likely to intervene in conflicts when they are seeking to protect a politically similar regime from a third nation that does not share their polity characteristics. Polity type is highly predictive of how states treat one another because of the tendency for like states to flock together because of shared norms.

Second, and more importantly, we believe that the specific policies pursued by governments should also explain their proclivity for conflict involvement and the likelihood that the USA will use force against them. Governments that are fair and responsive to their citizens do not provoke the scope or intensity of opposition that generates unrest at home and escalates into conflict with other regimes. For example, the states of Europe tend not to provoke militarized, international crises by their policies toward their own citizens, while some governments in Africa and Asia have become enmeshed in crises because of their repressive nature. Regimes that do not respect the human rights of their citizens are also typical of regimes that centralize power and possess far greater latitude to act repressively at home and aggressively abroad. Ultimately, repression and/or aggression are at the hub of most international crises and uses of force, and so we should find those states whose regimes utilize these tools as normal political practice will be the site of many of these crises of interest to the United States, and therefore will be targeted with military force.

> Hypothesis 1: *The United States will be more likely to use force the less democratic the target state.*[2]

> Hypothesis 2: *The United States will be more likely use force the less respectful the target state is toward its citizens' human rights.*[3]

Initial bivariate explorations

The dependent variable, FORCE, is coded "1" for each country in the world for each year in which the USA used force and "0" otherwise in the period 1976–1996. Data on the political use of force were gathered from Blechman and Kaplan (1978), Job and Ostrom (1986), Zelikow (1987), The Center for Naval Analyses: 'The Use of Naval Forces in the Post-War Era: U.S. Navy and U.S. Marine Corps Crisis Response Activity, 1946–1990', and the Global Security web site.[4] A political use of military force short of war is defined by Blechman and Kaplan (1978: 12) as

> physical actions ... taken by one or more components of the uniformed military services as part of a deliberate attempt by the national

authorities to influence, or to be prepared to influence, specific behavior of individuals in another nation without engaging in a continuing contest of violence.

Empirically-oriented researchers are well aware that viewing simple bivariate relationships can sometimes lead to erroneous conclusions, as seemingly important relationships can appear that are in fact spurious, or alternatively, that significant relationships can be hidden (i.e., Lewis-Beck 1980). However, the old maxim that "a picture is worth a thousand words" has a certain appeal, and our experience has taught us that sometimes simple visual analyses can lead to a greater understanding of patterns in the data than would be possible from the inspection of multivariate analyses alone.

By examining figures that show trends in countries' levels of democracy, and respect for human rights, we can gain an idea of the likelihood that hypotheses 1 and 2 are supported by data. In Figure 8.1 we depict the average Polity III democracy scores (a scale ranging from 0–10) during the time period under study, in years prior to US uses of force, at time t. Figure 8.1 paints an interesting picture of the relationship between democracy and US military actions. The mean democracy scores in cases where US actions were to later occur are much lower than those to be found in countries where no such use of force would happen. Six years prior to an impending US military action, the average democracy score was just under 0.4, very near the bottom of the democracy scale. Democracy scores in other countries at that time, and across the period were by no means stellar, with means of around 3.5 to 4, on the bottom half of the scale, but they were substantially greater than in the countries where the USA was to later intervene, and statistically significantly ($p < 0.001$).

Also interesting are the trends in both series across time. One sees an

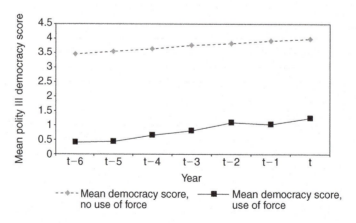

Figure 8.1 Mean polity democracy scores prior to a US use of force at time t.

upward trend in democracy in both series, indicative of a global trend toward democratization during this period of time. The upward trend in democracy is somewhat greater among nations that would later experience a US use of force, perhaps because countries on the "0" end of the Polity Democracy spectrum cannot possibly see decreases in their democracy scores, whereas a certain percentage of cases achieving higher scores are apt to do so. The mean democracy score at the time of the use of force is 1.26, as compared to 3.89 in cases where the USA does not use force, a difference which is still highly significant ($p < 0.001$). We can conclude from this analysis, then, that the US tends to use force in a subset of cases that are very low in democracy, a finding consistent with Hypothesis 1. Further, when one examines the overall trend toward democracy one may also notice that the progress tends to halt one year prior to US military actions, as the democracy scores actually decrease from 1.08 to 1.05 from t−2 to t−1. Admittedly this decrease is very small, but it is suggestive that perhaps in some instances US uses of force could result from *downturns* in democracy, in addition to levels in that variable at a particular point in time.

In Figure 8.2 we present trends in human rights scores, as measured by the Amnesty International Political Terror Scale, which ranges from 1 to 5 (where "1" is best for human rights practices and "5" is "worst"), and deals primarily with "personal integrity rights," the right not to be imprisoned, tortured, disappeared, executed, or murdered, either arbitrarily or for one's views. Here we see that countries that would experience US military actions are indeed substantially more repressive than others in the period leading up to that event. As in our first figure, differences between

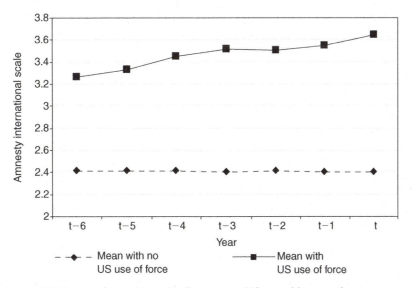

Figure 8.2 Human rights abuses leading up to a US use of force at time t.

the group experiencing uses of force and those that did not are statistically significant throughout the period ($p < 0.001$).

The trend in human rights abuses is also suggestive, as one sees substantial increases in human rights abuses leading up to the military action, from 3.26, six years prior to the use of force; to 3.52 two years prior; 3.55, one year prior; and to 3.64 in the year of the military action. It does appear that the United States uses force in a subset of countries with rather undemocratic institutions and practices. However, though such analyses are suggestive, they are subject to difficulties since potentially important relationships with other explanations of the US use of force may have been overlooked.

The effects of US military actions on human rights: initial bivariate examination of trends

Now we consider the effects of US military actions on human rights. Our first analysis of this issue, which is presented in Figure 8.3, allows us to examine the evolution of human rights practices in the six years subsequent to US interventions, taking place at time t. We look at the level of respect for human rights, in US uses of force in general. However, the effects of uses of force might differ, depending on what kind of force is used, and the number of forces committed. We might theorize that, if one of the purposes of the US use of force is to increase respect for human rights, as indicated in the analyses conducted above, the use of ground forces represents an important threshold in terms of the level of commitment, and that uses of force that cross that threshold are apt to have a greater impact than if only naval or air forces are used.

A number of interesting patterns become evident in Figure 8.3. First, quite consistent with the findings in above sections, one notices that the

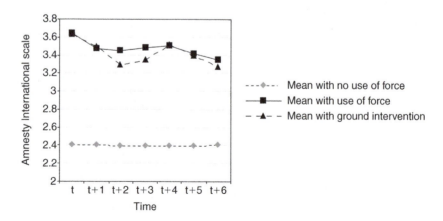

Figure 8.3 Human rights practices after US uses of force, 1976–1996.

mean human rights abuse scores for countries having experienced US military actions are substantially higher than those that have not throughout the seven-year period. This underscores our argument regarding the selection process that occurs as a result of the US using force in certain kinds of cases.

More interesting findings are evident in the trends once military action takes place. The downward trend in human rights abuse scores, from just above 3.6 to between 3.2 and 3.4 indicate moderate improvements in human dignity in the six years subsequent to US military actions. Further, we see that human rights abuse scores are somewhat lower in cases where ground forces are introduced, consistent with the reasoning presented above. Though the differences are rather small, this bivariate analysis when viewed alone may be interpreted as evidence to support the claim that US uses of force have been successful in improving human rights. There is good reason to be skeptical of such a claim, however. Previous research has shown that countries that have human rights scores in that range have a tendency to decrease over time, as such repression is difficult to maintain for long periods of time (Tate *et al.* 2000), so one might expect that a decrease in human rights abuse scores would have occurred even if no military action had taken place.

To test for this possibility, we created a "control group" consisting of a subset of countries with a similar mean human rights score at time t, which did not experience US uses of force. To make sure that the composition of the two sets of countries was as similar as possible, we took a random sample of the countries not experiencing military action, stratified according to the level of the dependent variable (Figure 8.4). Specifically, we

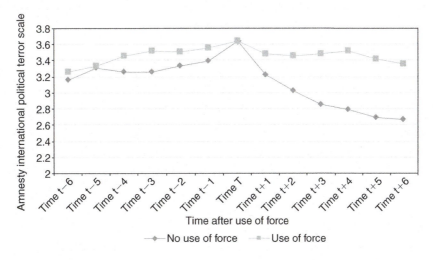

Figure 8.4 Human rights practices after US use of force: comparison with a control group.

chose four times, the number of cases, for each of the five points on the human rights scale, as were present in the group of countries that experienced uses of force. This resulted in two groups of countries in which levels of human rights abuse were identical (3.64) at time t. In one group US military action had occurred, and in another they had not. The results show that human rights abuses decrease substantially more quickly when the USA chooses not to use force. At time t+6 the sample of cases in which the USA had not used force had a mean human rights score of 2.67, as compared to the mean of 3.35 in countries which had experienced military action at the same point of time, a difference that was highly statistically significant ($p < 0.001$).

From these bivariate results we have learned that human rights conditions tend to improve in the wake of US military action. That said, this is most likely due to the countries that have most often been the target of these uses of force having relatively serious human rights problems prior to the intervention. In a subset of countries with similar histories of human rights abuse, which did not experience US military action, human rights conditions improvement occurred more quickly.

If we were to judge the effects of US uses of force on human rights solely on the basis of these simple pictures, the tendency would be to conclude that such actions worsened human rights conditions from what they would otherwise be by slowing their improvement. The possibility of misleading effects as a result of selection bias come into play here too, however, since the subset of countries experiencing uses of force have already been shown to be substantially different from those which did on a variety of different characteristics. A better idea of the actual effects of US uses of force can be gained by including other potential determinants of human rights in a multivariate model of human rights abuse, along with US uses of force. We will do so, in the next section.

Testing the effects of US military action in a multivariate model

To yield results in which we can have more confidence, we employ a more sophisticated statistical model.[5] We also employ a set of control variables derived from prior research on human rights (Poe and Tate 1994; Poe *et al.* 1999) including: (1) level of democracy; (2) per capita GNP; (3) logged population; (4) leftist government dummy variable; (5) military dictatorship dummy variable; (6) British colonial influence; (7) involvement in international war; (8) involvement in civil war; (9) organized nonviolent rebellion; and (10) organized violent rebellion. The results are available upon request. Here we simply describe the relationships we find between the use of force and human rights. We use three different measures of the US use of force. The first is measured simply as the occurrence of any US use of military force. The second is measured as a major level US use of force.[6] The third is measured as a use of military force involving the deployment of US ground forces.[7] We employ the latter two variables to determine if a stronger commitment of the US military is needed to affect human rights. Major military actions are those that involve multiple units of air, land and/or sea forces that would be expected to provide a more visible and assertive US military presence. We would also expect that in instances where presidents ordered the deployment of US ground forces that the US government would possess greater leverage over the policies of the target regime. Ground forces are in a much stronger position to affect change in a target country when they are used to secure a peace, patrol, and protect lives and property. Therefore, we expect that the more force used and the deployment of ground forces would be more associated with an increase in the protection of human rights. Each of these three, binary variables was lagged one-year, two-years and three-years to determine the length of time needed for force to actually influence, if at all, respect for human rights.

The effects of the three measures of uses of force on human rights are largely negligible. In the first set of measures we examined the effects of all uses of force irrespective of size or type. Regardless of how many years we lag the occurrence of a use of force (to allow time for human rights practices to change within a country), the coefficients for the use of force variables never attain statistical significance. Interestingly, the coefficient for the one-year, lagged variable is negative, while the coefficients at two- and three-year lags are positive. The impact of uses of force would appear to change over time. At first, the use of force may lead to an increase in respect for human rights, but later and perhaps after US forces have departed the scene, the target nation experiences increasing violations. One could imagine several possible scenarios associated with a use of force. If US forces have left the target nation, that regime may be returning to its previous and poor human rights policies, which may have triggered the use of force. Whatever positive influence US military forces may have on human rights may depend entirely on their continuing presence. Or, it may be that the introduction of US forces creates greater instability and political problems in the target country that lead to increasing violations of human rights over time. The use of force may provoke opposition or violence that the regime forcefully represses; it may be perceived by the government as a green light to engage in abusive human rights practices (especially if the use of force was in support of the regime); or it may lead to a general breakdown in respect for the rule of law.

Perhaps the effects of a use of force are contingent upon the size and type of military deployment. The President may need to order a substantial deployment of US military personnel to cause a target regime to modify its behavior. A flyover by the US Air Force, or a port visit by the US Navy may not signal the depth of commitment required to effect a fundamental change of human rights policies in the target regime. Therefore, we next examined the effects of major uses of military force on human rights. The findings are very similar to what we just found. First, none of the lagged measures of major uses of military force are statistically significant, although the coefficient for the one-year lag comes very close. We also see that the effect of a major use of force one year after its occurrence is negative – such deployments improve human rights. However, the coefficients for the two-year and three-year lags are positive. Over time, major uses of force tend to lead to decreasing protection of human rights.

We are also interested in evaluating the effects of uses of force involving ground troops. Again, we see that the coefficients for these variables at one-year, two-year and three-year lags are all statistically insignificant. However, the signs of the coefficients change twice in these estimates. One year after the deployment of ground forces, the effect is small, but positive, which indicates a decrease in protection of human rights. At two years, the coefficient for the lagged variable is negative, but at three years it becomes positive once again. While we do not wish to make too much of these findings due to the statistical insignificance of the coefficients, it may be that all such deployments are entirely dependent upon a host of other factors we do not measure, such as the purpose of the mission, the relationship between the United States and the target regime, and subsequent events.

One final possibility that occurs to us is that the duration of a dispute may exercise an impact on human rights and repression. Carothers (2000: 107) observed that intervening nations usually focus on the endpoint, i.e., an election, and not on the process of establishing necessary preconditions to substantive democracy, such as securing freedom of speech or protest thus, in effect, focusing on the symptoms instead of the causes of the problem. Short-term interventions, when the intervening party leaves as soon as order is restored or an election held, may not be effective in improving human rights for these reasons. In contrast, in long-term, or so-called "state building" enterprises there are efforts to rebuild a nation from the ground up, establishing new laws, and trying to cultivate new laws and norms in the target country. It could be that longer-term uses of force are more effective, resulting in greater respect of human rights in the target country, than in shorter-term uses of force. Alternatively, if US occupation is bad for human rights, then longer military actions might be found to be worse for human rights than shorter ones.

In order to test for these possibilities we created a new data set in which the unit of analysis is an event in which the USA used force. We then calculated a variable that measured the duration of each US military action, for which data were available, in days.[8] In order to observe the effect of duration of uses of force on human rights within those countries that experienced such actions, we re-ran again the base model, this time including the duration of the use of force, lagged one, two, and three, years respectively.

Once again, the findings offer us no firm evidence that the duration of

US military actions make a difference for better or for worse. The coefficient of the duration variable at lag one is closest to achieving statistical significance (p<.07, two-tailed) indicating there is a good possibility that duration has an effect. However, the positive sign indicates that the effect of a longer duration (if there is one) is probably to increase human rights abuses. Duration of the military action at the second lag has a negative coefficient, while at the third lag the coefficient becomes positive again. But these two variables do not approach conventional levels of statistical significance.

Conclusion

In this study we have examined two closely interrelated, but nevertheless distinct questions, "Why does the United States use force?" and, "What are the ramifications for these uses of force for human rights practices within the target countries?" Though they are distinct questions, to address one without the other can produce only an incomplete story of the relationship between human rights and the use of force.

Our findings are consistent with the claim that US military actions are motivated by the desire to promote human rights, as human rights appear to be one of the strongest predictors, if not the strongest predictor of US uses of force. But, unfortunately, from a normative perspective, the results also indicate that though the use of force by the US is partly motivated by the desire to improve human rights in target countries, these actions do not improve the substance of democracy in target nations; the degree to which citizens are free to speak, worship, or simply to live peacefully, free of the fear of imprisonment or acts of violence, by their governments.

We conducted a variety of analyses of the effects of uses of force on human rights. We examined the effects of all US uses of force. We then looked at a subset of the most serious uses of force, and then on those in which ground forces were used. Finally, we used a variable that discriminated between longer and shorter uses of force in countries that were the targets of military action. And in each of these analyses we examined the effects of uses of force at three separate lags. The results indicate rather unambiguously that such military actions do not have any desirable impact on human rights. Indeed, the findings suggested that if uses of force had any impact, it was toward greater human rights abuse in interventions of longer duration.

Rather than just assuming that we have explained as much as is possible, we believe that there are other relationships and angles to be explored. We caution against taking these results as verification of the extreme view of Luttwak (1999) and others, who would say that humanitarian interventions of almost any kind tend to make matters worse, by prolonging the inevitable. Regarding US military actions, we know that during the Cold War period, which constitutes most of this sample of data, though they might have been a consideration, human rights considerations were not always a top priority of US foreign policymakers. Indeed, such concerns were often sacrificed in the interest of larger, strategic objectives. Since the end of the Cold War, however, these interests have become much more important, and many uses of force have been undertaken primarily to confront human rights problems. Such cases need to be analyzed in more depth and with data for more recent years to provide us with a better picture of how much improvement in human rights we have seen (if any) as a consequence of military interventions since the end of the Cold War. Further, this study does not examine the effects of a wide variety of interventions undertaken by other countries, and by international governmental, and non-governmental organizations. Further research should look at the effectiveness of the variety of instruments used by the world community, in its attempt to foster improvements in the respect for human rights.

If we can draw one lesson from these analyses, it is that promoting human rights is difficult at best and fraught with complexities. While the results do not necessarily speak to what these complexities are, we may hazard a few guesses. First, there are practical difficulties. Military interventions often result in instability and sometimes greater violence, especially in their early stages, as institutions traditionally responsible for law and order may be pushed aside, damaged or even done away with. This in turn may well create a more permissive environment in which human rights abuses may flourish. Second, there are cultural complexities involved in advancing a human rights agenda on a society that may be at a minimum unprepared, and at worst, hostile to the imposition of a new set of moral and political values. The presence of the US military may inspire even greater opposition to the transference of such values than had they been promoted via other avenues, such as foreign aid, diplomacy, and the media. Third, there are strategic considerations that may militate against human rights improvements as US foreign policymakers may be more concerned with establishing a stable, friendly government rather than one that is protective of human rights, but unable to maintain law and order. Yet, despite the complexities inherent in the promotion of human rights, there may as yet be long-term improvements in many of the targeted nation. With the passage of time that will bring us more information on the effects of the post-Cold War interventions, we can begin to better understand the extent to which these uses of force have improved human rights, or whether the targeted nations would have been better off without such intervention.

Notes

1 This portion of "The Annual Defense Report" is found at http://www.dtic.mil/execsec/adr2000/chap1.html
2 The measurement of democracy is taken from the Polity IV dataset, courtsey of the Polity IV project at the University of Maryland. Data is from the Polity IV

website at http://www.cidcm.umd.edu/inscr/polity/index.htm. It is measured on the 0–10 scale where "10" is the most democratic.

3 Human rights data are taken from the International Human Rights Study Center website at http://www.psci.unt.edu/ihrsc/ courtesy of Steve Poe and Neal Tate. The human rights measure is a 1–5 scale with greater values indicating more repression of human rights to personal integrity.

4 http://www.globalsecurity.org/military/ops/index.html

5 We use a pooled time series model with panel-corrected standard errors and a lagged, endogenous variable to counter the effects of heteroskedasticity and autocorrelation.

6 Blechman and Kaplan (1978, 50) divide force levels into three broad groups: (1) Major force level including at least one of the following: (a) two or more aircraft carrier task groups; (b) more than one battalion ground unit; (c) one or more air combat wings; (2) Standard force level including at least one of the following: (a) one aircraft carrier task group; (b) a ground unit of no more than one battalion, but larger than one company; (c) one or more air combat squadrons, but less than one wing; (3) Minor force level including at least one of the following: (a) naval units without aircraft carriers; (b) ground units of no more than one company; (c) less than one air combat squadron.

7 Any US military intervention in which Blechman and Kaplan and the other sources used to obtain data on the use of force list the deployment of units of the US Army or US Marines are coded as a US use of force involving ground forces.

8 There were 110 instances of the use of force during the period under study. We were able to obtain lengths for 87 cases, which ranged from one day to 2,734 days. We coded cases that were still ongoing at the end of 1996 as missing. Also in some instances there was insufficient information to calculate the duration of an event, and those were coded as missing. We also lost some of the cases as a result of lagging this variable three years, leaving us with an N of 62. It should be noted that for ease of statistical manipulation, only one intervention was counted per country per year.

References

Apodaca, C. and Stohl, M. (1999) "United States Human Rights Policy and Foreign Assistance," *International Studies Quarterly* 43: 185–198.

Benoit, K. (1996) "Democracies Really Are More Pacific (In General): Reexamining Regime Type and War Involvement," *Journal of Conflict Resolution* 40 (December): 636–657.

Blanton, S.L. (1994) "Impact of Human Rights on U.S. Foreign Assistance to Latin America," *International Interactions* 19(4): 339–358.

Blanton, S.L. (2000) "Promoting Human Rights and Democracy in the Developing World: U.S. Rhetoric versus U.S. Arms Exports," *American Journal of Political Science* 44(1): 123–131.

Blechman, B. and Kaplan, S. (1978) *Force Without War*. Washington, DC: The Brookings Institution.

Bueno de Mesquita, B. and Lalman, D. (1992) *War and Reason*. New Haven, CT: Yale University Press.

Carothers, T. (2000) *Aiding Democracy Abroad*. Washington, DC: The Carnegie Endowment for International Peace.

Center for Naval Analyses (1991) "The Use of Naval Forces in the Post-War Era: U.S. Navy and U.S. Marine Corps Crisis Response Activity, 1946–1990," Alexandria, VA: Center for Naval Analyses.

Cingranelli, D.L. and Pasquarello, T. (1985). "Human Rights Practices and the U.S. Distribution of Foreign Aid to Latin American Countries," *American Journal of Political Science* 29: 539–63.

Fossedal, G.A. (1989) *The Democratic Imperative*. New York: Basic Books Inc.

Hermann, M. and Kegley, C. (1998) "The Use of U.S. Military Intervention to Promote Democracy: Evaluating the Record," *International Interactions* 24: 91–114.

Huth, P.K. (1998) "Major Power Intervention in International Crises," *Journal of Conflict Resolution* 42(December): 744–770.

Ikenberry, G.J. and Kupchan, C.A. (1990) "Socialization and Hegemonic Power," *International Organization* 44: 283–315.

Job, B.L. and Ostrom C.W. Jr. (1986) "Opportunity and Choice: The U.S. and the Political Use of Force: 1948–1976," paper presented at the 1986 Annual Meeting of the American Political Science Association, Washington, DC.

Krasner, S. (1978) *Defending the National Interest*. Princeton, NJ: Princeton University Press.

Leeds, B.A. and Davis, D. (1999) "Beneath the Surface: Regime Type and International Interaction, 1953–78," *Journal of Peace Research* 36: 5–21.

Lewis-Beck, M.S. (1980) *Applied Regression: An Introduction*. Beverly Hills, CA: Sage Publications.

Luttwak, E. (1999) "Give War a Chance," *Foreign Affairs* 78(4): 36–44.

Maoz, Z. and Russett, B. (1993) "Normative and Structural Causes of Democratic Peace 1946–1986," *American Political Science Review* 87: 624–638.

McCormick, J.M. and Mitchell, N. (1988) "Is U.S. Aid Really Linked to Human Rights in Latin America," *American Journal of Political Science* 32: 231–239.

McDougall, W.A. (1997) *Promised Land, Crusader State*. Boston, MA: Houston Mifflin Company.

Meernik, J. (1996) "U.S. Military Intervention and the Promotion of Democracy," *Journal of Peace Research* 33: 391–402.

Morgenthau, H.J. (1973) *Politics Among Nations*. 5th edn. New York: Alfred A. Knopf.

Owen, J.M. IV (1994) "How Liberalism Produces Democratic Peace," *International Security* 19: 87–125.

Owen, J.M. IV (2002) "The Foreign Imposition of Domestic Institutions," *International Organization* 56(Spring): 375–409.

Peceny, M. (1995) "Two Paths to the Promotion of Democracy During U.S. Military Interventions," *International Studies Quarterly* 39: 371–401.

Peceny, M. (1999) *Democracy at the point of Bayonets*. University Park, PA: Pennsylvania State University Press.

Poe, S.C. and Sirirangsi, R. (1994) "Human Rights and U.S. Economic Aid During the Reagan Years," *Social Science Quarterly* 75: 494–509.

Poe, S.C. and Tate, C.N. (1994) "Repression of Human Rights to Personal Integrity in the 1980s: A Global Analysis," *American Political Science Review* 88: 853–872.

Poe, S.C., Tate, C.N., and Keith, L.C. (1999) "Repression of the Human Right to Personal Integrity Revisited: A Global Crossnational Study Covering the Years 1976–1993," *International Studies Quarterly* 43: 291–315.

Prins, B.C. and Sprecher, C. (1999) "Institutional Constraints, Political Opposition, and Interstate Dispute Escalation: Evidence from Parliamentary Systems, 1946–89," *Journal of Peace Research* 36: 271–287.

Regan, P.M. (1995) "U.S. Economic Aid and Political Repression: An Empirical Evaluation of U.S. Foreign Policy," *Political Research Quarterly* 48: 613–628.

Smith, T. (1994) *America's Mission: The United States and the Worldwide Struggle for Democracy in the Twentieth Century*. Princeton, NJ: Princeton University Press.

Stohl, M. and Carleton, D. (1985) "The Foreign Policy of Human Rights: Rhetoric and Reality from Jimmy Carter to Ronald Reagan," *Human Rights Quarterly* 7: 205–229.

Stohl, M., Carleton, D., and Johnson, S. (1984) "Human Rights and U.S. Foreign Assistance from Nixon to Carter," *Journal of Peace Research* 21: 215–226.

Tate, C.N., Poe, S.C., Keith, L.C., and Lanier, D.N. (2000) "Domestic Threats: The Abuse of Personal Integrity," in C. Davenport (ed.) *Paths to State Repression: Human Rights Violations and Contentious Politics*. Lanham, MD: Rowman and Littlefield.

Whitcomb, R. (1998) *The American Approach to Foreign Affairs*. Westport, CT: Praeger Publishers.

Zelikow, P.D. (1987) "The United States and the Use of Force: A Historical Summary," in George K. Osborn, A. Clark IV, D.J. Kaufman, and D.E. Cote (eds.) *Democracy, Strategy and Vietnam*. Lexington, MA: Lexington Books.

9 Can truth reconcile divided nations?

James L. Gibson

Introduction

In recent years, interest in the use of truth commissions as a mechanism of transitional justice and the consolidation of democratic change has blossomed.[1] From Sierra Leone to Greensboro, North Carolina, a preferred means of dealing with past injustices and abuses is the creation of a process by which truth can be discovered and certified. The hope of these processes is that the truth will facilitate healing, leading to reconciliation, and ultimately the substitution of peaceful political competition for violent and destructive confrontations. It is little wonder then that wartorn countries like Iraq (and many others) are considering the possibility of implementing some sort of truth process.

Unfortunately, truth commissions are more widely embraced than is warranted by systematic evidence. One might imagine, for instance, that the success or failure of such commissions has been widely and rigorously investigated, but that is not so. Indeed, beyond fragmentary anecdotal evidence (and fascinating accounts of the day-to-day operation of truth commissions[2]), no truth process anywhere in the world has been subjected to a systematic effort at evaluation. We simply do not know whether truth processes are an effective means of bringing about political transformation.

Until now. In a recently published book, *Overcoming Apartheid: Can Truth Reconcile a Divided Nation?*, I report an analysis of the effectiveness of South Africa's truth and reconciliation process. Based on a nationally representative sample of more than 3,700 South Africans – interviewed face-to-face for approximately 90 minutes, in their language of choice – this study contends that, when evaluated in terms of the objectives enunciated in the law creating the Truth and Reconciliation Commission (TRC), the South African process stacks up reasonably well. Certainly the TRC failed along some dimensions – as in failing to deliver retribution against those responsible for the criminal defense of the apartheid state – but, in general, reconciliation seems to be the consequence of the truth process South Africa embarked upon during the mid-1990s.

The argument and evidence in *Overcoming Apartheid* are a bit complicated, as befits a book of 450 pages, and this is not the forum in which to rehearse the detailed statistical findings of that analysis. Instead, the aim of this article is to accept the findings of that book and then to highlight the lessons that emerge from South Africa's truth and reconciliation process. In particular, I identify several specific factors that contributed to the success of South Africa's truth and reconciliation process. These factors are discussed here with an eye toward their possible applicability to other troubled polities attempting to overcome their legacies of hatred, violence, and authoritarianism. I conclude that, although the South African model should not be replicated *in toto* in other troubled places, many important lessons emerge from their effort to build reconciliation out of truth. It is perhaps useful to begin this analysis with a brief overview of the truth and reconciliation process in South Africa.

Truth and reconciliation in South Africa: history and formal objectives

Ending apartheid in South Africa came at a considerable cost to those who had long struggled against the oppressive system. In South Africa, in contrast to other nations emerging from a tyrannical past (e.g., Argentina and Uganda), the *ancien régime* was not defeated. This meant that the transition had to be brokered. One of the central issues in the talks over the transformation of the apartheid state was amnesty. The National Party and the leaders of other powerful white-dominated institutions (e.g., the security forces) made amnesty a non-negotiable centerpiece of their demands (see Omar 1996). Without the promise of amnesty for the crimes (and criminals) of apartheid, the transition to democracy would stall, perhaps even with a resumption of the political violence so widespread in the 1980s. The creation of the Truth and Reconciliation Commission (TRC), with the power to grant amnesty, was the price the liberation forces had to pay in order to secure a peaceful transition to majority rule (Rwelamira 1996).

The Truth and Reconciliation Commission was provided for by the Postamble/Endnote to the Interim Constitution of 1993 and was enacted by the new parliament in 1995 as the "Promotion of National Unity and Reconciliation Act" (No. 34, 1995). That statute called for the establishment of a Truth and Reconciliation Commission, with separate Committees on Human Rights Violations, Amnesty, and Reparations and Rehabilitation. The TRC began functioning shortly thereafter.

South Africa's TRC is unique in many important respects. Hayner (2000: 33) distinguishes the South African truth and reconciliation process in the following way:

a public process of disclosure by perpetrators and public hearings for victims; an amnesty process that reviewed individual applications and avoided any blanket amnesty; and a process that was intensely focused on national healing and reconciliation, with the intent of moving a country from its repressive past to a peaceful future, where former opponents could work side by side.

Few, if any, truth commissions throughout the world have all of the characteristics and objectives of South Africa's TRC.

The truth and reconciliation process was expected to last only two years. Instead, the TRC was in operation for six years. In 2001, President Thabo Mbeki dissolved the Amnesty Committee, effective May 31, 2001. At the same time, his proclamation revived the TRC for six months for the purpose of preparing two supplementary volumes to the Final Report (which was issued in 1998). These volumes address the experiences of the victims and the work of the Amnesty Committee.

The creation of the TRC was certainly controversial, with many (including Amnesty International) arguing that international law and convention forbade granting amnesty for crimes against humanity, as well as for torture and similar offenses (their slogan was: "No amnesty, no amnesia, just justice," quoted in Verwoerd 1997).[3] Nonetheless, the South African Constitutional Court upheld the constitutionality of the act (*Azanian Peoples Organization (AZAPO) and others* v. *President of the Republic of South Africa and others* CCT 117/96 (25 July 1996)), and the TRC began functioning in 1995.[4]

Some evidence suggests that the truth and reconciliation process was deeply unpopular among some South Africans. For instance, critics charge that the process has been characterized by little remorse or penance among the perpetrators, that not all of the guilty came forward to admit their crimes (e.g., P.W. Botha), and generally that whites have been unwilling to accept responsibility for apartheid. A host of other criticisms has also been laid against the details of the process employed by the TRC (e.g., Jeffery 1999).

The TRC was established to achieve a general purpose as well as several specific objectives. The goal "of the Commission shall be to promote national unity and reconciliation in a spirit of understanding which transcends the conflicts and divisions of the past" (National Unity and Reconciliation Act, Section (3) (1)). The specific means of achieving this goal include:

> establishing as complete a picture as possible of the causes, nature and extent of the gross violations of human rights which were committed during the period ... including antecedents, circumstances, factors and context of such violations, as well as perspectives of the victims and the motives and perspectives of the persons responsible for the commission of the violations, by conducing investigations and holding hearings.
>
> (National Unity and Reconciliation Act, Section (3) (1) (a))

In calling for a "complete picture" of the past, the law specifically addresses the need to create a collective memory for South Africa.

> A society cannot reconcile itself on the grounds of a divided memory
> ... Clearly, key aspects of the historical and ethical past must be put
> on the public record in such a manner that no one can in good faith
> deny the past. Without truth and acknowledgment, reconciliation is
> not possible.
>
> (Zalaquett 1997: 13)

A second mandate for the TRC involved:

> facilitating the granting of amnesty to persons who make full disclo-
> sure of all the relevant facts related to acts associated with a political
> objective and comply with the requirement of this Act.
>
> (National Unity and Reconciliation Act, Section (3) (1) (b))

This objective obviously concerns the deeds of individual victims and perpetrators, but, to many, over time came also to address the larger issue of
apartheid itself. For instance:

> the enormity of the crime of apartheid as a system of social engin-
> eering must be revealed in all its nakedness, including the distortions
> wrought upon some of those who, in their fight against this evil, lost
> their way and engaged [in] the very human rights violations so
> systematically practised [sic] by their oppressors.
>
> (Human Rights Commission, "HRC Statement," 31/07/93, cited in
> Hay 1998: 55)

The TRC was also charged with

> establishing and making known the fate or whereabouts of victims and
> restoring the human and civil dignity of such victims by granting them
> an opportunity to relate their own accounts to the violations of which
> they are the victims, and by recommending reparation measures in
> respect of them.
>
> (National Unity and Reconciliation Act, Section (3) (1) (c))

The purpose identified in this section is that of achieving reconciliation by
restoring lost dignity to victims, as well as to provide for compensation for
the victims.

Finally, the fourth objective called for the production of a report by the
TRC addressing the first three issues, and making recommendations contributing to a political culture in South Africa that is respectful of the
human rights of all citizens. Thus, the most general goal of the truth and

reconciliation process in South Africa was to enhance the likelihood of reconciliation. Reconciliation was not given a great deal of specific content, although the framers of the process clearly sought to shape the views of individual South Africans, as in getting them to accept the collective memory about the country's past and to endorse an expansive definition of human rights.

The success of truth and reconciliation in South Africa

I begin by postulating that South Africa's truth and reconciliation process succeeded in achieving many of the important objectives set for the process. At a simplistic level, this is self-evidently true. Few expected South Africa's transition to democracy to be accomplished without widespread violence. Tetlock (1998) reports that only 11 of 26 experts on South Africa correctly predicted the peaceful demise of the apartheid system. Indeed, that South Africa would celebrate its first ten years of democracy in 2004 would have been virtually inconceivable to experts in the 1980s. The transition period was certainly contentious, with many dying in the process, and few believe that South Africa has reached a democratic pinnacle today. But to most, the transition is nothing short of miraculous.[5]

The simple answer to the question of why South Africa succeeded includes the truth and reconciliation process. Many credit the TRC and the accompanying activities with creating a more reconciled society, allowing the transition to move forward. The truth and reconciliation process got South Africa over an initial hump so crucial when processes of democratic reform are initiated[6] – a hump still in the distant future for many societies – and in doing so, it allowed democratic reform to get a foothold in South Africa's political culture.[7]

In *Overcoming Apartheid*, I provide a far more systematic assessment of the truth → reconciliation hypothesis. I define a reconciled South African as one who eschews racial stereotyping, treating people respectfully, as individuals, not as members of a racial group, is tolerant of those with whom he or she disagrees, subscribes to a set of beliefs about the universal application of human rights protections to all South African citizens, and who recognizes the legitimacy of South Africa's political institutions and is predisposed to accept and acquiesce to their policy rulings. Thus, the concept refers to reconciliation between *people*, among *groups*, with basic constitutional *principles*, and with the *institutions* essential to the new South African democracy.

The statistical analysis in *Overcoming Apartheid* indicates that slightly less than one-half of South Africans score as at least somewhat reconciled, as measured according to this conceptualization. Racial differences, however, are substantial, as depicted in Figure 9.1. Based on these indicators, one might draw the following conclusions about the level of

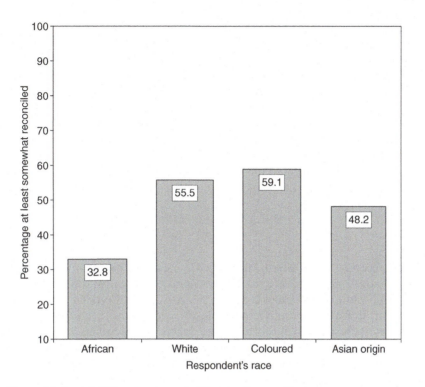

Figure 9.1 Racial differences in overall levels of reconciliation.

reconciliation prevalent among South Africa's various racial groups: Africans – Not very reconciled; Whites – Somewhat reconciled; Coloured South Africans – Somewhat reconciled; and South Africans of Asian origin – Somewhat reconciled. That is, Coloured South Africans are most reconciled, followed by whites, then South Africans of Asian origin, and, finally, Africans. I find the following percentages of each group are at least somewhat reconciled: 33 percent for Africans, 56 percent for whites, 59 percent for Coloured people, and 48 percent for those of Asian origin (see Figure 9.1). Thus, whites, Coloured people, and those of Asian origin hold similar, moderately reconciled views, but Africans are significantly less reconciled. In terms of the various ethnic/linguistic groups, the most reconciled are English-speaking Coloured people (75 percent), followed by English-speaking whites (64 percent). The least-reconciled South Africans are North Sotho-speaking blacks (17 percent). Thus, enormous variability exists in levels of reconciliation across the various groups.

The effect of the truth and reconciliation process may have been to get people to question their beliefs about good and evil in the past and present in South Africa. As the Commission proclaimed:

[O]ne can say that the information in the hands of the Commission made it impossible to claim, for example, that: the practice of torture by the state security forces was not systematic and widespread; that only a few "rotten eggs" or "bad apples" committed gross violations of human rights; that the state was not directly and indirectly involved in "black-on-black" violence; that the chemical and biological warfare programme was only of a defensive nature; that slogans by sections of the liberation movement did not contribute to killings of "settlers" or farmers; and that the accounts of gross human rights violations in the African National Congress (ANC) camps were the consequence of state disinformation. Thus, disinformation about the past that had been accepted as truth by some members of society lost much of its credibility.

(Truth and Reconciliation Commission 1998, Final Report,
Volume 1, 111–112)

If one accepted the positions of the TRC, one might have come to see the struggle over apartheid as one of pretty good good against pretty bad bad, not as absolute good versus infinite evil. It is hard to reconcile with infinite evil; it is perhaps more palatable to reconcile with bad that is not entirely evil (especially if there is some degree of repentance). Truth may have opened the door to reconciliation by encouraging people to abandon their views that South Africa includes people of world views so distant that they cannot be reconcilable. The revelations of the truth and reconciliation process may have encouraged self-reflection and self-criticism, resulting in more moderate views of the adversaries in the struggle. As Gobodo-Madikizela asserts, to demonize one's enemies as monsters is too easy – it lets them off too easily (2003: 119); further, "to dismiss perpetrators simply as evildoers and monsters shuts the door to the kind of dialogue that leads to an enduring peace" (ibid.: 125). Continuing, she argues:

Daring, on the other hand, to look the enemy in the eye and allow oneself to read signs of pain and cues of contrition or regret where one might almost have preferred to continue seeing only hatred is the one possibility we have for steering individuals and societies toward replacing long-standing stalemates out of a nation's past with genuine engagement. Hope is where transformation begins; without it, a society cannot take its first steps toward reconstructing its self-identity as a society of tolerance and coexistence.

(ibid.: 125–126)

Thus, several types of evidence, ranging from anecdotal accounts to complex statistical analysis lead to the conclusion that truth did indeed contribute to a more reconciled South Africa.

Factors contributing to South Africa's success

The target of the process: changing society

The single most important attribute of the truth and reconciliation process in South Africa was that the entire process was designed as an effort at *societal* change. For instance, according to the TRC: "Reconciliation requires that *all South Africans* accept moral and political responsibility for nurturing a culture of human rights and democracy within which political and socio-economic conflicts are addressed both seriously and in a non-violent manner" (Truth and Reconciliation Commission, Volume 5, Chapter 9, p. 435, emphasis added). In an effort to address this mandate, the Final Report of the TRC included in its recommendations a section on the "promotion of a human rights culture" (TRC, Volume 5, Chapter 8, Recommendations). Although the TRC was obviously concerned with the fate of victims and perpetrators, its genius was that it defined its ultimate objective in terms of transforming South African society. The target of its activities was therefore society, which is of course overwhelmingly composed of bystanders, not activists.

I should fully acknowledge that my analysis of truth and reconciliation places rather minor emphasis on victims and perpetrators and rather major emphasis on societal transformation. I entirely support schemes to compensate victims, and to expose the deeds of perpetrators. But the highest goal of such transitional processes is the consolidation of democratic reform (a position Snyder and Vinjamuri (2004) refer to as a "logic of consequences").

One consequence of this definition of the purpose of the process is that the truth and reconciliation process was pursued in every little nook and cranny of the South African countryside. The Commission did not merely sit comfortably in Johannesburg, Cape Town, and Durban, but instead took its proceedings to the hinterland through public hearings in which people were able to come forth and tell their stories of abuse under apartheid. The consequence was that virtually no segment of South African society could ignore the activities of the truth and reconciliation process.[8]

The process was abetted by the mass media, which took a tremendous interest in the activities of the TRC. Not only did the proceedings of the TRC fill the radio airwaves for years, but one of the most widely watched television shows during the mid-1990s depicted the activities of the Commission. With the media saturation of society, virtually every South African had the opportunity to learn about and judge the truth and reconciliation process.

In general, strong impediments always exist to new information generating attitude change (e.g., Zaller 1991). However, the information provided by the truth and reconciliation process had several attributes rendering it likely to be influential. First, information was widely accessible. I mean this not only in terms of the quantity of information available – which by all accounts was absolutely overwhelming – but also in terms of the type of information broadcast. The South African media focused overwhelmingly on the human interest side of the TRC's activities, in contrast to the broader ideological and intellectual goals in which the TRC was also interested. South Africans learned of the suffering of ordinary people through the TRC. What they learned was often extremely graphic – as in Policeman Benzein's demonstration of his notorious "wet bag" method of torture, broadcast widely throughout South Africa. It was the type of fare often addictive to ordinary people, and few in South Africa could have escaped exposure to the highly moving and personalized reports of the activities of the truth and reconciliation process.

It is also important that information about the truth and reconciliation process in South Africa typically had no conspicuous ideological content; no obvious message was being sold. Consequently, reports on the TRC did not necessarily raise the sort of defensive alarms that often make new information impotent in terms of bringing about attitude change.[9] This flows in part from the human interest dimensions of the reports, but also in part from the conscious desire on the part of the TRC to reach all segments of society. Surely, the truth and reconciliation process was used by some to launch ideological attacks on either the apartheid system or the liberation movement, but much of what the TRC put before the South African people was simple and subtle; it had to do with bad guys hurting good guys.[10] Without an obvious and explicit ideological veneer, many of the messages and stories of the TRC were attractive and palatable to South Africans of many different ideological persuasions.

The information presented to South Africans by the TRC was also typically unrebutted, in part because miscreants were coming before the TRC to admit their crimes and to be awarded amnesty. Certainly conflict was occasionally involved (e.g., some victims challenged the motives of the perpetrators, arguing for instance that they were economic not political and therefore not covered by the amnesty legislation). But generally the intense denials that often cloud political controversies were limited in the case of the TRC.

Thus, many of the factors generally contributing to social persuasion reinforce the possibility that the truth and reconciliation process might have created attitude change. The information was salient and interesting, not as threatening as it might have been, thereby avoiding defense mechanisms, subtle in its messages, and largely not greeted by counterarguments. These are just the conditions likely to give rise to social persuasion.

Story-telling instead of trials

The issue of whether to try to hold human rights abusers accountable through legal proceedings is enormously complex, with many legitimate factors contributing to the decision on whether to prosecute.[11] Consequently, I wish to avoid a full discussion of those issues here. But I do nonetheless note that if one wishes to communicate with the mass public – to tell stories, to get them to understand the nature of their past – then trials are unlikely to be effective. Far more compelling is the testimony of ordinary people in their own narratives; the stories that people tell, in their own words, can have an enormous impact on bystanders. Even the hardest apartheid heart could not help but have been moved by some of the tales of abuse and suffering told by the survivors of apartheid atrocities.[12] Even the most militant MK operative must have experienced a twinge of remorse when learning of the terrible damage done to civilians by liberation explosives.[13] The theory of a "just war," in which the ends justify many means, is an abstraction that loses some of its potency when confronted with real people who had their lives destroyed during the struggle. If one wishes to ensure that all segments of a society recognize the pain inflicted, often unfairly, on their enemies during the struggle, then these story-telling proceedings are invaluable.

I must also acknowledge that due process suffers under the story-telling format used by the South African TRC (and indeed due process issues were litigated in South Africa). One solution to due process compromises is to minimize the harm done to those who are accused, although some might have little concern for fully protecting those seeking amnesty for gross human violations from due process compromises. Justice in transitional processes is an aggregate concept, and certain types of injustices can be compensated for by other types of justice. In the end, the criteria by which such processes ought to be judged are surely whether *on balance* more justice than injustice results, and whether the process contributes to the consolidation of democratic reform.[14]

Independence and evenhandedness

The TRC was sued by nearly every major political party in South Africa, from the African National Congress (ANC) to the National Party (NP – the party of apartheid). The commission quite reasonably treats this as evidence of its evenhandedness (see Villa-Vicencio and Verwoerd 2000: 287). Through its willingness to pursue gross human violators irrespective of their ideology, the TRC demonstrated its commitment to a universalistic conception of the meaning of human rights. Although some dubbed this a "poisonous evenhandedness," one of the factors contributing most to the legitimacy of the process was it willingness to blame all parties in the struggle, rejecting the notion that a "just war" justifies or excuses atrocities.

Crucial to the ability to blame all sides in the struggle was the independence of the Commission, and essential to its independence was the nature of the TRC's leadership. Although Archbishop Desmond Tutu has been criticized for injecting his own religious ideology into what some view as a largely secular process (Wilson 2001), and thereby moving "forgiveness" to the forefront of reconciliation,[15] there can be little doubt that Tutu's impeccable integrity and commitment to the liberation of South Africa shielded the TRC from many partisan attacks.

That the TRC was willing to blame all who committed gross human rights violations points as well to the significance of procedural justice in truth and reconciliation processes. The perception of procedural fairness is perhaps the most important asset of truth processes, since perceived fairness enhances legitimacy (see, for example, Tyler and Huo 2002). The TRC blundered several times – as in its decision to grant blanket amnesty to the leaders of the ANC, a decision overturned by the Constitutional Court – but generally the commission was willing to give all parties a voice in the process. This is especially important for victims, since being allowed to tell one's story is a crucial step on the road to the restoration of individual dignity.

A strategy of pursuing "victor's justice" – in which the victors are held to different standards than the vanquished – undermines the legitimacy of truth processes. If a truth and reconciliation process is to be recognized as fair, it must be committed to unearthing and documenting human rights abuses irrespective of the justifications given for such abuses.

Changing views of apartheid in South Africa

Consider how the truth and reconciliation process might have worked among South African whites. White people could have learned from the truth and reconciliation process that the defense of the apartheid state included many indefensible actions. Many of the revelations unearthed by the TRC involved extreme excesses in the political repression the state applied against dissidents. Whether they should have known or not, many white South Africans claim to have been shocked by these revelations, claiming to have never imagined that the state would go as far as it did to crush resistance to apartheid.[16] For instance, when asked about this, a group of white South Africans in one of our focus groups[17] had the following replies:

> Yes, all these things when they came out at the TRC, I thought, my
>   God, where was I living? Was that in South Africa?
> It's a very good point.
> The whites, you didn't know any of that was going on. You looked on
>   apartheid and you were comfortable because you could go to the
>   shops and go where you liked.

It was a very clever system.

It was wonderful, but I didn't know these things were happening. I was shocked to learn what was going on. But that was the government we were living under.

I remember having arguments with my father. He was saying, "Don't believe everything you get told." I'm telling him, "This is happening to my friends" and he kept saying they were Communists and ...

That's it, you see! Because that is what the justification for all this was, to us.

It was the brainwashing.

Moderator: So there are quite a lot of people here, let me understand this nicely, you're saying that to some or to a large extent you weren't actually aware of the atrocities until you saw ...

I think we were aware of people being separated, separate toilets, buses, you know this.

The superficial things.

But, in my opinion ... I can remember growing up, hearing drums on the farm, having a wonderful time and to me, that was some of their choice.

They were happy living in these ...

Yes, they were happy. We were ignorant in a sense of knowing what actually really went on.

Perhaps some whites, even those who still cannot accept that apartheid was a crime against humanity, have come to view the implementation of apartheid, or at least its defense, as criminal. At a minimum, it seems quite unlikely that the defenders of apartheid were as heroic and legitimate after the revelations of the truth and reconciliation process. The "just war" in defense of apartheid seems less just, after the exposés of the TRC.

White South Africans have also learned that liberation does not lead to Communism. The TRC did not have to teach whites this lesson; history was sufficient. With the breakdown of the world-wide Communist movement, with the moderation of both the Mandela and Mbeki governments, few whites today would equate ANC rule with the rule of godless Communists.

Whites cannot help but have been impressed by the magnanimity and graciousness of Nelson Mandela during the early days of the transition. Mandela's continuous pleas for tolerance and reconciliation – not to mention his well-publicized donning of a rugby shirt (the sport of choice among whites) – have undoubtedly contributed to more benign racial attitudes among whites.

Whites may also have come to accept some of the guilt and blame for the benefits they enjoyed under apartheid and for the costs the system imposed on the vast majority of South Africans. Though some whites may have been unaware of the atrocities committed by their state against the liberation forces, no whites could claim to be unaware of the enormous subsidy apartheid provided for their standard of living. Thus, whites attentive to the truth and reconciliation process basically learned that their side was less than noble in creating and defending apartheid, and that the opposition was perhaps less radically evil in its efforts to create a new political system in South Africa.

The truth and reconciliation process may have contributed also to attitude change among blacks, although because the revelations of the process were often not new news to blacks, attitude change may not have been as radical or as widespread. Prior to the TRC, blacks in South Africa were entirely aware of the evil of apartheid, and the TRC did little to dispel this knowledge. But the truth and reconciliation process may have also taught blacks that horrible things were done – against blacks and against whites – in the name of liberation. In many respects, the campaign of ungovernability in the 1980s turned blacks against blacks, with great pressures toward conformity (reinforced by the horrific crime of "necklacing"), and with some degree of gangsterism occurring under the guise of the struggle (e.g., Marks 2001; see also Gobodo-Madikizela 2003: 147). We put the following question to the subjects in one of our African focus groups:

> *Moderator: (Reads second statement:) Those struggling for and against apartheid did terrible things to others. What do you think of that?*
> It's very true, both sides have blood on their hands.
> Even the so-called liberators had very inhumane methods that they used when they wanted to put through a message – in camps abroad and within the country. A lot of people were hurt in the townships, if you were successful you were accused of selling out.
> We as blacks don't empower our people, whites lift each other up. When we blacks get to the top, we forget our own.
>
> *Moderator: Anyone else?*
> It's true, both sides did bad things.
>
> *Moderator: You only mention the liberation movements, why not the white regime?*
> That is obvious, with them we don't even need to mention it, because we know exactly what happened.
>
> *Moderator: But was it justified for both camps to do what they did?*
> Not at all.
> But in those days there was no time to think about whether the actions were justified or not.
>
> *Moderator: So both sides did wrong?*
> Yes.
> Two wrongs don't make a right.

Moreover, the truth and reconciliation process was important for blacks because it often confirmed what many had regarded as "disinformation" created by the apartheid regime. In the 1980s, one never knew what to believe. Some Africans were also no doubt moved by revelations of terrorism directed against innocent white civilians. Many black South Africans most likely came away from the truth and reconciliation process believing that the struggle against apartheid was indeed a "just war" but many unjust actions were taken in the name of liberation.

Moreover, black South Africans have surely learned that apartheid is not the sole source of the myriad problems facing blacks. Perhaps it is true that apartheid caused poverty which in turn causes AIDS (as President Mbeki argues), but few in South Africa accept this connection today. The end of apartheid did little to offer immediate relief to the millions of South Africans living in abject poverty. Thus, one can imagine that the possibility of reconciliation with whites was opened by encouraging Africans to rethink the view that apartheid was a system of infinite evil that was brought down by a movement of ultimate good.

Furthermore, with the fall of the forced segregation of apartheid has come at least some increase in inter-racial interactions within South Africa. One must be careful not to overstate the point, but blacks encountering whites in situations of social equality was very rare before 1994 and has been less rare since 1994. Not only has the frequency of inter-group contact surely increased since the transition, but so too has the quality of the interaction, especially in terms of formal equality (and to a lesser degree, power). The opportunity for blacks and whites to get to know each other has blossomed since the transition (even if taking advantage of the opportunity has been unevenly distributed). This likely contributes to greater possibilities for reconciliation. Thus, the effect of the truth and reconciliation process may have been to get people to question their beliefs about good and evil in the past and present South Africa.

Conclusion

It is certainly true that the independence and evenhandedness of the South African truth and reconciliation process were abetted by several characteristics of the South African case. That the transition was negotiated between the apartheid and liberation forces meant that the "vanquished" maintained considerable political power. A vigilant and diverse mass media carefully scrutinized (and usually criticized) every action of the TRC. South Africa is a country in which most citizens do not view themselves as victimized by the apartheid system (Gibson 2004), and the lack of an enormous class of victims certainly makes reconciliation easier. And South Africa's curiously strong commitment to the rule of law made appeals to legal universalism in the application of human rights principles attractive to many citizens. All of these attributes contributed to the success of the South African truth and reconciliation process. Replicating these factors in other societies may well be difficult if not impossible.

On the other hand, the South African experience teaches several important lessons. Perhaps most important, reconciliation ought to be thought of as focusing on the entire society, not just victims and perpetrators. The experiences of those directly involved in the struggle must be publicized and legitimized so that the bystanders – the overwhelming majority of most conflicted societies – can learn the lessons of reconciliation.

The most important such lesson is that all sides have legitimate grievances; not in equal number, nor with equal responsibility or culpability. But the crucial lesson of transitional justice ought to be that no party to violent conflicts ought to be allowed to violate human rights with impunity. Principles of human rights must be upheld even when the cause of the perpetrator is just. Even those struggling against a regime as evil as apartheid (or the regime of Saddam Hussein) must be bound by basic human rights principles.

That no side is excused does not mean that retribution is necessary. The need for retributive justice is only one component of a large set of justice expectations and demands. Some types of justice are fungible; procedural justice may even substitute for the failure to achieve distributive justice. Governments must not ignore the justice demands of their citizens; but they should be cognizant that the denial of one form of justice can be compensated for with another form of justice.

Discussions about truth commissions often contrast two polar opposites: vindicating the past by strict enforcement of human rights regulations through prosecutions of miscreants versus pragmatic amnesties recognizing the greater importance of the future than the past (Snyder and Vinjamuri (2003) quite appropriately refer to these as stressing either the "logic of appropriateness" versus the "logic of consequences"). In this chapter, I have identified a third, compromise pathway: strict condemnation of all who violate universal human rights standards, but without extensive prosecution (perhaps to be referred to as a "logic of rational hypocrisy"). In this fashion, the principle of universalism is compromised to a lesser degree, while at the same time pragmatic considerations prevail in documenting the past but preparing for the future.

In the final analysis, truth and reconciliation processes are not a "one size fits all" palliative. For many reasons, the South African experience should not be replicated lock, stock, and barrel in other parts of the world. The process in South Africa was expensive, perhaps too expensive for many countries attempting to dig themselves out of the mire of civil war, and as it turns out, a relatively small proportion of the South African population believes itself to have been seriously victimized by apartheid (in the end, only 20,000 or so official victims of gross human rights violations were identified). Moreover, it was enormously time-consuming, and it relied upon what seems to be the boundless patience of ordinary South Africans. The South African truth and reconciliation process was designed to respond to the specific circumstances of that society, and that is surely the first desideratum for all transitional efforts.

But whatever the local circumstances of those contemplating such efforts at reconciliation, the lessons of the South African experience ought to be heeded. In societies torn by a history of violent conflict, the past must be overcome. Transitional systems should never forget that the consolidation of democratic reform is the ultimate objective, and that advancing the cause of democracy cannot prosper without some degree of reconciliation among citizens, groups, and cultures.

Acknowledgments

This is a revised version of a paper delivered at the conference "After the Storm: Reconstructing States, Reconciling Societies," University of North Texas, Denton, Texas, January 14–15, 2005. This research has been supported by the Law and Social Sciences Program of the National Science Foundation (SES 9906576). Any opinions, findings, and conclusions or recommendations expressed in this material are those of the author and do not necessarily reflect the views of the National Science Foundation. The project is a collaborative effort between Amanda Gouws, Department of Political Science, the University of Stellenbosch (South Africa), and me. I am indebted to Charles Villa-Vicencio, Helen Macdonald, Paul Haupt, Nyameka Goniwe, Fanie du Toit, Erik Doxtader, and the staff of the Institute for Justice and Reconciliation (South Africa), where I am a Distinguished Visiting Research Scholar, for the many helpful discussions that have informed my understanding of the truth and reconciliation process in South Africa. Most of the research on which this chapter relies was conducted while I was a Visiting Scholar at the Russell Sage Foundation, to which I am extremely grateful. I also appreciate the research assistance of Eric Lomazoff, of the Russell Sage Foundation.

Notes

1 The most comprehensive description of the truth commissions throughout the world can be found in the work of Hayner (2001). In a pathbreaking book, she documents and compares the attributes of all 21 truth commissions that had been created by the turn of the century, from the Uganda commission in 1974 to the Sierra Leone Truth and Reconciliation Commission of 2000–2001.

2 For instance, Boraine (2000) gives the insider's view of the politics of South Africa's Truth and Reconciliation Commission. So too does Orr (2000), although her story is both more personal and more connected to specific cases before the TRC. The transformation of an individual commissioner is documented by Gobodo-Madikizela's (2003) account of her meetings with one of apartheid's worst assassins. Several highly informative anthologies on truth

commissions have been published. In the South African case, none is better than that compiled by Villa-Vicencio and Verwoerd (2000).

3 For objections to the truth and reconciliation process, see Ngidi (1998). The Spring 1998 issue of *Siyaya!* is devoted to the TRC and provides several interesting articles critical of the process.

4 On the motives of the Biko family in challenging the TRC legislation, see Biko (2000).

5 On the South African "miracle," see Sparks (2003). The struggle against apartheid was itself bloody – and conventional wisdom is that more South Africans died in political violence in the 1990–1994 period than in all other periods of South African history – but few prognosticators expected that the apartheid state would be defeated without anything short of a full-blown civil war.

6 Political scientists typically differentiate between the initiation of and consolidation of democratic reforms. For instance, Diamond (1999: 65) notes that the consolidation of democratic reform is only possible when

> political competitors . . . come to regard democracy (and the laws, procedures, and institutions it specifies) as "the only game in town," the only viable framework for governing the society and advancing their own interests. At the mass level, there must be a broad normative and behavioral consensus – one that cuts across class, ethnicity, nationality, and other cleavages – on the legitimacy of the constitutional system, however poor or unsatisfying its performance may be at any point in time.

7 On South African political culture see Gibson and Gouws (2003).

8 Gibson (2004) documents the high level of awareness of the TRC in South Africa. However, although few black, white, and Asian South Africans were unaware of the TRC, fully one-third of Coloured people claimed to be unaware of the activities of the TRC. Perhaps this reflects the perception among some Coloured people that the events and history addressed by the TRC are not of much relevance to them.

9 An exception may be found in the white Afrikaans community. Afrikaners tended to view the TRC as an "ANC witch hunt," and the Afrikaans-language press continuously vilified the Commission. Villa-Vicencio and Verwoerd (2000: 284) describe this as a "sustained campaign to undermine the legitimacy" of the TRC and its work.

10 As Iyengar and Simon (2000: 156) observe, the image of President Ford attempting to eat a tamale without first shucking it was a very clear signal to Hispanics in the USA of the sensitivity of the president to this constituency. Subtle messages are often more effective at social persuasion than more explicit appeals to attitude change.

11 In the South African case, prosecution was nearly impossible because the apartheid state was in near total control of the apparatus and files of government from 1990 to 1994. See Harris (2000) on the destruction of vital files by agents of the apartheid state. On the failed Malan prosecution, see Van Zyl (2000).

12 No better collection of stories can be found than those chronicled in Krog (1998).

13 The MK was the military wing of the ANC.

14 For a most useful and insightful analysis of the numerous issues surrounding amnesties, see Slye (2000a, 2000b).

15 Wilson is especially critical of the religious veneer often associated with the truth and reconciliation process:

it is misguided to delegitimize human rights at the national level by detaching them from a retributive understanding of justice and attaching them to a religious notion of reconciliation-forgiveness, a regrettable amnesty law and an elite project of nation-building. Democratizing regimes should not seek legitimacy through nation-building, efforts to forge a moral unity and communitarian discourses, but on the basis of accountability and justice defined as proportional retribution and procedural fairness. The role of human rights and the rule of law in all this is to create the bedrock of accountability upon which democratic legitimacy is built.

(2001: 230)

16 Pumla Gobodo-Madikizela, a member of the Human Rights Violations Committee of the TRC, concludes that it is plausible that whites did not know of many of the reprehensible activities of the apartheid government. See Gobodo-Madikizela (2003: 26, 109). She refers to this as an "apartheid of the mind."

17 During June 2000, six focus groups were held, two each in Cape Town, Durban, and Johannesburg. Focus group participants, who of course could not constitute a representative sample of any population, were recruited by the survey firm staff and were paid to participate in the discussions.

References

Biko, N. (2000) "Amnesty and Denial," in C. Villa-Vicencio and W. Verwoerd (eds.) *Looking Back Reaching Forward: Reflections on the Truth and Reconciliation Commission of South Africa*. Cape Town: University of Cape Town Press, pp. 193–198.

Boraine, A. (2000) *A Country Unmasked: Inside South Africa's Truth and Reconciliation Commission*. Oxford: Oxford University Press.

Diamond, L. (1999) *Developing Democracy: Toward Consolidation*. Baltimore, MD: Johns Hopkins University Press.

Gibson, J.L. (2004) *Overcoming Apartheid: Can Truth Reconcile a Divided Nation?* New York: Russell Sage Foundation.

Gibson, J.L. (2005) "The Truth About Truth and Reconciliation in South Africa," *International Political Science Review* (October): forthcoming.

Gibson, J.L. and Gouws, A. (2003) *Overcoming Intolerance in South Africa: Experiments in Democratic Persuasion*. New York: Cambridge University Press.

Gobodo-Madikizela, P. (2003) *A Human Being Died That Night: A South African Story of Forgiveness*. Boston: Houghton Mifflin Company.

Harris, V. (2000) "'They Should Have Destroyed More': The Destruction of Public Records by the South African State in the Final Years of Apartheid, 1990–94," *Transformation* 42: 29–56.

Hay, M. (1998) *Ukubuyisana: Reconciliation in South Africa*. Pietermaritzburg: Cluster Publications.

Hayner, P.B. (2000) "Same Species, Different Animal: How South Africa Compares to Truth Commissions Worldwide," in C. Villa-Vicencio and W. Verwoerd (eds.) *Looking Back Reaching Forward: Reflections on the Truth and Reconciliation Commission of South Africa*. Cape Town: University of Cape Town Press.

Hayner, P.B. (2001) *Unspeakable Truths: Facing the Challenge of Truth Commissions*. New York: Routledge.

Iyengar, S. and Simon, A.F. (2000) "New Perspectives and Evidence on Political Communication and Campaign Effects," *Annual Review of Psychology* 51: 149–169.

Jeffery, A. (1999) *The Truth About the Truth Commission*. Johannesburg: South African Institute of Race Relations.

Krog, A. (1998) *Country of My Skull*. Johannesburg: Random House.

Marks, M. (2001) *Young Warriors: Youth Politics, Identity and Violence in South Africa*. Johannesburg: Witwatersrand University Press.

Ngidi, S. (1998) "Bitter Pill of Amnesty," *Siyaya!* 3 (Spring): 24–25. [No issue number]

Omar, A.M. (1996) "Forward," in M.R. Rwelamira and G. Werle (eds.) *Confronting Past Injustices: Approaches to Amnesty, Punishment, Reparation and Restitution in South Africa and Germany*. Durban: Butterworths.

Orr, W. (2000) *From Biko to Basson: Wendy Orr's Search for the Soul of South Africa as a Commissioner of the TRC*. Saxonwold: Contra Press.

Rwelamira, M.R. (1996) "Punishing Past Human Rights Violations: Considerations in the South African Context," in M.R. Rwelamira and G. Werle (eds.) *Confronting Past Injustices: Approaches to Amnesty, Punishment, Reparation and Restitution in South Africa and Germany*. Durban: Butterworths.

Slye, R. (2000a) "Justice and Amnesty," in C. Villa-Vicencio and W. Verwoerd (eds.) *Looking Back Reaching Forward: Reflections on the Truth and Reconciliation Commission of South Africa*. Cape Town: University of Cape Town Press, pp. 174–183.

Slye, R. (2000b) "Amnesty, Truth, and Reconciliation: Reflections on the South African Amnesty Process," in Robert I. Rotberg and Dennis Thompson (eds.) *Truth v. Justice: The Morality of Truth Commissions*. Princeton, NJ: Princeton University Press, pp. 170–188.

Snyder, J. and Vinjamuri, L. (2003) "Trials and Errors: Principle and Pragmatism in Strategies of International Justice," *International Security* 28 (3, Winter): 5–44.

Sparks, A. (2003) *Beyond the Miracle: Inside the New South Africa*. Chicago: University of Chicago Press.

Tetlock, P.E. (1998) "Close-Call Counterfactuals and Belief-System Defenses: I Was Not Almost Wrong But I Was Almost Right," *Journal of Personality and Social Psychology* 75 (3): 639–652.

Truth and Reconciliation Commission (1998) *Truth and Reconciliation Commission of South Africa Report*. Cape Town: Juta.

Tyler, T.R. and Huo, Y.J. (2002) *Trust in the Law: Encouraging Public Cooperation with the Police and Courts*. New York: Russell Sage Foundation.

Van Zyl, P. (2000) "Justice Without Punishment: Guaranteeing Human Rights in Transitional Societies," in C. Villa-Vicencio and W. Verwoerd (eds.) *Looking Back Reaching Forward: Reflections on the Truth and Reconciliation Commission of South Africa*. Cape Town: University of Cape Town Press, pp. 42–57.

Verwoerd, W. (1997) "Justice After Apartheid? Reflections on the South African Truth and Reconciliation Commission," paper delivered at the Firth International Conference on Ethics and Development, "Globalization, Self-Determination and Justice in Development," Madras, India, 2–9 January.

Villa-Vicencio, C. (2000) "Getting On with Life: A Move Towards Reconciliation," in C. Villa-Vicencio and W. Verwoerd (eds.) *Looking Back Reaching Forward: Reflections on the Truth and Reconciliation Commission of South Africa*. Cape Town: University of Cape Town Press, pp. 199–209.

Villa-Vicencio, C. and Verwoerd, W. (eds.) (2000) *Looking Back Reaching Forward: Reflections on the Truth and Reconciliation Commission of South Africa.* Cape Town: University of Cape Town Press.

Wilson, R.A. (2001) *The Politics of Truth and Reconciliation in South Africa: Legitimizing the Post-Apartheid States.* New York: Cambridge University Press.

Zalaquett, J. (1997) "Why Deal With the Past?' in Alex Boraine, Janet Levy, and Ronel Scheffer (eds.) *Dealing with the Past: Truth and Reconciliation in South Africa.* Second Edition. Cape Town: Institute for Democracy in South Africa, pp. 8–15.

Zaller, J. (1991) *The Nature and Origins of Mass Opinion.* Cambridge: Cambridge University Press.

10 Violence, participation, and democratic norms

Prospects for democratic consolidation in post-conflict Central America

John A. Booth and Patricia Bayer Richard

Political violence wracked Central America from the 1970s through the mid-1990s and took hundreds of thousands of lives. Five of six nations entered the 1970s with authoritarian governments. Only Costa Rica practiced constitutional electoral democracy and consistently respected human rights. Three countries experienced civil wars driven by a combination of economic crisis and increasing political mobilization against authoritarian rule, and political unrest spread across most of the region. In 1979 Nicaraguan rebels led by the Sandinistas overthrew the Somoza regime and began an 11-year revolution that ended when Nicaraguans voted out the revolutionary government in 1990. US intervention and financing nourished Nicaraguan counterinsurgents who fought the revolutionary government throughout the 1980s. In El Salvador, a military coup overthrew a military government in late 1979, spawning a leftist rebellion and extensive US involvement on behalf of the government. This war lasted until 1992, eventually ending in a negotiated settlement after a slow transition to formal electoral democracy. Guatemala's military regimes fought a counterinsurgency war against leftist rebels from the 1960's through 1996. Until the mid-1980s the military repressed civilian opposition, but then slowly liberalized the regime and transferred power to civilians; negotiations ended the war in 1996. Honduras's military regime began liberalizing in the early 1980s; this shift of power toward civilians likely averted civil war. Panama's military-dominated government suppressed opposition parties until an invasion by the United States in 1989 ousted Manuel Noriega from power and ushered in electoral democracy.

These developments raise vital questions about Central America and the effects of civil wars the world over. How might peace be sustained in the three nations that experienced civil wars? Is democracy the key to preventing the reemergence of civil war or other extreme political violence? Does long-term peace require democracy, as Doyle and Sambanis (2000) contend? Is the democracy that has developed in Central America likely to consolidate itself and thus diminish the risk of a return to authoritarianism? To what extent do the popular culture and behavior of Central Americans contribute to democratic consolidation? What actions might elites and foreign actors take to promote democratic consolidation? To address these questions we focus on survey research to elucidate the extent to which democratic political cultures have emerged in the region's six countries. The lessons learned here have significant implications for post-conflict societies elsewhere.

During the violence and repression of the 1970s and 1980s, conditions in authoritarian Central American countries did not favor survey research, especially on sensitive questions about political beliefs and behavior. In the early 1990s, however, the Central American Peace Accords and the presence of several new civilian governments made survey research possible. Based on comparable surveys conducted in six Central American nations in the early 1990s,[1] we studied citizens' political behaviors and opinions. In 2004 a new set of similar surveys were conducted in the same countries.[2] The 2004 data enable us to examine changes in political attitudes and behaviors and to see whether democratic political culture has broadened and deepened. Will these electoral democracies, having operated as such for a decade or more, manifest similar attitudinal and behavioral characteristics to those encountered in the early 1990s? Have citizen political engagement and attitudes reached a point that will render unlikely a return to authoritarianism and civil war?

Violence

As noted above, by 2004 formal electoral democracy had been established for two decades or longer in all six countries in the region. The civil wars that afflicted El Salvador, Guatemala and Nicaragua in the 1970s and 1980s had ended. We therefore assumed that by 2004 the political contexts of the formerly most violent Central American countries would have become much less violent than in the early 1990s. We expected that with lessened violence would come enhanced democratic norms, and greater political participation, civil society activism, and political support for regimes.

Despite the end of the civil wars and adoption of formal electoral democracy, political violence in Central America has diminished rather less than we expected. Table 10.1 presents Gibney's (2005a, 2005b) Political Terror Scale (PTS), which assesses the level of political violence within a country over time. Coders rank countries on a five-level scale ranging from 1.00 – "a secure rule of law, people are not imprisoned for their views, and torture is rare or exceptional. Political murders are extremely rare" – up through 5.00 –

> [t]he terrors of level 4 ["murders, disappearances, and torture are a common part of life"] have been expanded to the whole population.

Table 10.1 Evolution of political violence in Central America*

	Costa Rica	El Salvador	Guatemala	Honduras	Nicaragua	Panama	Region
Political Terror Scale 1990	1.00	4.00	4.00	3.00	4.00	2.00	3.00
Political Terror Scale 2003	1.00	3.00	3.00	3.00	3.00	2.00	2.50
Net Change in Political Terror Scale, 1991 to 2003	0.00	−1.00	−1.00	0.00	−1.00	0.00	−0.50
Political Terror Scale, mean 1981–1990	1.00	4.00	4.10	2.80	3.90	2.50	3.05
Political Terror Scale, mean 1994–2003	1.00	2.60	3.50	2.80	2.80	1.90	2.43
Change in Political Terror Scale mean 1981–1990 to 1994–2003	0.00	−1.40	−0.60	0.00	−1.10	−0.60	−0.62

Source: Gibney (2005b).

*Note on scale values:

Level 1: Countries under a secure rule of law, people are not imprisoned for their view, and torture is rare or exceptional. Political murders are extremely rare; Level 2: There is a limited amount of imprisonment for nonviolent political activity. However, few persons are affected, torture and beatings are exceptional. Political murder is rare; Level 3: There is extensive political imprisonment, or a recent history of such imprisonment. Execution or other political murders and brutality may be common. Unlimited detention, with or without a trial, for political views is accepted; Level 4: The practices of level 3 are expanded to larger numbers. Murders, disappearances, and torture are a common part of life. In spite of its generality, on this level terror affects those who interest themselves in politics or ideas; Level 5: The terrors of level 4 have been expanded to the whole population. The leaders of these societies place no limits on the means or thoroughness with which they pursue personal or ideological goals (Gibney 2005a).

The leaders of these societies place no limits on the means or thoroughness with which they pursue personal or ideological goals.

(Gibney 2005a)

Table 10.1 includes the PTS scores for the six Central American countries for 1990 and 2003 (just prior to each of our two waves of surveys). We find the expected high levels of terror or violence in 1990, but by 2003 see only a modest violence decline of one point in three countries, Nicaragua, El Salvador, and Guatemala, each of which had had civil wars. Among the countries that had not experienced civil wars, each remained at the same level, Costa Rica at a low violence level (1.00), Panama at 2.00, and Honduras at 3.00. Region wide, the average improvement between 1990 and 2003 was only a half point on the political terror scale. We also calculated the average PTS scores for the decade prior to each survey. The picture is slightly more nuanced, but basically similar. The PTS regional average between the two decades declined 0.62 points. Costa Rica remained stable at a low level of violence across these decades at 1.00. Honduras too, was stable, but at an intermediate violence level of 2.80. El Salvador experienced the biggest between-period change in violence (−1.40), followed by Nicaragua (−1.10) and Guatemala and Panama both (−0.60). Thus all the civil war countries improved on their levels of violence.

These data belie our supposition that democratization and settling civil wars would sharply reduce violence. The horrific figures of deaths from combat and mass killings during the civil wars had indeed largely vanished by the early 2000s. But, despite this, several governments have failed to establish public security or effectively protect their citizens in the post-conflict environment (Kincaid 2000). In the early 2000s several countries experienced continuing disappearances or murders of party personnel or candidates, indicating that not all political elites had embraced democratic rules of the game. There were also high levels of gang violence in El Salvador and Honduras, spawned in part by large numbers of returning émigrés from the United States who became involved in urban gangs there. The strength and capability of police forces in several countries failed to keep up with the rise in criminality in the aftermath of formal peace and reform of security forces. Ill-trained and understaffed police have recently responded to gangs and to large numbers of homeless street children with the same solution – extrajudicial killings. National security personnel in some countries had become involved in narcotics smuggling. Finally, ex-police cashiered under terms of the peace accords in El Salvador and Guatemala became involved in criminal activities including carjackings and kidnappings for ransom (Dye *et al.* 2000; Spence *et al.* 2001; Freedom House 2003a, 2003b, 2003c, 2003d, 2003e, 2003f; Robinson 2003; Booth *et al.* 2006). The inability of these formally democratic governments to ensure security and prevent violence bodes ill for their democratic consolidation and peace.

In summary, Central America's violence, rather than disappearing changed old modalities of terror and insecurity to new ones. Civil wars' armed clashes between insurgents and regime forces and dictatorship's intense repression of perceived opponents have mostly gone, but gang violence, official anti-gang repression, high crime rates, lynchings, renegade ex-police, and persistent violent harassment of political figures and activists replaced them. Formal peace brought only modest reductions in violence, and for many Central Americans life remained startlingly insecure.

In addition, although civil wars have ended, the quality of democracy established in Central America has been mediocre in several cases. Freedom House democracy scores[3] (a low score indicating greater rights and liberties) showed modest improvements between 1993 and 2003 (Table 10.2).[4] Panama improved the most (from four down to one on political rights and from three to two on civil liberties. The three civil war countries each moved one point in a positive direction: Nicaragua and El Salvador on political rights and Guatemala on civil liberties. Honduras worsened a point on political rights, and Costa Rica lost a point on civil liberties. Costa Rica nevertheless remained what Freedom House calls "fully free" and Panama joined it in that category. The remaining Central American countries remained "partly free." This judgment that only "partial freedom" prevails in Central America's post-civil war, "low-intensity democracies" (Booth *et al.* 2006) reflects their continued violence.

In summary, then, from the early 1990s to the early 2000s Costa Rica maintained and Panama moved toward full freedom. This contrasts with the other four nations where formal democracy and peace accords ended the combat and repression of civil war, but did not end other kinds of political, social, and criminal violence. New types of violence (vigilantism, the killing of "undesirable" gang members and street urchins by police) and some old types of violence (extrajudicial political killings, death squads, military involvement in internal security activities) remain or have grown since the early 1990s. On the other hand, Freedom House and other observers describe Central American citizens as free to elect or change their governments, and characterize recent elections as relatively or very free and fair in all six countries (Freedom House 2003a, 2003b, 2003c, 2003d, 2003e, 2003f; Booth *et al.* 2006.) Thus, despite formal democracy, there remains in Central America a significant disjuncture between Panama and Costa Rica with the least violent histories and best democratic liberties performances, and the other four countries with their more violent histories and more repressive recent performances.

Analysis[5]

Our aim here is to explore comparatively the impact of violence on levels of political participation and key democratic norms in 2004, and to

Table 10.2 Freedom House scores for Central American countries, 1993 and 2003

Freedom House measures	Costa Rica	El Salvador	Guatemala	Honduras	Nicaragua	Panama
Political rights 1993	1	3	4	2	4	4
Civil liberties 1993	1	3	5	3	3	3
Political rights 2003	1	2	4	3	3	1
Civil liberties 2003	2	3	4	3	3	2

Source: Freedom House (2003a, 2003b, 2003c, 2003d, 2003e, 2003f).

Note
Scale range 1 = best performance, 7 = worst performance.

compare these patterns with those from the 1990s. We seek to explain to what extent the evident shortcomings of several of these post-civil war regimes may have affected citizens' participation and support for democracy. This will allow us to proffer some conclusions about the effects of political violence in post-conflict Central America and to make some suggestions about policies that might enhance the prospects for the consolidation of democracy in the region.

Participation

Classical democratic theory treats political participation as the key to democracy. Societies are more democratic when more of their citizens take part in politics, their political activities are more varied, and the arenas affected by citizen action are broader (Pateman 1970; Cohen 1973). Political participation includes not only engagement around elections (voting and campaigning), but such other activities as civil society (group) engagement, community activism, contacting public officials, and political protest. We expected participation to increase in post-civil war countries with their lowered state repression and formal democracy. Expanded participation has special importance in post-civil war democracies as vehicles through which citizens engage their governments and resolve conflicts. Table 10.3 presents evidence from 2004 on Central Americans' participation in their political systems.

Being registered to vote ranged from 76 to 99 percent, reflecting differences in national policy: some countries require voter registration (Costa Rica and Nicaragua) and issue a mandatory combined national identity-voter registration card. Others separate national civil registration and voter registration.[6] Guatemala's lower registration rate reflects a low effort to encourage citizens to become voters. We suspected that the Ladino (Hispanic) population would have a much higher registration rate than indigenous in Guatemala, but the difference was only 4 percent. Our two waves of surveys showed an upward trend in registered voters of several percentage points in Costa Rica, El Salvador and Nicaragua.[7] El Salvador had the greatest increase (14 percent), driven by the implementation of a new voter and identification system and massive re-registration drive for the 2004 elections. In Panama urban voter registration declined 7 percent, perhaps owing to the cooling of electoral passions after the hotly contested pre-invasion election of 1989.

Self-reported voter turnout in each country's most recent presidential election was around 75 percent, except for Guatemala at 65 percent. Since a mere 1 percent fewer indigenous Guatemalans reported voting than Ladinos, it was not disproportionately low indigenous turnout that reduced overall voting there.

In all countries, Central Americans outvote US citizens. We surmise that for Central Americans having free elections offered a refreshing

Table 10.3 Political participation rates by country, Central American nations, 2004

Type of political participation	Costa Rica	El Salvador	Guatemala	Honduras	Nicaragua	Panama
Voting behavior						
Registered to vote (%)	99	94	76	91	87	87
Voted in last Presidential election (%)	74	76	65	73	75	76
Attend political party meetings (%)	6	9	12	19	20	18
Campaigning						
Attempted to persuade someone how to vote (%)	30	21	28	25	19	30
Worked for a political campaign or candidate (%)	16	8	10	15	14	11
Communal activism						
Attend community improvement group* (%)	14	19	27	28	18	18
Worked with others to solve community problem (%)	34	31	34	37	29	38
Civil society activism*						
Church-related group (%)	52	39	69	69	51	30
School-related group (%)	44	36	36	45	41	18
Business-professional gp. (%)	7	5	9	7	9	7
Mean group activism **(%)	34	26	38	41	33	18
Contacting public officials						
Local official (%)	32	34	32	22	30	17
Legislative deputy (%)	11	8	8	11	9	20
Protest participation (%)	15	6	11	9	18	20

Source: Data from the Latin American Public Opinion Project at Vanderbilt University (2004), multinational survey, funded by the US Agency for International Development.

Notes
* Percentages are for reporting attendance at meetings of each group "from time to time" or more frequently, at least an intermediate or higher level of involvement.
** Average of all three types of groups listed above (church, school and business-professional) for at least the intermediate-level of involvement ("from time to time").

difference from political oppression and therefore much valued. Relatively high levels of turnout may represent a referendum on democracy and a preference for it and for peace. The more intimate political arenas of these small countries may also favor high turnout. Over the period covered by the surveys, though, while turnout rates remained stable in Panama, they declined elsewhere in the region, in Guatemala and Nicaragua by a few percentage points and reaching a 15 percent decline in Costa Rica and 18 percent in Honduras.[8] In marked contrast, however, urban Salvadorans reported a 23 percent rise in turnout, greater even than its increase in voter registration.

Partisan activity such as attending political party meetings requires more time and effort than voting. Fewer than one in 16 Costa Ricans reported attending such meetings while about one in five in Honduras, Nicaragua, and Panama did so. The low attendance reported in Costa Rica may stem partly from the two major parties having adopted primary elections in the 1980s. This reduced the parties' use of local meetings and brought other significant changes in the party system. The once-dominant National Liberation Party lost adherents and experienced severe electoral reversals in the 1998 and 2002 elections. Citizens may thus have disengaged from Costa Rica's parties because of growing disaffection with the party system and because both dominant parties experienced major corruption scandals since the mid-1990s (Rovira Mas 2000; Sánchez 2003; Booth 2005). Citizens in Guatemala and El Salvador, whose transitions to formal democracy are the region's most recent and where violent repression afflicted certain parties' members and political candidates, may remain more reluctant to expose themselves as party activists by attending meetings than those in Nicaragua, Honduras, and Panama where party activity was much freer and more open during much of the 1980s and 1990s.[9]

In actual campaigning, about 30 percent of Costa Ricans, Guatemalans and Panamanians had tried to convince others how to vote while only about 20 percent of Salvadorans and Nicaraguans did so. Central Americans vary modestly in the percentages who reported working in political campaigns (8 to 16 percent), but El Salvador, with historically high repression levels, is again low.

Communal activism – collective self-help or community improvement work – allows citizens to address local problems and needs and has had a vibrant history in Central America. Communal activism persisted even during intense political conflict and repression, apparently not appearing as a challenge to authoritarian regimes (Booth and Richard 2004). More than one in five survey respondents at least occasionally attended a communal organization meeting and one in three had "contributed or tried to contribute to the solution of some problem" of their communities within the previous two years. Guatemalans and Hondurans were most involved in community groups. Between the two surveys reported attendance at communal association meetings had declined about 10 to 12 percent in urban Costa Rica, Guatemala and Nicaragua but remained steady elsewhere.

Participation in formal organizations (civil society) offers people a way to promote their interests collectively. Table 10.3 compares the percentage of citizens attending meetings at least "from time to time" in church-related, school-related, and business and professional organizations. The overall mean group activism level (constructed by averaging the scores for all three types of groups) shows that Panamanians reported far less group activity than the rest of their Central American neighbors, and Hondurans the most.

Compared to the 1990s, urban Panamanians and Salvadorans reported doing considerably less church-group activity (15 and 26 percent less, respectively). Costa Ricans and Nicaraguans reported modest increases (5 to 7 percent), while Guatemalans and Hondurans reported substantial increases (16 and 20 percent growth, respectively). This sharp increase in Guatemala and Honduras may stem from a widely observed growth of evangelical Protestant proselytism and the formation of many new Protestant congregations in the 1990s. In El Salvador, the opening of alternate channels of political activism may have decreased the appeal or need of church-related activity. We also find urban populations reporting slight declines in school-related activism across the region but a much greater 22 percent drop in El Salvador. Involvement in professional and business groups also declined region wide between the surveys.

In most countries, citizens contact public officials to demand services, seek benefits or to call government's attention to some problem. Table 10.3 shows that about one Central American in four reported contacting a local public official. The frequency of activity is similar for Costa Rica, El Salvador, Guatemala, and Nicaragua, but lower for Honduras and especially Panama. In contrast, Panamanians were most likely to contact legislators. Panamanian legislators may have been more responsive to their constituents than those of other countries. The distinct preference of Guatemalans and Salvadorans to contact local officials may reflect the higher recent repression levels in both countries than elsewhere in the region. Previous research has shown that participation in the local arena (municipal government and local organizations) provides venues for citizen activism even in very repressive regimes, possibly because it is less threatening to national authorities.

As to protest behavior, Table 10.3 reveals that the Central American countries split into higher and lower protest countries. Fifteen to 20 percent of Nicaraguans, Costa Ricans, and Panamanians reported protesting compared to between 6 to 11 percent of Salvadorans, Guatemalans, and Hondurans. The history of violent repression of political opposition may account for fewer protesters in El Salvador, Guatemala, and Honduras. In contrast, despite its extensive political violence, Nicaragua experiences frequent demonstrations as working-class groups, unions, and organizations linked to the Sandinista party protested neo-liberal austerity privatization proposals of post-1990 governments (Dye *et al.* 2000; Deonandan 2004). Costa Rica also has a lively record of citizens demonstrating and of positive government response to protest (Booth 1998), which can offer a lesson to the post-conflict regimes: Non-violent protest is healthy for democracy.

In sum, according to 2004 survey data, Central Americans engaged the political system through high voter turnout, campaigning, attendance at party meetings, contacting officials, and even protesting. To understand what other factors might have influenced political participation we analyzed other variables in the survey. For a within-system participation variable (all the participation variables discussed above except protesting) we found that, other variables held constant, higher systemic levels of political terror reduced participation rates, clearly revealing a civil war "hangover" effect. Respondents who were economically better off and women had reduced participation. Perceiving the political system to allow free participation, being older, and (most strongly) having more education increased participation.[10] It is instructive to note that several of these variables shaping participation can be influenced by national political elites, especially access to education and levels of political violence and repression. These factors provided important keys to increased democratic participation in Central America and indicate that ruling elites' choices about public policy and governmental behavior remained as central to citizen participation in 2004 as they had in the early 1990s.

Attitudes

Latin American political culture has long had authoritarian components including citizen intolerance of regime critics, antidemocratic norms, and preference for strong leaders (Dealy 1974; Morse 1974; Wiarda 1981). Central American countries shared these traits, which were likely reinforced by protracted authoritarian rule in several countries. Research from the late 1980s, however, reported higher democratic norms than anticipated among Nicaraguans – equal to those of their Costa Rican neighbors – despite Nicaragua's lesser experience with democracy (Seligson and Booth 1993). Citizens of other countries in the region had democratic norms by the early 1990s (Booth and Richard 1998a, 1998b). This discrepancy between cultural tradition and recent findings calls for us to assess the balance between authoritarian and democratic norms. We especially want to know whether the commitment to democracy persisted or grew after the end of civil wars.

We asked respondents whether their country needed "a strong leader who does not need to be elected or worry about elections." As Table 10.4 reveals, between 6 and 22 percent of Central Americans agreed with this

Table 10.4 Political attitudes by country, Central America, 2004

Attitudes	Costa Rica	El Salvador	Guatemala	Honduras	Nicaragua	Panama
Authoritarianism						
"We need a strong leader who does not need to be elected." (% agreeing)	7	6	18	22	13	10
Support for military coups						
"There are some circumstances under which a military coup may be justified." (% agreeing)	48	64	46	55	32	47
Support for general political participation rights* (index, range = 1–100)	81	70	66	72	78	83
Tolerance for participation rights for regime critics ** (index, range = 1–100)	62	56	52	60	59	68
Support for civil disobedience and confrontational political methods *** (index, range =1–100)	25	28	29	34	30	29
System Support						
General System Support **** (index, range = 1–100)	71	62	51	53	51	54
Specific Institutional Support ***** (index, range 1–100)	58	57	45	48	44	50

Source: Data from 2004 Survey by US Agency for International Development. See source for Table 10.3.

Notes

* This index incorporates approval of three behaviors: taking part in a legal demonstration, in a group working to solve communal problems, and in campaigning for a candidate or party.

** This index incorporates approval of four behaviors by critics of the regime: being allowed to vote, carry out peaceful demonstrations, run for public office, and give a speech on television.

*** This index incorporates approval of four behaviors: taking part in street blockages, invading of private property, taking over factories, offices, or buildings, or taking part in a group that wishes to overthrow an elected government by violent means.

**** This index incorporates level of approval of national political institutions, protection of basic rights, pride in the system, and obligation to support the political system.

***** This index incorporates citizen support/approval for 9 different specific government institutions (elections office, legislature, "the government," political parties, supreme court, municipal government, and elections, etc.).

patently authoritarian statement, a viewpoint likely dangerous to democracy if widely held. In Honduras and Guatemala, about one in five held this view.

The survey also asked: "Are there ever any circumstances under which a military coup might be justified?" Region-wide, about half of the respondents agreed with this non-democratic position. Nicaraguans embraced this idea the least (32 percent), but Salvadorans (64 percent) and Hondurans (55 percent) were much more receptive. Costa Rica, which has had no military rule for eight decades and no coups d' etat since the 1940s, surprised us with almost half of its respondents envisioning circumstances that might justify a coup. Indeed, Costa Ricans' response on this item is similar to that expressed in the much more coup-afflicted Panama.

When asked what specific hypothetical problems might justify a military takeover of their governments, Central Americans mentioned official corruption (61 percent), crime (56 percent), and inflation (55 percent). These findings reveal that, across the region, Central Americans' commitment to civilian rule remained partly contingent on regime performance. Threats to their security (crime and inflation) and public corruption deeply troubled many. Should crime, corruption, or inflation (or all three) become sufficiently bad, armed forces or other plotters against the constitutional order might find many citizens who would support a coup d'état claiming to address these problems. A possibly analogous case is Weimar Germany. The combination of a structurally democratic state with terrible economic performance created conditions leading to public support for Hitler and the breakdown of democracy.

Turning to democratic norms, Table 10.4 reports the averages for an index of support for basic political participation rights for citizens of a democracy. On a scale of one to 100 (from the least to the most democratic), the urban citizens of all six countries averaged well in the positive end of the scale. Panamanians, Costa Ricans and Nicaraguans scored the highest and Guatemalans lowest. Comparing support for general participation rights between decades, we found a decline in scores region wide ranging from two to ten points. Central Americans had not abandoned their support for general participation rights as of 2004, but the decline of support for participation rights raises some concern about the prospects for democratic consolidation. This finding, like the support level for coups, suggests that support for democracy in 2004 remained fragile in the face of the poor political and economic performance of several regimes.

On a measure of tolerance for participation rights for regime critics (those "who speak badly of our form of government") on a similar one to 100 scale, Central Americans expressed less support than they did for general participation rights. The tolerance index taps into support for a challenging precept of democracy: allowing regime critics to take part in politics. Panamanians were the most tolerant (mean score of 68), followed by Costa Ricans, Hondurans and Nicaraguans with scores around 60 and

Salvadorans (56) and Guatemalans (52). Across the two decades no mean-
ingful changes in tolerance levels occurred among urban Costa Ricans,
Panamanians or Nicaraguans. In Honduras, however, the tolerance
average declined ten points. Combined with a similar decline in support
for general participation rights in Honduras, this suggests a diminished
popular commitment to democracy. In positive contrast, tolerance scale
scores rose six points in El Salvador and seven in Guatemala, a positive
development in the two lowest-tolerance and post-civil war countries.

We also asked citizens whether they supported various confrontational
political behaviors including political violence. While political confrontation may sometimes be needed to create, nurture or maintain democracy,
such tactics seldom enjoy widespread support. If engaged in to extremes
they may threaten a democratic system. Taking part in a "group wishing to
violently overthrow an elected government" – one of the items in this
index – may indeed be inimical to democracy itself. On a similar one to
100 scale, the region-wide index average is below 29, indicating a widely
shared bias against such techniques. Hondurans were the most favorable
toward confrontational tactics (34 index mean), and Costa Ricans the least
(25).

Comparing support for confrontational political methods over time, we
found an increase everywhere but Honduras. In Panama support had
nearly doubled to 29 scale points in 2004, and in the remaining countries,
support rose roughly seven points from their early 1990s levels. As civil
wars ended and formal democracy generalized, urban Central Americans
grew more supportive of confrontational tactics. This may be partly
because more democratic institutions reduced the danger of such confrontation. Interestingly, though, the trend also applies for Costa Ricans
where there was little danger earlier. Perhaps, then, some of the increase
stemmed from reaction against the effects of neo-liberal economic
reforms. Under pressure from foreign lending institutions and governments, debt-strapped governments in the 1990s cut public sector services
and jobs and privatized public sector enterprises. Protests provided
affected workers and consumers one of the few tools to influence public
policy. We are not surprised that sympathy for confrontational tactics rose
simultaneously with protests against tough economic austerity measures.

Comparing findings over time

Another way to assess how ending civil wars and formal democratization
have affected political participation and attitudes in the region is to
examine repression's effects on some of the key variables laid out above.
Our earlier research showed that repression had a strongly depressing
effect on participation and democratic norms. Taking advantage of both
surveys, we can explore the relative effects of political repression, measured by the Political Terror Scale, on participation and attitudes in the

early 1990s and in 2004 using a multiple regression analysis, controlling for the effects of national gross domestic product per capita; respondents' sex, age, standard of living, and education); civil society engagement, exposure to news media, interpersonal trust, and diffuse support for the political system.[11] Assuming that the effect of high levels of political violence decays slowly, our measure is the average political terror scale score for the decade prior to each of the surveys (1981–1990 and 1994–2003).[12]

The partial replication of the 1990s analyses for these variables using the PTS to measure political repression produces results very similar to those reported in our prior work (Booth and Richard 1996, 1998a, 1998b; Richard and Booth 2000). Table 10.5 reveals that repression in the 1990s lowered political participation, democratic norms, and support for civil disobedience while elevating citizens' willingness to suppress civil liberties.[13]

Turning to the comparative analysis over time of repression's effects (Table 10.5), the most striking finding is that repression's impact on political participation declines over time. Even though violence levels remained fairly high in post-conflict Central America, the emergence of formal democracy, modest civil liberties improvements, and the disappearance of formal combat between regimes and insurgents have apparently lowered many barriers to political engagement. Repression's depressing effect on support for civil disobedience and confrontational political methods also declined between the early 1990s and 2004, likely for similar reasons. We surmise that a qualitative shift in the political climate of at least two of the post-civil war countries, Guatemala and El Salvador, toward less extensive and systematic repression of perceived opponents and less violent government-insurgent warfare has opened the political climate for participation in general and makes expression of support for dissent and protest more acceptable. Thus "peace" and formal democratization have enlarged political space.

In sharp contrast, the depressing effect of violence on basic democratic norms in the decade before each survey more than doubled between the early 1990s and 2004 and its effect on Central Americans' willingness to suppress civil liberties also increased. Thus the violence reflected in the 2004 survey – albeit more disorganized and less regime- and insurgent-managed than in the early 1990s – actually undermined rather than reinforced democratic norms more than earlier repression. Perversely, the somewhat less violent environments of the early 2000s – marked by the disorganized and random violence of police killings of gang members, violent crime, occasional political assassinations, and vigilantism – reduced democratic values more than the climates of organized repression and civil war of the 1980s and early 1990s. Military regimes took the blame for the repression of the 1970s and 1980s, which made formal democracy attractive to Central Americans. In the early 2000s, however, the great risk of the high violence levels is that they erode democratic norms and undermine the credibility and legitimacy of the region's inept democracies.

Table 10.5 Multiple regression models of political terror's effects, early 1990s and 2004

	Political participation[a]		Democratic norms[b]		Civil disobedience[d]		Censor/suppr. civil liberties[e]	
	1990s	2004	1990s	2004	1990s	2004	1990s	2004
Political terror (in the decade before each survey)	**−0.344**	**−0.069**	**−0.186**	**−0.351**	**−0.191**	**−0.089**	**0.149**	**0.191**
National gross domestic product/capita in survey yr.	−0.053	−0.004	−0.031	**−0.226**	**−0.207**	**−0.131**	0.011	**0.192**
Sex (male = 1, female = 2)	**−0.122**	**−0.087**	**−0.064**	**−0.081**	−0.012	−0.018	−0.003	**0.031**
Age	**0.048**	**0.118**	**0.053**	0.022	**−0.082**	**−0.167**	**−0.119**	**−0.064**
Standard of living[f]	**−0.064**	**−0.107**	−0.012	**0.036**	**−0.095**	**−0.061**	0.015	**−0.055**
Years of education	**0.040**	**0.136**	**0.179**	**0.150**	0.001	**−0.097**	**−0.095**	**−0.108**
Civil society activism[g]	**0.371**	**0.282**	**0.081**	−0.005	**0.064**	0.015	−0.019	−0.002
Level of news media contact[h]	**0.057**	**0.098**	0.027	**0.032**	**0.050**	**0.025**	0.015	0.011
Level of interpersonal trust[i]	0.010	−0.010	0.026	0.003	−0.002	−0.018	0.001	0.014
Diffuse support for the political system[j]	−0.003	**0.041**	0.022	**0.103**	**−0.223**	−0.024	0.016	**0.083**

Sources: Early 1990s and 2004 Central American Surveys (1990s data urban only, 2004 data national samples).

Notes

* Cell values presented in each column are beta coefficients, which indicate the relative independent contribution of each variable in the left-hand column to the dependent variable (indicated in the column headings); coefficients in **boldface** are significant at p>0.05 (unlikely to occur by chance more than one time in twenty).

a These indices combine registering to vote, voting, contacting public officials, campaign activity, and communal activism. They exclude civil society activism.

b These identical indices include respondents' support for general political participation rights and tolerance for the rights of regime critics. They combine support for general participation rights and tolerance for regime critics' rights (Table 10.4).

c Respondent agreement that "there are some circumstances under which a military coup may be justified."

d Index that combines respondents' approval of civil disobedience and confrontational means (demonstrations, occupation of buildings, blocking streets, and participating in a group violently seeking to overthrow the regime).

e Respondents' approval of the suppression of civil liberties (including censorship, prohibition of demonstrations and prohibition of political meetings).

f Index of living standard calculated from possession of certain artifacts in home (appliances, televisions, automobiles, etc.)

g Index calculated from respondent's reported frequency of attendance at meetings of church-related, school-related, and business/professional groups.

h Index based on respondent's level of reported exposure to news media (newspaper, radio, television).

i Index calculated from three questions indicating respondent's degree of agreement that others are fundamentally trustworthy.

j Index of respondent's trust or confidence in national political institutions (e.g., courts, legislature, etc.) and the protection of the respondent's basic rights by the political system.

Conclusion and policy implications

The end of both formal, highly organized regime-against-insurgent violence and systematic state terror campaigns in several Central American countries and the advent of formal electoral democracy have reduced the overall amount of political violence in Central America and reshaped the nature of violence. Disparate violence (less structured by competition over state power) from multiple sources still earned Central American nations high political terror scores in the early 2000s; some of this violence was clearly political and some of it criminal. Some emanated from within the state (especially the police) and some from the non-state actors (gangs and lynch mobs). Despite the end of civil war and regime violence and despite the onset of democracy, therefore, violence persists in post-conflict Central America.

According to 2004 survey data, Central Americans engaged the political system through voting, campaigning, attending party meetings, contacting officials, and protesting. Regional trends from the early 1990s to 2004 indicate that voter registration rose, but voter turnout declined. The main exception was in El Salvador where turnout increased considerably in the last presidential election. Voter turnout declines seem unsurprising given that elections had higher stakes and greater importance in the earlier period, especially as expressions of hopes for the end of conflict. Communal activism declined in several countries, as did school-related and business and professional group involvement, also suggesting that depoliticization and demobilization have occurred in the calming of the political waters since the early 1990s. Citizens who once collaborated in groups and community projects to improve their lives while evading the dangerous arena of national electoral politics have perhaps found such civil society engagement less necessary today.

Very importantly, we found a marked decline in violence's depressing effect on political participation over time. We conclude that democratization and the end of civil war and state repression have effectively freed up citizens for conventional forms of political participation. Violence had not vanished from Central America, but governments in the early 2000s were not actively terrorizing large groups of people and organizations out of the political arena. Thus the decline of civil war and of massive state-managed repression has allowed participation to occur more easily. In this sense, democracy and political peace have positively afforded citizen engagement and augur well for democratic consolidation.

The 2004 survey data show that most Central Americans rejected authoritarian values and held strongly democratic norms, although about half of them nevertheless believed that certain circumstances could justify a coup d'état. Trends from the early 1990s to 2004 reveal, however, that democratic norms actually declined somewhat while support for confrontational politics rose. Diffuse support for the regimes of the region remained at only middling levels in 2004 except in Costa Rica and in El Salvador, where political violence had declined the most and diffuse support levels had increased sharply. On balance, these findings hold forth mixed prospects for continued peace and democracy.

Our most striking finding is that, unlike participation, political violence more sharply reduced democratic norms and increased support for suppressing democratic liberties in 2004 than in 1991. Under the more organized state-*versus*-insurgent violence of the early 1990s, political terror undermined support for civil liberties, to be sure, but the relatively disorganized violence of the early 2000s actually undermined democratic values even more. This suggests that sociopolitical disorder may erode democratic norms and undermine consolidation more than heavy repression. Indeed, Henderson and Singer (2000) found an inverted U-shaped relationship between democracy and conflict, with semi-democracies and high levels of conflict found together. Citizens disgruntled with the poor job their democratic governments are doing of providing social stability and curtailing crime appear to have lost some of their support for democracy. Combined with Central Americans' support for coups and their weakened democratic values, this has truly troubling implications for future peace and democracy. Sustaining the peace after civil war takes more than an end to organized violence. Both time and institutional capacity are needed to establish a deeply rooted democratic culture. Without such a culture, crises can quickly undermine support for democratic values, freedoms, and rights and enable a return to civil war or authoritarian rule.

How might Central American governments and elites and providers of foreign assistance consolidate democracy in the region? Ending civil wars has already clearly enhanced democratic political participation, but support for democracy has diminished rather than grown. What should be done? Our findings suggest a number of courses of action to sustain the peace and inoculate against relapse, although some are beyond the easy reach of Central American policy makers.

Shoring up eroding public commitment to democracy appears to require enhanced regime performance. *Central American states should strengthen their capacities to reduce the excessive levels of crime, corruption, human rights abuse and social disorder.* After the Cold War ended, so did Central America's civil wars. In the 1990s the international assistance community largely turned away from the area except to insist on austere neo-liberal economic and free trade policies (Robinson 2003; Booth *et al.* 2006). Developed nations and international institutions have not provided assistance for Central American economies to grow faster and more equitably. They also stripped these states of funds and programs needed to improve citizen security and reduce social pathology.

To undo these errors and strengthen states, *international donors should provide more economic and technical assistance to improve crime prevention and better train and socialize police forces and others in the judicial system.* We have seen the inadequacy of ending civil war if fear of repression is replaced by fear of criminal violence. *Additionally, international donors should modify policies to promote equitable economic growth.* When new democracies fail to deliver economically, citizens may grow cynical about democratic government and reduce their support for democratic values. Failed expectations for real improvement in living conditions create fertile ground for non-democratic actors.

The largest challenge facing Central American states, like most post conflict societies, is to find both the will and the funds for these initiatives. These governments and economies are very poor (particularly Nicaragua and Honduras). Moreover they face an international economic assistance community and local political-economic elites with powerful neo-liberal biases against increased public spending and broader social service roles for governments. Yet, by strengthening and professionalizing the police forces and thereby reducing the level of criminal violence, by investing in judicial reform, economic development, education, family services, by bolstering governmental capacity and institution-building, the governments and the international community would reduce the chances of authoritarian recidivism and a return to civil war. We sadly suspect, however, that efforts to generate and direct increased domestic public spending or international aid to these arenas will be minimal in the foreseeable future. Popular support for democracy may, therefore, continue its downward trend. The likelihood of unrest may grow, and the prospects for democratic consolidation may fade.

Acknowledgments

We thank James Meernik and Dave Mason for their helpful comments on an earlier draft of this chapter.

Notes

1 In mid-1991 surveys were conducted among the urban voting-age populations of El Salvador, Honduras, Nicaragua, and Panama. In 1992 a similar survey was conducted in Guatemala, followed in 1995 by another in Costa Rica. In each a stratified (by socio-economic level) cluster sample of dwelling units was drawn from the national capital and other major urban centers. Interviewees were chosen using randomizing procedures and following sex and age quotas. We collected a total of 4,089 face-to-face interviews region-wide, but national sample ns varied from 500 to 900. To prevent larger country ns from distorting findings in this analysis, the country samples have here been weighted equally to approximately 700 each (total n=4,198). We believe our early 1990s samples reflected the opinions of the urban populations of Central America (capital cities and other major cities and towns).

We gratefully acknowledge the support for the collection of these data by the North-South Center of the University of Miami, the Howard Heinz Endowment-Center for Latin American Studies of the University of Pittsburgh Research Grants on Current Latin American Issues, University of North Texas Faculty Development Grants and Faculty Research programs, the Andrew Melon Foundation, the Tinker Foundation, the Heinz Foundation, and the University of Pittsburgh. The project was designed and much of the data were collected by a team including Mitchell A. Seligson of the University of Pittsburgh and John Booth. Team members who also directed fieldwork were Ricardo Córdova, Andrew Stein, Annabelle Conroy, Orlando Pérez, and Cynthia Chalker. Guatemala fieldwork was conducted by the Asociación de Investigación y Estudios Sociales (ASIES) of Guatemala. Invaluable assistance and collaboration were provided by the following institutions in Central America: Costa Rica: Consejo Superior Universitaria Centroamericana (CSUCA), Maestría en Sociología, and the Universidad de Costa Rica, Departments of Statistics and Political Science; Nicaragua: Instituto de Estudios Internacionales (IEI), Universidad Centroamericana; Honduras, Centro de Estudio y Promoción del Desarrollo (CEPROD), and Centro de Documentación de Honduras; Panama, Centro de Estudios Latinoamericanos "Justo Arosemena" (CELA); and El Salvador, Centro de Investigación y Acción Social (CINAS), and the Instituto de Estudios Latinoamericanos (IDELA).

2 The 2004 survey data were collected by research teams from six Central American countries plus Colombia and Mexico in April 2004. The survey was funded by the U.S. Agency for International Development and conducted under the leadership of Mitchell A. Seligson of Vanderbilt University. We report here only on the six Central American nations. Each nation was surveyed, using a large core of identical survey items; most of those employed in this chapter were identical to items used in the early 1990s surveys described in note 1. In each country a stratified (by socioeconomic level) cluster sample of dwelling units was drawn from the sample frame of national sampling units. Interviewees were chosen using randomizing procedures and following sex and age quotas. The results closely approximate national probability samples of at least 1,500 respondents from each nation, for a total of 9,366 interviews from the six Central American nations (12,403 with Colombia and Mexico included). As in the early 1990s results, in the data reported here each national sample size is weighted to 1,500 respondents, for a Central American regional sample of 9,000. Respondents were of voting age and citizens of the country in which the interviews were conducted. (The authors sincerely thank USAID, who have released these data as under public domain, and Professor Seligson for his co-operation in providing these data for analysis.)

3 The Gastil index, a seven-point scale used by Freedom House, has become widely accepted as a standard measure providing a basic classification of political rights and civil liberties.

4 Freedom House's political rights category assesses how much voters may freely choose among candidates not imposed by the state; neither militaries nor monarchs should exercise much sway in elections. The civil liberties scores assess whether citizens enjoy a panoply of civil liberties – freedoms of expression, assembly, association, education, religion.

5 The discussion in this analysis section draws heavily on and extends the findings and discussion reported in Booth *et al.* (2006), Chapter 9.

6 Costa Rica's highly institutionalized Tribunal Supremo de Elecciones (Supreme Electoral Tribunal – TSE) has operated effectively for several decades and achieved 99 percent registration of Costa Ricans in 2004. Lower registration rates elsewhere appear to occur because other countries have made less conscientious efforts to register all eligible citizens (Guatemala), the newness and inexperience of some civil registries (Nicaragua), and changing

rules and procedures. The lowest national rate of voter registration (76 percent) was in Guatemala, where voting was not mandatory.

7 Note that all such comparisons reported here compare the early 1990s urban samples with only 2004 urban samples to avoid possible distortions in comparing dissimilar populations.

8 The turnout decline in Costa Rica, consistent with national election bureau turnout reports, has been widely noted and analyzed elsewhere (Booth 2005; Seligson 2002).

9 While surveys from the 1990s revealed that Central Americans had generally low confidence in parties, that situation seems to have changed somewhat, especially for El Salvador. On a 1.0 (very low) to 7.0 (very high) self-evaluation of one's "trust in parties," the following mean scores were obtained by country from the 2004 survey: Costa Rica 3.1; El Salvador 3.4; Guatemala and Panama 2.8, Honduras 2.9, and Nicaragua 2.7. El Salvador's parties, given their links to past political violence, scored surprisingly well at 3.4 out of 7.0 – the highest self-reported trust in parties level in the entire region.

10 Results of a multiple regression analysis of the 2004 survey using a measure of overall participation (combining the variables reported in Table 10.1 into a single participation index) as the dependent variable, and with sex, age, educational attainment, standard of living, crime victimization, perceived freedom to participate in politics, perceived level of civil liberties, level of national economic development, and system-level repression as independent variables; results not shown to conserve space.

11 Multiple regression analysis indicates the independent effects (holding other variables effects constant) of each of several independent variables on a dependent variable. Thus the cell values in Table 10.5 (beta coefficients) indicate and allow comparison of the relative, independent contribution (the value) and direction (the sign) of each independent variable (e.g., sex, age) to changes in the dependent variables (e.g., participation, democratic norms).

12 This repression measure, similar to the one we used in earlier studies, incorporates measures of violence over the decade prior to the survey. Annual violence estimates come from Gibney's Political Terror Scale scores (Gibney 2005a, 2005b). Each country's respondents receive their respective national violence score (Table 10.1) as a contextual measure of the climate of violence within they live. To test for similarity between this repression measure and our previous one (e.g., Booth and Richard 1996), we analyzed their intercorrelation. Pearson's r between them for the 1981–1990 period is 0.882, indicating close correspondence.

13 We found that repression had no effect on coup justification in the early 1990s, and only a very small positive effect in 2004, so we excluded the model from Table 10.5 to conserve space.

References

Booth, J.A. (1998) *Costa Rica: Quest for Democracy*, Boulder, CO: Westview Press.

Booth, J.A. (2005 forthcoming) "Political Parties in Costa Rica," in P. Webb, S. White, and D. Stansfield (eds.) *Political Parties in Transitional Democracies*. Oxford: Oxford University Press.

Booth, J.A. and Richard, P.B. (1996) "Repression, Participation, and Democratic Norms in Urban Central America," *American Journal of Political Science* 40: 1205–1232.

Booth, J.A. and Richard, P.B. (1998a) "Civil Society, Political Capital, and Democratization in Central America," *Journal of Politics* 60: 780–800.

Booth, J.A. and Richard, P.B. (1998b) "Civil Society and Political Context in Central America,' *American Behavioral Scientist* 42: 33–46.

Booth, J.A. and Richard, P.B. (2000) "Civil Society and Democratic Transition," in Thomas W. Walker and Ariel C. Armony (eds.) *Repression, Resistance, and Democratic Transition in Central America*. Wilmington, DE: Scholarly Resources.

Booth, J.A. and Richard, P.B. (2004) "Civil Society and Social Capital Formation in Central America: Context versus Intensity of Involvement," paper presented at the Midwest Political Science Association Meeting, Chicago, IL, April 15.

Booth, J.A. and Richard, P.B. (2006 forthcoming) "Revolution's Legacy: Residual Effects on Nicaraguan Participation and Attitudes in Comparative Context," *Latin American Politics and Society* 48.

Booth, J.A., Wade, C.J., and Walker, T.W. (2006) *Understanding Central America: Global Forces, Rebellion and Regime Change*. 4th edn. Boulder, CO: Westview Press.

Cohen, C. (1973) *Democracy*. New York: The Free Press.

Dealy, G. (1974) "The Tradition of Monistic Democracy in Latin America," in Howard J. Wiarda (ed.) *Politics and Social Change in Latin America: The Distinct Tradition*. Amherst, MA: University of Massachusetts Press.

Deonandan, K. (2004) "The Assault on Pluralism," in David Close and Kalowatie Deonandan (eds.) *Undoing Democracy The Politics of Electoral Caudillismo*. Lanham, MD: Lexington Books.

Doyle, M. and Sambanis, N. (2000) "International Peacebuilding: A Theoretical and Quantitative Analysis," *American Political Science Review* 94: 779–801.

Dye, D.R. with Spence, J. and Vickers, G. (2000) *Patchwork Democracy: Nicaraguan Politics Ten Years After the Fall*. Cambridge, MA: Hemisphere Initiatives.

Freedom House (2003a) *Freedom in the World*. <http://freedomhouse.org/research/Freeworld/2003/countryratings/costarica.htm>, accessed March 13, 2005.

Freedom House (2003b) *Freedom in the World*. <http://freedomhouse.org/research/Freeworld/2003/countryratings/elsalvador.htm>, accessed March 13, 2005.

Freedom House (2003c) *Freedom in the World*. <http://freedomhouse.org/research/Freeworld/2003/countryratings/guatemala.htm>, accessed March 13, 2005.

Freedom House (2003d) *Freedom in the World*. <http://freedomhouse.org/research/Freeworld/2003/countryratings/honduras.htm>, accessed March 13, 2005.

Freedom House (2003e) *Freedom in the World*. <http://freedomhouse.org/research/Freeworld/2003/countryratings/nicaragua.htm>, accessed March 13, 2005.

Freedom House (2003f) *Freedom in the World*. <http://freedomhouse.org/research/Freeworld/2003/countryratings/panama.htm>, accessed March 13, 2005.

Gibney, M. (2005a) "Notes on Levels of Political Terror Scale," <www.unca.edu/politicalscience/faculty-staff/gibney_docs/Political Terror Scale.doc>, accessed March 12, 2005.

Gibney, M. (2005b) Political Terror Scale, University of North Carolina Asheville, <www.unca.edu/politicalscience/faculty-staff/gibney_docs/pts.xls>, accessed March 12, 2005.

Henderson, E. and Singer, J.D. (2000) "Civil War in the Post-Colonial World, 1946–1992," *Journal of Peace Research* 37: 245–299.

Inglehart, R. (1988) "The Renaissance of Political Culture," *American Political Science Review* 82: 1203–30.

Inglehart, R. and Norris, P. (2003) *Rising Tide: Gender Equality and Cultural Change Around the World.* Cambridge: Cambridge University Press.

Kincaid, A.D. (2000) "Demilitarization and Security in El Salvador and Guatemala: Convergences of Success and Crisis," *Journal of Interamerican Studies and World Affairs* 42: 39–58.

Morse, R.M. (1974) "The Heritage of Latin America," in Howard J. Wiarda (ed.) *Politics and Social Change in Latin America: The Distinct Tradition.* Amherst, MA: University of Massachusetts Press.

Pateman, C. (1970) *Participation and Democratic Theory.* Cambridge: Cambridge University Press.

Putnam, R.D. (2000) *Bowling Alone: The Collapse and Revival of American Community.* (New York: Simon and Schuster).

Richard, P.B. and Booth, J.A. (2000) "Civil Society and Democratic Transition," in Thomas W. Walker and Ariel Armony (eds.) *Repression, Resistance, and Democratic Transition in Central America.* Wilmington, DE: Scholarly Review Books.

Robinson, W.I. (1996) *Promoting Polyarchy: Globalization, U.S. Intervention, and Hegemony.* Cambridge: Cambridge University Press.

Robinson, W.I. (2003) *Transnational Conflicts: Central America, Social Change, and Globalization.* London: Verso.

Rovira Mas, J. (2000) "Elecciones generales en Costa Rica: Primero de febrero de 1998. ¿Se debilita el bipartidismo?" Paper presented at the XXII International Congress of the Latin American Studies Association, Miami, FL, March 16–18.

Sánchez, F.F. (2003) "Dealignment in Costa Rica: A Case Study of Electoral Change," doctoral thesis, University of Oxford.

Seligson, M.A. (2002) "Trouble in Paradise: The Impact of the Erosion of System Support in Costa Rica, 1978–1999," *Latin America Research Review* 37: 160–185.

Seligson, M.A. and Booth, J.A. (1993) "Political Culture and Regime Type: Evidence from Nicaragua and Costa Rica," *Journal of Politics* 55: 777–792.

Spence, J., Lanchin, M., and Thale, G. (2001) *From Elections to Earthquakes: Reform and Participation in Post-War El Salvador.* Cambridge, MA: Hemisphere Initiatives.

Wiarda, H.J. (1981) *Corporatism and National Development in Latin America.* Boulder, CO: Westview Press.

11 Post-conflict economic development and sustaining the peace

Seonjou Kang

Introduction

In recent history, civil wars have broken out exclusively in the developing world.[1] According to the Correlates of War Project's data sets, 103 civil wars were fought in developing countries from 1946 to 1997 (Sarkees 2000). This effect was especially heightened in the past 15 years, during which 80 percent of the world's poorest countries have experienced a civil war (World Bank 2005). These statistics suggest that against their social and political backdrop, many developing countries have been trapped in a vicious circle of poverty and violence; poverty causes violence, violence causes more poverty, and the chain goes on. A corollary to this rule in the developing world is economic development as a solution to break away. If developing countries that have experienced civil wars successfully recover from war's destruction and develop further, they are less likely to experience a recurrence of civil war.

This brings post-conflict economic reconstruction to our attention. Certainly conflict-affected countries undertook economic reconstruction with the onset of peace, but their success appears to be uncertain. In reality, few civil-war countries adequately recovered from war destruction, and many of them actually relapsed into violence over time.[2] The recurrence of civil wars indicates that developing countries are incapable of achieving economic recovery from civil wars on their own. To begin with, developing countries lack tangible and intangible resources useful for economic growth (i.e., economic, human, and social capital), and the worsened conditions after civil war hamper their efforts to reconstruct the economies. Therefore, in order to prescribe economic development as a means to prevent civil wars, it is necessary to understand the process and prospects for post-conflict economic growth. What conditions do developing countries inherit from civil wars, and to what extent do they systematically hinder economic reconstruction? Under what conditions can those countries achieve adequate economic reconstruction and carry it into long-term growth? And, how can the international community assist their efforts? All these questions call for well thought-out answers. This chapter will guide the reader down the path toward better answers found through further inquiry.

This chapter is structured in the following manner. First, we discuss the economic environment in which civil-war countries become situated after the shooting stops. This will help us understand these difficulties that post-conflict countries face in economic reconstruction. Second, we discuss international assistance for post-conflict countries as a way of lessening the difficulties that they face. Premised on this discussion, we further identify conditions necessary to make international assistance more effective. Finally, we close the chapter by reiterating its central arguments and other potentially important factors to be considered for post-conflict economic growth.

Environment for post-conflict economic reconstruction

Studies devoted to understanding the causes and evolution of civil wars commonly tell us that deep poverty, fractionalized ethnic groups, and undemocratic polities are associated with civil wars in the developing world (see Henderson and Singer 2000; Hegre *et al.* 2001; Collier and Hoeffler 2002a; Reynal-Querol 2002; Fearon and Laitin 2003). At the onset and evolution stages of civil war, the three common causes are inter-twined, feeding one another to create more violence and leaving long-lasting scars behind. Economically, civil-war countries have been characterized by low income, slow economic growth, and heavy depen-dence on exports of primary, especially lootable, commodities such as gold, diamond, and oil for foreign income; socially, those countries have been ethnically fragmented;[3] and politically, they have been ruled under authoritarian regimes. Reflecting both ethnic rivalry of the pre-colonial times and the adverse institutional legacy of European colonialism, wealth obtained from exports of primary commodities was unequally distributed along ethnic lines, and political regimes did not function as a widely agreed framework for distributing wealth or addressing inequality in a peaceful manner in the country. Thus, motivated both by greed for the rents from lootable commodities and by grievances for unjustifiable poverty and inequality, ethnic groups resorted to violence in order to get around blocked political channels.

Once civil wars have ended, conflict-torn countries are faced with the challenge of rebuilding their societies. Due to the violence committed against fellow citizens and risk of renewed violence, devastation from civil wars requires careful post-conflict management in all aspects of life, including politics, economy, security, health, and reconciliation. The fact that poverty was at the heart of most civil wars, however, suggests that future internal peace in former civil-war societies hinges on how fast their economies will recover from civil war and transform it into economic development. Since those countries experienced civil wars for economic reasons, former civil-war combatants may otherwise take up arms again in order to secure their shares of scarce resources. Such a possibility is clearly demonstrated by Elbadawi and Sambanis (2002), who simulated that poverty persistently increases the risk of civil wars at medium-levels of ethnic fragmentation, whereas economic development can effectively defeat such risk at all levels of ethnic fragmentation. Thus, poverty alleviation and further economic development are critical to defusing militarized conflicts in former civil-war countries.

In assessing the process and prospects for economic growth in civil-war countries, it is necessary first to check what useful and/or detrimental factors those countries inherit from civil wars. Following a strand in the study of the relationship between interstate wars and economic growth, we wonder whether the end of civil war can present opportunities to the countries concerned.[4] That is, before civil war, many developing countries suffer rent-seeking, distributional coalitions, which have ossifying effects on economic performance. It is thus possible that civil war disrupts the negative pre-war distributional coalitions and allows societies to implement more efficient and fair government policies (Olson 1982). The creation of a new government at the end of a civil war can also enhance the prospects for economic growth through reconciliation among ethnic groups and by building institutional capacity for growth. And, the destruction of infrastructure allows new, state-of-the-art facilities to be built, which could provide for greater economic gains (Kugler and Arbetman 1989). Therefore, though devastating at first, civil wars might provide the countries with some opportunities to advance their economies while addressing the revealed root causes of civil wars.

Although certain positive effects on economic growth can be expected from civil wars, there are reasons to suspect that civil wars are uniquely more detrimental than useful for the countries concerned. First, "civil wars, which are entirely fought on the territory of the country, are liable to be more damaging than international wars, and have a smaller peace dividend from the end of fighting" (Collier 1999: 168). Civil-war countries were poor before war, and hence there is little expectation that resources are left in the society for reconstruction upon the end of war. According to Collier, civil wars lower national income (GDP, gross domestic production) in four major ways: destroying, disrupting, diverting, and depleting national resources. These negative economic effects of civil wars can be regionally contagious, too. "Civil wars have significant, but modest, negative influences on GDP per capita, both at home and in neighboring countries" (Murdoch and Sandler 2002: 92). This occurs because neighboring countries' trade with civil-war countries is disrupted, and refugees from civil-war countries strain already scarce resources in the neighboring countries. Thus, what is expected, especially during the immediate post-civil war period, is severe resource shortage at both domestic and regional levels, which will hamper post-civil war economic take-off unless there is relief from abroad under way.

Second, the very fact that a country has undergone a civil war creates a prejudice that the society is prone to violence (Collier 1999). Since the end of a civil war hardly means the end of ethnic fragmentation in the society, such prejudice will translate into risk perception by economic actors due to renewed violence in post-civil war countries. In business, risk perception is a major component of investment decisions. Perceived risks in former civil-war countries in addition to their poor economic conditions can suppress investment necessary for economic growth. For proper economic growth after the shooting stops, it is essential to redirect resources from war efforts to civilian economic activities and to repatriate assets from foreign countries for domestic investment. However, the fear of renewed conflict coupled with existing ethnic fragmentation in the society may hinder the economic activities of both locals and foreigners from fully reverting to the pre-war levels (ibid.). Thus, the restoration of peace does not necessarily restore the pre-war economy, much less economic development.

Finally, civil wars in the developing world originate from forces and events internal to the state and produce outcomes that are internally oriented. While interstate wars threaten the existence of other states through territorial occupation, which potentially destabilizes the international system, civil wars are over lesser issues that are resolved without threatening the existence of another state and are thus less destabilizing to the international system (Herbst 1990). This is especially true to the extent that civil wars are exclusively waged in the developing world. This internal nature of civil war distinctively places responsibilities for post-conflict economic reconstruction on the civil-war countries. In other words, the involvement of the international community in post-conflict economic reconstruction is neither warranted nor automatic. The civil-war countries themselves have to create whatever environments are conducive to economic recovery and accomplish the myriad tasks needed to grow. International assistance will be available if major powers are directly or indirectly involved in the conflict and if they are willing to take the leadership to mitigate or overcome the effects of civil wars on the economy.

The presence and actual influence of detrimental factors on civil-war countries can be confirmed in economic growth rates. For the period 1960–2002, the average growth rates of GDP in the developing countries that did not experience civil wars at all were about 5–7 percent annually. On the other hand, in the developing countries that experienced at least one civil war, their average growth rates during post-civil war periods were not only lower than those of non-civil war countries, but were also in the negative double digits if their civil wars were very lengthy and bloody (see Kang and Meernik 2005, Figure 1). War destruction coupled with the uniquely detrimental conditions after civil wars, which create war hangover effects, appears to have made it difficult for civil war countries to achieve economic take-off and has resulted in persistently low GDP growth. Thus, given the difficulty and complexity of post-civil war economic growth, it is imperative to examine what assistance is available at the international level for former civil-war countries to reconstruct their economies and build a lasting peace.

Post-civil war economic reconstruction and foreign aid

Post-conflict economic reconstruction is paradoxical: While economic reconstruction bears tremendous importance to the future of civil-war countries, at the same time it poses formidable challenges to them in terms of time and scale. The World Bank (2005) estimates that it can take a generation or more for former civil-war countries just to return to pre-war living standards, even with rapid progress. If we think of development beyond reconstruction in former civil-war countries, which signifies betterment in the quality of life through economic, social, political, and cultural progress, there is little doubt that it will take multiple generations. While post-civil war reconstruction requires a great deal of resources (capital) over time, countries that experienced civil wars are unable to supply the necessary capital domestically (i.e., the government and/or the private sector) due to pre-war poverty and destruction from wars. The governments cannot generate public revenue from taxation because most economic activities are disrupted. And private investors, local and international, will not invest until they see clear signs of peace and stability due to the perceived risk of renewed violence.

Under such circumstances, the urgently needed capital for economic reconstruction has to be transfused from the outside, and foreign aid is one means for accomplishing this. The role that foreign aid can play in post-conflict economic growth could not be better demonstrated than with the Marshall Plan after World War II, which provided Western Europe with $20 billion over five years from 1948. Considering the region's pre-war economic development, it is not difficult to project what the region could have achieved even without the Marshall Plan. Nonetheless, the Marshall Plan helped the region quickly tap its potential for post-war economic growth so that it was at or near pre-war level in two years of the Plan and, by late 1950s, was exceeding it. It is beyond doubt that this successful reconstruction became the foundation for unprecedented prosperity and peace in the region in the upcoming decades (see Dornbusch *et al.* 1993; Schain 2001).

Foreign aid for civil-war countries can have similar effects. Foreign aid will meet post-civil war countries' urgent needs for capital in a timely manner. With little expectation that capital will be replenished from domestic sources, the immediate effect of foreign aid is to relax the budget constraints of the governments that emerge from civil wars, thereby giving them opportunities to initiate growth (Svensson 1999). The capital injected from abroad will be used for both humanitarian relief and developmental investment. Foreign aid also includes technical assistance for management and production, which post-civil war economies will need for long-term growth based on industrialization. If former civil-war countries capitalize on these positive externalities of foreign aid and recover quickly, internal peace is more likely to last. Collier and Hoeffler (2002b) find that foreign aid helps former civil-war countries diversify their economies (lowering dependence on exports of primary commodities for foreign income) and boost output growth, which in turn contributes to lowering the risks of civil war.

The sources of aid for post-conflict countries include two types – bilateral aid from major countries and multilateral development aid from the UN, the World Bank, the IMF, and Regional Development Banks. Collectively, the former are the members of Development Assistance Committee (DAC) within OECD. Post-conflict aid from the World Bank is not surprising since the Bank itself was created to assist post-conflict reconstruction in Europe. However, the World Bank has recently set up a new account called the Post-Conflict Fund (PCF), particularly for reconstruction of post-conflict developing countries. The World Bank also maintains a collaborative relationship with bilateral donors through the Multi-Donor Trust Fund (MDTF). The MDTF is set up with grants from bilateral and multilateral development organizations for individual national-building cases, and the World Bank serves as a fiduciary trustee and executer of comprehensive post-conflict reconstruction programs.[5]

Post-conflict assistance has two priorities: humanitarian relief and reconstruction. The former is commonly required since civil wars often involve humanitarian disasters and mass population dislocations internally and/or across borders (refugees). Humanitarian relief includes care for the victims, restoration of essential security for resettlement, and basic social services (Muscat 2002). For the period 1999–2003, humanitarian assistance in real terms from DAC countries was about $5.7 billion, 10 percent of total bilateral aid (Development Initiatives 2004). Those numbers can be larger if non-earmarked donations from the DAC countries to multilateral relief organizations such as UN agencies and to charitable non-governmental organizations (NGOs) are counted. In actual delivery of humanitarian relief, however, the UN may have a comparative advantage over other bilateral and multilateral aid agencies because the UN organizes its humanitarian activities under the agencies that were created particularly for that purpose, the UN High Commissioner for Refugees (UNHCR) and the Office for the Coordination of Humanitarian Affairs (OCHA). These agencies have field offices around the world standing by to respond and a dense network of co-operation with NGOs. Also, another advantage of these agencies is that their relief activities can be internally coordinated with UN peacekeeping operations, which provide logistical support and protection of victims.[6]

The importance of humanitarian relief is that it restores the normalcy of life. During civil war, economic activities virtually stop, and resources are dispersed. Hence, humanitarian aid with immediately consumable goods has the greatest welfare impact on the survivors (Demekas *et al.* 2002). Especially since most survivors of civil wars are socially and economically vulnerable groups (i.e., women and children), addressing their welfare through humanitarian relief is critical for the next phases of post-conflict reconstruction. Furthermore, humanitarian relief during post-conflict periods can motivate development depending on how it is structured. Based on experiences of a community in El Salvador in the mid-1990s, where World Food Program (WFP)'s food-for-work aid resulted in community development, Mancusi-Materi (2000) argues that humanitarian relief not only ameliorates living conditions at the individual level, but also enhances people's awareness of economic conditions and control over the processes to change them. Since economic growth beyond post-conflict economic recovery will depend on how fast civil-war countries build local capacity, humanitarian relief is deemed to do the groundwork for it.

As the immediate emergency phase of post-conflict comes to an end, post-conflict assistance moves onto the other priority – the repair and rebuilding of destroyed infrastructure. In economics, the accumulation of physical capital is known to be the factor invariably related to economic growth on which current and future productive activities are built (see Levine and Renelt 1992).[7] However, accumulation of physical capital requires investment of large amounts of financial capital over time. Hence, mobilizing financial capital underlies economic reconstruction. As mentioned above, neither the governments nor the private sectors of civil-war countries can supply the needed capital, and international private capital will be reluctant to invest in former civil-war countries due to risk perception.[8] Under these circumstances, bilateral and multilateral development aid, which is less profit-oriented than private capital, can help with large-scale investment in post-conflict countries. Official aid aimed at reconstruction of infrastructure can improve the prospects for long-term growth by directly affecting the productive capacity of post-conflict countries. This will also help post-conflict countries attract international private capital later.[9]

The contribution of foreign aid to reconstructing infrastructure can be captured with the share of aid incorporated in accumulating physical capital. Developing countries depend heavily on foreign aid for physical capital formation during normal times (50 percent on average), and this number can be much higher during post-conflict periods. For instance, in Rwanda, the share of bilateral aid in physical capital formation was on average about 95 percent through 1993. After a civil war in 1994, the share of bilateral aid in physical capital formation jumped to 530 percent over three years. Similarly in Nicaragua, the numbers changed from 16 percent through 1989 to 170 percent in 1990 and the next six years when the Sandinistas' government was defeated in a free election.[10] Rebuilding infrastructure is emphasized in World Bank post-conflict assistance, too: thus, 69 percent ($27 million) of the PCF was disbursed on early reconstruction for the period 1997–2001 (World Bank 2002).

How beneficial has foreign aid been to post-conflict economic growth? Foreign aid is generally assessed to have failed to achieve its intended goals: poverty alleviation and economic development.[11] Post-conflict aid, however, can be different because of the extraordinary circumstances in which the aid is offered. Specifically, the humanitarian relief and reconstruction aspects of post-conflict aid are more likely to generate positive effects on the economy, directly boosting productivity (Demekas *et al.* 2002). Empirically, the positive effects of foreign aid to post-civil war countries are shown in Collier and Hoeffler's (2002c) study of 27 countries that experienced large-scale civil wars. They found that as foreign aid (measured as a share of recipient country's GDP) increases by 1 percent, GDP per capita grows about 0.1 percent, with statistical significance. A tangible example of this is Mozambique, which is often cited as an example of successful post-conflict economic growth. After its 16-year civil war ended with a peace agreement in 1992, the average annual growth rates of GDP over the next nine years was 9.25 percent (except 2000 due to a massive flood). This success was driven by (re)construction of transportation/communication infrastructure and manufacturing facilities (27 percent of GDP), with the help of foreign aid concentrated in those sectors (OECD 2004). In the early phase of reconstruction, foreign aid was given to Mozambique on average at 60 percent of its GDP and at 360 percent of its physical capital formation. A significant portion of economic growth also came from restored agricultural production (20 percent of GDP), which benefited from the reconstruction of infrastructure. During that period, GDP per capita grew at 6.5 percent annually, which suggests income benefits from employment in infrastructure construction and the revived agricultural sector. Although this remarkable growth has not taken Mozambique out of poverty yet, OECD (2004) predicts that its prospects for growth will be good as it continues to stabilize both the political and economic environments favorable for investment (i.e., liberalization and privatization).

The positive effects of post-conflict aid on economic growth, however, should be interpreted with caution because of hidden non-linearity. The nonlinear effects of foreign aid on post-civil war economic growth means that as the size of foreign aid rises, recipient economies respond positively to it at first, then begin to taper off after foreign aid reaches a certain point. More specifically, according to a study conducted by Kang and Meernik (2005), for every extra dollar of foreign aid per capita (i.e., division of foreign aid by a recipient country's population), growth in GDP increases by 0.007 percent per year during post-civil war periods until aid per capita reaches about US $184.[12] After that point, economic growth tends downward even if increasingly large amounts of aid are given. The diminishing return on foreign aid can be explained in two ways: first, among nations that have emerged from civil wars, their ability to absorb aid may be limited, and additional aid dollars beyond a saturation point no longer help. Foreign aid is certainly essential at first to provide humanitarian needs and rebuild infrastructure. In the long term, however, economic growth will depend more on private investment and technological innovation coupled with sound macroeconomic conditions and development in human capital than on additional foreign aid. Foreign aid can help position a war-torn society for reconstruction and growth, but it probably cannot replace those long-term growth factors. Second, "aid is fungible and tends to increase government spending proportionately" (Burnside and Dollar 2000: 848). The recipient governments spend the budget saved from the areas that donors finance in other areas, and larger government spending, in total, adversely affects economic growth in the end while crowding out private investment. Therefore, donors need to carefully design and install post-conflict aid in the fashion that facilitates private sector development (Demekas *et al.* 2002).

Making post-conflict aid work better: donor practice

Despite the positive externalities of foreign aid for post-conflict economic growth, certain counterproductive aspects of foreign aid for post-civil war countries need to be improved. First, foreign aid for post-conflict countries is selective. While multilateral aid is more sensitive to poverty and more conditional upon policy changes in recipient countries, bilateral foreign aid during normal times is known for strategic, thus less conditional, distribution based on donors' national interests (see Akram 2003; Meernik *et al.* 1998; Schraeder *et al.* 1998). Considering that, it is not surprising that bilateral aid has had a negligible impact on recipients' economic development. When it comes to assisting war-torn countries, we might expect the pattern of distribution to be different. Contrary to that expectation, however, aid for post-conflict countries is no exception. Like foreign aid during normal times, Kang and Meernik (2004) find that the distribution of bilateral aid to post-conflict countries from the DAC countries has been determined by political-economic assessments of the past and the future relationship with recipient countries as well as conflict-related humanitarian needs. This implies that even humanitarian relief, which will be the first step for rebuilding the economy, is linked to donors' strategic considerations, and thus post-civil war economic growth can be hampered from the early stage.

In addition, the pattern of aid-giving has to be revisited. Donor countries tend to increase aid for countries that recently experienced conflicts to extraordinarily high levels, whether in a per capita scale or in the relative size of the recipient economy. However, once the emergency phase is over, donors cut aid quickly. In Rwanda, for example, foreign aid jumped from 11 percent of GDP before the war to 95 percent of GDP immediately after the war but declined to 17 percent within three years. Kang and

Meernik's study (2004) shows that the DAC countries increased aid by \$5 per capita more in the five years after a conflict than in the five years prior to the conflict. If the post-conflict period is further analyzed year by year, aid generally increases through the fourth post-conflict year and starts declining from the fifth year.[13] This is, however, not an efficient pattern of aid allocation. Although civil wars lower capital stock, post-civil war countries' capacity to absorb aid does not expand immediately with the onset of peace. Collier and Hoeffler (2002c) find that for the first three post-conflict years, absorptive capacity is no greater than normal but gradually rises in the next seven years. Thus, for the greatest results from foreign aid, the pattern of aid-giving to post-conflict countries has to be reversed. Instead of pouring a large aid for a short-term period immediately following the peace settlement and tapering off over the next years, donors should gradually increase aid over medium- and long-term periods after a civil war ends. This pattern will also be more conducive to the long-term economic development of the recipient countries, if we consider the sequence of post-conflict reconstruction and resource needs together. Humanitarian relief comes first but lasts only for the short-term. On the other hand, infrastructure reconstruction, coming next, builds actual productive capacity and requires larger amounts of capital. Therefore, increased aid over medium- and long-term periods can help better economic recovery and growth in post-civil war countries.

Post-conflict aid and governance of recipient countries

The positive effects of post-conflict aid will not be possible without co-operation from recipient countries. The area that requires co-operation most from recipient countries is governance or institutional capacity, which must be built from scratch.[14] Given the failure of foreign aid to achieve its intended goals, the donor community has increasingly emphasized good governance as a prerequisite for foreign aid success and directed assistance toward recipients qualified as demonstrating such.[15] The quality of governance in a country is assessed on six dimensions: voice and accountability, political stability, government effectiveness, regulatory quality, rule of law, and control of corruption (Kaufmann and Kraay 2002). The first reason that donors believe that foreign aid will be more effective in countries showing those qualities is that foreign aid eventually depends on the recipient government for administration and delivery. Foreign aid becomes part of the government's resources although donors earmark it for specific spending areas. Thus, the quality of the recipient government will influence the effectiveness of foreign aid to a certain degree. Particularly, since foreign aid is unearned extra income for recipient governments, without good governance in place, those governments will have incentives to use foreign aid in satisfying their own non-productive goals (Svensson 1999).

Second, good governance makes a difference to macroeconomic management in monetary and fiscal affairs. Even if foreign aid is spent as designated by donors and produces intended outcomes, generally poor macroeconomic conditions caused by poor governance can wash out the positive effects of foreign aid. Especially, given the tendency of foreign aid to increase government spending, good governance is a mechanism necessary to counter that tendency by controlling government spending prudently. Finally, good governance provides a stable environment for private economic activities and thus for long-term development. As already mentioned, foreign aid ushers recipient countries along growth paths, and long-term growth depends on innovations within the private sector. Poor governance not only hinders the growth paths from opening to the private sector but also directly harms indigenous private economic activities with market-unfriendly policies. And the reader will recall that the positive effects of foreign aid on post-conflict reconstruction found by Collier and Hoeffler (2002c) were conditioned upon a healthy political environment. The success of Mozambique was also coupled with implementation of policies favorable to private investment. Therefore, good governance is a necessary condition to ensure the effectiveness of foreign aid in productive areas under well-managed macroeconomic conditions.

Beside its general importance, good governance in post-conflict countries has to be stressed particularly for resource management in relation to the causes of civil wars. Some developing countries are resource-abundant, but poverty and inequality induced by poor governance led them to civil wars. In a similar vein, unless good governance is put in place, increased resources from post-conflict aid can be used to reignite civil wars through corruption or outright diversion to rearmament (Anderson 1999; Muscat 2002). This possibility is realized through the following mechanism. Among other things, allocating government resources is endogenous to the political process. In democratic regimes, the allocation of government resources corresponds with competing groups' abilities to deliver votes to politicians (Dixit and Londregan 1995); in authoritarian regimes, on the other hand, the government itself selects target groups for government spending, which is usually based on politicians' ethnic and regional affiliations (Bueno de Mesquita *et al.* 1999). The end of a civil war hardly means the end of ethnic fragmentation, and each ethnic group remains a competing interest group in post-civil war societies. Poor governance during post-conflict periods will make the government susceptible to ethnic competition over resource allocation or even permit the government to illegally use resources in soliciting ethnic support. As the government distributes resources in such a way, it raises the cost of governing but reduces public goods enjoyed by the entire society (Alesina *et al.* 1998). Through this process, post-conflict aid, as included in government spending, is not only spent for non-developmental purposes, but also helps renew violence in former civil-war countries. Therefore, good governance is required to prevent post-conflict aid from producing adverse economic and political consequences through ethnicity-driven, inefficient public policies.

Good governance is also required for post-civil war countries to manage the extra resources generated by debt reduction. The DAC countries and the IMF/World Bank reduced former civil-war countries' debt as part of their post-conflict assistance for them.[16] Generally, external debt deprives the country of opportunities to invest in growth since a substantial portion of national income is transferred abroad for debt servicing (Krugman 1988; Sachs 1989). For post-civil war countries, debt service deprives them of opportunities to enjoy a peace dividend because national income from normalized economic activities is transferred abroad instead of being invested in reconstruction. Furthermore, since most debt in those countries is sovereign, debt service limits government resources available for providing public goods. Thus, it is logically expected that debt reduction for former civil-war countries will lower the risks of conflict by releasing resources from debt service and enabling the governments to make income transfers, which will address the grievances of rebels (Addison and Murshed 2003). Nonetheless, this expectation will materialize only if good governance is established in post-civil war countries. Like foreign aid, reduced debt service means unearned extra income for post-civil war countries. Without good governance in place, the governments have incentives to use the resources freed from debt service for non-developmental purposes instead of administering them for the production of public goods. Therefore, in the short term, good governance is required as a way of ensuring that extra resources from debt reduction will be used for productive activities. And by way of this, good governance will contribute to solving the chronic debt problems in developing countries in the longer term.

Finally, good governance is required to remedy the dependence on primary commodities for income, a cause of civil war. The problems caused by heavy dependence on primary commodities are two-fold: first, economically, countries dependent on primary commodities are more vulnerable to external shocks than less dependent ones because primary commodity prices fluctuate wildly (Collier 2002). Further, dependence on primary commodities can hinder long-term economic development because it reduces investment in the sectors of the economy that have positive externalities such as manufacturing and physical/human capital accumulation (Sachs and Warner 1999). On the political front, dependence on primary commodities tends to cause poor governance in the country. As the government monopolizes revenues extracted from primary commodities, the government becomes self-sufficient, i.e., there is no need to levy taxes in order to run the country. Tax collection symbolizes the consensus between the government and the governed over the public goods that the society will produce (La Porta *et al.* 1999). However, if the government need not levy taxes because of the rents from primary commodities, it becomes autonomous from societal pressure and less accountable for policy failures and even illegal activities (Jensen and Wantchekon 2004).

Given these problems of dependence on primary commodities, good governance can provide solutions in two ways, thus reducing risks of civil war. First, civil-war countries inevitably have to depend on primary commodities for their livelihood at least for a while. During that period, good governance can change the way that the rents from primary commodities are distributed in the country, mitigating their negative effects. Improved governance will function as a framework for allocating wealth and addressing inequality in a peaceful manner. For the longer term, the economy needs to diversify for development, and policy innovations for diversification will be possible under good governance. Diversification of an economy is not merely a shift from extractive industries to manufacturing; it means forming a new consensus regarding change in the national economy and the priorities for allocating government resources, by which certain groups of people in the nation will be negatively affected. This implies that there will be political opposition to derail economic diversification, and thus good governance is necessary to devise diversification plans that can gain a consensus in the nation. The effectiveness of foreign aid aimed at assisting economic diversification of post-conflict economies will also depend on such national plans devised through good governance.

Given the role of good governance in post-civil war countries, a question that inevitably arises is, "Under what conditions can former civil-war countries establish good governance?" An answer may lie with democratization. The aforementioned six dimensions of governance are by and large a mirror image of democracy. Governance should be understood as part of a political regime – democratic or authoritarian – rather than a stand-alone issue.[17] Political regime type differentiates the mechanism through which societal demands become policies – so-called top-down or bottom-up methods. Political regime type also differentiates the ability of the society to hold the government accountable for policy failures through voting or some other measures. Thus, the quality of governance during post-civil war periods will depend on whether the political regime that emerges from a civil war is democratic or not. Democracy, by establishing separation of power within the government and permitting the public to participate in the selection of political leaders, encourages and reinforces good governance, in which the leaders are held directly accountable to the electorate.

The effects of democratization on post-conflict governance and thus economic growth are four-fold. First, democratization legitimizes the power of the government and thus influences the degree of compliance from the governed. Even if the new government attained power through violence, its subsequent efforts to democratize the nation and share power with the defeated party will solidify the power and legitimacy of the government, thus reducing risks of insurgency. Second, democratization widens public influence on policy-making, and its open political process increases pressure on the government for good performance. As its legitimacy and power depend on support from the general public, not particular ethnic groups, democratic regimes cannot afford policy failures and will exert themselves to implement innovative policies. It is this characteristic of democracy that brings about much needed changes in public policies in order to address ethnic inequality and dependence on primary commodities. Third, periodic elections and checks-and-balances in democratic regimes make leadership changes peaceful and less disruptive to economic activities (Przeworski 1991). Elections also encourage the leadership to implement risk-averse policies in fiscal and monetary matters (Quinn and Woolley 2001). Post-civil war countries desperately need stable economic environments for economic activities, and the preference for stability built into democracy can help build such an environment. Finally, democratization will encourage and support productive economic activities by the private sector. Although post-conflict reconstruction is intrinsically a top-down process after the private sector is destroyed by civil war (Schiavo-Campo 2003), reviving the private sector quickly is important for long-term development. The political culture of democracy, which respects individual rights and private property rights, will provide a stable environment for private economic agents, whether local or foreign, to invest, save, build, and engage in economically beneficial activities with little fear of arbitrary governmental intervention (North 1990). Also, democratic governments are more likely to use resources to provide public goods required for innovation by the private sector such as education, public health, and infrastructure, thereby contributing to economic growth (Baum and Lake 2003).

Good governance and democratization are needed to build the institutional capacity to effectively absorb foreign aid. Civil war destroys not only physical structures but also institutional structures – political, economic, social, and administrative – which keep human interaction constructive and predictable (Schiavo-Campo 2003). In rebuilding those institutional structures, the creation of a new democratic government by the winning party (if any) in the war appears to hold the key. Though it takes time to establish it, democratic governance brings much needed economic and political stability to civil-war countries, from which many areas of post-conflict reconstruction – such as foreign aid, private economic activities, and NGOs – will benefit. Democratic governance also disentangles the intertwined root causes of civil wars – poverty, ethnic fragmentation, and dependence on primary commodities – resulting in economic development and internal peace. Hence, there is a strong imperative to link the building of democratic institutions to post-conflict reconstruction.

Conclusion

If we summarize the economic consequences of civil wars in one word, it would be "paradoxical." While post-conflict economic reconstruction bears tremendous importance to the future of the countries concerned, those countries do not have the ability to meet the challenges in front of them. Deepened poverty and risk perception after civil war leave those countries virtually helpless. Given this, international assistance to rehabilitate the economy is critical. Foreign aid is important for setting the stage for civil-war countries to start economic recovery by addressing urgent humanitarian relief and reconstruction of infrastructure. This will also be the first step to defeat risks of civil wars. Thus, despite the internal orientation of civil wars, the involvement of the international community in cleaning up the mess of civil wars is imperative.

Because of the extraordinary circumstances under which aid is arranged, many areas that are vital for post-conflict economic growth can be helped by foreign aid. Nonetheless, post-conflict aid still has a range of policy issues to improve in order to maximize its positive externalities. With the onset of peace, post-conflict economies' capacity to absorb aid is no greater than normal. While post-conflict aid responds to humanitarian needs first, it needs to be balanced with longer-term growth goals, which depend on building productive capacity with reconstructed infrastructure. And even if increasingly large amounts of aid are given, positive responses from recipient countries will not increase linearly. Therefore, disbursement of post-conflict aid needs to be well sequenced over medium- and long-term periods after civil wars end. In addition to the assistance from the international community, the key to successful post-conflict economic growth also lies in the extent to which the governments emerging from civil wars perform to undo the damages of civil wars. Especially, the effectiveness of foreign aid is contingent on the governance of the recipient countries during post-civil war periods. Substantial reforms in governance are crucial to capitalizing on opportunities provided by foreign aid.

Finally, it is worth noting that foreign aid is a necessary, but not sufficient, condition for post-civil war economic growth. Although the role of foreign aid in humanitarian relief and infrastructure reconstruction is certainly essential, long-term positive economic outcomes will depend on the performance of the private sector, local and international. Private economic activities will complement and concretize the growth paths ushered in by official foreign aid. However, for private economic activities to flourish in post-conflict countries, the governments need to provide security and enact policies to support them. Therefore, both donor and recipient countries should co-operate to design post-conflict aid with a view to facilitating private sector development.

Notes

1 Based on income criteria, this includes civil wars in former Yugoslavia, spin-off states from the former Soviet Union, and Russia in the 1990s.
2 The 103 civil wars in the Correlates of War data sets were waged in 55 countries, of which 25 countries (46 percent) experienced more than one civil war.
3 While ethnic fragmentation is widely accepted as a cause of civil war, some scholars question this. For example, Collier (1996) and Fearon and Laitin (2003) find that controlling for income, ethnically diverse societies are no more prone to civil war than the rest, and civil wars are far more likely to be caused by economic opportunities than by grievances.
4 Literature on the linkage of war to economic growth is well reviewed by Van Raemdonck and Diehl (1989). It suffices to note here that in the study of the linkage between interstate war and economic growth, no generalized theory has been established. Depending on the timing, duration, and other factors contributing to war, the net impact of war on economic growth may vary. Conversely, this indicates that policy choices during post-war periods influence economic growth a great deal.
5 High-profile MDTFs for post-conflict situations, for example, are Sierra Leone, the West Bank and Gaza, Bosnia, East Timor, Afghanistan, and Iraq.
6 Though not discussed here due to the focus of this chapter on foreign aid, it should be noted that the international community can assist post-conflict economic growth through multinational peacekeeping operations. Multinational peacekeeping operations, which typically involve monitoring cease-fires, separation of warring parties, and disarmament, can reduce the risks of civil war and thus provide a stable environment that is essential for economic activities.
7 Physical capital means durable goods such as infrastructures, equipment, and inventories of intermediate and finished goods that are used to make final goods.
8 However, it should be noted that the time-frame of private investment in post-conflict countries differs by industrial sectors. Depending on their potential security risk (i.e., being targeted for attack) and returns, private capital in petroleum/mining and mobile communication sectors comes back relatively sooner (see Bray 2005).
9 It should be noted that donor countries have incentives to invest in reconstructing infrastructure in order to help their national firms invest in post-conflict countries.
10 The data of aid in physical capital formation and economic growth rates of recipient countries mentioned later are found in World Development Indicator (2003).
11 For the most up-to-date assessment of the effects of foreign aid on economic development, see Arvin and Barillas (2002), Boone (1996), and Burnside and Dollar (2000).
12 A similar result was found by Collier and Hoeffler (2002c), though their measurement of foreign aid is the share of aid to GDP.
13 Collier *et al.* (2003) also obtained a similar result, which shows that aid from all sources tends to increase more in the first two years after a conflict and then begins to decrease in subsequent years. Thus, while our findings differ on the precise point at which aid begins to level off and diminish, both studies find that after an initial, sizeable increase in foreign aid, the donor community provides less and less over time.
14 Governance is also termed policy environment, the quality of government, and government performance. This chapter will use all these terms interchangeably.
15 Donors' emphasis on good governance, for instance, can be found in OECD

(2001), USAID (2002), World Bank (1998). For empirical evidence of governance and the effectiveness of foreign aid, see Burnside and Dollar (2000). However, it is noteworthy that the validity of good governance as a condition for foreign aid success has recently been questioned by Easterly *et al.* (2003).

16 Visit www.imf.org/external/np/hipc/2001/pc/042001.pdf for the list of countries whose debt was partially forgiven by the IMF/World Bank.

17 Good governance is determined by more than democratization. Culture and history also determine the quality of governance. For a comprehensive survey of the determinants of good governance, see La Porta *et al.* (1999).

References

Addison, T. and Murshed, S.M. (2003) "Debt relief and civil war," *Journal of Peace Research* 40: 159–176.

Akram, T. (2003) "The international foreign aid regime: Who gets foreign aid and how much?," *Applied Economics* 35: 1351–1356.

Alesina, A., Baqir, R. and Easterly, W. (1998) "Public goods and ethnic divisions," *NBER Working Paper* 6009. Cambridge, MA: National Bureau of Economic Research. Available at www.nber.org.

Anderson, M.B. (1999) *Do No Harm: How Aid Can Support Peace or War.* Boulder, CO: Lynne Rienner Publishers.

Arvin, B.M. and Barillas, F. (2002) "Foreign aid, poverty reduction, and democracy," *Applied Economics* 34: 2151–2156.

Baum, M.A. and Lake, D.A. (2003) "The political economy of growth: Democracy and human capital," *American Journal of Political Science* 47: 333–347.

Boone, P. (1996) "Politics and the effectiveness of foreign aid," *European Economic Review* 40: 289–329.

Bray, J. (2005) "International companies and post-conflict reconstruction," *Working Paper* 31819 (*Social Development Papers* No. 79; *Conflict Prevention and Reconstruction Working Paper* No. 22). Washington, DC: World Bank. Available at www-wds.worldbank.org.

Bueno de Mesquita, B., Morrow, J.D., Siversson, R., and Smith, A. (1999) "Policy failure and political survival: The contribution of political institutions," *Journal of Conflict Resolution* 43: 147–161.

Burnside, C. and Dollar, D. (2000) "Aid, policies, and growth," *American Economic Review* 90: 847–868.

Collier, P. (1996) "Economic causes of civil war and their implications for policy," in C.A. Crocker and F.O. Hampson (eds.) *Managing Global Chaos: Sources of and Responses to International Conflict.* Washington, DC: United States Institute of Peace Press.

Collier, P. (1999) "On the economic consequences of civil war," *Oxford Economic Papers* 51: 169–83.

Collier, P. (2002) "Primary commodity dependence and Africa's future," *Working Paper* 28111. Washington, DC: World Bank. Available at www.wds.worldbank.org.

Collier, P. and Hoeffler, A. (2002a) "On the incidence of civil war in Africa," *Journal of Conflict Resolution* 46: 13–28.

Collier, P. and Hoeffler, A. (2002b) "Aid, policy and peace: reducing the risks of civil conflict," *Working Paper* 28125. Washington, DC: World Bank. Available at www-wds.worldbank.org.

Collier, P. and Hoeffler, A. (2002c) "Aid, policy and growth in post conflict societies," *Policy Research Working Paper* WPS 2902. Washington, DC: World Bank. Available at www-wds.worldbank.org.

Collier, P., Elliot, L., Hegre, H., Hoeffler, A., Reynal-Querol, M., and Sambanis, N. (2003) *Breaking the Conflict Trap: Civil War and Development Policy*. New York: Oxford University Press.

Demekas, D.G., McHugh, J., and Kosma, T. (2002) "The economics of post-conflict aid," *IMF Working Paper* WP/02/198. Washington, DC: International Monetary Fund. Available at www.imf.org.

Development Initiatives (2004) "Global humanitarian assistance: Some updated trends." Available at http://www.globalhumanitarianassistance.org/ghupdate 19o.pdf.

Dixit, A. and Londregan, J. (1995) "Redistributive politics and economic efficiency," *American Political Science Review* 89: 856–866.

Dornbusch, R., Nölling, W., and Layard, R. (1993) *Postwar Economic Reconstruction and Lessons for the East Today*. Cambridge, MA: The MIT Press.

Easterly, W., Levine, R., and Roodman, R. (2003) "New data, new doubts: a comment on Burnside and Dollar's 'Aid, policies, and growth,'" *Center for Global Development Working Paper* 26. Washington, DC: Center for Global Development. Available at www.cgdev.org.

Elbadawi, I. and Sambanis, N. (2002) "How much war will we see? Explaining the prevalence of civil war," *Journal of Conflict Resolution* 46: 307–334.

Fearon, J.D. and Laitin, D.D. (2003) "Ethnicity, insurgency, and civil war," *American Political Science Review* 97: 75–90.

Hegre, H., Ellingsen, T., Gates, S., and Gleditsch, N.P. (2001) "Toward a democratic civil peace? Democracy, political change, and civil war, 1816–1992," *American Political Science Review* 95: 33–48.

Henderson, E.A. and Singer, J.D. (2000) "Civil war in the post-colonial world, 1946–92," *Journal of Peace Research* 37: 275–299.

Herbst, J. (1990) "War and the state in Africa," *International Security* 14: 117–139.

IMF and World Bank (2001) "Assistance to post-conflict countries and the HIPC Framework." Available at http://www.imf.org/external/np/hipc/2001/pc/042001. pdf.

Jensen, N. and Wantchekon, L. (2004) "Resource wealth and political regimes in Africa," *Comparative Political Studies* 37: 816–841.

Kang, S. and Meernik, J. (2004) "Determinants of post-conflict economic assistance," *Journal of Peace Research* 41: 149–166.

Kang, S. and Meernik, J. (2005) "Civil war destruction and the prospects for economic growth," *The Journal of Politics* 67: 88–109.

Kaufmann, D. and Kraay, A. (2002) "Governance indicators, aid allocation, and the Millennium Challenge Account." Available at http://www.worldbank.org/ wbi/governance/pdf/gov_indicators_aid.pdf.

Krugman, P. (1988) "Financing vs. Forgiving a debt overhang," *Journal of Development Economics* 29: 253–68.

Kugler, J. and Arbetman, M. (1989) "Exploring the phoenix factor with the collective goods perspective," *Journal of Conflict Resolution* 33: 84–112.

La Porta, R., Lopez-de-Silanes, F., Shleifer, A., and Vishny, R.W. (1999) "The quality of Government," *Journal of Law, Economics, and Organization* 15: 222–279.

Levine, R. and Renelt, D. (1992) "A sensitivity analysis of cross-country growth regressions," *American Economic Review* 82: 942–963.

Mancusi-Materi, E. (2000) "Food aid for social development in post-conflict situations," *Development* 43: 106–112.

Meernik, J.D., Krueger, E.L., and Poe, S.C. (1998) "Testing models of United States foreign policy: Foreign aid during and after the cold war," *The Journal of Politics* 60: 63–85.

Murdoch, J. and Sandler, T. (2002) "Economic growth, civil wars, and spatial spillovers," *Journal of Conflict Resolution* 46: 91–110.

Muscat, R.J. (2002) *Investing in Peace: How Development Aid Can Prevent or Promote Conflict.* Armonk, NY: M. E. Sharpe.

North, D. (1990) *Institutions, Institutional Change and Economic Performance.* Cambridge: Cambridge University Press.

OECD (2001) "Helping prevent violent conflict." Available at http://www.oecd. org/dataoecd/15/54/1886146.pdf as found on 29 August 2003.

OECD (2004) *African Economic Outlook 2003/2004 – Country Studies: Mozambique.* Available at http://www.oecd.org/dataoecd/24/23/32430193.pdf.

Olson, M. (1982) *The Rise and Decline of Nations.* New Haven, CT: Yale University Press.

Przeworski, A. (1991) *Democracy and the Market: Political and Economic Reforms in Eastern Europe and Latin America.* Cambridge: Cambridge University Press.

Quinn, D.P. and Woolley, J.T. (2001) "Democracy and national economic performance: the preference for stability," *American Journal of Political Science* 45: 634–657.

Reynal-Querol, M. (2002) "Ethnicity, political system, and civil wars," *Journal of Conflict Resolution* 46: 29–54.

Sachs, J. (1989) "Conditionality, debt relief, and the developing country debt crisis," in J. Sachs, (ed.) *Developing Country Debt and Economic Performance: The International Financial System.* Chicago: University of Chicago Press, pp. 255–295.

Sachs, J. and Warner, A. (1999) "The big push, natural resource booms and growth," *Journal of Development Economics* 39: 43–76.

Sarkees, M. (2000) "The Correlates of War data on war: an update to 1997," *Conflict Management and Peace Science* 18: 123–44.

Schain, M. (2001) *The Marshall Plan: Fifty Years After.* New York: Palgrave.

Schiavo-Campo, S. (2003) "Financing and aid management arrangement in post-conflict situations," *Working Paper* 26689 (*Conflict Prevention and Reconstruction Working Paper* No. 6). Washington, DC: World Bank. Available at http://www-wds.worldbank.org.

Schraeder, P., Taylor, B., and Hook, S. (1998) "Clarifying the foreign aid puzzle: a comparison of American, Japanese, French, and Swedish aid flows," *World Politics* 50: 294–323.

Svensson, J. (1999) "Aid, growth and democracy," *Economics and Politics* 11: 275–297.

USAID (2002) "Millennium Challenge Account," Available at http://www.usaid.gov/press/releases/2002/fs_mca.html.

Van Raemdonck, D.C. and Diehl, P.F. (1989) "After the shooting stops: insights on postwar economic growth," *Journal of Peace Research* 26: 249–264.

World Bank (1998) *Assessing Aid: What Works, What Doesn't, and Why?* New York: Oxford University Press.

World Bank (2002) *Evaluation of the Post-Conflict Fund.* Available at http://www.worldbank.org.

World Bank (2003) *World Development Indicator.* CD-Rom.

World Bank (2004) *PCF Annual Report.* Available at http://www.worldbank.org.

World Bank (2005) "Post conflict: Building peace through development." Available at http://web.worldbank.org/WBSITE/EXTERNAL/NEWS.

12 The economics of sustaining the peace

Breaking the Conflict Trap – civil war and development policy

Constance V. Elliott and V. Lani Elliott

Introduction

Recent empirical studies have altered our understanding of modern, internal war, its conduct, aftermath and what the international community can do to help prevent repeat conflicts and build peace.[1] We focus on one of those studies, *Breaking the Conflict Trap: Civil War and Development Policy* (Collier *et al.* 2003) but draw upon the related findings of the Political Instability Task Force (Goldstone *et al.* 2000)[2] and the work of individual authorities where appropriate. While we stress economics – the studies use many methods from economics and the data often measure economic variables – the research programs are interdisciplinary. For this reason, we offer comments in explanatory end notes that may help identify opportunities for related work in other disciplines.

Space does not permit a summary of this body of recent empirical research. Instead, we discuss the findings that, in our judgment, have the greatest, most lasting relevance for policymakers and analysts.

Collective action is a key to the economic study of a society's stability. Some important aspects of the economic analysis of collective action began relatively recently (Samuelson 1954: 387–389; 1955: 350–356; Tiebout 1956: 416–424; Buchanan and Tullock 1965; Olson 1965, 1982). Questions remain about the validity of economic man in collective action analysis, largely because of the self-maximizing assumption: "Economic man" looks out for himself. This idea of rational, self-maximizing behavior has been criticized as being too narrow for the study of collective activity. Yet analysts from other disciplines, especially those using game theory, also use the assumption. For example, rational actor/rational choice theory depends heavily on game theory.[3]

We suggest that the self-maximizing assumption is not the problem and is, in fact, quite defensible.[4] Instead the problem is a narrow definition of rationality that does not readily accommodate collective activity, co-operation, and can raise problems for interdisciplinary analysis (Downs 1957: 4–11).[5] It may be helpful to readers to use an approach to economic man based on the idea that each individual knows what they want, their own preferences, better than anyone else can and chooses accordingly. Economists are concerned with what most people do most of the time and people generally co-operate (Coase 1960: 1–44).[6] Our definition can accommodate the decisions about their preferences that individuals make as members of groups, that is, when engaged in collective activity. Collective action is not then outwith the range of economic analysis.

The violent aftermath of peace

Sustained peace first requires a peace, hopefully one that can be sustained. Perhaps the most disturbing findings in *Breaking the Conflict Trap* (hereafter "*The Conflict Trap*") are about what happens once there is peace. Within five years after an internal war ends, more than 30 percent of affected countries lapse back into collective violence. In Africa, war follows peace within five years 50 percent of the time. Economic growth is required for countries to avoid internal war. Thus, most internal wars occur in poorer countries. Tragically, these wars hamper, even destroy, the ability to grow and develop. This is "The Conflict Trap." If sustained peace does not necessarily follow from negotiated settlements, how then do we proceed?

A natural, frequent reaction to internal wars outside one's own country, especially when fighting re-starts, is to say "it's their problem," that of the country within which the violence occurs. Another is that "we" cannot just move in, take over and become the world's policeman. These arguments often stress costs. A more sophisticated but similar argument refers to national sovereignty,[7] a formative precept of international organizations like the UN and international financial institutions such as the International Monetary Fund (IMF), the World Bank and the regional development banks. The treaties and agreements establishing these organizations bind us, preventing intervention according to this more sophisticated argument.

These arguments and others notwithstanding, "The Conflict Trap" has a long, international reach. Regardless of how costs are viewed or national sovereignty valued, the problems resulting from internal wars are not confined to the affected country or even to its "neighborhood."

These internal wars create externalities, "international public 'bads'" imposed on other countries by the country within which the civil war occurs and often beyond the ability of any single country to resolve. The effects of internal wars spill across a region or neighborhood, with destabilizing impacts reaching up to 800 kilometers beyond the affected country's borders (Murdoch and Sandler 2004: 138–151). A war within one country and the inevitable build-up in that country's military strength cause neighboring countries to build their own military, resulting in arms races. These arms races – which may be necessary for short-term survival – divert resources from the processes of economic growth.

An even more vexing problem may be costs that cannot be limited to the region. Even in out-of-the-way places, internal wars can have a global reach. War has changed and the humanitarian issues have intensified while the ability to ignore them has declined. The costs internal wars impose on the world include an increased spread of disease, such as malaria and HIV/AIDS; the proliferation of illicit narcotics production with its attendant costs, and political terrorism. For example, people displaced by war are often forced to transit areas with diseases to which they have little immunity. These diseases spread rapidly under the conditions of hardship the displaced usually endure. The magnitude of the problem overwhelms public health facilities. This is true both within the country in which the war takes place and, when displaced groups cross national borders, the country of asylum. An indicator of the magnitude of this problem is that for every 1,000 refugees crossing an international boundary, 1,400 cases of malaria result (Collier *et al.* 2003: 2). Epidemiological research suggests that the initial spread of HIV was closely associated with the 1979 civil war in Uganda and the large number of rapes along the border with Tanzania (ibid.: 47). Public health systems are stressed and break down in warring and asylum countries. The response of aid donors extends costs to the industrialized nations and when international organizations, such as the UN's World Health Organization (WHO), become involved, the costs are imposed on a larger group of nations.

Roughly 95 percent of the global production of illegal narcotics is located in countries experiencing internal war (ibid.: 179). Like those who produce and traffic in illicit narcotics, international terrorists also need areas outside of government control for large-scale training camps, such as those that Al Qaeda ran in Afghanistan or that existed in Lebanon.

The nature of these external costs, the "externalities" of internal wars, makes ignoring the wars impossible. Simply put, the world cannot afford to leave them alone because the participants in these wars impose costs on many if not all other nations. This is hardly a humanitarian view.

What the numbers show

The Conflict Trap found, among many other things that the nature of war has changed dramatically. Wars have turned inward, become more frequent and last longer. Since 1945 few countries have escaped some form of internal war, many falling victim since the end of the Cold War. A growing proportion of the world's internal wars are occurring in the world's poorest countries and affecting about 1.1 billion people. That figure represents about one-sixth of the world's population, yet that same group is involved in about five-sixths of the world's internal wars (ibid.: 103, 121–122, 186).[8]

As the incidence of internal wars has increased the heaviest burdens of war have shifted away from combatants. During World War II nine combatants died for each non-combatant. In today's era of internal war, the ratio of combatant to non-combatant deaths is exactly reversed. This reversal is due in significant part to disease. The shift is not simply forced onto non-combatants; it is forced most acutely upon those non-combatants least able to protect themselves – mothers and children, the aged and the infirm. Thus, the burdens of internal war fall heaviest on the weakest and poorest individuals within the weakest and poorest countries. The trend is intensifying. Those who now bear the heaviest burden of internal war and who have probably the greatest interest in establishing and maintaining peace are weak and so have little influence over those who decide whether to fight or not. Those who decide, the combatants, have relatively little interest in peace because they bear less of the cost.

The typical internal conflict studied by the World Bank lasted approximately seven years and left a legacy of persistent poverty and disease. Negative effects of these wars have extended far beyond the actual fighting, spilling over into neighboring countries and even to industrialized countries as well.

Perhaps surprisingly, the study found that neither ethnic nor religious diversity nor income inequality increased the likelihood that a country would fall into civil war (Collier *et al.* 2003: 66).[9] The Political Instability Taskforce (PITF), however, found ethnicity was indeed a component in state failure (Goldstone *et al.* 2000: 35). Note that state failure is a condition related but not identical to, civil war. In addition, the PITF dealt with ethnic conflict as a type of conflict more than as a cause of civil war. We believe this could eventually complement rather than contradict *The Conflict Trap*'s findings but caution that there are sufficient differences here to warrant great care in drawing comparisons on this issue.

The PITF found that the type of governmental regime was also important in terms of state failure (Goldstone *et al.*: 40). The least stable form of regime was a weak democracy followed by a weak autocracy. Strong versions of either were much more resistant to state failure and excessive instability. Governments do not last unless they have a great deal of popular support or are prepared to impose order through force. Few countries enjoy stability based on widespread popular support so the incentive for governmental repression of some form is not uncommon.

For the average country studied by *The Conflict Trap*, the risk of civil war during any five-year period was about 6 percent. But the risk was alarmingly higher if the economy was poor (had low per capita income), declining and dependent on natural resource exports (Collier *et al.* 2003: 37). For a country like the former Zaire in the late 1990s, with deep poverty, a collapsing economy, and huge mineral exploitation, *The Conflict Trap* reported that the risk of civil war was nearly 80 percent (ibid.: 139).

Empirical studies show that if countries do not achieve and sustain high economic growth rates for extended periods they are vulnerable to instability, often falling into internal war (Collier and Hoeffler 2004: 563–595). Even so, while economic growth is necessary, it is not sufficient to fix the problem, especially after great instability and violence. The conditions needed for economic and political success are far too closely related to allow simplistic policy choices, which treat one arena while ignoring the other. But economic growth is certainly a valuable indicator and should be emphasized.

Patterns of performance across regions over the past 40 years have been quite different (Collier *et al.* 2003: 57–58, 81). *The Conflict Trap* identifies three trends from the period:

1   Increased number of African civil wars.
2   Contraction of many African economies.
3   Diversification of many developing economies.

The performance of the economies of Sub-Saharan Africa since independence gives them special prominence among the poorest nations and the increase in African civil wars is related to economic growth or its absence and to dependence on primary commodities. During this 40-year period much of the developing world has broken out of primary commodity dependence into reliance on manufactured exports. Significant parts of the developing world outside Africa have increased per capita incomes, although many countries have experienced such increases erratically. Internal wars in these regions have generally declined. In Africa they have not. Large parts of Africa have or have had negative economic growth rates; their economies have contracted on both an absolute and per capita basis. Africa has become poorer (ibid.: 115–118) and today the economies of Sub-Saharan Africa are at least as dependent on primary commodities now as they were 30 years ago. As Sub-Saharan African poverty has deepened, the pattern of internal war in the region has become distinct from those of other regions (Mason *et. al.* forthcoming; Weingarten 2000). It has a higher intensity and greater loss of life although over a shorter time span (Sambanis and Elbadawi, December 2000: 244–269).

This leads to a finding that is not intuitive at all, until one looks beneath the surface. That significant oil deposits have been discovered in West Africa would seem to offer hope. But the discovery of a highly desired resource such as oil actually is a barrier to improved economic performance. In some cases, such as alluvial diamonds, high value, easily transported resources can enhance the chances of internal war because they can be turned to the finance of opposition movements with relative ease. The financial power of a primary commodity such as oil within a less developed economy can simply overwhelm other economic processes that generate popular participation in the economy if not the political activities of a country. Where the basic social, political and economic arrangements are not robust, the result is financial power concentrated in the hands of a limited number of people at the expense of a dynamic set of economic processes. These are conditions that can and all too often do contribute to the dynamics that undermine or prevent stability.

High value commodities can be especially pernicious in their impact on a fragile economy. The negative impact of dependence on a primary commodity for a large share of exports is not limited to oil or other high valued items though. If a basic grain crop provides a dominant share of a country's exports that country too is vulnerable to instability and internal war. To some extent, the problem is a lack of diversification. Very likely, although the empirical findings do not necessarily confirm this point, it is related to the level of participation of the general population in the day-to-day activities of the economy. We raise this as a cautionary point for policy analysis.

The strong link between dependence on natural resources and the risk of civil war and, more generally, of failed development deserves attention. *The Conflict Trap* found that the link is due to several reasons, including poor use of resources by governments, resentment and rebel group finance.

It is sometimes necessary to allocate resources to governments, that is, to act collectively in the acquisition of goods and services that markets do not provide, but for which legitimate demand exists within the polity. Yet by definition, even at their most efficient levels of operation governments use resources less efficiently than does the market.[10] Central governments are the least efficient users of resources among governments. When governments then use resources poorly the problem is compounded.

The poor use of resources by a government is a problem not uncommon in less developed countries. Poor government use of resources combines inefficiency and corruption; both point toward popular resentment and may lend further credence to Gurr's ideas on relative deprivation and cognitive dissonance (Gurr 1970).[11]

Poorer countries have too few resources from the outset. They have to use their available resources with the greatest possible efficiency to generate economic growth. But the trend is for at least a reduction in allocational efficiency if not maximizing the inefficiency with which resources are used.

Rebel group finance can have an immediate, tangible effect on stability. To conduct their opposition to governments, rebel groups must be financially viable. This does not necessarily mean that they become profit-seeking enterprises, although illicit narcotics production in unstable countries offers evidence that they sometimes do. The more important point is that these opposition groups need revenue and if foreign donors will not make funds available they must seek money where they can find it. The alluvial diamond trade in West Africa and the "Logs of War" in Cambodia and Thailand (Collier *et al.* 2003: 42, 145) are some examples of creative finance by opposition movements. Some, such as Sendero Luminoso in Peru and the FARC in Colombia have turned to illicit narcotics and today, as noted, estimates of the production of controlled substances in countries undergoing internal wars range up to about 95 percent of total world production of these substances. This is an example not only of failure to achieve and sustain peace but of the failure to achieve economic growth as well.

An important finding of the World Bank research is that a major source of funding for rebel groups is diasporas, especially those in rich countries. These groups "do not suffer the consequences of violence, nor are they in day-to-day contact and accommodation with 'the enemy.'" They tend to be more extreme than their counterparts in the country of origin and use support for extremism as a means of "asserting continued identity" with their homeland. *The Conflict Trap* draws examples from the Eritrean People's Liberation Front's "taxes" on ethnic compatriots around the world, the Tamil Tigers fundraising in North America and the Kosovo Liberation Army's support from Albanians throughout Europe (ibid.: 74–75).

Support for the Irish Republican Army (IRA) in the United States, even after a radical element gained power within the organization is also a compelling example. After the September 11, 2001 terrorist attacks on the United States the flow of funds to both the IRA and the Tamil Tigers were restricted, in one case (the IRA) by former donors and in the other (the Tamil Tigers) when government intervention limited access. In both cases, with access to funds limited, fighting subsided and serious peace negotiations took place. In the case of the IRA the process was carried through at least in part because better informed and newly sensitized American supporters apparently brought pressure on the combatants. Restrictions on the flow of funds to the Tamil Tigers were eased and negotiations became less effective.

What we can learn from the empirical studies

The findings of the empirical research programs agree that the problem of internal war is wide spread and that Sub-Saharan African countries are affected beyond world norms. Colombia, Georgia, Indonesia and Nepal serve to demonstrate the worldwide presence of these wars.

The basic policy implications from examination of the data seem clear. It is tempting to rework the old French Foreign Legion motto of "March or die!" into "Grow or fight!" but, while dramatic, that would be simplistic. Economic growth is certainly necessary but it is as much an indicator of as a contributor to success or failure. Peace within countries requires both political and economic success. By "political" we expressly mean the development of the institutional arrangements, the rules that help individuals co-operate voluntarily across some range of activities. Understanding this finding is important so that we can avoid "either/or" reasoning about political and economic development that is likely to lead to policy failure. So, while following economic growth as an indicator, nations must also perform and develop the processes that generate vital growth in order to avoid falling into internal war. These processes involve collective actions to acquire public goods. Collective actions tend to be classified as political activity yet they have fundamental implications for economics, often being pre- or co-requisites of economic success. Economic processes and their results at the very least affect political processes and the stability of system and order. We suggest that the bridge between the two is the set of agreements people accept to constitute their joint activities.

In dealing with the problems identified by *The Conflict Trap* the cost of failure is great; the probability of long-term success in either political or economic efforts without success in the other is small. Governance and economic growth are strongly related although it is simplistic to argue that good governance is sufficient in and of itself to address the problems of peace and conflict. It is impolitic to argue in favor of nation-building perhaps but, among the countries caught in or approaching *The Conflict Trap*, the alternative to building nations is to continue having the externalities of their internal wars imposed on their neighbors and the rest of the world, especially aid donors and nations capable of projecting force regionally or globally. Those who miss the requirement to build nations may not fully understand the problem.

The implications for the social and policy-related disciplines are basic. Analysts can increase their accuracy and ability to offer relevant advice. This will help policy decision makers improve their chances of success by recognizing the political economy of problems surrounding instability. Policymakers can also increase chances of success by paying greater attention to the dynamics of the political economy of a country or region as a whole rather than just its politics or just its economy. Neither analyst or policymaker will be able to accomplish these ends satisfactorily until there is a means of alerting the polity, political leaders and decision-makers of the need for intervention much further in advance than they are now.

Earlier warning requires a greater understanding of the processes that cause co-operation to break down in a society, order to erode and violent, collective conflict to take place. To gain this earlier awareness and the potentially wider scope of options, decision-makers must require analysts to look further upstream in the dynamic processes by which stability grows or fails. Questions can no longer be limited to how to mobilize or prevent the mobilization of the marginal opponent. The requirements must include questions about why people are ceasing to co-operate. This is, in part, a function of the individual benefit/cost calculus (Tullock, in Milde and Monissen 1985: 139–148; Buchanan and Faith 1987: 1023–1031; Marcoullier and Young 1995: 630–646). For analysts to be able to deliver timely reports, the need for empirical work is evident and empirical work requires the "ground-truthing" of case studies. But even perfect warning is of little value without action and that is a function of leadership and popular will, not of textbooks.

What is to be done?

The recommendations for future action made in *The Conflict Trap* are heavily weighted toward the roles of foreign assistance donors, especially in making aid available when it can be used and in the most useful forms for the conditions faced. Some of *The Conflict Trap*'s findings suggest that aid needs to be increased in post-conflict countries. There are cases where this is true. However, *The Conflict Trap* is also concerned about the pattern of aid.

The research shows that the critical years for post-conflict countries are not the initial years that make the 24-hour news cycle. At that time, the aid community rushes in with large amounts of money and resources; much frustration and criticism arises because all the funds cannot be spent and suffering continues – often on television screens in the wealthier nations. For example, why could the highway in Afghanistan not be built for so long? Afghanistan did not have the absorptive capacity and the aid donors had great difficulty in carrying out their roles for this and other reasons.

In most cases, countries do not have needed absorptive capacity except for strictly humanitarian – and military – help until post-conflict years four and five. In years one and two they have humanitarian needs and the ability to attract headlines. Not surprisingly assistance becomes available in this early period. Yet that is when countries have the least ability to use or absorb aid. When they reach the point that they can really start to put assistance to use the donors and their money have moved on to another crisis on cable and broadcast news. Budgetary restrictions on when funds can be appropriated, obligated and put to use reduced the overall effectiveness of the aid, especially in reducing a country's vulnerability to recidivist conflict.

The aid problems are not just in post-conflict settings. When countries first obtain independence, they have a period of political fragility. Their political institutions are new and easily challenged. They therefore tend to go through a fairly high-risk phase. Those phases of independence occur at different stages in different regions. For example, the break-up of the Soviet empire occurred much later than the break-up of the French and British empires. Thus there are different timetables for political instability factors in different regions.

The Conflict Trap includes recommendations for cutting off funds to rebel groups, a point that we accept but only with reservations. These are governments that cannot be reformed and are so bad they must be removed by virtually whatever means are available, including civil war. The genocidal communist regime of the Khmer Rouge in Cambodia, the kleptocracy of the former Zaire and the apartheid regime in South Africa are only the most obvious examples. Just as it is with opposition groups, sometimes it is necessary to de-fund governments or to bring great pressure to bear on them to bring about necessary changes. The economic issues in these cases center more on financial concerns and trade.

Another important foreign assistance issue is the nature or form of the assistance given. Balanced programs that involve both specifically targeted or project assistance and broader programmatic funds are needed to achieve overall economic success (Commission on Security and Economic Assistance 1983). According to USAID's evaluation system, policy reform, without which economic growth is unlikely if not impossible, cannot be consistently achieved through the use of project assistance (Devres Associates 1986). Program assistance is necessary. The US has been the primary source of program assistance historically and made effective use of this form of assistance in the aid programs for the "Asian Tigers" as well as in stabilization efforts related to Containment during the Cold War. There are two accounts from which US program assistance is drawn: the Economic Support Fund (ESF) and Public Law 480 or the Food for Peace Act, Title I. Over the past 30 years both of these accounts have been redirected as the ability of USAID to manage American foreign assistance programs has come into question. World Bank attempts to step into this role with its sector adjustment lending were less than successful. A modest component of US assistance to Africa was set aside for program assistance under the Development Fund for Africa (DFA) in the late 1980s. The DFA succumbed to bureaucratic and political resistance in the 1990s. As a result, the availability of resources needed to underwrite policy reforms is limited. If donors are to help nations break out of "The Conflict Trap" this situation must be changed.

Why are we only learning these lessons now?

We are learning the lessons from empirical research now because of hard-won advances in theory across the social sciences, particularly in economics. Theoretical advances have coincided with significant improvements in data quality, quantity and availability (Heston *et al.* 2002).

After the collapse of the Soviet Union ended the Cold War in 1989, continuing improvement in the quality and availability of data made quantitative studies of internal war more possible. The political climate also changed enough to reduce resistance to such studies, although some resistance still exists within economics accompanied by resistance to accept quantitative analysis and economic reasoning on the subject matter by other disciplines. Concurrently, an upsurge in internal wars following the Cold War's end (Collier *et al.* 2003: 37), took many by surprise in both the policy and social science communities. The upsurge, especially among the countries of the former Soviet Bloc and those of Sub-Saharan Africa, made new studies necessary. This need was especially evident in Africa where the greatest number of the most intense internal wars has occurred (ibid.: 115). Losses from violent conflicts, both in terms of human lives and of past foreign assistance outlays have been large. Political instability spilled across national boundaries, creating regional and, sometimes, global security concerns. Researchers and policy analysts were compelled to allocate significant resources to the study of conflict and its causes.

The scale of conflict contagion in Sub-Saharan Africa was sufficient to demand new work but, neither collective violence nor its study was confined to Africa alone. During this period, South-eastern Europe – especially the Former Yugoslavia (ibid.: 40) – also suffered several internal wars and economists did not neglect them.[12] But while the number of studies grew, some lacked direction, analytical coherence and, in some cases, substance and relevance. Perhaps of even greater importance, the evolving literature was, as Hirshleifer observed, "disjoint" (Hirshleifer, in Hartley and Sandler 1995: 191–212) and even within disciplines learning was not cumulative (Lichbach 1992: 341). The economics profession failed to incorporate historical lessons on instability and internal war after the end of the Second Indo-China War in 1975. The resulting lack of knowledge of internal war among economists along with the analytical barriers that had developed in the social science disciplines made progress in the empirical study of these phenomena and their causal and resulting conditions difficult. Overspecialization caused other notable difficulties in communications across disciplines. As a result, those with the most powerful analytical methods – economics – and those with the greatest depth and breadth of knowledge – the other social sciences and the military art – often faced significant barriers when attempting to communicate, much less collaborate.

The first major post-Cold War program to study internal war was an interdisciplinary task force on state failure sponsored by the U.S. Government.[13] Set up in 1994 and originally called the State Failure Task Force, it continues today as the Political Instability Task Force (PITF). The PITF combines economic analysis and quantitative methods with authoritative knowledge from several disciplines.

The level of post-Cold War conflict around the world spurred the Carnegie Foundation to establish a Commission on Preventing Deadly Conflict, also in 1994. The Commission addressed economic factors but its analytical methods were more closely related to foreign policy analysis than to any specific social science discipline. The methods used by the Commission included some straightforward applications of defense economics. The Commission issued its final report in 1997 and ceased operations in 1999 (Carnegie Commission 1997).[14]

As the Carnegie Commission ended the World Bank brought the noted Africa scholar and economist, Paul Collier of Oxford University's Center for the Study of African Economies, to direct an interdisciplinary research program on "The Economics of Civil War, Crime and Political

Violence."[15] He mobilized a community of respected scholars from several disciplines, including policy analysts.[16] Collier then led the Bank's program for four years, investigating a wide variety of issues and catalyzing the formation of an important interdisciplinary research community. The program culminated in a major World Bank Policy Review published in book form as *Breaking the Conflict Trap*. The study analyzed 52 major civil wars that occurred between 1960 and 1999 (Collier *et al.* 2003: 58).[17] The World Bank has set new priorities that appear to de-emphasize its own findings about instability and internal war. Perhaps this will change when the former Deputy US Secretary of Defense, Ambassador Paul Wolfowitz, takes office as the Bank's president, although we have no reason to predict such change.

The sole major effort in this area is now the PITF. (The research program on the economic study of terrorism led by Sandler also continues and is certainly relevant but not central to this discussion.)

Prescriptive concepts

An important variable for donors and host governments to consider in working toward a system that prevents at least the relapse into conflict comes from prior empirical work. Economically successful countries do a number of the same things in common and economically unsuccessful countries do as well. These two sets of common practices were very different (Reynolds 1985). A defining difference among the common practices of these two groups was the share of a country's wealth allocated to its public sector.[18]

Long-term resolution of the problems of the poorest countries certainly must deal with relevant financial concerns but there are broader economic and political issues to address as well. The economic issues generally come down to production and participation.

Production in the poorest countries is not sufficient for the people of those countries to be free from a continuing threat of violence. Poor economies produce too little due to inefficient allocation of available resources, especially domestic ones, but also suffer an absolute insufficiency of resources. Foreign assistance resources are unlikely to increase sufficiently to relieve the conditions that underlie instability. Since economic growth results from either increasing the supply of resources or from the reallocation of resources from less to more efficient uses, or a combination of the two, the source of economic growth for poor economies must then come at least partly from an increase in how efficiently they use their own resources. A priority then for solving the problem of internal war is improving the efficiency with which resources are used by poor societies.

Market economies consistently produce the greatest output and enjoy the highest sustained growth rates because the market is the most efficient resource allocation system. If societies are to improve the efficiency with which they use resources, they must organize to meet the needs of their individual citizens for goods and services as market societies. The poorer the country, the greater its need to develop efficient markets yet, according to *The Conflict Trap*, the poorer the country, the less likely it is to make itself into a market society.

Many of the steps necessary to promote the use of markets must be made by the public sector and involve provision of public goods.[19] An early step in improving the efficiency with which an economy allocates resources is improving the functioning of existing markets. One priority in this area is establishing and improving financial markets, the functioning of markets that impact on the efficiency with which other markets function through improved information flow, expanded access and in the packaging and discounting of risk. Financial markets expand popular participation in the ownership of the means of production, as well as improving and expanding the linkage of domestic to international markets. They also make the reform of macroeconomic policy more effective. Promoting the establishment and expansion of financial markets requires providing for institutional needs. Collier has noted the need to understand why people trust or distrust their institutions.[20]

Court systems are necessary to make the legal systems effective and, therefore, credible to investors and traders, and they must be both fair and adequately administered. Both the institution of the law and the organization for its enforcement, the courts, must be made relevant to the needs of financial markets and more effective.

The most efficient allocation of resources within the public sector is that which best matches the preference mix for public goods and services of those served. The structure of the public sector that is most efficient in the provision of the public goods mix of a given country is very important.

Determining the least inefficient structure of the public sector requires assessment of the need and effective demand for specific public goods and the development of some means of establishing relative priorities. Donor priorities should be based at least partly on how a structure or a specific public good contributes to the overall goal of stimulating economic growth.

When you cannot run or hide

Certainly there is a need for effective peace negotiations, but the incentives to negotiate in good faith and to find resolution for difficult problems do not appear to favor resolution. A negotiating table is a venue for combatants and their agents, war fighters, brokers and diplomats, all of whom tend to be exempt from the heaviest costs of internal war. The noncombatants who bear the heaviest costs, costs that continue long after the fighting stops in these longest of wars, lack power and influence militarily, politically and economically. They have no say within their own countries, or in the *fora* where decisions are made, about whether fighting continues or stops, even though those decisions may well determine their ability to survive. They are unheard within their own countries beyond the village or refugee camp that shelters them. As a result, combatants and negotiators can and too often do ignore them. Yet, in an age of almost instant global communication, where networks are driven by the unending 24-hour news cycle, the weak have a special voice in the world's industrialized democracies. Perhaps unheard within their own precincts, their only voice, the only means of influence they can have is on global television broadcasts.

Because the general public is the audience of these broadcasts, elected representatives in the world's republics respond. The option to "let them fight it out among themselves" fades. Assistance then will likely be sent to countries with what are becoming very internationalized internal wars, so long as those burdened most by a war reach the news. The options available to appointed foreign policy and national security decision-makers become constrained due to public scrutiny. Early interventions sometimes offer a great range of policy options and implementing methods. Late interventions are very often confined to a set of methods involving the deployment of troops to provide protection or and, sometimes, to deliver the assistance.

Even assistance meant to bolster security requires some minimum level of security for workers to deliver necessary commodities and supplies. When assistance must be delivered under hostile or simply anarchic conditions, military deployments are necessary to provide security. Military deployments usually require some level of US involvement if for no other reason than transportation capacity. After the "Black Hawk Down" incident in Somalia, US policymakers have, hopefully, learned that the Powell Doctrine of overwhelming force is necessary in humanitarian deployments as well as in more conventional military operations. The costs of such deployments are significant but the issue of putting one's young countrymen at risk represents a profoundly more important cost.

Protecting the unprotected means placing one's own young people at risk. There are few options in any region that do not include US involvement. Given the natural tendency of decision-makers to continually seek better understanding of a situation that may be beyond an outsider's ability to grasp, the likelihood of late intervention is virtually assured much of the time. However it may be justified, policy procrastination delays response and reduces the few options available. Many, if not most, responses then will have a requirement to put US troops on the ground and in harm's way.

Given the nature of internal wars, we risk becoming involved while the incentive to prevent or simply end hostilities sits most heavily on the shoulders of everyone except those who can end them. Further, we do so with the incentive to "free ride" firmly implanted in the incentive structures facing countries that are not necessarily directly involved. Analysts must warn much earlier. Policymakers have to demand and see that they get the needed alerts far enough in advance to permit strategic options that include but are not limited to "stay home" or "send troops." Policymakers must then discipline themselves to act.

Acknowledgments

The views expressed in this chapter are the authors' and do not represent those of the World Bank, the United States Government, its departments and agencies, Data Net, Inc. or any other organization. The chapter draws on conversations with the co-authors of *Breaking the Conflict Trap: Civil War and Development Policy*, Paul Collier of Oxford University, Håvard Hegre of the Peace Research Institute of Oslo (PRIO), Anke Hoeffler of Oxford University's Center for the Study of African Economies, Marta Reynal-Querol of the World Bank Group and Nicholas Sambanis of Yale University. At the World Bank, Ibrahim Elbadawi, who was central to the research program that produced the book, has also contributed greatly to our understanding, as have Ian Bannon and Colin Scott. We are also indebted to participants in two workshops, the first at the University of North Texas (UNT) in November 2003 from which this volume is derived and the second held on the findings of *Breaking the Conflict Trap* in April 2004 by the Social Science Research Council under the direction of John Tirman. We are grateful as well to Professor T. David Mason of UNT, Wayne Brough, Chief Economist of Citizens for A Sound Economy, and Henry Wooster of the US Department of State, for their advice in developing the body of reasoning that underlies our work. We have made extensive use of Professor Collier's comments at the May 14, 2003 press conference in Paris signaling *Breaking the Conflict Trap*'s publication as well as the comments at the time made by Dr. Bannon. However, we have incorporated findings of other researchers and expressed our own judgments throughout the chapter. In both cases the other co-authors of *Breaking the Conflict Trap* and those from whom we have learned so much may well not agree. So, for whatever is correct herein (especially if the reader agrees with it), we gratefully acknowledge the co-authors of *Breaking the Conflict Trap* as well as those mentioned above. The burden for all in this chapter that is controversial and, of course, for mistakes is ours.

Notes

1 The major empirical research programs dealing with relevant subject matter are the Political Instability Task Force, the World Bank's Project on the Economics of Civil Wars, Crime and Political Violence and the work of Paul Collier, who originally directed the World Bank Project, and Anke Hoeffler at the Center for the Study of African Economies at Oxford University. These programs have been informed by the findings of the: Carnegie Commission on

Deadly Conflict; Woodrow Wilson International Center for Scholars projects on Conflict Prevention (which effectively succeeded the Carnegie Commission) as well as Environmental Change and Security Project; University of Maryland's Center for International Development and Conflict Management; Peace Research Institutes of Oslo (PRIO) and of Stockholm (SIPRI); S.E.N.S.E. Project of the Institute for Defense Analyses; a large body of work done under the auspices of the Rand Corporation; and the work of Todd Sandler and various co-authors, notably Walter Enders, James Murdoch, and Dan Arce applying quantitative methods from economics to the study of terrorism. It is important to note the contributions of programs to improve and gather data, especially those of Ted Robert Gurr of the University of Maryland, Barbara Haarf of the U.S. Naval Academy, the University of Michigan social science database program and the Penn World Tables project. The work done to establish, maintain and improve relevant databases on terrorism by Sandler and Edward F. Mickolous has proved to have considerable value. The improved quality, lengthening streams and increased availability of data were cornerstones of the efforts to apply quantitative measures that were at the heart of the empirical research programs.

2 For purposes of disclosure, V.L. Elliott is currently a consultant to the Political Instability Task Force and was a participant in its predecessor, the State Failure Task Force, from 1999 to 2002.

3 Cournot-Nash equilibrium is the condition in non-co-operative, repeating games where no player can gain anything by changing his strategy in future iterations. Antoine-Augustin Cournot was the first to describe imperfectly competitive equilibria in his *Recherches sur les principes mathématiques de la théorie des richesses (1838; Researches into the Mathematical Principles of the Theory of Wealth)*, with his formulation of duopoly, a market with only two players. From Cournot's viewpoint, this equilibrium describes a condition in which market price is reached in situations like duopoly. John Nash's seminal work *Non-Cooperative Games* (1950, explicitly proved such equilibria existed in iterative games. (For a good description readers may wish to refer to http://www.answers.com/main/ntquery?method=4&dsid=2222&dekey=Nash+e quilibrium.) Myerson (1999) disputes the correctness of the joint naming, arguing that while Cournot did discover the theory of imperfect competition, including the price theory of non-co-operative solutions, and recognized elements of non-co-operative equilibria, he did not explicitly develop the theory of non-co-operative equilibria itself. Myerson's dispute is not central to this piece but future researchers should address his argument to determine whether it applies to their reasoning. For a full discussion of the development of game theory, see Leonard (1994 and 1995).

4 The functional goal of the social sciences is not just to predict human behavior in the abstract, but to analyze social institutions and evaluate proposals for specific institutional reforms. "When our task is to look for potential flaws in a social institution, it can be very helpful to analyze the institution under an assumption that the agents in the institution are not themselves flawed. Otherwise, if we find that flawed individuals may come to grief in this institutional structure, we cannot say whether our finding is an argument for reform or an argument for better education of individuals. Thus, economists have found it useful to assume a certain perfection of individuals, in order to see more clearly when social problems must be solved by institutional reform.... To do any kind of analytical social theory, we must formulate a model that includes both a description of the institutions that we are studying and a prediction of individuals' likely behavior in these institutions. To be able to handle normative questions, there must also be some concept of human welfare in our model. If

we assume that some individuals are not movitated to maximize their own welfare (as measured in our model) or that some individuals do not understand their environment (as predicted in our analysis), then any loss of welfare that we find in our analysis can be blamed on dysfunctional or misinformed individual behavior, rather than on the structure of social institutions. Thus, an argument for reform of social institutions (rather than for reeducation of individuals) is most persuasive when it is based on a model that assumes that individuals intelligently understand their environment and rationally act to maximize their own welfare. So, applied social theorists should find it useful to scrutinize social institutions under the assumption that every member of society will act, within their domain of control, to maximize welfare as they evaluate it, given the predicted behavior of others" (Myerson 1999: 1069).

5 Anthony Downs gave two definitions of rationality, one narrow and one broad. Stan Taylor indicated that some of the earliest modern attempts by economists to deal with instability and internal war, such as the work of Thomas Ireland, used the narrow definition that Downs argued economists must use. Tullock and then Silver used the broader definition. Both encountered substantial problems. These were due partly to the limits of economics' quantitative tools. Much of the economics literature in this area follows Ireland's use of a more narrow definition of rationality although he is not often cited. At the time this chapter was being written, David M. Levy of George Mason University's Center for the Study of Public Choice, was working on a demonstration that economists can indeed use arguments involving broad or "weak" rationality while using the mathematics that have traditionally described narrow or "strong" rationality. Source: conversations with the author.

6 Coase found that people will seldom fail to co-operate with one another when co-operation is to their mutual advantage, so long as no transaction costs are involved. Usually, however, some transaction costs are involved and Coase saw the role of institutions – the rules – as the means of facilitating co-operation when this is the case. Since co-operation generally takes the form of collective or group activity. When costs of membership are real, members require an agreement on the assignment of benefits (rights) and costs (duties and responsibilities) before joining a group. The agreement itself thus constitutes the group. This agreement and an attendant means of preference revelation (e.g., voting) are at the heart of any calculation of the acceptability – the legitimacy – of the group to its members.

7 The Treaty of Westphalia established the modern concept of national sovereignty in 1648. Policies of preemptive intervention are assumed by many to be at odds with this precept of international relations.

8 Collier also addressed this point in his Paris press conference on May 14, 2003.

9 Income inequalities and the distribution of land are not causal factors with regard to civil war. This was first reported by Collier and Hoeffler in their Oxford University Center for the Study of African Economies Working Papers on "Greed and Grievance in Civil War." The citation in *Breaking the Conflict Trap* is for a 2001–02 working paper series. The research dates back to at least 1999 and there may have been precursors to these working papers at the World Bank although we have not seen them. Collier and Hoeffler revisited the question in an Oxford Economics Papers article of the same title, published in 2004. The results were the same. This finding places *Breaking the Conflict Trap* seemingly at odds with the empirical results of the PITF and the theoretical arguments of Ted Robert Gurr concerning relative deprivation and Amartya Sen (see the opening page of his 1973 book, *On Economic Inequality*) as well as related arguments from those in the traditions following Marx. We note again that the PITF's findings were related to state failure not civil war however, and

the theoretical arguments were not empirical. The state failure/civil war application differences call for both replication and analytical resolution. Regarding theoretical arguments, we suggest that the burden then rests with those making such arguments to demonstrate why the empirical work that does not support the theory is in error.

10 Among the fields of specialization in economics that address this subject in considerable depth are fiscal federalism and public choice.

11 For a current examination of the subject of government financial management see: R. Barry Johnston and John M. Abbott, eds., *Deterring Abuse of the Financial System* (2005).

12 See, for example, the referenced bodies of work by Bookman and by Kuran respectively.

13 The Heritage Foundation set up a temporary working group on special operations during the early 1990s and it dealt with counterinsurgency issues. However, while recognizing the need for study beyond its mandate, this working group did not extend its work into the areas covered by the Carnegie Commission, the PITF or the Collier-led program at the World Bank.

14 The Woodrow Wilson International Center for Scholars' Conflict Prevention Project explicitly builds on the work of the Carnegie Commission on Preventing Deadly Conflict. Again, for purposes of disclosure, V.L. Elliott has taken part in the WWIC Conflict Prevention Project since 1999.

15 This is another project in which V.L. Elliott participated, from 1999 until 2002 as a conference attendee and invited member of the advisory board and, in 2002–3 as a consultant and co-author of *Breaking the Conflict Trap*.

16 The core team members of the World Bank program are listed as: Jean-Paul Azam, Robert H. Bates, Paul Collier, Michael Doyle, Ibrahim Elbadawi, Scott Gates, Roberta Gatti, Edward Glaeser, Nils Petter Gleditsch, Håvard Hegre, Jeffrey Herbst, Anke Hoeffler, Daniel Lederman, Norman Loayza, Michael L. Ross, Nicholas Sambanis and Mark Woodward. Sandler, Jack Goldstone, James Fearon, David Laitin, Jane Hull Lute, Marta Querol-Reynal, Stergios Skaperdas, and Barbara Walter were among other participants.

17 Collier and co-author Anke Hoeffler have continued their investigations since returning to Oxford (Collier and Hoeffler 2004: 563–95). Co-authors Nicholas Sambanis (Sambanis and Collier 2002: 1–170), Yale University, and Håvard Hegre (Hegre 2004: 243–252), PRIO, have also continued their empirical research in this subject matter.

18 See the referenced body of work by Daniel Landau.

19 The types of public good to which we refer include: 1. Security of person and property that includes territorial defense and maintenance of internal order but which goes beyond that rudimentary level of individual security by explicitly recognizing the individual's right to own and control the allocation and use of property; 2. Institutional needs, including a fair, workable set of laws governing contracts, exchange and investment; a just and timely means of adjudicating these laws; and 3. Production/marketing standards; a set of macroeconomic policies that stimulate growth, and provide price stability.

20 We define institutions as rules, which may be cultural, as in traditions, political, as in laws, or economic, as in policies. With institutions there are often accompanying organizational development requirements that may include the central bank or Finance Ministry or provincial governments.). Using our definition, institutional needs include: Explicit recognition of the individual's right to own and control the allocation and use of property; a fair, workable set of laws governing contracts, exchange and investment; a just and timely means of adjudicating these laws; production/marketing standards; a set of macroeconomic policies which stimulate growth, and control inflation; a basic set of physical

infrastructure which links production areas with the principal sources of demand. Institutional priorities in promoting market use would be: 1. Encouragement of markets that improve the efficiency of other markets, such as financial markets; 2. Improving the conditions that affect several markets, e.g., information flow, physical access, level and quality of labor and management skills, reduction of debilitating disease in key production areas, etc.; 3. Improving the efficiency with which existing markets function; 4. Diversification of production in order to establish new markets; and 5. Improving and expanding the linkage of domestic markets to international markets. (Globalization critics notwithstanding, openness to trade is a positive condition identified by both the World Bank and the PITF.)

References

Bookman, M. (1990) "The Economic Basis of Regional Autarchy in Yugoslavia," *Soviet Studies* 42(1): 93–109.

Bookman, M. (1992a) *The Economics of Secession*. New York: St Martin's Press.

Bookman, M. (1992b) "Economic Issues Underlying Secession: The Case of Slovenia and Slovakia," *Communist Economies and Economic Transformation* 4(1): 111–134.

Bookman, M. (1994a) "War and Peace: The Divergent Breakups of Yugoslavia and Czechoslovakia," *Journal of Peace Research* 31(2): 175–187.

Bookman, M. (1994b) "Yugoslav Sanctions Destabilize the Balkans," *Zlatno Slovo* 1(1): 25–32.

Bookman, M. (1994c) *Economic Decline and Nationalism in the Balkans*. New York: St Martin's Press.

Bookman, M. (1997) *The Demographic Struggle for Power*. London: Frank Cass Publishers.

Buchanan, J. and Faith, R. (1987) "Secession and the Limits of Taxation," *American Economic Review* 77(5): 1023–1031.

Buchanan, J., Faith, R., and Tullock, G. (1965) *The Calculus of Consent: Logical Foundations of Constitutional Democracy*. Ann Arbor, MI: The University of Michigan Press.

Carnegie Commission on Preventing Deadly Conflict (1997) *Preventing Deadly Conflict Final Report*. New York: Carnegie Corporation of New York, December.

Coase, R. (1960) "The Problem of Social Cost," *The Journal of Law and Economics* 3: 1–44.

Collier, P. (2003) Press conference, Paris, May 14.

Collier, P., Elliott, V., Hegre, H., Hoeffler, A., Reynal-Querol, M., and Sambanis, N. (2003) *Breaking the Conflict Trap: Civil War and Development Policy*. A World Bank Policy Review. Washington, DC: The World Bank Group and Oxford University Press.

Collier, P. and Hoeffler, A. (2004) "Greed and Grievance in Civil War," *Oxford Economics Papers* 56: 563–595.

Commission on Security and Economic Assistance (Carlucci Commission) (1983) *A Report to the Secretary of State*. Washington, DC.

Cournot, A. (1927) *Researches into the Mathematical Principles of the Theory of Wealth*. Trans. Nathaniel T. Bacon. New York: The Macmillan Co.

Devres Associates (1986) "Synthesis of A.I.D. Evaluation Reports: FY 85 and FY

86. Draft." Washington, DC: US Agency for International Development PPC/CDIE's.

Downs, A. (1957) *An Economic Theory of Democracy*. New York: Harper and Row.

Goldstone, J., Gurr, T., Haarf, B., Levy, M., Marshall, M., Bates, R., Epstein, D., Kahl, C., Surko, P., Ulfelder, J., and Unger, A., in consultation with Christenson, M., Dabelko, G., Esty, D., and Parris, T. (2000) *State Failure Task Force Report: Phase III Findings*. McLean, VA: Science Applications International Corporation (SAIC).

Gurr, T. (1970) *Why Men Rebel*. Princeton, NJ: Princeton University Press.

Hartley, K. and Sandler, T. (eds.) (1995) *The Handbook of Defense Economics*. New York: Elsevier.

Hegre, Håvard (ed.) (2004) "The Duration and Termination of Civil War," *Journal of Peace Research* 41(3): 243–252.

Heston, A., Summers, R., and Aten, B. (2002) *Penn World Table Version 6.1*, Center for International Comparisons at the University of Pennsylvania (CICUP). Online. Available HTTP: <http://pwt.econ.upenn.edu/php_site/pwt_index.php> Accessed May 8, 2005.

Ireland, T. (1967) "Rationale for Revolt," *Papers in Non-market Decision Making* 49–66.

Johnston, R. and Abbott, J. (eds.) (2005) *Deterring Abuse of the Financial System: Elements of an Emerging International Integrity Standard*. Washington, DC: The International Monetary Fund.

Koppel, C. and Sharma, S. (2003) *Preventing the Next Wave of Conflict: Understanding Non-traditional Threats to Global Stability*. Report of the Non-Traditional Threats Working Group of the Conflict Prevention Project. Washington, DC: The Woodrow Wilston International Center for Scholars.

Kuran, T. (1991a) "The East European Revolution of 1989: Is It Surprising That We Were Surprised?," *American Economic Review* 81: 121–125.

Kuran, T. (1991b) "Now Out of Never: The Element of Surprise in the East European Revolution of 1989," *World Politics* 44: 7–48.

Kuran, T. (1993) "Seeds of Racial Explosion," *Society* 30: 55–67.

Kuran, T. (1995a) "The Inevitability of Future Revolutionary Surprises," *American Journal of Sociology* 100(6): 1528–1551.

Kuran, T. (1995b) *Private Truths, Public Lies: The Social Consequences of Preference Falsification*. Cambridge, MA: Harvard University Press.

Kuran, T. (1998a) "Ethnic Norms and Their Transformation Through Reputational Cascades," *Journal of Legal Studies* 27: 623–659.

Kuran, T. (1998b) "Insincere Deliberation and Democratic Failure," *Critical Review* 12(4): 529–544.

Landau, D. (1983) "Government Expenditure and Economic Growth: A Cross Country Study," *Southern Economic Journal* 49: 783–792.

Landau, D. (1985) "Government and Economic Growth in the Developed Countries: 1952–1976," *Public Choice* 47: 459–477.

Landau, D. (1986) "Government and Economic Growth in the Less Developed Countries: An Empirical Study for 1960–80," *Economic Development and Cultural Change* 35: 35–76.

Landau, D. (1990) "The Pattern of Economic Policies in LDCs: A Public Choice Explanation," *The Cato Journal* 10(2): 573–602.

Landau, D. (1995) "Do Country Characteristics Matter for Economic Growth Among the Developed Countries," *Atlantic Economic Journal* 23(2): 113–121.

Landau, D. (1997) "Government Expenditure, Human Capital Creation and Economic Growth," *Journal of Public Budgeting, Accounting and Financial Management* 9(3): 467–487.

Leonard, R. (1994) "Reading Cournot, Reading Nash: The Creation and Stabilisation of the Nash Equilibrium," *The Economic Journal* 104: 492–511.

Leonard, R. (1995) "From Parlor Games to Social Science: Von Neumann, Morgenstern and the Creation of Game Theory, 1928–1944," *The Journal of Economic Literature* 33(2): 730–761.

Lichbach, M. (1992) "Nobody Cites Nobody Else: Mathematical Models of Domestic Political Conflict," *Defence Economics* 3(4): 341–357.

Marcouillir, D. and Young, L. (1995) "The Black Hole of Graft: The Predatory State and the Informal Economy," *American Economic Review* 85(3): 630–646.

Mason, T., Weingarten, J., and Lindstrom, R. (forthcoming) "Structure Versus Grievance as Determinants of Ethnic Civil War."

Milde, H. and Monissen, H. (eds.) (1985) *Rationale Wirtschaftspolitik in Komplexen Gesellschaften*. Stuttgart: Verlag W. Kohlhammer.

Murdoch, J. and Sandler, T. (2004) "Civil Wars and Economic Growth: Spatial Dispersion," *The American Political Science Review* 138–151.

Myerson, R.B. (1999) "Nash Equilibrium and the History of Economic Theory," *The Journal of Economic Literature* 37(3): 1067–1082.

Olson, M. (1971) *The Logic of Collective Action: Public Goods and the Theory of Groups*. Cambridge, MA: Harvard University Press.

Olson, M. (1982) *The Rise and Decline of Nations: Growth, Stagflation and Social Rigidities*. New Haven, CT: Yale University Press.

Reynolds, L. (1985) *Economic Growth in the Third World: 1850–1980*. New Haven, CT: Yale University Press.

Sambanis, N. and Collier, P. (eds.) (2002) Special Issue, *Journal of Conflict Resolution* 46(1): 1–170.

Sambanis, N. and Elbadawei, I. (2000) "Why Are There So Many Civil Wars in Africa? Understanding and Preventing Violent Conflict," *Journal of African Economies* 9(3): 244–269.

Samuelson, P. (1954) "The Pure Theory of Public Expenditure," *The Review of Economics and Statistics* 36: 387–389.

Samuelson, P. (1955) "Diagrammatic Exposition of a Theory of Public Expenditure," *The Review of Economics and Statistics* 38: 350–356.

Samuelson, P. (1958) "Aspects of Public Expenditure Theories," *The Review of Economics and Statistics* 40: 332–338.

Sen, A. ([1973] 1997) *On Economic Inequality*. Oxford: Oxford University Press.

Silver, M. (1974) "Political Revolutions and Repression: An Economic Approach," *Public Choice* 14: 63–71.

Tiebout, C. (1956) "A Pure Theory of Local Expenditures," *The Journal of Political Economy* 45(5): 416–424.

Tullock, G. (1971) "The Paradox of Revolution," *Public Choice* 11: 89–99.

Tullock, G. (1974) *The Social Dilemma: The Economics of War and Peace*. Blacksburg, VA: Public Choice Center.

Tullock, G. (1985) "A New Proposal for Decentralizing Government Activity," in

H. Milde and H. Monissen (eds.) *Rationale Wirtschaftspolitik in Komplexen Gesellschaften.* Stuttgart: Verlag W. Kohlhammer, pp 139–148.

Tullock, G. (1994) *The New Federalist.* Vancouver: The Fraser Institute.

Weingarten, J. (2000) "Regional Differences in Ethnic Conflict: Structural versus Grievance-based Explanations," paper presented at American Political Science Association Annual Meeting, Washington, DC.

13 Conclusion

James D. Meernik and T. David Mason

It should come as no surprise that the authors of the chapters in this volume all describe a process of ending violence and peacebuilding that is difficult, expensive and fraught with hazards. Done right, it can set a nation on the path toward reconciliation, reconstruction, peace and prosperity. Done wrong, it may well lead to renewed fighting and more human suffering. When the aggregate response falls somewhere in between, as it most often does, the results are mixed and the post-conflict society will find its injuries in varying states of recuperation and continually at risk of subsequent outbreaks of violence and other problems. Nations navigating through this uncertain zone of neither war nor peace, neither recovery nor relapse will find it a constant struggle to right their society and the ship of state. Yet, as is apparent from the findings of this volume, it is this gray zone in which many, if not most, nations emerging from conflict tend to languish. Our aim in this chapter is not so much to prescribe a specific course of treatment, but to describe the general lessons we have learned about the manner in which the post-conflict society and the international community can best approach the reconciliation and reconstruction process and escape this gray zone. We are most concerned with highlighting those general themes brought out by the authors regarding what the international community and the post conflict society should consider as they evaluate the appropriate response.

The conditions that put a nation at risk for civil war are themselves exacerbated by war. Therefore, as Mason and Quinn point out, peacebuilding must involve forms of intervention that dismantle the conditions of dual sovereignty that make renewed civil war possible. And reconstruction and reconciliation must focus on reducing the incentives of former combatants to choose a resumption of armed conflict over sustaining the peace. Successful reconciliation and reconstruction demand a diverse array of resources in costly and sizeable amounts. It also requires a level of effort and commitment by all parties to stay the course even when setbacks occur. So much for the obvious. How it is all done, however, matters as much as what is done. The international community can sink all the money and expertise into a post-conflict society it can afford, and yet leave its people only marginally better off than before. As Seonjou Kang shows in her chapter, as Elliott and Elliott do in theirs, if post-conflict development assistance is to promote economic growth, there must be an environment of good governance. External resources should be focused on humanitarian relief in the short-run and the development of infrastructure over the middle and long-run. When the international community, both IGOs and NGOs, rushes into a post-conflict society after the guns are silenced with fat wallets and a desire to have an immediate impact, some good can be done, but at often an overly inflated price because such societies are ill-equipped to absorb so much assistance so quickly. Much energy and money is often used unwisely in the first flush of peace. And when the media spotlight is dimmed and the aid workers depart for the next international hot spot, they leave behind a post-conflict society that often has not reached the point of economic take-off where more significant, ongoing investment would place it on the pathway toward stability and recovery. Despite this, we find that all too often aid tapers off after the first few years, and the post-conflict society is left to compete for foreign capital in the open market against nations that have not experienced the devastation of civil war and, therefore, are more attractive (and less risky) as investment opportunities. More judicious timing and targeting of foreign assistance would reap the far greater benefits of self-sustained growth and thus be much more cost effective.

It also matters which external actor is leading the recovery efforts. Peceny and Pickering show that the United Nations, which tends to enter post-conflict nations in order to support a society that has made peace and acquiesced to the role of the UN in recovery efforts, has the best track record of promoting democracy. Democratization, and in particular good governance, as we already know is crucial to the effective utilization of foreign assistance. Democratic checks on public officials make them more accountable and thus less able to engage in the sort of rent-seeking behaviors that can divert development assistance into their own bank accounts, bleed the economy dry, and bring about the degeneration of a fledgling democracy into an authoritarian relapse.

When the United States intervenes, even to replace an authoritarian government with a more democratic one, it is often successful too and performs better than the British and the French in their interventions. These are, however, very different types of missions than those undertaken by the UN. Whereas the UN comes in at the invitation of the host country and with plans for peacebuilding agreed upon by all or most parties, the US efforts at democratization have mostly involved the US acting unilaterally in opposition to the interests of the host government. Both methods may bring democracy. However, it would seem that the UN missions should have a greater chance of success, given the acquiescence of the host country that then provides a mantle of legitimacy to the operation. OSCE operations, as illustrated by Bruce George, also show great promise for the same reasons that UN operations tend to work better than unilateral efforts at democratization. OSCE missions are generally comprehensive, multilateral, and though the impetus for the "invitation" to provide peace-building may have originated in a more violent military intervention, the level of expertise and resources the OSCE enjoys should outweigh the costs. The OSCE also has a successful track record of election monitoring and bringing pressure to bear on recalcitrant dictators bent on clinging to power, as we saw in the Ukraine in late 2004.

But while some such interventions may bring about greater levels of democratization, the uses of force led by the United States do not appear to improve a nation's human rights record as shown by Meernik, Poe and Shaikh. It is probably easier to engineer and install the formal institutions of democracy – including constitutions, election systems, legislatures and a state bureaucracy – than it is to change the substance of democracy – including the manner in which governments treat their citizens and the extent to which citizens tolerate one another's diversity. Such lessons may take years or even generations to reach full fruition, especially in nations where hatred and intolerance have been hardened by years of war, torture, disappearances, extra-judicial killings and the like. It bears repeating that efforts to remake a society and cultivate a democratic political culture occur only over many years, probably at least a generation or more. Yet, often the most crucial work involved in building a culture of tolerance begins only after the initial wave of international assistance and public enthusiasm for peace has died down. This is especially the case with the promotion of human rights. Certainly doing away with laws in the United States that mandated the legal separation of the races did not end racism.

Even when military intervention leads to greater levels of democracy in one nation, it is possible that the regional spillover effects present dangers to nations in the neighborhood. Enterline and Greig show that only when the democracy established by an intervention becomes a "bright beacon" – a more stable and complete form of democracy – can we expect enhanced regional peace and prosperity, but even then not necessarily greater levels of democratization in neighboring states. On the other hand, if the newly created democracy is only "dimly lit," it exerts a negative impact on regional peace, prosperity and democratization by becoming a source of instability. The lessons for US and other foreign policymakers in Iraq are quite obvious. Either the experiment in democratization in that country is thoroughly and continuously nurtured to the point of its emergence as a "bright beacon," or the hoped for spread of democratization in the Middle East will not occur; indeed, a failed Iraqi experiment is likely to spread instability and conflict to other nations in the region. Thus, imposed democratization that is carried out thoroughly and patiently should yield significant benefits. But policymakers who believe that democratization can be done on the cheap will not only be disappointed; they will inherit a region even more conflictual than it was before.

These are the lessons we learn from Hartzell and Mullenbach as well. International peacebuilding efforts must be thorough and multidimensional. The greater the level of institutionalization of the economic, military, political and territorial components of a peacebuilding effort, the greater the likelihood of its success. The de-mining effort that was inadequately funded may not bring about the return of farmers to their land, which in turn makes the society less self-sufficient economically and then eventually leads rebels to take up arms once again. Thoroughness and, as Mullenbach points out, coordination are critical in peacebuilding efforts. It bears repeating that as in all elements of peacebuilding, if it is worth doing, it is worth doing right. Nonetheless, as these authors also demonstrate, the fact that such peacebuilding efforts do provide for a variety of forms of relief and conflict resolution makes them more likely to be successful. Should one aspect of the settlement prove lacking, or should the parties to the conflict find another element politically difficult to implement, if there are enough other components of the peacebuilding effort still on track, recovery is yet possible. Still, predicting which elements of a peacebuilding plan can safely be set aside or only partially completed will likely be quite difficult. If the wrong choices are made regarding what elements might be set aside or sacrificed, or if compensatory action to make up for deficiencies fails, the entire plan may be jeopardized.

What ingredients for successful reconciliation and reconstruction may be found within the post-conflict society? Do peace and prosperity depend entirely on the efforts of the international community? It certainly seems to be the case that some nations are better positioned than others to be success stories. Gibson shows in his discussion of the Truth and Reconciliation Commission in South Africa that many of the critical elements of the effectiveness of that institution were to be found in the willingness of the parties to the conflict to accept the need for and the powers of the TRC. And while later many politicians in all parties found reason to object to some of the TRC's actions, the Commission successfully fulfilled its mandate and has been held up as a model for the rest of the world. We must wonder, however, whether the factors that made the South African TRC successful were not present all along in that society. A desire on the part of many for an even-handed truth telling and exemplary leadership certainly contributed to the South African success story. Whether such good intentions exist or can be evoked in other post-conflict societies is debatable. Could such a commission have been created in Bosnia after its three and one-half year war; or in Rwanda after its genocide? The odds would seem to favor more economically well-developed societies in which the parties have reached a negotiated settlement and are honestly ready to confront the past in order to build a more prosperous future.

Perhaps of all the challenges facing post-conflict societies the most crucial is fostering a respect for law and order after widespread violence marked by the commission of atrocities that have been the norm for so long. Closely coupled with this effort is the need to reintegrate back into the mainstream of society those who did the fighting and others for whom weapons have become readily available. No group is in a better position to wreak havoc with all aspects of reconciliation and reconstruction than the former combatants. Yet, as the Booth and Richard chapter shows us, just because the *political* violence may have formally ended with a truce or peace settlement, does not mean that other forms of even more pernicious and destabilizing violence will not arise. Former combatants who may be marginalized, or have few job prospects may put to use their war-fighting skills in criminal activity as has been the case in some Central American nations, Iraq, Afghanistan, Liberia and elsewhere. Indeed, in Bosnia, many of the combatants were originally drawn from criminal gangs, and it should come as no surprise when they return to their former ways. Thus, in the short run it will be critical to reduce access to the machinery of war-making, to integrate former combatants into civilian life by giving them a stake in the legal economy, and to ensure that the police have adequate personnel, training, and resources. Over the long term it is equally critical that respect for human rights and the rule of law be fostered in order to prevent political and economic violence. Such work, as we can see in the case of present-day Iraq, will likely take years.

Trends in peacebuilding

As Paul Diehl shows, peacebuilding efforts by the international community and, in particular, the United Nations, have gone through various periods of development. With the winding down of the Cold War we saw first an increase in such efforts, followed by something of disillusionment with peacebuilding, as in Somalia, and disappointment with the continued savagery of humankind, as in Rwanda. Yet since then there have been renewed attempts at peacebuilding and calls for even more such actions in other emerging conflict and post-conflict nations. As Diehl points out, these operations have expanded in number and are more geographically dispersed than ever before. The major powers are more heavily invested, and they now often involve attempts at peacebuilding without the full consent of the host government, especially in the case of failed states such as Bosnia, Somalia, Liberia, and Kosovo. All these issues are worth further exploration for peacebuilding is not simply a matter of the relationship between the affected parties and the international community. Rather, to the extent that new and different modalities of peacebuilding develop, and as such efforts increase in frequency and breadth, the competition for scarce resources and expertise increases, but not necessarily the learning that should come with such heightened activity. The effects of such changes are global and systemic, not just local, as the quality of any one peacebuilding effort and the quantity of peacebuilding resources devoted to it become increasingly conditioned on the nature and frequency of other such operations.

Major power involvement in peacebuilding is a double-edged sword. When nations with considerable resources and expertise become involved in these operations, we would expect that the political, financial and military commitment to post-conflict societies would increase commensurately. Whether it is the United States and NATO in Bosnia and Kosovo; the Australians in East Timor or the British in Sierra Leone, major power involvement can bring about better coordination of sizeable amounts of peacebuilding assistance. It can lead to greater international awareness and representation of the affected parties. And it can provide for greater levels of accountability. Yet, as we know, major powers bring their own interests and political baggage into these post-conflict societies. Often, the perception that their actions are in service of their own interests and not necessarily those of the host country can interfere with the imperative of neutrality and even-handedness that makes fractious groups willing to abide by the terms of a peace settlement. Major power involvement risks adding another layer of politics to already complicated peace agreements. In the best of all possible worlds the major powers would leave their politics at the water's edge and subordinate their own self-interests to the interest of building a sustainable peace in the target country. How often such major power involvement approaches that level of benevolence is debatable. Certainly there are grounds for all parties to be skeptical. If the affected groups in post-conflict societies can all agree that major power involvement is necessary, one major prerequisite for peacebuilding success would at least be met. But ensuring that major powers, especially the United States, do not seek to fit a peacebuilding operation into their own political agenda will be a continual source of controversy that may well divert attention from the more pressing needs of the people put most at risk by the prospects of a failed peace.

Does it make sense for the international community to set aside sovereignty and implement peacebuilding missions where there is no central state authority – that is, in a failed state? If there are no national authorities answerable to the international community, let alone their own citizens, there may be no alternative. State failure, however, takes many forms ranging from the near complete anarchy of a Somalia to the functioning government of Cambodia that temporarily steps aside while international caretakers assume power for a specified period of time and for a specified set of responsibilities. Humanitarian disasters and horrific widespread human rights abuses may well call for an international response regardless of the interests of the host nation. When the affected parties, as in Cambodia or Kosovo agree or acquiesce to international involvement, such missions may well work. But what of those nations such as Congo or Sudan, where there is a state apparatus, but it does not enjoy control over some or most parts of its domain? At what point does the international community decide that sovereignty be damned – lives must be saved? When the major powers have interests at stake in such deep interventions, barely a passing glance may be given to sovereignty. Absent such interests, sovereignty and especially local self-determination are high on the list of rationales offered by world leaders, disingenuously or otherwise, for lack of involvement. Thus, the issue really may come back again to commitment. With major power or substantial UN involvement (which generally requires major power assent), mountains can be moved and objections overridden. Societies at war that do not command such support can usually look forward to more of the same.

Of all the trends Diehl points to in the evolution of peacebuilding, perhaps none is more important than the increasing frequency and geographical dispersion of these missions. To the extent that there is real and deep commitment underlying these operations, we would hope that this development indicates a greater willingness on the part of both post-conflict societies and the international community to build peace. That IGOs and NGOs are willing to invest their time and energy in peacebuilding the world over also portends well for those parts of the globe, like Africa, that seem to be perpetually on the back burner of international affairs. But while the upsurge in peacebuilding may well point the way toward a more peaceful world, we ought to consider just why this trend is occurring. Of course, there is no shortage of conflicts and post-conflict societies in need of international assistance that may simply be finally given the attention they deserve. Yet, if the increasing frequency and breadth of these operations have more to do with international politics, the consequences could be much more troublesome. We know that these operations generally only work when resources and expertise are utilized wisely along the lines described earlier. But if the increasing call for peacebuilding operations is not accompanied by increased funding, the international community may find its resources spread too thinly to do much good. Furthermore, if the increasing frequency of peacebuilding operations is also due in part to contagion and imitation effects, the consequences could be even more damaging. If post-conflict society A receives a peacebuilding mission and as a result the advocates for post-conflict society B demand similar treatment, irrespective of its real desire to make peace and absorb assistance, we run the risk that the entire notion of peacebuilding becomes overly politicized and turned into some variant of pork barrel politics. And as Diehl points out, there does not appear to be a great deal of learning occurring within the international peacebuilding community regarding the most appropriate and efficacious peacebuilding actions. Thus, even if there is adequate funding for the expanded number of peacebuilding operations, if the actors involved have not taken steps to regularly assess the effectiveness of these missions, there is an increasing likelihood that scarce resources will not be utilized appropriately.

Looking for such objective and hard-headed appraisals of fairly delicate political issues involving the relief of the millions suffering the effects of civil wars and other conflicts is a tall order, especially when new emergencies seem to arise all the time. Even if the peacebuilding providers are not able to be constantly updating their knowledge bank, however, the academic community can certainly contribute to this enterprise. Indeed, much of the research in international relations today seems to be more concerned with how peace can be created and sustained than with what causes wars. This development should provide some degree of optimism both for what it signals regarding the way in which global events inspire research, and for the prospects for the development of a sizeable and (hopefully) systematic body of knowledge on peacebuilding. And though there are a number of reasons for wariness and skepticism regarding peacebuilding operations, the bottom line is that now there is a better chance than ever to help post conflict societies. We know more now than ever before about what works. The diminution of conflict among major powers means that their resources can be devoted to helping societies end wars rather than fight them. All things considered, there is much reason for hope.

Final thoughts

Like good social scientists, however, we close with some caveats and notes of caution, some of which derive from the issues of peacebuilding that have not been addressed by the chapters in this volume. Peacebuilding involves a plethora of activities that essentially seek to ameliorate the root causes of conflict. To reiterate, among these efforts one might find reform or reinvention of the governmental system, generally with an eye toward increased public participation and democratization; reformation and rebuilding an economy; improvement of human rights; return of refugees to their homes; revitalization of civil society; some form of truth telling whether through truth commissions or tribunals; as well as a host of military activities (e.g., cease fire monitoring; supervision of the surrender of arms and their safeguarding; de-mining). More often than not, these efforts move forward simultaneously both because societal needs are so great, but also because they are carried out by a variety of local and international groups with their own agendas. But should there be a proper sequencing of events? Is there some sort of hierarchy of peacebuilding needs where more fundamental wants are given more prompt and thorough attention? Such basic human needs as food and shelter must obviously be addressed in the short term in order to prevent loss of life. But is it better to focus on establishing feeding stations to confront hunger, or is it more useful to return people to their villages and provide them with the resources needed to plant their crops so that eventually they can feed themselves and others? What if their fields are still laced with landmines? Is it best to set up the institutions of democratic governance first to develop a free and legitimate regime, or would scarce resources better be utilized in re-energizing and creating civil society to promote democratic values and human rights? The chapters in this volume have examined many of these questions, and they tell us something about the likelihood of success for such endeavors. But scholars would be well advised to consider whether there is some sort of optimal sequencing of peacebuilding activities, even if on a case-by-case basis. Understanding what percentage of the peacebuilding effort/resources should be devoted to each of these myriad tasks at any point in time and how such efforts should be adjusted over time and in response to the success/failure of other actions is critical. Simply throwing money at the most high-profile and visible needs may do little good and might even foster greater skepticism of peacebuilding generally if such actions do not produce their intended outcomes.

The sequencing of peacebuilding priorities directly ties into another vital question facing those charged with rebuilding nations – whose interests will take precedence in the claim to scarce resources and political commitment? When the representatives of IGOs, NGOs and foreign governments descend on post-conflict societies they bring with them their own experiences and preferences regarding the most critical needs facing these nations and the best methods for addressing them. But the people who have lived through the trauma of political violence also have their own agendas that do not always fit with the interests of external actors. For example, in the aftermath of the 1994 genocide in Rwanda, its post-genocide government sought substantial international assistance to rebuild the shattered nation. Yet, because of concerns over the Rwandan government's treatment of suspected genocidaires and because of the tremendous international preoccupation with the simultaneous refugee crisis in (then) Zaire, comparatively little aid was forthcoming. While the intentions of international aid agencies in evaluating the extent to which international norms trump local needs may be morally or political justifiable, they nonetheless set outsiders against insiders and may provoke resentment. IGOs and states have bureaucratic rules and regulations they must follow in determining who gets aid and how much they get. After satisfying these multifarious requirements they may assure the home government that all funds were properly accounted for and none fell into the wrong hands. Although the money may not fall into the wrong hands, it is not always clear that it makes it into the right hands. NGOs as well have their boards and donors to which they must report and depend upon for funding. A failure to look after their interests, or an unwillingness to charge into the latest international trouble spot to help the victims and get on the news, may well result in a drop-off in contributions. An awareness of these dilemmas is critical for our own assessment of what works and what does not work in peacebuilding for, like most scholars, we tend to focus on the efforts of international groups in peacebuilding (in part because we have much better data on these activities). Without knowledge of the compatibility and complementarity of international and local interests, however, we must be careful in drawing conclusions about the efficacy of either's peacebuilding efforts.

Continuing in the same vein, it is especially useful to consider how the international community is spending funds for peacebuilding that directly benefit the intended recipients. The costs of rebuilding a nation can be astronomically high, if it is even calculable. Invariably, despite pledges and promises to contribute vast sums of money, far less ever makes it into the field in the form of projects that produce tangible improvements in people's lives. Large sums of aid money are spent not on the people and society harmed by conflicts, nor are those funds applied with the most efficiency. Aid dollars often go to fund studies, to purchase and maintain a transportation infrastructure for aid workers, to pay local translators and experts, and to subsidize outside consultants and experts. Much of this work is entirely necessary and justifiable, and we do not wish to engage in any kind of IGO bashing here. It is also an inescapable fact, however, that such spending insures both that less money is spent on tangible projects of improvement, and that the local economy becomes somewhat distorted into one oriented toward servicing the aid community. Therefore, when we examine the impact of international efforts at peacebuilding, we must remember that such assistance is like an iceberg. Our scholarly attention is generally directed toward that part of the effort that is above the surface and visible – the projects themselves – while much of the time, energy and money that constitutes the international peacebuilding effort is directed toward overhead and other expenses. We make this argument neither to disparage the intentions of those who dedicate their lives to improving the lives of others, nor to call into question the need for such work. Rather, we aim to highlight one of the principal limitations of peacebuilding that *may* sometimes make it appear as though such work does not improve post-conflict societies. That is, because our findings may not always point to substantial improvements from these activities, we should not conclude that they do not work. The problem may well be that while the assistance that goes toward digging a new village well, or helping refugees to return home does work, violence may still return because not enough resources and assistance were directed toward these types of activities where they are most needed.

Of all the problems and pitfalls to occur in peacebuilding, perhaps none are more vexing and difficult to confront as those that stem from the law of unintended consequences. The science we employed in these chapters and the analysis that goes into policymaking are inexact. We cannot possibly hope to measure all the variables that distinguish peacebuilding successes from peacebuilding failures. Even when we have a reasonably informed appreciation of the potential consequences of individual programs and policies, predicting the effects that peacebuilding activities exert on each other involves more hope than science. The post-conflict society is like a patient who is prescribed a variety of pills by his doctor –

the international community. We often do not have any way of appreciating the interactive effects of these medicines. Thus, we must recognize that our findings come with the constant caveat, *ceteris paribus* – all other things being equal. We must always bear in mind that the product of these activities – whether peace or violence follows – is not always traceable directly back to them. Rather, we see correlation, not necessarily causation between peacebuilding efforts and subsequent events.

We are sure of one thing. Violence costs more than peace. Organizations, governments and taxpayers may groan at the seemingly never-ending need for more money to help repair the seemingly never-ending list of nations emerging from war. But it is important to remember that these efforts are supposed to be both curative and preventative. Peacebuilding aims to cure, however imperfectly, what ails a nation so that future conflict can be prevented. The costs of these conflicts are so large and varied (and not always immediately apparent as Elliott and Elliott show) as to be almost incalculable. And where once we might have believed the costs are borne just by those who experienced the violence, because of the events of September 11, we know that these costs are paid by people the world over. And this connection is just one rather obvious one to draw. There are far more relationships between your lives and the lives of people in other countries living through war. Whether these spillover, contagion, or indirect effects result in higher oil prices, greater opium and cocaine production, environmental degradation, international trafficking in children as soldiers and prostitutes to name but a very few, they all affect our lives and our pocketbooks. It only makes sense for all self-interested individuals to pay attention to these issues of war, peace and peacebuilding. Our purpose has been to provide the reader with the most thorough and timely knowledge on how to create peace out of war and how to sustain the conditions in which it flourishes. We take the position that regardless of one's political views and goals, we are all best served by an informed and systematic discussion of these phenomena. And while we do reach conclusions, the application of this knowledge is left to the reader. Our aim has been to contribute to an understanding of how to sustain the peace in the hope that with more knowledge, we are all better off.

Index

Made in the USA
Coppell, TX
03 July 2021